LAW IN LITERATURE

LAW IN LITERATURE:
Legal Themes in Drama

edited by
Elizabeth Villiers Gemmette

The Whitston Publishing Company
Troy, New York
1995

Copyright 1995
Elizabeth Villiers Gemmette

Library of Congress Catalog Card Number 95-61175

ISBN 0-87875-468-7 (cloth); 0-87875-471-7 (paper)

Printed in the United States of America

Cover Illustration: Charles Macklin as Shylock
By an unknown engraver; published by Wenman, 1776
Reproduced by courtesy of the
Shakespeare Centre Library, Stratford-upon-Avon

Acknowledgments

This Piece of Land by Lou Rivers. Reprinted by permission of the author, originally printed by the American Theatre Company, New York City, December 19, 1975, and published in *The Best Short Plays*, 1977, by Chilton Book Company, and edited by Stanley Richards. The first production was produced by Richard Kuss with Gwen Simmons as Rosa, Nate King as Perry, Herb Duval as Mr. Charlie, and Jay Hargrove as Leroy. Ray Shelton played Mr. Morgan. Donald Shannon was the Singer. Ruth Grant was Miss Nancy and Ed Smith played the Deacon. Ed Smith also served as stage manager. Rights of production, stage or otherwise, must be obtained from the author.

Contents

Preface vii

Part I. **Greek Plays of the 5th Century B.C.**

    1. *The Eumenides* 1
       Aeschylus, translated by E. D. A. Morshead
    2. *Antigone*
       Sophocles, translated by R. C. Jebb 42

Part II. **Shakespearean Plays of the Late Elizabethan and Early Jacobean Periods**

    3. *The Merchant of Venice* 88
       William Shakespeare
    4. *Measure for Measure* 188
       William Shakespeare

Part III. **English Plays of the 17th and 18th Century**

    5. *The Fatal Dowry* 306
       Philip Massinger
    6. *The London Merchant, or The History of George Barnwell* 420
       George Lillo

Part IV. **American One-Act Plays of the 20th Century**

    7. *Trifles* 496
       Susan Glaspell
    8. *This Piece of Land* 518
       Lou Rivers

Preface

Law in Literature: Legal Themes in Drama was written as a companion volume to *Law in Literature: Legal Themes in Short Stories*. It was stated in the Preface to *Law in Literature: Legal Themes in Short Stories* that one purpose for that text was to provide material for use in law and literature courses, material which could then be supplemented with other works—novels, poetry, and plays. This volume now brings together eight plays which can be used to supplement and enhance the materials in *Law in Literature: Legal Themes in Short Stories*. The preface to that earlier work also indicated that the book was intended for students of law, students of literature, lawyers and others participating in the legal profession, and the lay public. Similarly, *Law in Literature: Legal Themes in Drama* can be enjoyed by all of the same readers, and it has the added audience of those particularly interested in reading, teaching, or producing plays.

To compile an anthology comprised of forty law-related stories involved some decision-making as to what pieces should be chosen to illustrate particular topics, but the more difficult task was to find just the right stories to fit into the rubrics which were created for the presentation of legal themes throughout the text. Making choices for this anthology was different in several ways. First of all, the longer length of plays necessitated selection of fewer pieces—in this case eight plays, rather than the forty short stories which appeared in the earlier work. Secondly, drama, unlike the short story, is an art form which has existed since the ancient Greeks; therefore, the anthologist faces more difficult choices. Which period should be covered? Which writers should be included? Which of their works should be selected?

Obviously, the first criterion in the selection of these plays was that they all be law-related, but this did not help to limit or shorten the time period from which to select texts because even the plays of the ancient Greeks exhibit man's early fascination with legal topics. In selecting from the greek plays, space constraints permitted the inclusion of only *The Eumenides* by Aeschylus and *Antigone* by Sophocles. Although these are the two Greek plays chosen most often to be taught by law and literature professors, there are other works which it was difficult to omit—Aeschylus' *Agamemnon* and *The Choephori*, which together with *The Eumenides* comprise the trilogy known as the *Oresteia*; Sophocles' *Oedipus the King* and *Oedipus at Colonus*, which together with *Antigone* form the trilogy about Oedipus and his children; Aristophanes' *Lysistrata* and *The Wasps*—the former showing women successfully attaining peace, and the latter satirizing the Greek legal system; and Euripides' *Alcestis* and *Medea*, more plays addressing the role of women in Greek society.

The next time period to produce a plethora of plays is marked by the Elizabethan and Jacobean periods, most notably the works of William Shakespeare. Again, the difficulty lay not in finding suitable works for inclusion in this anthology but in deciding what to omit. The most obvious choices for inclusion in this anthology were *The Merchant of Venice* and *Measure for Measure*, but what about *Hamlet*, *Henry IV*, *Henry V*, and *Henry VII*, *Julius Caesar*, *King John*, *King Lear*, *Macbeth*, *Othello*, *Richard II*, and *Richard III*, to name but a few. Readers are encouraged to explore these and other plays by Shakespeare for their rich legal themes.

Space constraints allowed the inclusion of only two plays out of all the works written by others during and after Shakespeare's day to the present time. To say that the two plays selected—Massinger's *The Fatal Dowry*, and Lillo's *The London Merchant, or The History of George Barnwell*—were chosen for the quality of the works and for the rich selection of legal themes that they afford the reader, is to leave the most difficult question unanswered—what was again omitted? Robert Greene's *London and England* dealing with usury and his *James the Fourth* in which a lawyer is blamed for civil ills; Middleton's *The Phoenix* depicting Tangle, "an old, crafty client, who, by the puzzle of suits and shifting courts, has more tricks and starting-holes than the dizzy pates of fifteen attorneys"; Massinger's *The Old Law*; Jonson's *The Fox*; Shirley's *Honoria and Mammon*; works by Beaumont and Fletcher, Wycherly, Congreve, and Knowles. From Knowles comes the hint that it is time to move on. As a character in his *The Love Chase* proclaims to a lawyer:

> How many words you take to tell few things!
> Again, again say over what, said once,
> Methinks were told enough.

Turning to modern times, we see that the 20th century is replete with one-act plays which work in fine contrast to the other plays in this anthology as they illustrate how briefly and succinctly a theme can be dealt with both on the written page and in live theater. They also provide an opportunity for short classroom productions or dramatic readings which are more manageable than presentations of the longer plays included earlier in this collection. Once again, the choices were endless, but Susan Glaspell's *Trifles* and Lou Rivers' *This Piece of Land* were chosen for their legal themes and for their further contributions to our understanding of discrimination and the need for equality.

Aeschylus

The Eumenides

Characters in the Play

The Pythian Priestess
Apollo
Orestes
The Ghost of Clytemnestra
Chorus of Furies
Athena
Attendants of Athena
Twelve Athenian Citizens

(SCENE.—*Before the temple of* Apollo *at Delphi. The* Pythian Priestess *enters and approaches the doors of the temple.*)

The Pythian Priestess:
    First, in this prayer, of all the gods I name
    The prophet-mother Earth; and Themis next,
    Second who sat—for so with truth is said—
    On this her mother's shrine oracular.
    Then by her grace, who unconstrained allowed,
    There sat thereon another child of Earth—
    Titanian Phoebe. She, in after time,
    Gave o'er the throne, as birthgift to a god,
    Phoebus, who in his own bears Phoebe's name.
    He from the lake and ridge of Delos' isle
    Steered to the port of Pallas' Attic shores,
    The home of ships; and thence he passed and came
    Unto this land and to Parnassus' shrine.
    And at his side, with awe revering him,

There went the children of Hephaestus' seed,
The hewers of the sacred way, who tame
The stubborn tract that erst was wilderness.
    And all this folk, and Delphos, chieftain-king
Of this their land, with honour gave him home;
And in his breast Zeus set a prophet's soul,
And gave to him this throne, whereon he sits,
Fourth prophet of the shrine, and, Loxias hight,
Gives voice to that which Zeus his sire decrees.

Such gods I name in my preluding prayer,
And after them, I call with honour due
On Pallas, wardress of the fane, and Nymphs
Who dwell around the rock Corycian,
Where in the hollow cave, the wild birds' haunt,
Wander the feet of lesser gods; and there,
Right well I know it, Bromian Bacchus dwells,
Since he in godship led his Maenad host,
Devising death for Pentheus, whom they rent
Piecemeal, as hare among the hounds. And last,
I call on Pleistus' springs, Poseidon's might,
And Zeus most high, the great Accomplisher.
Then as a seeress to the sacred chair
I pass and sit; and may the powers divine
Make this mine entrance fruitful in response
Beyond each former advent, triply blest.
And if there stand without, from Hellas bound,
Men seeking oracles, let each pass in
In order of the lot, as use allows;
For the god guides whate'er my tongue proclaims.

(She goes into the interior of the temple; after a short interval, she returns in great fear.)

Things fell to speak of, fell for eyes to see,
Have sped me forth again from Loxias' shrine,
With strength unstrung, moving erect no more,
But aiding with my hands my failing feet,
Unnerved by fear. A beldame's force is naught—
Is as a child's, when age and fear combine.
For as I pace towards the inmost fane
Bay-filleted by many a suppliant's hand,

Lo, at the central altar I descry
One crouching as for refuge—yea, a man
Abhorred of heaven; and from his hands, wherein
A sword new-drawn he holds, blood reeked and fell:
A wand he bears, the olive's topmost bough,
Twined as of purpose with a deep close tuft
Of whitest wool. This, that I plainly saw,
Plainly I tell. But lo, in front of him,
Crouched on the altar-steps, a grisly band
Of women slumbers—not like women they,
But Gorgons rather; nay, that word is weak,
Nor may I match the Gorgons' shape with theirs!
Such have I seen in painted semblance erst—
Winged Harpies, snatching food from Phineus' board,—
But these are wingless, black, and all their shape
The eye's abomination to behold.
Fell is the breath—let none draw nigh to it—
Wherewith they snort in slumber; from their eyes
Exude the damned drops of poisonous ire:
And such their garb as none should dare to bring
To statues of the gods or homes of men.
I wot not of the tribe wherefrom can come
So fell a legion, nor in what land Earth
Could rear, unharmed, such creatures, nor avow
That she had travailed and had brought forth death.
But, for the rest, be all these things a care
Unto the mighty Loxias, the lord
Of this our shrine: healer and prophet he,
Discerner he of portents, and the cleanser
Of other homes—behold, his own to cleanse!

(*She goes out. The central doors open, disclosing the interior of the temple.* Orestes *clings to the central altar; the* Furies *lie slumbering at a little distance;* Apollo *and* Hermes *appear from the innermost shrine.*)

Apollo (*to* Orestes):
Lo, I desert thee never: to the end,
Hard at thy side as now, or sundered far,
I am thy guard, and to thine enemies
Implacably oppose me: look on them,
These greedy fiends, beneath my craft subdued!
See, they are fallen on sleep, these beldames old,

> Unto whose grim and wizened maidenhood
> Nor god nor man nor beast can e'er draw near.
> Yea, evil were they born, for evil's doom,
> Evil the dark abyss of Tartarus
> Wherein they dwell, and they themselves the hate
> Of men on earth, and of Olympian gods.
> But thou, flee far and with unfaltering speed;
> For they shall hunt thee through the mainland wide
> Where'er throughout the tract of travelled earth
> Thy foot may roam, and o'er and o'er the seas
> And island homes of men. Faint not nor fail,
> Too soon and timidly within thy breast
> Shepherding thoughts forlorn of this thy toil;
> But unto Pallas' city go, and there
> Crouch at her shrine, and in thine arms enfold
> Her ancient image: there we well shall find
> Meet judges for this cause and suasive pleas,
> Skilled to contrive for thee deliverance
> From all this woe. Be such my pledge to thee,
> For by my hest thou didst thy mother slay.

Orestes:
> O king Apollo, since right well thou know'st
> What justice bids, have heed, fulfill the same,—
> Thy strength is all-sufficient to achieve.

Apollo:
> Have thou too heed, nor let thy fear prevail
> Above thy will. And do thou guard him, Hermes,
> Whose blood is brother unto mine, whose sire
> The same high God. Men call thee guide and guard,
> Guide therefore thou and guard my suppliant;
> For Zeus himself reveres the outlaw's right,
> Boon of fair escort, upon man conferred.

(Apollo, Hermes, *and* Orestes *go out. The* Ghost of Clytemnestra *rises.*)

Ghost of Clytemnestra:
> Sleep on! awake! what skills your sleep to me—
> Me, among all the dead by you dishonoured—
> Me from whom never, in the world of death,

Dieth this course, 'Tis she who smote and slew,
And shamed and scorned I roam? Awake, and hear
My plaint of dead men's hate intolerable.
Me, sternly slain by them that should have loved,
Me doth no god arouse him to avenge,
Hewn down in blood by matricidal hands.
Mark ye these wounds from which the heart's blood ran,
And by whose hand, bethink ye! for the sense
When shut in sleep hath then the spirit-sight,
But in the day the inward eye is blind.
List, ye who drank so oft with lapping tongue
The wineless draught by me outpoured to soothe
Your vengeful ire! how oft on kindled shrine
I laid the feast of darkness, at the hour
Abhorred of every god but you alone!
Lo, all my service trampled down and scorned!
And he hath baulked your chase, as stag the hounds;
Yea, lightly bounding from the circling toils,
Hath wried his face in scorn, and flieth far.
Awake and hear—for mine own soul I cry—
Awake, ye powers of hell! the wandering ghost
That once was Clytemnestra calls—Arise!

(The Furies *mutter grimly, as in a dream.*)
  Mutter and murmur! He hath flown afar—
  My kin have gods to guard them, I have none!

      (*The* Furies *mutter as before.*)

O drowsed in sleep too deep to heed my pain!
Orestes flies, who me, his mother, slew.

      (*The* Furies *give a confused cry.*)

Yelping, and drowsed again? Up and be doing
That which alone is yours, the deed of hell!

      (*The* Furies *give another cry.*)

Lo, sleep and toil, the sworn confederates,
Have quelled your dragon-anger, once so fell!

The Furies *(muttering more fiercely and loudly)*:
 Seize, seize, seize, seize—mark, yonder!

Ghost:
 In dreams ye chase a prey, and like some hound,
 That even in sleep doth ply his woodland toil,
 Ye bell and bay. What do ye, sleeping here?
 Be not o'ercome with toil, nor, sleep-subdued,
 Be heedless of my wrong. Up! thrill your heart
 With the just chidings of my tongue,—such words
 Are as a spur to purpose firmly held.
 Blow forth on him the breath of wrath and blood,
 Scorch him with reek of fire that burns in you,
 Waste him with new pursuit—swift, hound him down!

(The Ghost sinks.)

First Fury *(awaking)*:
 Up! rouse another as I rouse thee; up!
  Sleep'st thou? Rise up, and spurning sleep away,
  See we if false to us this prelude rang.

Chorus of Furies *(singing)*:

          strophe 1

 Alack, alack, O sisters, we have toiled,
  O much and vainly have we toiled and borne!
 Vainly! and all we wrought the gods have foiled,
  And turned us to scorn!
He hath slipped from the net, whom we chased: he hath 'scaped us who should be our prey—
O'ermastered by slumber we sang, and our quarry hath stolen away!

         antistrophe 1
Thou, child of the high God Zeus, Apollo, hast robbed us and wronged;
Thou, a youth, hast down-trodden the right that to godship more ancient belonged;
Thou hast cherished thy suppliant man; the slayer, the God-forsaken,
The bane of a parent, by craft from out of our grasp thou hast taken;
A god, thou hast stolen from us the avengers a matricide son—
And who shall consider thy deed and say, *It is rightfully done?*

strophe 2

    The sound of chiding scorn
     Came from the land of dream;
Deep to mine inmost heart I felt it thrill and burn,
   Thrust as a strong-grasped goad, to urge
     Onward the chariot's team.
   Thrilled, chilled with bitter inward pain
I stand as one beneath the doomsman's scourge.

antistrophe 2

Shame on the younger gods who tread down right,
    Sitting on thrones of might!
Woe on the altar of earth's central fane!
    Clotted on step and shrine,
Behold, the guilt of blood, the ghastly stain!

strophe 3

  Woe upon thee, Apollo! uncontrolled,
   Unbidden, hast thou, prophet-god, imbrued
   The pure prophetic shrine with wrongful blood!
  For thou too heinous a respect didst hold
Of man, too little heed of powers divine!
  And us the Fates, the ancients of the earth,
    Didst deem as nothing worth.

antistrophe 3

Scornful to me thou art, yet shalt not fend
  My wrath from him; though unto hell he flee,
    There too are we!
  And he the blood-defiled, should feel and rue,
Though I were not, fiend-wrath that shall not end,
Descending on his head who foully slew.

   (Apollo *enters from the inner shrine.*)

Apollo:
  Out! I command you. Out from this my home—
  Haste, tarry not! Out from the mystic shrine,
  Lest thy lot be to take into thy breast
  The winged bright dart that from my golden string
  Speeds hissing as a snake,—lest, pierced and thrilled
  With agony, thou shouldst spew forth again

Black frothy heart's-blood, drawn from mortal men,
Belching the gory clots sucked forth from wounds.
These be no halls where such as you can prowl—
Go where men lay on men the doom of blood,
Heads lopped from necks, eyes from their spheres plucked
    out,
Hacked flesh, the flower of youthful seed crushed out,
Feet hewn away, and hands, and death beneath
The smiting stone, low moans and piteous
Of men impaled—Hark, hear ye for what feast
Ye hanker ever, and the loathing gods
Do spit upon your craving? Lo, your shape
Is all too fitted to your greed; the cave
Where lurks some lion, lapping gore, were home
More meet for you. Avaunt from sacred shrines,
Nor bring pollution by your touch on all
That nears you. Hence! and roam unshepherded—
No god there is to tend such herd as you.

Leader of the Chorus:
O king Apollo, in our turn hear us.
Thou hast not only part in these ill things,
But are chief cause and doer of the same.

Apollo:
How? stretch thy speech to tell this, and have done.

Leader:
Thine oracle bade this man slay his mother.

Apollo:
I bade him quit his sire's death,—wherefore not?

Leader:
Then didst thou aid and guard red-handed crime.

Apollo:
Yea, and I bade him to this temple flee.

Leader:
And yet forsooth dost chide us following him!

Apollo:
Ay—not for you it is, to near this fane.

Leader:
Yet is such office ours, imposed by fate.

Apollo:
What office? vaunt the thing ye deem so fair.

Leader:
From home to home we chase the matricide.

Apollo:
What? to avenge a wife who slays her lord?

Leader:
That is not blood outpoured by kindred hands.

Apollo:
How darkly ye dishonour and annul
The troth to which the high accomplishers,
Hera and Zeus, do honour. Yea, and thus
Is Aphrodite to dishonour cast,
The queen of rapture unto mortal men.
Know, that above the marriage-bed ordained
For man and woman standeth Right as guard,
Enhancing sanctity of trothplight sworn;
Therefore, if thou art placable to those
Who have their consort slain, nor will'st to turn
On them the eye of wrath, unjust art thou
In hounding to his doom the man who slew
His mother. Lo, I know thee full of wrath
Against one deed, but all too placable
Unto the other, minishing the crime.
But in this cause shall Pallas guard the right.

Leader:
Deem not my quest shall ever quit that man.

Apollo:
Follow then, make thee double toil in vain!

Leader:
    Think not by speech mine office to curtail.

Apollo:
    None hast thou, that I would accept of thee!

Leader:
    Yea, high thine honour by the throne of Zeus:
    But I, drawn on by scent of mother's blood,
    Seek vengeance on this man and hound him down.

(The Chorus *goes in pursuit of* Orestes.*)*

Apollo:
    But I will stand beside him; 'tis for me
    To guard my suppliant: gods and men alike
    Do dread the curse of such an one betrayed,
    And in me Fear and Will say *Leave him not.*
    (He goes into the temple.)

(The scene changes to Athens. In the foreground is the Temple of Athena *on the Acropolis; her statue stands in the centre;* Orestes *is seen clinging to it.)*

Orestes:
    Look on me, queen Athena; lo, I come
    By Loxias' behest; thou of thy grace
    Receive me, driven of avenging powers—
    Not now a red-hand slayer unannealed,
    But with guilt fading, half-effaced, outworn
    On many homes and paths of mortal men.
    For to the limit of each land, each sea,
    I roamed, obedient to Apollo's hest,
    And come at last, O Goddess, to thy fane,
    And clinging to thine image, bide my doom.

(The Chorus of Furies *enters, questing like hounds.)*

Leader of the Chorus:
    Ho! clear is here the trace of him we seek:
    Follow the track of blood, the silent sign!
    Like to some hound that hunts a wounded fawn,

We snuff along the scent of dripping gore,
And inwardly we pant for many a day
Toiling in chase that shall fordo the man;
For o'er and o'er the wide land have I ranged,
And o'er the wide sea, flying without wings,
Swift as a sail I pressed upon his track,
Who now hard by is crouching, well I wot,
For scent of mortal blood allures me here.

Chorus (*chanting*):
>Follow, seek him—round and round
>Scent and snuff and scan the ground,
>Lest unharmed he slip away,
>He who did his mother slay!
>Hist—he is there! See him his arms entwine
>Around the image of the maid divine—
>>Thus aided, for the deed he wrought
>>Unto the judgment wills he to be brought.

It may not be! a mother's blood, poured forth
>Upon the stained earth,
None gathers up: it lies—bear witness, Hell!—
>For aye indelible!
And thou who sheddest it shalt give thine own
>That shedding to atone!
Yea, from thy living limbs I suck it out,
>Red, clotted, gout by gout,—
A draught abhorred of men and gods; but I
>Will drain it, suck thee dry;
Yea, I will waste thee living, nerve and vein;
>Yea, for thy mother slain,
Will drag thee downward, there where thou shalt dree
>The weird of agony!
And thou and whosoe'er of men hath sinned—
>Hath wronged or God, or friend,
Or parent,—learn ye how to all and each
>The arm of doom can reach!
Sternly requiteth, in the world beneath,
>The judgment-seat of Death;
Yea, Death, beholding every man's endeavour,
>Recordeth it for ever.

Orestes:
> I, schooled in many miseries, have learnt
> How many refuges of cleansing shrines
> There be; I know when law allowth speech
> And when imposeth silence. Lo, I stand
> Fixed now to speak, for he whose word is wise
> Commands the same. Look, how the stain of blood
> Is dull upon mine hand and wastes away,
> And laved and lost therewith is the deep curse
> Of matricide; for while the guilt was new,
> 'Twas banished from me at Apollo's hearth,
> Atoned and purified by death of swine.
> Long were my word if I should sum the tale,
> How oft since then among my fellow-men
> I stood and brought no curse. Time cleanses all—
> Time, the coeval of all things that are.
>
> Now from pure lips, in words of omen fair,
> I call Athena, lady of this land,
> To come, my champion: so, in aftertime,
> She shall not fail of love and service leal,
> Not won by war, from me and from my land
> And all the folk of Argos, vowed to her.
>
> Now, be she far away in Libyan land
> Where flows from Triton's lake her natal wave,—
> Stand she with planted feet, or in some hour
> Of rest conceal them, champion of her friends
> Where'er she be,—or whether o'er the plain
> Phlegraean she look forth, as warrior bold—
> I cry to her to come, wher'er she be,
> (And she, as goddess, from afar can hear)
> And aid and free me, set among my foes.

Leader of the Chorus:
> Thee not Apollo nor Athena's strength
> Can save from perishing, a castaway
> Amid the Lost, where no delight shall meet
> Thy soul—a bloodless prey of nether powers,
> A shadow among shadows. Answerest thou
> Nothing? dost cast away my words with scorn,
> Thou, prey prepared and dedicate to me?
> Not as a victim slain upon the shrine,
> But living shalt thou see thy flesh my food.

Hear now the binding chant that makes thee mine.

Chorus (*chanting*):
>Weave the weird dance,—behold the hour
>>To utter forth the chant of hell,
>>Our sway among mankind to tell,
>
>The guidance of our power.
>Of Justice are we ministers,
>>And whosoe'er of men may stand
>>Lifting a pure unsullied hand,
>
>That man no doom of ours incurs,
>>And walks thro' all his mortal path
>>Untouched by woe, unharmed by wrath.
>>But if, as yonder man, he hath
>>Blood on the hands he strives to hide,
>>We stand avengers at his side,
>
>Decreeing, *Thou hast wronged the dead:*
>*We are doom's witnesses to thee.*
>The price of blood, his hands have shed,
>We wring from him; in life, in death,
>>Hard at his side are we!

strophe I

Night, Mother Night, who brought me forth, a torment
>To living men and dead,

Hear me, O hear! by Leto's stripling son
>I am dishonoured:

He hath ta'en from me him who cowers in refuge,
>To me made consecrate,—

A rightful victim, him who slew his mother.
>Given o'er to me and fate.

refrain I

>Hear the hymn of hell,
>>O'er the victim sounding,—
>
>Chant of frenzy, chant of ill,
>>Sense and will confounding!
>
>Round the soul entwining
>>Without lute or lyre—
>
>Soul in madness pining,
>>Wasting as with fire!

antistrophe 1

Fate, all-pervading Fate, this service spun, commanding
    That I should bide therein:
Whosoe'er of mortals, made perverse and lawless,
    Is stained with blood of kin,
By his side are we, and hunt him ever onward,
    Till to the Silent Land,
The realm of death, he cometh; neither yonder
    In freedom shall he stand.

refrain 1

    Hear the hymn of hell,
        O'er the victim sounding,
    Chant of frenzy, chant of ill,
        Sense and will confounding!
    Round the soul entwining
        Without lute or lyre—
    Soul in madness pining,
        Wasting as with fire!

strophe 2

When from womb of Night we sprang, on us this labour
    Was laid and shall abide.
Gods immortal are ye, yet beware ye touch not
    That which is our pride!
None may come beside us gathered round the blood-feast—
    For us no garments white
Gleam on a festal day; for us a darker fate is,
    Another darker rite.

refrain 2

That is mine hour when falls an ancient line—
    When in the household's heart
The God of blood doth slay by kindred hands,—
    Then do we bear our part:
On him who slays we sweep with chasing cry:
    Though he be triply strong,
We wear and waste him; blood atones for blood,
    New pain for ancient wrong.

antistrophe 2

I hold this task—'tis mine, and not another's.
    The very gods on high,
Though they can silence and annul the prayers

Of those who on us cry,
They may not strive with us who stand apart,
　　A race by Zeus abhorred,
Blood-boltered, held unworthy of the council
　　And converse of Heaven's lord.

strophe 3

Therefore the more I leap upon my prey;
　　Upon their head I bound;
My foot is hard; as one that trips a runner
　　I cast them to the ground;
Yea, to the depth of doom intolerable;
　　And they who erst were great,
And upon earth held high their pride and glory,
　　Are brought to low estate.
In underworld they waste and are diminished,
　　The while around them fleet
Dark wavings of my robes, and subtly woven,
　　The paces of my feet.

antistrophe 3

Who falls infatuate, he sees not neither knows he
　　That we are at his side;
So closely round about him, darkly flitting,
　　The cloud of guilt doth glide.
Heavily 'tis uttered, how around his hearthstone
　　The mirk of hell doth rise.

strophe 4

Stern and fixed the law is; we have hands t' achieve it,
　　Cunning to devise.
Queens are we and mindful of our solemn vengeance.
　　Not by tear or prayer
Shall a man avert it. In unhonoured darkness,
　　Far from gods, we fare,
Lit unto our task with torch of sunless regions,
　　And o'er a deadly way—
Deadly to the living as to those who see not
　　Life and light of day—
Hunt we and press onward.

antistrophe 4

Who of mortals hearing
Doth not quake for awe,
Hearing all that Fate thro' hand of God hath given us
For ordinance and law?
Yea, this right to us, in dark abysm and backward
Of ages it befel:
None shall wrong mine office, tho' in nether regions
And sunless dark I dwell.

(Athena *enters.*)

Athena:
Far off I heard the clamour of your cry,
As by Scamander's side I set my foot
Asserting right upon the land given o'er
To me by those who o'er Achaea's host
Held sway and leadership: no scanty part
Of all they won by spear and sword, to me
They gave it, land and all that grew thereon,
As chosen heirloom for my Theseus' clan.
Thence summoned, sped I with a tireless foot,—
Hummed on the wind, instead of wings, the fold
Of this mine aegis, by my feet propelled,
As, linked to mettled horses, speeds a car.
And now, beholding here Earth's nether brood,
I fear it nought, yet are mine eyes amazed
With wonder. Who are ye? of all I ask,
And of this stranger to my statue clinging.
But ye—your shape is like no human form,
Like to no goddess whom the gods behold,
Like to no shape which mortal women wear.
Yet to stand by and chide a monstrous form
Is all unjust—from such words Right revolts.

Leader of the Chorus:
O child of Zeus, one word shall tell thee all.
We are the children of eternal Night,
And Furies in the underworld are called.

Athena:
I know your lineage now and eke your name.

Leader:
  Yea, and eftsoons indeed my rights shalt know.

Athena:
  Fain would I learn them; speak them clearly forth.

Leader:
  We chase from home the murderers of men.

Athena:
  And where at last can he that slew make pause?

Leader:
  Where this is law—*All joy abandon here.*

Athena:
  Say, do ye bay this man to such a flight?

Leader:
  Yea, for of choice he did his mother slay.

Athena:
  Urged by no fear of other wrath and doom?

Leader:
  What spur can rightly goad to matricide?

Athena:
  Two stand to plead—one only have I heard.

Leader:
  He will not swear nor challenge us to oath.

Athena:
  The form of justice, not its deed, thou willest.

Leader:
  Prove thou that word; thou art not scant of skill.

Athena:
  I say that oaths shall not enforce the wrong.

Leader:
>Then test the cause, judge and award the right.

Athena:
>Will ye to me then this decision trust?

Leader:
>Yea, reverencing true child of worthy sire.

Athena *(to* Orestes*):*
>O man unknown, make thou thy plea in turn.
>Speak forth thy land, thy lineage, and thy woes;
>Then, if thou canst, avert this bitter blame—
>If, as I deem, in confidence of right
>Thou sittest hard beside my holy place,
>Clasping this statue, as Ixion sat,
>A sacred suppliant for Zeus to cleanse,—
>To all this answer me in words made plain.

Orestes:
>O queen Athena, first from thy last words
>Will I a great solicitude remove.
>Not one blood-guilty am I; no foul stain
>Clings to thine image from my clinging hand;
>Whereof one potent proof I have to tell.
>Lo, the law stands—*The slayer shall not plead,*
>*Till by the hand of him who cleanses blood*
>*A suckling creature's blood besprinkle him.*
>Long since have I this expiation done,—
>In many a home, slain beasts and running streams
>Have cleansed me. Thus I speak away that fear.
>Next, of my lineage quickly thou shalt learn:
>An Argive am I, and right well thou know'st
>My sire, that Agamemnon who arrayed
>The fleet and them that went therein to war—
>That chief with whom thy hand combined to crush
>To an uncitied heap what once was Troy;
>That Agamemnon, when he homeward came,
>Was brought unto no honourable death,
>Slain by the dark-souled wife who brought me forth
>To him,—enwound and slain in wily nets,
>Blazoned with blood that in the laver ran.

And I, returning from an exiled youth,
Slew her, my mother—lo, it stands avowed!
With blood for blood avenging my loved sire;
And in this deed doth Loxias bear part,
Decreeing agonies, to goad my will,
Unless by me the guilty found their doom.
Do thou decide if right or wrong were done—
Thy dooming, whatsoe'er it be, contents me.

Athena:
Too mighty is this matter, whosoe'er
Of mortals claims to judge hereof aright.
Yea, me, even me, eternal Right forbids
To judge the issues of blood-guilt, and wrath
That follows swift behind. This too gives pause,
That thou as one with all due rites performed
Dost come, unsinning, pure, unto my shrine.
Whate'er thou art, in this my city's name,
As uncondemned, I take thee to my side,—
Yet have these foes of thine such dues by fate,
I may not banish them: and if they fail,
O'erthrown in judgment of the cause, forthwith
Their anger's poison shall infect the land—
A dropping plague-spot of eternal ill.
Thus stand we with a woe on either hand:
Stay they, or go at my commandment forth,
Perplexity or pain must needs befall.
Yet, as on me Fate hath imposed the cause,
I choose unto me judges that shall be
An ordinance for ever, set to rule
The dues of blood-guilt, upon oath declared.
But ye, call forth your witness and your proof,
Words strong for justice, fortified by oath;
And I, whoe'er are truest in my town,
Them will I choose and bring, and straitly charge,
Look on this cause, discriminating well,
And pledge your oath to utter nought of wrong.

(Athena *withdraws.*)

Chorus *(singing)*:

strophe I

  Now are they all undone, the ancient laws,
    If here the slayer's cause
  Prevail; new wrong for ancient right shall be
    If matricide go free.
  Henceforth a deed like his by all shall stand,
    Too ready to the hand:
  Too oft shall parents in the aftertime
    Rue and lament this crime,—
  Taught, not in false imagining, to feel
    Their children's thrusting steel:
  No more the wrath, that erst on murder fell
    From us, the queens of Hell,
  Shall fall, no more our watching gaze impend—
    Death shall smite unrestrained.

antistrophe I

  Henceforth shall one unto another cry
  Lo, they are stricken, lo, they fall and die
 Around me! and that other answers him,
  O thou that lookest that thy woes should cease,
    Behold, with dark increase
  They throng and press upon thee; yea, and dim
    Is all the cure, and every comfort vain!

strophe 2

  Let none henceforth cry out, when falls the blow
    Of sudden-smiting woe,
  Cry out in sad reiterated strain
 O Justice, aid! aid, O ye thrones of Hell!
    So though a father or a mother wail
  New-smitten by a son, it shall no more avail,
 Since, overthrown by wrong, the fane of Justice fell!

antistrophe 2

  Know, that a throne there is that may not pass away,
    And one that sitteth on it—even Fear,
  Searching with steadfast eyes man's inner soul:
  Wisdom is child of pain, and born with many a tear;
    But who henceforth,
  What man of mortal men, what nation upon earth,

That holdeth nought in awe nor in the light
Of inner reverence, shall worship Right
    As in the older day?

strophe 3

Praise not, O man, the life beyond control,
Nor that which bows unto a tyrant's sway.
    Know that the middle way
Is dearest unto God, and they thereon who wend,
    They shall achieve the end;
But they who wander or to left or right
    Are sinners in his sight.
    Take to thy heart this one, this soothfast word—
    Of wantonness impiety is sire;
    Only from calm control and sanity unstirred
Cometh true weal, the goal of every man's desire.

antistrophe 3

Yea, whatsoe'er befall, hold thou this word of mine:
    Bow down at Justice' shrine,
    Turn thou thine eyes away from earthly lure
Nor with a godless foot that altar spurn.
For as thou dost shall Fate do in return,
    And the great doom is sure.
Therefore let each adore a parent's trust,
    And each with loyalty revere the guest
    That in his halls doth rest.

strophe 4

For whoso uncompelled doth follow what is just,
    He ne'er shall be unblest;
    Yea, never to the gulf of doom
    That man shall come.

But he whose will is set against the gods,
    Who treads beyond the law with foot impure,
Till o'er the wreck of Right confusion broods,—
    Know that for him, though now he sail secure,
The day of storm shall be; then shall he strive and fail
    Down from the shivered yard to furl the sail,

antistrophe 4

And call on Powers, that heed him nought, to save,
And vainly wrestle with the whirling wave.
    Hot was his heart with pride—
    I shall not fall, he cried.
    But him with watching scorn
    The god beholds, forlorn,
Tangled in toils of Fate beyond escape,
Hopeless of haven safe beyond the cape—
Till all his wealth and bliss of bygone day
    Upon the reef of Rightful Doom is hurled,
    And he is rapt away
Unwept, for ever, to the dead forgotten world.

(Athena *enters, with* twelve Athenian citizens. *A large crowd follows.*)

Athena:
    O herald, make proclaim, bid all men come.
    Then let the shrill blast of the Tyrrhene trump,
    Fulfilled with mortal breath, thro' the wide air
    Peal a loud summons, bidding all men heed.
    For, till my judges fill this judgment-seat,
    Silence behoves,—that this whole city learn,
    What for all time mine ordinance commands,
    And these men, that the cause be judged aright.

(Apollo *enters.*)

Leader of the Chorus:
    O king Apollo, rule what is thine own,
    But in this thing what share pertains to thee?

Apollo:
    First, as a witness come I, for this man
    Is suppliant of mine by sacred right,
    Guest of my holy hearth and cleansed by me
    Of blood-guilt: then, to set me at his side
    And in his cause bear part, as part I bore
    Erst in his deed, whereby his mother fell.
    Let whoso knoweth now announce the cause.

Athena *(to the Chorus)*:
    'Tis I announce the cause—first speech be yours;
    For rightfully shall they whose plaint is tried
    Tell the tale first and set the matter clear.

Leader:
    Though we be many, brief shall be our tale.
                         (To Orestes.*)*
    Answer thou, setting word to match with word;
    And first avow—hast thou thy mother slain?

Orestes:
    I slew her. I deny no word hereof.

Leader:
    Three falls decide the wrestle—this is one.

Orestes:
    Thou vauntest thee—but o'er no final fall.

Leader:
    Yet must thou tell the manner of thy deed.

Orestes:
    Drawn sword in hand, I gashed her neck. 'Tis told.

Leader:
    But by whose word, whose craft, wert thou impelled?

Orestes:
    By oracles of him who here attests me.

Leader:
    The prophet-god bade thee thy mother slay?

Orestes:
    Yea, and thro' him less ill I fared, till now.

Leader:
    If the vote grip thee, thou shalt change that word.

Orestes:
>Strong is my hope; my buried sire shall aid.

Leader:
>Go to now, trust the dead, a matricide!

Orestes:
>Yea, for in her combined two stains of sin.

Leader:
>How? speak this clearly to the judges' mind.

Orestes:
>Slaying her husband, she did slay my sire.

Leader:
>Therefore thou livest; death assoils her deed.

Orestes:
>Then while she lived why didst thou hunt her not?

Leader:
>She was not kin by blood to him she slew.

Orestes:
>And I, am I by blood my mother's kin?

Leader:
>O cursed with murder's guilt, how else wert thou
>The burden of her womb? Dost thou forswear
>Thy mother's kinship, closest bond of love?

Orestes:
>It is thine hour, Apollo—speak the law,
>Averring if this deed were justly done;
>For done it is, and clear and undenied.
>But if to thee this murder's cause seem right
>Or wrongful, speak—that I to these may tell.

Apollo:
>To you, Athena's mighty council-court,
>Justly for justice will I plead, even I,

The prophet-god, nor cheat you by one word.
For never spake I from my prophet-seat
One word, of man, of woman, or of state,
Save what the Father of Olympian gods
Commanded unto me. I rede you then,
Bethink you of my plea, how strong it stands,
And follow the decree of Zeus our sire,—
For oaths prevail not over Zeus' command.

Leader:
Go to; thou sayest that from Zeus befell
The oracle that this Orestes bade
With vengeance quit the slaying of his sire,
And hold as nought his mother's right of kin!

Apollo:
Yea, for it stands not with a common death,
That he should die, a chieftain and a king
Decked with the sceptre which high heaven confers—
Die, and by female hands, not smitten down
By a far-shooting bow, held stalwartly
By some strong Amazon. Another doom
Was his: O Pallas, hear, and ye who sit
In judgment, to discern this thing aright!—
She with a specious voice of welcome true
Hailed him, returning from the mighty mart
Where war for life gives fame, triumphant home;
Then o'er the laver, as he bathed himself,
She spread from head to foot a covering net,
And in the endless mesh of cunning robes
Enwound and trapped her lord, and smote him down.
Lo, ye have heard what doom this chieftain met,
The majesty of Greece, the fleet's high lord:
Such as I tell it, let it gall your ears,
Who stand as judges to decide this cause.

Leader:
Zeus, as thou sayest, holds a father's death
As first of crimes,—yet he of his own act
Cast into chains his father, Cronus old:
How suits that deed with that which now ye tell?
O ye who judge, I bid ye mark my words!

Apollo:
>O monsters loathed of all, O scorn of gods,
>He that hath bound may loose: a cure there is,
>Yea, many a plan that can unbind the chain.
>But when the thirsty dust sucks up man's blood
>Once shed in death, he shall arise no more.
>No chant nor charm for this my Sire hath wrought.
>All else there is, he moulds and shifts at will,
>Not scant of strength nor breath, whate'er he do.

Leader:
>Think yet, for what acquittal thou dost plead:
>He who hath shed a mother's kindred blood,
>Shall he in Argos dwell, where dwelt his sire?
>How shall he stand before the city's shrines,
>How share the clansmen's holy lustral bowl?

Apollo:
>This too I answer; mark a soothfast word
>Not the true parent is the woman's womb
>That bears the child; she doth but nurse the seed
>New-sown: the male is parent; she for him,
>As stranger for a stranger, hoards the germ
>Of life, unless the god its promise blight.
>And proof hereof before you will I set.
>Birth may from fathers, without mothers, be:
>See at your side a witness of the same,
>Athena, daughter of Olympian Zeus,
>Never within the darkness of the womb
>Fostered nor fashioned, but a bud more bright
>Than any goddess in her breast might bear.
>And I, O Pallas, howsoe'er I may,
>Henceforth will glorify thy town, thy clan,
>And for this end have sent my suppliant here
>Unto thy shrine; that he from this time forth
>Be loyal unto thee for evermore,
>O goddess-queen, and thou unto thy side
>Mayst win and hold him faithful, and his line,
>And that for aye this pledge and troth remain
>To children's children of Athenian seed.

Athena:
    Enough is said; I bid the judges now
    With pure intent deliver just award.

Leader:
    We too have shot our every shaft of speech,
    And now abide to hear the doom of law.

Athena (to Apollo and Orestes):
    Say, how ordaining shall I 'scape your blame?

Apollo:
    I spake, ye heard; enough. O stranger men,
    Heed well your oath as ye decide the cause.

Athena:
    O men of Athens, ye who first do judge
    The law of bloodshed, hear me now ordain.
    Here to all time for Aegeus' Attic host
    Shall stand this council-court of judges sworn,
    Here the tribunal, set on Ares' Hill
    Where camped of old the tented Amazons,
    What time in hate of Theseus they assailed
    Athens, and set against her citadel
    A counterwork of new sky-pointing towers,
    And there to Ares held their sacrifice,
    Where now the rock hath name, even Ares' Hill.
    And hence shall Reverence and her kinsman Fear
    Pass to each free man's heart, by day and night
    Enjoining, *Thou shalt do no unjust thing*,
    So long as law stands as it stood of old
    Unmarred by civic change. Look you, the spring
    Is pure; but foul it once with influx vile
    And muddy clay, and none can drink thereof.
    Therefore, O citizens, I bid ye bow
    In awe to this command, *Let no man live
    Uncurbed by law nor curbed by tyranny;*
    Nor banish ye the monarchy of Awe
    Beyond the walls; untouched by fear divine,
    No man doth justice in the world of men.
    Therefore in purity and holy dread
    Stand and revere; so shall ye have and hold

A saving bulwark of the state and land,
Such as no man hath ever elsewhere known,
Nor in far Scythia, nor in Pelops' realm.
Thus I ordain it now, a council-court
Pure and unsullied by the lust of gain,
Sacred and swift to vengeance, wakeful ever
To champion men who sleep, the country's guard.
Thus have I spoken, thus to mine own clan
Commended it for ever. Ye who judge,
Arise, take each his vote, mete out the right,
Your oath revering. Lo, my word is said.

(The twelve judges come forward, one by one, to the urns of decision; the first votes; as each of the others follows, the Leader *and* Apollo *speak alternately.)*

Leader:
    I rede ye well, beware! nor put to shame,
    In aught, this grievous company of hell.

Apollo:
    I too would warn you, fear mine oracles—
    From Zeus they are,—nor make them void of fruit.

Leader:
    Presumptuous is thy claim, blood-guilt to judge,
    And false henceforth thine oracles shall be.

Apollo:
    Failed then the counsels of my sire, when turned
    Ixion, first of slayers, to his side?

Leader:
    These are but words; but I, if justice fail me,
    Will haunt this land in grim and deadly deed.

Apollo:
    Scorn of the younger and the elder gods
    Art thou: 'tis I that shall prevail anon.

Leader:
    Thus didst thou too of old in Pheres' halls,
    O'erreaching Fate to make a mortal deathless.

Apollo:
>Was it not well, my worshipper to aid,
>Then most of all when hardest was the need?

Leader:
>I say thou didst annul the lots of life,
>Cheating with wine the deities of eld.

Apollo:
>I say thou shalt anon, thy pleadings foiled,
>Spit venom vainly on thine enemies.

Leader:
>Since this young god o'errides mine ancient right,
>I tarry but to claim your law, not knowing
>If wrath of mine shall blast your state or spare.

Athena:
>Mine is the right to add the final vote,
>And I award it to Orestes' cause.
>For me no mother bore within her womb,
>And, save for wedlock evermore eschewed,
>I vouch myself the champion of the man,
>Not of the woman, yea, with all my soul,—
>In heart, as birth, a father's child alone.
>Thus will I not too heinously regard
>A woman's death who did her husband slay,
>The guardian of her home; and if the votes
>Equal do fall, Orestes shall prevail.
>
>Ye of the judges who are named thereto,
>Swiftly shake forth the lots from either urn.

>>*(Two judges come forward, one to each urn.)*

Orestes:
>O bright Apollo, what shall be the end?

Leader:
>O Night, dark mother mine, dost mark these things?

Orestes:
>Now shall my doom be life, or strangling cords.

Leader:
>And mine, lost honour or a wider sway.

Apollo:
>O stranger judges, sum aright the count
>Of votes cast forth, and, parting them, take heed
>Ye err not in decision. The default
>Of one vote only bringeth ruin deep,
>One, cast aright, doth stablish house and home.

Athena:
>Behold, this man is free from guilt of blood,
>For half the votes condemn him, half set free!

Orestes:
>O Pallas, light and safety of my home,
>Thou, thou hast given me back to dwell once more
>In that my fatherland, amerced of which
>I wandered; now shall Grecian lips say this,
>*The man is Argive once again, and dwells*
>*Again within his father's wealthy hall,*
>*By Pallas saved, by Loxias, and by Him,*
>*The great third savior, Zeus omnipotent—*
>Who thus in pity for my father's fate
>Doth pluck me from my doom, beholding these,
>Confederates of my mother. Lo, I pass
>To mine own home, but proffering this vow
>Unto thy land and people: *Nevermore,*
>*Thro' all the manifold years of Time to be,*
>*Shall any chieftain of mine Argive land*
>*Bear hitherward his spears for fight arrayed.*
>For we, though lapped in earth we then shall lie,
>By thwart adversities will work our will
>On them who shall transgress this oath of mine,
>Paths of despair and journeyings ill-starred
>For them ordaining, till their task they rue.
>But if this oath be rightly kept, to them
>Will we the dead be full of grace, the while
>With loyal league they honour Pallas' town.
>And now farewell, thou and thy city's folk—
>Firm be thine arms' grasp, closing with thy foes,
>And, strong to save, bring victory to thy spear.

(Orestes *and* Apollo *depart.*)

Chorus *(chanting)*:
    Woe on you, younger gods! the ancient right
    Ye have o'erridden, rent it from my hands.
    I am dishonoured of you, thrust to scorn!
        But heavily my wrath
  Shall on this land fling forth the drops that blast and burn,
    Venom of vengeance, that shall work such scathe
    As I have suffered; where that dew shall fall,
        Shall leafless blight arise,
    Wasting Earth's offspring,—Justice, hear my call!—
    And thorough all the land in deadly wise
    Shall scatter venom, to exude again
        In pestilence on men.
    What cry avails me now, what deed of blood,
    Unto this land what dark despite?
        Alack, alack, forlorn
    Are we, a bitter injury have borne!
    Alack, O sisters, O dishonoured brood
        Of mother Night!

Athena:
    Nay, bow ye to my words, chafe not nor moan:
    Ye are not worsted nor disgraced; behold,
    With balanced vote the cause had issue fair,
    Nor in the end did aught dishonour thee.
    But thus the will of Zeus shone clearly forth,
    And his own prophet-god avouched the same,
    Orestes slew: his slaying is atoned.
    Therefore I pray you, not upon this land
    Shoot forth the dart of vengeance; be appeased,
    Nor blast the land with blight, nor loose thereon
    Drops of eternal venom, direful darts
    Wasting and marring nature's seed of growth.
    For I, the queen of Athens' sacred right,
    Do pledge to you a holy sanctuary
    Deep in the heart of this my land, made just
    By your indwelling presence, while ye sit
    Hard by your sacred shrines that gleam with oil
    Of sacrifice, and by this folk adored.

Chorus (*chanting*):
>>Woe on you, younger gods! the ancient right
>>Ye have o'erridden, rent it from my hands.
>>I am dishonoured of you, thrust to scorn!
>>>But heavily my wrath
>Shall on this land fling forth the drops that blast and burn,
>>Venom of vengeance, that shall work such scathe
>>As I have suffered; where that dew shall fall,
>>>Shall leafless blight arise,
>>Wasting Earth's offspring,—Justice, hear my call!—
>>And thorough all the land in deadly wise
>>Shall scatter venom, to exude again
>>>In pestilence on men.
>>What cry avails me now, what deed of blood,
>>Unto this land what dark despite?
>>>Alack, alack, forlorn
>>Are we, a bitter injury have borne!
>>>Alack, O sisters, O dishonoured brood
>>>Of mother Night!

Athena:
>>Dishonoured are ye not; turn not, I pray,
>>As goddesses your swelling wrath on men,
>>Nor make the friendly earth despiteful to them.
>>I too have Zeus for champion—'tis enough—
>>I only of all goddesses do know
>>To ope the chamber where his thunderbolts
>>Lie stored and sealed; but here is no such need.
>>Nay, be appeased, nor cast upon the ground
>>The malice of thy tongue, to blast the world;
>>Calm thou thy bitter wrath's black inward surge,
>>For high shall be thine honour, set beside me
>>For ever in this land, whose fertile lap
>>Shall pour its teeming firstfruits unto you,
>>Gifts for fair childbirth and for wedlock's crown:
>>Thus honoured, praise my spoken pledge for aye.

Chorus (*chanting*):
>>I, I dishonoured in this earth to dwell,—
>>Ancient of days and wisdom! I breathe forth
>>Poison and breath of frenzied ire. O Earth,
>>>Woe, woe for thee, for me!

From side to side what pains be these that thrill?
Hearken, O mother Night, my wrath, mine agony!
Whom from mine ancient rights the gods have thrust,
      And brought me to the dust—
Woe, woe is me!—with craft invincible.

Athena:
Older art thou than I, and I will bear
With this thy fury. Know, although thou be
More wise in ancient wisdom, yet have I
From Zeus no scanted measure of the same,
Wherefore take heed unto this prophecy—
If to another land of alien men
Ye go, too late shall ye feel longing deep
For mine. The rolling tides of time bring round
A day of brighter glory for this town;
And thou, enshrined in honour by the halls
Where dwelt Erechtheus, shalt a worship win
From men and from the train of womankind,
Greater than any tribe elsewhere shall pay.
Cast thou not therefore on this soil of mine
Whetstones that sharpen souls to bloodshedding,
The burning goads of youthful hearts, made hot
With frenzy of the spirit, not of wine.
Nor pluck as 'twere the heart from cocks that strive,
To set it in the breast of citizens
Of mine, a war-god's spirit, keen for fight,
Made stern against their country and their kin.
The man who grievously doth lust for fame,
War, full, immitigable, let him wage
Against the stranger; but of kindred birds
I hold the challenge hateful. Such the boon
I proffer thee—within this land of lands,
Most loved of gods, with me to show and share
Fair mercy, gratitude and grace as fair.

Chorus (*chanting*):
    I, I dishonoured in this earth to dwell,—
Ancient of days and wisdom! I breathe forth
Poison and breath of frenzied ire. O Earth,
      Woe, woe for thee, for me!
From side to side what pains be these that thrill?

Hearken, O mother Night, my wrath, mine agony!
Whom from mine ancient rights the gods have thrust
    And brought me to the dust—
Woe, woe is me!—with craft invincible.

Athena:
I will not weary of soft words to thee,
That never mayst thou say, *Behold me spurned,*
An elder by a younger diety,
And from this land rejected and forlorn,
Unhonoured by the men who dwell therein.
But, if Persuasion's grace be sacred to thee,
Soft in the soothing accents of my tongue,
Tarry, I pray thee; yet, if go thou wilt,
Not rightfully wilt thou on this my town
Sway down the scale that beareth wrath and teen
Or wasting plague upon this folk. 'Tis thine,
If so thou wilt, inheritress to be
Of this my land, its utmost grace to win.

Leader of the Chorus:
O queen, what refuge dost thou promise me?

Athena:
Refuge untouched by bale: take thou my boon.

Leader:
What, if I take it, shall mine honour be?

Athena:
No house shall prosper without grace of thine.

Leader:
Canst thou achieve and grant such power to me?

Athena:
Yea, for my hand shall bless thy worshippers.

Leader:
And wilt thou pledge me this for time eterne?

Athena:
> Yea: none can bid me pledge beyond my power.

Leader:
> Lo, I desist from wrath, appeased by thee.

Athena:
> Then in the land's heart shalt thou win thee friends.

Leader:
> What chant dost bid me raise, to greet the land?

Athena:
> Such as aspires towards a victory
> Unrued by any: chants from breast of earth,
> From wave, from sky; and let the wild winds' breath
> Pass with soft sunlight o'er the lap of land,—
> Strong wax the fruits of earth, fair teem the kine,
> Unfailing, for my town's prosperity,
> And constant be the growth of mortal seed.
> But more and more root out the impious,
> For as a gardener fosters what he sows,
> So foster I this race, whom righteousness
> Doth fend from sorrow. Such the proffered boon.
> But I, if wars must be, and their loud clash
> And carnage, for my town, will ne'er endure
> That aught but victory shall crown her fame.

Chorus *(chanting):*
> Lo, I accept it; at her very side
>   Doth Pallas bid me dwell:
> I will not wrong the city of her pride,
> Which even Almighty Zeus and Ares hold
>   Heaven's earthly citadel,
> Loved home of Grecian gods, the young, the old,
>   The sanctuary divine,
>   The shield of every shrine!
> For Athens I say forth a gracious prophecy,—
>   The glory of the sunlight and the skies
>   Shall bid from earth arise
> Warm wavelets of new life and glad prosperity.

Athena *(chanting)*:
>Behold, with gracious heart well pleased
>>I for my citizens do grant
>>Fulfilment of this covenant:
>And here, their wrath at length appeased,
>>These mighty dieties shall stay.
>For theirs it is by right to sway
>The lot that rules our mortal day,
>>And he who hath not inly felt
>Their stern decree, ere long on him,
>Not knowing why and whence, the grim
>>Life-crushing blow is dealt.
>The father's sin upon the child
>Descends, and sin is silent death,
>And leads him on the downward path,
>>By stealth beguiled,
>Unto the Furies: though his state
>On earth were high, and loud his boast,
>>Victim of silent ire and hate
>>He dwells among the Lost.

Chorus *(chanting)*:
>To my blessing now give ear.—
>Scorching blight nor singed air
>Never blast thine olives fair!
>Drouth, that wasteth bud and plant,
>Keep to thine own place. Avaunt,
>Famine fell, and come not hither
>Stealthily to waste and wither!
>Let the land, in season due,
>Twice her waxing fruits renew;
>Teem the kine in double measure;
>Rich in new god-given treasure;
>Here let men the powers adore
>For sudden gifts unhoped before!

Athena *(chanting)*:
>O hearken, warders of the wall
>That guards mine Athens, what a dower
>Is unto her ordained and given!
>For mighty is the Furies' power,
>And deep-revered in courts of heaven

    And realms of hell; and clear to all
        They weave thy doom, mortality!
    And some in joy and peace shall sing;
    But unto other some they bring
        Sad life and tear-dimmed eye.

Chorus (*chanting*):
    And far away I ban thee and remove,
        Untimely death of youths too soon brought low!
    And to each maid, O gods, when time is come for love,
        Grant ye a warrior's heart, a wedded life to know.
    Ye too, O Fates, children of mother Night,
        Whose children too are we, O goddesses
    Of just award, of all by sacred right
        Queens, who in time and in eternity
    Do rule, a present power for righteousness,
        Honoured beyond all Gods, hear ye and grant my cry!

Athena (*chanting*):
        And I too, I with joy am fain,
        Hearing your voice this gift ordain
        Unto my land. High thanks be thine,
        Persuasion, who with eyes divine
        Into my tongue didst look thy strength,
        To bend and to appease at length
            Those who would not be comforted.
        Zeus, king of parley, doth prevail,
        And ye and I will strive nor fail,
            That good may stand in evil's stead,
        And lasting bliss for bale.

Chorus (*chanting*):
        And nevermore these walls within
        Shall echo fierce sedition's din,
            Unslaked with blood and crime;
        The thirsty dust shall nevermore
        Suck up the darkly streaming gore
        Of civic broils, shed out in wrath
        And vengeance, crying death for death!
        But man with man and state with state
        Shall vow *The pledge of common hate*
        And common friendship, that for man

Hath oft made blessing out of ban,
Be ours unto all time.

Athena *(chanting):*
>Skill they, or not, the path to find
>Of favouring speech and presage kind?
>Yea, even from these, who, grim and stern,
>>Glared anger upon you of old,
>O citizens, ye now shall earn
>>A recompense right manifold.
>Deck them aright, extol them high,
>Be loyal to their loyalty,
>>And ye shall make your town and land
>>Sure, propped on Justice' saving hand,
>>And Fame's eternity.

Chorus *(chanting):*
>>Hail ye, all hail! and yet again, all hail,
>>O Athens, happy in a weal secured!
>O ye who sit by Zeus' right hand, nor fail
>>Of wisdom set among you and assured,
>Loved of the well-loved Goddess-Maid! the King
>Of gods doth reverence you, beneath her guarding wing.

Athena *(chanting):*
>All hail unto each honoured guest!
>Whom to the chambers of your rest
>'Tis mine to lead, and to provide
>The hallowed torch, the guard and guide.
>Pass down, the while these altars glow
>With sacred fire, to earth below
>>And your appointed shrine.
>There dwelling, from the land restrain
>The force of fate, the breath of bane,
>But waft on us the gift and gain
>>Of Victory divine!
>And ye, the men of Cranaos' seed,
>I bid you now with reverence lead
>These alien Powers that thus are made
>Athenian evermore. To you
>Fair be their will henceforth, to do
>>Whate'er may bless and aid!

Chorus *(chanting):*
>Hail to you all! hail yet again,
>All who love Athens, gods and men,
>>Adoring her as Pallas' home!
>And while ye reverence what ye grant—
>My sacred shrine and hidden haunt—
>>Blameless and blissful be your doom!

Athena:
>Once more I praise the promise of your vows,
>And now I bid the golden torches' glow
>Pass down before you to the hidden depth
>Of earth, by mine own sacred servants borne,
>My loyal guards of statue and of shrine.
>Come forth, O flower of Theseus' Attic land,
>O glorious band of children and of wives,
>And ye, O train of matrons crowned with eld!
>Deck you with festal robes of scarlet dye
>In honour of this day: O gleaming torch,
>Lead onward, that these gracious powers of earth
>Henceforth be seen to bless the life of men.

(Athena *leads the procession downwards into the Cave of the* Furies, *now* Eumenides, *under the Areopagus: as they go, the escort of women and children chant aloud.*)

Chant:
>With loyalty we lead you; proudly go,
>Night's childless children, to your home below!
>>*(O citizens, awhile from words forbear!)*
>To darkness' deep primeval lair,
>Far in Earth's bosom, downward fare,
>>Adored with prayer and sacrifice.
>>*(O citizens, forbear your cries!)*
>Pass hitherward, ye powers of Dread,
>With all your former wrath allayed,
>>Into the heart of this loved land;
>With joy unto your temple wend,
>The while upon your steps attend
>>The flames that feed upon the brand—
>*(Now, now ring out your chant, your joy's acclaim!)*
>>Behind them, as they downward fare,
>>Let holy hands libations bear,

And torches' sacred flame.
All-seeing Zeus and Fate come down
To battle fair for Pallas' town!
Ring out your chant, ring out your joy's acclaim!

Comments and Questions

1. "The Eumenides," meaning "the gracious ones" or "the well-disposed" or "the kindly ones," is a propitiatory euphemism for "The Furies" which means that the term is used in order to appease or gain the good will of the avenging hags from hell whose purpose is to inflict famines and pestilences, to sting the conscience of the guilty, and to execute curses cast upon criminals. What is the central theme of Athena's argument to the Furies in which she works to persuade them to accept the verdict and to cease their relentless quest for revenge against Orestes?

2. The Furies make the argument that they are not charged with avenging the killing of a husband because he is not a blood relative to his wife but that they must avenge the murder of a relative by blood. In this case, they argue that the death of Agamemnon by Clytemnestra is not to be avenged by them while the death of Clytemnestra by her son Orestes is their concern. What would their position be if Agamemnon had killed Clytemnestra and Orestes had then killed Agamemnon? What would Apollo's argument be in defense of Orestes then?

3. Apollo rebuts the argument of the Furies that Orestes is guilty of killing a parent, and, therefore, subject to their wrath, by countering that women are not parents but mere vessels for the seeds of man. Does this argument make this a sexist or anti-female play? If so, how would you argue to Apollo that his argument is specious? Why is Athena persuaded that Apollo is right? Can a woman carry a baby

without being the child's parent? How does this question lead to moral, legal, and ethical considerations in today's society?

4. Athena asks the Furies whether or not Orestes was urged by fear of wrath and doom, and the Furies respond that nothing can goad to matricide. Are they only concerned with the murder of a mother? What about the killing of Agamemnon by Clytemnestra? How would you attempt to defend Orestes if you were his attorney?

5. Athena states that it is not a particularly heinous crime to kill a killer. Is this the argument used most often to justify capital punishment? Is it more acceptable for the state to avenge a murder than it is for the wronged to do so? If so, why? Do you understand and accept the moral code under which Orestes functions? How does his behavior compare and contrast with that of Antigone? Remember Antigone's adherence to Divine law rather than positive law. Is it a reliance on Divine law and the notion that it is not a particularly heinous crime to kill a killer that motivates pro-life advocates who engage in the killing of pro-choice doctors and clinicians?

Sophocles

Antigone

Characters in the Play

Antigone, *daughter of Oedipus.*
Ismene, *daughter of Oedipus.*
Creon, *King of Thebes.*
Eurydice, *his wife.*
Haemon, *his son.*
Teiresias, *the blind prophet.*
Guard, *set to watch the corpse of Polyneices.*
First Messenger.
Second Messenger, *from the house.*
Chorus of Theban Elders.

(SCENE.—*The same as in the Oedipus the King, an open space before the royal palace, once that of Oedipus, at Thebes. The backscene represents the front of the palace, with three doors, of which the central and largest is the principal entrance into the house. The time is at daybreak on the morning after the fall of the two brothers, Eteocles and Polyneices, and the flight of the defeated Argives.* Antigone *calls* Ismene *forth from the palace, in order to speak to her alone.)*

Antigone:
Ismene, sister, mine own dear sister, knowest thou what ill there is, of all bequeaths by Oedipus, that Zeus fulfils not for us twain while we live? Nothing painful is there, nothing fraught with ruin, no shame, no dishonour, that I have not seen in thy woes and mine.

And now what new edict is this which they tell, that our Captain hath just published to all Thebes? Knowest thou aught? Hast thou heard? Or is it hidden from thee that our friends are threatened with the doom of our foes?

Ismene:
No word of friends, Antigone, gladsome or painful, hath come to me, since we two sisters were bereft of brothers twain, killed in one day by a twofold blow; and since in this last night the Argive host hath fled, I know no more, whether my fortune be brighter, or more grievous.

Antigone:
I knew it well, and therefore sought to bring thee beyond the gates of the court, that thou mightest hear alone.

Ismene:
What is it? 'Tis plain that thou art brooding on some dark tidings.

Antigone:
What, hath not Creon destined our brothers, the one to honoured burial, the other to unburied shame? Eteocles, they say, with due observance of right and custom, he hath laid in the earth, for his honour among the dead below. But the hapless corpse of Polyneices—as rumour saith, it hath been published to the town that none shall entomb him or mourn, but leave unwept, unsepulchred, a welcome store for the birds, as they espy him, to feast on at will.

Such, 'tis said, is the edict that the good Creon hath set forth for thee and for me,—yes, for *me*,—and is coming hither to proclaim it clearly to those who know it not; nor counts the matter light, but, whoso disobeys in aught, his doom is death by stoning before all the folk. Thou knowest it now; and thou wilt soon show whether thou art nobly bred, or the base daughter of a noble line.

Ismene:
Poor sister,—and if things stand thus, what could I help to do or undo?

Antigone:
Consider if thou wilt share the toil and the deed.

Ismene:
In what venture? What can be thy meaning?

Antigone:
Wilt thou aid this hand to lift the dead?

Ismene:
Thou wouldst bury him,—when 'tis forbidden to Thebes?

Antigone:
I will do my part,—and thine, if thou wilt not,—to a brother. False to him will I never be found.

Ismene:
Ah, over-bold! when Creon hath forbidden?

Antigone:
Nay, he hath no right to keep me from mine own.

Ismene:
Ah me! think, sister, how our father perished, amid hate and scorn, when sins bared by his own search had moved him to strike both eyes with self-blinding hand; then the mother wife, two names in one, with twisted noose did despite unto her life; and last, our two brothers in one day,—each shedding, hapless one, a kinsman's blood,—wrought out with mutual hands their common doom. And now *we* in turn— we two left all alone—think how we shall perish, more miserably than all the rest, if, in defiance of the law, we brave a king's decree or his powers. Nay, we must remember, first, that we were born women, as who should not strive with men; next that we are ruled of the stronger, so that we must obey in these things, and in things yet sorer. I, therefore, asking the Spirits Infernal to pardon, seeing that force is put on me herein, will hearken to our rulers; for 'tis witless to be over busy.

Antigone:
I will not urge thee,—no, nor, if thou yet shouldst have the mind, wouldst thou be welcome as a worker with *me*. Nay, be what thou wilt; but I will bury him: well for me to die in doing that. I shall rest, a loved one with him whom I have loved, sinless in my crime; for I owe a longer allegiance to

the dead than to the living: in that world I shall abide for ever. But if *thou* wilt, be guilty of dishonouring laws which the gods have stablished in honour.

Ismene:
I do them no dishonour; but to defy the State,—I have no strength for that.

Antigone:
Such be thy plea:—I, then, will go to heap the earth above the brother whom I love.

Ismene:
Alas, unhappy one! How I fear for thee!

Antigone:
Fear not for me: guide thine own fate aright.

Ismene:
At least, then, disclose this plan to none, but hide it closely,—and so, too, will I.

Antigone:
Oh, denounce it! Thou wilt be far more hateful for thy silence, if thou proclaim not these things to all.

Ismene:
Thou hast a hot heart for chilling deeds.

Antigone:
I know that I please where I am most bound to please.

Ismene:
Aye, if thou canst; but thou wouldst what thou canst not.

Antigone:
Why, then, when my strength fails, I shall have done.

Ismene:
A hopeless quest should not be made at all.

Antigone:
If thus thou speakest, thou wilt have hatred from me, and

will justly be subject to the lasting hatred of the dead. But leave me, and the folly that is mine alone, to suffer this dread thing; for I shall not suffer aught so dreadful as an ignoble death.

Ismene:
Go, then, if thou must; and of this be sure,—that, though thine errand is foolish, to thy dear ones thou art truly dear.

(*Exit* Antigone *on the spectators' left.* Ismene *retires into the palace by one of the two side-doors. When they have departed, the* Chorus *of Theban Elders enters.*)

Chorus (*singing*):

strophe I

Beam of the sun, fairest light that ever dawned on Thebe of the seven gates, thou hast shone forth at last, eye of golden day, arisen above Dirce's streams! The warrior of the white shield, who came from Argos in his panoply, hath been stirred by thee to headlong flight, in swifter career;

Leader of the Chorus:

systema I

who set forth against our land by reason of the vexed claims of Polyneices; and, like shrill-screaming eagle, he flew over into our land, in snow-white pinion sheathed, with an armed throng, and with plumage of helms.

Chorus:

antistrophe I

He paused above our dwellings; he ravened around our sevenfold portals with spears athirst for blood; but he went hence, or ever his jaws were glutted with our gore, or the Fire-god's pine-fed flame had seized our crown of towers. So fierce was the noise of battle raised behind him, a thing too hard for him to conquer, as he wrestled with his dragon foe.

Leader:

systema 2

For Zeus utterly abhors the boasts of a proud tongue; and when he beheld them coming on in a great stream, in the haughty pride of clanging gold, he smote with brandished fire one who was now hasting to shout victory at his goal upon our ramparts.

Chorus:

strophe 2

Swung down, he fell on the earth with a crash, torch in hand, he who so lately, in the frenzy of the mad onset, was raging against us with the blasts of his tempestuous hate. But those threats fared not as he hoped; and to other foes the mighty War-god dispensed their several dooms, dealing havoc around, a mighty helper at our need.

Leader:

systema 3

For seven captains at seven gates, matched against seven, left the tribute of their panoplies to Zeus who turns the battle; save those two of cruel fate, who, born of one sire and one mother, set against each other their twain conquering spears, and are sharers in a common death.

Chorus:

antistrophe 2

But since Victory of glorious name hath come to us, with joy responsive to the joy of Thebe whose chariots are many, let us enjoy forgetfulness after the late wars, and visit all the temples of the gods with night-long dance and song; and may Bacchus be our leader, whose dancing shakes the land of Thebe.

Leader:

systema 4

But lo, the king of the land comes yonder, Creon, son of Menoeceus, our new ruler by the new fortunes that the gods have given; what counsel is he pondering, that he hath proposed this special conference of elders, summoned by his general mandate?

(Enter Creon, *from the central doors of the palace, in the garb of king, with two attendants.*)

Creon:
>Sirs, the vessel of our State, after being tossed on wild waves, hath once more been safely steadied by the gods: and ye, out of all the folk, have been called apart by my summons, because I knew, first of all, how true and constant was your reverence for the royal power of Laius; how, again, when Oedipus was ruler of our land, and when he had perished, your steadfast loyalty still upheld their children. Since, then, his sons have fallen in one day by a twofold doom,—each smitten by the other, each stained with a brother's blood,—I now possess the throne and all its powers, by nearness of kinship to the dead.
>
>No man can be fully known, in soul and spirit and mind, until he hath been seen versed in rule and law-giving. For if any, being supreme guide of the State, cleaves not to the best counsels, but, through some fear, keeps his lips locked, I hold, and have ever held, him most base; and if any makes a friend of more account than his fatherland, that man hath no place in my regard. For I—be Zeus my witness, who sees all things always—would not be silent if I saw ruin, instead of safety, coming to the citizens; nor would I ever deem the country's foe a friend to myself; remembering this, that our country is the ship that bears us safe, and that only while she prospers in our voyage can we make true friends.
>
>Such are the rules by which I guard this city's greatness. And in accord with them is the edict which I have now published to the folk touching the sons of Oedipus;—that Eteocles, who hath fallen fighting for our city, in all renown of arms, shall be entombed, and crowned with every rite that follows the noblest dead to their rest. But for his brother, Polyneices,—who came back from exile, and sought to consume utterly with fire the city of his fathers and the shrines of his fathers' gods,—sought to taste of kindred blood, and to lead the remnant into slavery;—touching this man, it hath been proclaimed to our people that none shall grace him with sepulture or lament, but leave him unburied, a corpse for birds and dogs to eat, a ghastly sight of shame.
>
>Such the spirit of my dealing; and never, by deed of mine, shall the wicked stand in honour before the just; but whoso hath good will to Thebes, he shall be honoured of me, in his life and in his death.

Leader of the Chorus:
> Such is thy pleasure, Creon, son of Menoeceus, touching this city's foe, and its friend; and thou hast power, I ween, to take what order thou wilt, both for the dead, and for all us who live.

Creon:
> See, then, that ye be guardians of the mandate.

Leader:
> Lay the burden of this task on some younger man.

Creon:
> Nay, watchers of the corpse have been found.

Leader:
> What, then, is this further charge that thou wouldst give?

Creon:
> That ye side not with the breakers of these commands.

Leader:
> No man is so foolish that he is enamoured of death.

Creon:
> In sooth, that is the meed; yet lucre hath oft ruined men through their hopes.

> *(A* Guard *enters from the spectators' left.)*

Guard:
> My liege, I will not say that I come breathless from speed, or that I have plied a nimble fool; for often did my thoughts make me pause, and wheel round in my path, to return. My mind was holding large discourse with me; 'Fool, why goest thou to thy certain doom?' 'Wretch, tarrying again? And if Creon hears this from another, must not thou smart for it?' So debating, I went on my way with lagging steps, and thus a short road was made long. At last, however, it carried the day that I should come hither—to thee; and, though my tale be nought, yet will I tell it; for I come with a good grip on one hope,—that I can suffer nothing but what is my fate.

Creon:
And what is it that disquiets thee thus?

Guard:
I wish to tell thee first about myself—I did not do the deed—I did not see the doer—it were not right that I should come to any harm.

Creon:
Thou hast a shrewd eye for thy mark; well dost thou fence thyself round against the blame; clearly thou hast some strange thing to tell.

Guard:
Aye, truly; dread news makes one pause long.

Creon:
Then tell it, wilt thou, and so get thee gone?

Guard:
Well, this is it.—The corpse—some one hath just given it burial, and gone away,—after sprinkling thirsty dust on the flesh, with such other rites as piety enjoins.

Creon:
What sayest thou? What living man hath dared this deed?

Guard:
I know not; no stroke of pickaxe was seen there, no earth thrown up by mattock; the ground was hard and dry, unbroken, without track of wheels; the doer was one who had left no trace. And when the first day-watchman showed it to us, sore wonder fell on all. The dead man was veiled from us; not shut within a tomb, but lightly strewn with dust, as by the hand of one who shunned a curse. And no sign met the eye as though any beast of prey or any dog had come nigh to him, or torn him.

Then evil words flew fast and loud among us, guard accusing guard; and it would e'en have come to blows at last, nor was there any to hinder. Every man was the culprit, and no one was convicted, but all disclaimed knowledge of the deed. And we were ready to take red-hot iron in our hands;—to walk through fire;—to make oath by the gods that we had not done the deed,—that we were not privy to the planning or the doing.

At last, when all our searching was fruitless, one spake, who made us all bend our faces on the earth in fear; for we saw not how we could gainsay him, or escape mischance if we obeyed. His counsel was that this deed must be reported to thee, and not hidden. And this seemed best; and the lot doomed my hapless self to win this prize. So here I stand,—as unwelcome as unwilling, well I wot; for no man delights in the bearer of bad news.

Leader:
O king, my thoughts have long been whispering, can this deed, perchance, be e'en the work of gods?

Creon:
Cease, ere thy words fill me utterly with wrath, lest thou be found at once an old man and foolish. For thou sayest what is not to be borne, in saying that the gods have care for this corpse. Was it for high reward of trusty service that they sought to hide his nakedness, who came to burn their pillared shrines and sacred treasures, to burn their land, and scatter its laws to the winds? Or dost thou behold the gods honouring the wicked? It cannot be. No! From the first there were certain in the town that muttered against me, chafing at this edict, wagging their heads in secret; and kept not their necks duly under the yoke, like men contented with my sway.

'Tis by them, well I know, that these have been beguiled and bribed to do this deed. Nothing so evil as money ever grew to be current among men. This lays cities low, this drives men from their homes, this trains and warps honest souls till they set themselves to works of shame; this still teaches folk to practise villainies, and to know every godless deed.

But all the men who wrought this thing for hire have made it sure that, soon or late, they shall pay the price. Now, as Zeus still hath my reverence, know this—I tell it thee on my oath:—If ye find not the very author of this burial, and produce him before mine eyes, death alone shall not be enough for you, till first, hung up alive, ye have revealed this outrage,—that henceforth ye may thieve with better knowledge whence lucre should be won, and learn that it is not well to love gain from every source. For thou wilt find that ill-gotten pelf brings more men to ruin than to weal.

Guard:
May I speak? Or shall I just turn and go?

Creon:
Knowest thou not that even now thy voice offends?

Guard:
Is thy smart in the ears, or in the soul?

Creon:
And why wouldst thou define the seat of my pain?

Guard:
The doer vexes thy mind, but I, thine ears.

Creon:
Ah, thou art a born babbler, 'tis well seen.

Guard:
May be, but never the doer of this deed.

Creon:
Yea, and more,—the seller of thy life for silver.

Guard:
Alas! 'Tis sad, truly, that he who judges should misjudge.

Creon:
Let thy fancy play with 'judgment' as it will;—but, if ye show me not the doers of these things, ye shall avow that dastardly gains work sorrows.

(Creon *goes into the palace.*)

Guard:
Well, may he be found! so 'twere best. But, be he caught or

be he not—fortune must settle that—truly thou wilt not see me here again. Saved, even now, beyond hope and thought, I owe the gods great thanks.

(The Guard *goes out on the spectators' left.)*

Chorus *(singing)*:

strophe I

Wonders are many, and none is more wonderful than man; the power that crosses the white sea, driven by the stormy south-wind, making a path under surges that threaten to engulf him; and Earth, the eldest of the gods, the immortal, the unwearied, doth he wear, turning the soil with the offspring of horses, as the ploughs go to and fro from year to year.

antistrophe I

And the light-hearted race of birds, and the tribes of savage beasts, and the sea-brood of the deep, he snares in the meshes of his woven toils, he leads captive, man excellent in wit. And he masters by his arts the beast whose lair is in the wilds, who roams the hills; he tames the horse of shaggy mane, he puts the yoke upon its neck, he tames the tireless mountain bull.

strophe 2

And speech, and wind-swift thought, and all the moods that mould a state, hath he taught himself; and how to flee the arrows of the frost, when 'tis hard lodging under the clear sky, and the arrows of the rushing rain; yea, he hath resource for all; without resource he meets nothing that must come: only against Death shall he càll for aid in vain; but from baffling maladies he hath devised escapes.

antistrophe 2

Cunning beyond fancy's dream is the fertile skill which brings him, now to evil, now to good. When he honours the laws of the land, and that justice which he hath sworn by the gods to uphold, proudly stands his city: no city hath he who, for his rashness, dwells with sin. Never may he share my hearth, never think my thoughts, who doth these things!

(Enter the Guard *on the spectators' left, leading in* Antigone.*)*

Leader of the Chorus:
    What portent from the gods is this?—my soul is amazed. I know her—how can I deny that yon maiden is Antigone?
        O hapless, and child of hapless sire,—of Oedipus! What means this? Thou brought a prisoner?—thou, disloyal to the king's laws, and taken in folly?

Guard:
    Here she is, the doer of the deed:—we caught this girl burying him:—but where is Creon?

(Creon enters hurriedly from the palace.)

Leader:
    Lo, he comes forth again from the house, at our need.

Creon:
    What is it? What hath chanced, that makes my coming timely?

Guard:
    O king, against nothing should men pledge their word; for the afterthought belies the first intent. I could have vowed that I should not soon be here again,—scared by thy threats, with which I had just been lashed: but,—since the joy that surprises and transcends our hopes is like in fulness to no other pleasure,—I have come, though 'tis in breach of my sworn oath, bringing this maid; who was taken showing grace to the dead. This time there was no casting of lots; no, this luck hath fallen to me, and to none else. And now, sire, take her thyself, question her, examine her, as thou wilt; but I have a right to free and final quittance of this trouble.

Creon:
    And thy prisoner here—how and whence hast thou taken her?

Guard:
    She was burying the man; thou knowest all.

Creon:
> Dost thou mean what thou sayest? Dost thou speak aright?

Guard:
> I saw her burying the corpse that thou hadst forbidden to bury. Is that plain and clear?

Creon:
> And how was she seen? how taken in the act?

Guard:
> It befell on this wise. When we had come to the place,—with those dread menaces of thine upon us,—we swept away all the dust that covered the corpse, and bared the dank body well; and then sat us down on the brow of the hill, to windward, heedful that the smell from him should not strike us; every man was wide awake, and kept his neighbour alert with torrents of threats, if anyone should be careless of this task.
>
> So went it, until the sun's bright orb stood in mid heaven, and the heat began to burn: and then suddenly a whirlwind lifted from the earth a storm of dust, a trouble in the sky, and filled the plain, marring all the leafage of its woods; and the wide air was choked therewith: we closed our eyes, and bore the plague from the gods.
>
> And when, after a long while, this storm had passed, the maid was seen; and she cried aloud with the sharp cry of a bird in its bitterness,—even as when, within the empty nest, it sees the bed stripped of its nestlings. So she also, when she saw the corpse bare, lifted up a voice of wailing, and called down curses on the doers of that deed. And straightway she brought thirsty dust in her hands; and from a shapely ewer of bronze, held high, with thrice-poured drink-offering she crowned the dead.
>
> We rushed forward when we saw it, and at once closed upon our quarry, who was in no wise dismayed. Then we taxed her with her past and present doings; and she stood not on denial of aught,—at once to my joy and to my pain. To have escaped from ills one's self is a great joy; but 'tis painful to bring friends to ill. Howbeit, all such things are of less account to me than mine own safety.

Creon:
>Thou—thou whose face is bent to earth—dost thou avow, or disavow, this deed?

Antigone:
>I avow it; I make no denial.

Creon *(to* Guard*)*:
>Thou canst betake thee whither thou wilt, free and clear of a grave charge.
>
>>*(Exit* Guard.*)*
>
>*(To* Antigone.*)* Now, tell me thou—not in many words, but briefly—knewest thou that an edict had forbidden this?

Antigone:
>I knew it: could I help it? It was public.

Creon:
>And thou didst indeed dare to transgress that law?

Antigone:
>Yes; for it was not Zeus that had published me that edict; not such are the laws set among men by the Justice who dwells with the gods below; nor deemed I that thy decrees were of such force, that a mortal could override the unwritten and unfailing statutes of heaven. For their life is not of to-day or yesterday, but from all time, and no man knows when they were first put forth.
>
>Not through dread of any human pride could I answer to the gods for breaking *these*. Die I must,—I knew that well (how should I not?)—even without thy edicts. But if I am to die before my time, I count that a gain: for when any one lives, as I do, compassed about with evils, can such an one find aught but gain in death?
>
>So for me to meet this doom is trifling grief; but if I had suffered my mother's son to lie in death an unburied corpse, that would have grieved me; for this, I am not grieved. And if my present deeds are foolish in thy sight, it may be that a foolish judge arraigns my folly.

Leader of the Chorus:
> The maid shows herself passionate child of passionate sire, and knows not how to bend before troubles.

Creon:
> Yet I would have thee know that o'er-stubborn spirits are most often humbled; 'tis the stiffest iron, baked to hardness in the fire, that thou shalt oftenest see snapped and shivered; and I have known horses that show temper brought to order by a little curb; there is no room for pride, when thou art thy neighbour's slave.—This girl was already versed in insolence when she transgressed the laws that had been set forth; and, that done, lo, a second insult,—to vaunt of this, and exult in her deed.
>
> Now verily I am no man, she is the man, if this victory shall rest with her, and bring no penalty. No! be she sister's child, or nearer to me in blood than any that worships Zeus at the altar of our house,—she and her kinsfolk shall not avoid a doom most dire; for indeed I charge that other with a like share in the plotting of this burial.
>
> And summon her—for I saw her e'en now within,—raving, and not mistress of her wits. So oft, before the deed, the mind stands self-convicted in its treason, when folks are plotting mischief in the dark. But verily this, too, is hateful,—when one who hath been caught in wickedness then seeks to make the crime a glory.

Antigone:
> Wouldst thou do more than take and slay me?

Creon:
> No more, indeed; having that, I have all.

Antigone:
> Why then dost thou delay? In thy discourse there is nought that pleases me,—never may there be!—and so my words must needs be unpleasing to thee. And yet, for glory—whence could I have won a nobler, than by giving burial to mine own brother? All here would own that they thought it well, were not their lips sealed by fear. But royalty, blest in so much besides, hath the power to do and say what it will.

Creon:
   Thou differest from all these Thebans in that view.

Antigone:
   These also share it; but they curb their tongues for thee.

Creon:
   And art thou not ashamed to act apart from them?

Antigone:
   No; there is nothing shameful in piety to a brother.

Creon:
   Was it not a brother, too, that died in the opposite cause?

Antigone:
   Brother by the same mother and the same sire.

Creon:
   Why, then, dost thou render a grace that is impious in his sight?

Antigone:
   The dead man will not say that he so deems it.

Creon:
   Yea, if thou makest him but equal in honour with the wicked.

Antigone:
   It was his brother, not his slave, that perished.

Creon:
   Wasting this land; while *he* fell as its champion.

Antigone:
   Nevertheless, Hades desires these rites.

Creon:
   But the good desires not a like portion with the evil.

Antigone:
Who knows but this seems blameless in the world below?

Creon:
A foe is never a friend—not even in death.

Antigone:
'Tis not my nature to join in hating, but in loving.

Creon:
Pass, then, to the world of the dead, and, if thou must needs love them, love them. While I live, no woman shall rule me.

(Enter Ismene *from the house, led in by two attendants.)*

Chorus *(chanting)*:
Lo, yonder Ismene comes forth, shedding such tears as fond sisters weep; a cloud upon her brow casts its shadow over her darkly-flushing face, and breaks in rain on her fair cheek.

Creon:
And thou, who, lurking like a viper in my house, wast secretly draining my life-blood, while I knew not that I was nurturing two pests, to rise against my throne—come, tell me now, wilt thou also confess thy part in this burial, or wilt thou forswear all knowledge of it?

Ismene:
I have done the deed,—if she allows my claim,—and share the burden of the charge.

Antigone:
Nay, justice will not suffer thee to do that: thou didst not consent to the deed, nor did I give thee part in it.

Ismene:
But, now that ills beset thee, I am not ashamed to sail the sea of trouble at thy side.

Antigone:
Whose was the deed, Hades and the dead are witnesses: a friend in words is not the friend that I love.

Ismene:
> Nay, sister, reject me not, but let me die with thee, and duly honour the dead.

Antigone:
> Share not thou my death, nor claim deeds to which thou hast not put thy hand: my death will suffice.

Ismene:
> And what life is dear to me, bereft of thee?

Antigone:
> Ask Creon; all thy care is for him.

Ismene:
> Why vex me thus, when it avails thee nought?

Antigone:
> Indeed, if I mock, 'tis with pain that I mock thee.

Ismene:
> Tell me,—how can I serve thee, even now?

Antigone:
> Save thyself: I grudge not thy escape.

Ismene:
> Ah, woe is me! And shall I have no share in thy fate?

Antigone:
> Thy choice was to live; mine, to die.

Ismene:
> At least thy choice was not made without my protest.

Antigone:
> One world approved thy wisdom; another, mine.

Ismene:
> Howbeit, the offence is the same for both of us.

Antigone:
> Be of good cheer; thou livest; but my life hath long been given to death, that so I might serve the dead.

Creon:
> Lo, one of these maidens hath newly shown herself foolish, as the other hath been since her life began.

Ismene:
> Yea, O king, such reason as nature may have given abides not with the unfortunate, but goes astray.

Creon:
> Thine did, when thou chosest vile deeds with the vile.

Ismene:
> What life could I endure, without her presence?

Creon:
> Nay, speak not of her 'presence'; she lives no more.

Ismene:
> But wilt thou slay the betrothed of thine own son?

Creon:
> Nay, there are other fields for him to plough.

Ismene:
> But there can never be such love as bound him to her.

Creon:
> I like not an evil wife for my son.

Antigone:
> Haemon, beloved! How thy father wrongs thee!

Creon:
> Enough, enough of thee and of thy marriage!

Leader of the Chorus:
> Wilt thou indeed rob thy son of this maiden?

Creon:
'Tis Death that shall stay these bridals for me.

Leader:
'Tis determined, it seems, that she shall die.

Creon:
Determined, yes, for thee and for me.—*(To the two attendants.)* No more delay—servants, take them within! Henceforth they must be women, and not range at large; for verily even the bold seek to fly, when they see Death now closing on their life.

(Exeunt attendants, guarding Antigone *and* Ismeme.—Creon *remains.)*

Chorus (singing):

strophe 1

Blest are they whose days have not tasted of evil. For when a house hath once been shaken from heaven, there the curse fails nevermore, passing from life to life of the race; even as, when the surge is driven over the darkness of the deep by the fierce breath of Thracian seawinds, it rolls up the black sand from the depths, and there is a sullen roar from wind-vexed headlands that front the blows of the storm.

antistrophe 1

I see that from olden time the sorrows in the house of the Labdacidae are heaped upon the sorrows of the dead; and generation is not freed by generation, but some god strikes them down, and the race hath no deliverance.

For now that hope of which the light had been spread above the last root of the house of Oedipus—that hope, in turn, is brought low—by the blood-stained dust due to the gods infernal, and by folly in speech, and frenzy at the heart.

strophe 2

Thy power, O Zeus, what human trespass can limit? That power which neither Sleep, the all-ensnaring, nor the untiring months of the gods can master; but thou, a ruler to whom time brings not old age, dwellest in the dazzling splendour of Olympus.

And through the future, near and far, as through the

past, shall this law hold good: Nothing that is vast enters into the life of mortals without a curse.

antistrophe 2
For that hope whose wanderings are so wide is to many men a comfort, but to many a false lure of giddy desires; and the disappointment comes on one who knoweth nought till he burn his foot against the hot fire.

For with wisdom hath some one given forth the famous saying, that evil seems good, soon or late, to him whose mind the god draws to mischief; and but for the briefest space doth he fare free of woe.

Leader of the Chorus:
But lo, Haemon, the last of thy sons;—comes he grieving for the doom of his promised bride, Antigone, and bitter for the baffled hope of his marriage?

(Enter Haemon)

Creon:
We shall know soon, better than seers could tell us.—My son, hearing the fixed doom of thy betrothed, art thou come in rage against thy father? Or have I thy good will, act how I may?

Haemon:
Father, I am thine; and thou, in thy wisdom, tracest for me rules which I shall follow. No marriage shall be deemed by me a greater gain than thy good guidance.

Creon:
Yea, this, my son, should be thy heart's fixed law,—in all things to obey thy father's will. 'Tis for this that men pray to see dutiful children grow up around them in their homes,— that such may requite their father's foe with evil, and honour, as their father doth, his friend. But he who begets unprofitable children—what shall we say that he hath sown, but troubles for himself, and much triumph for his foes? Then do not thou, my son, at pleasure's beck, dethrone thy reason for a woman's sake; knowing that this is a joy that soon grows cold in clasping arms,—an evil woman to share

thy bed and thy home. For what wound could strike deeper than a false friend? Nay, with loathing, and as if she were thine enemy, let this girl go to find a husband in the house of Hades. For since I have taken her, alone of all the city, in open disobedience, I will not make myself a liar to my people—I will slay her.

So let her appeal as she will to the majesty of kindred blood. If I am to nurture mine own kindred in naughtiness, needs must I bear with it in aliens. He who does his duty in his own household will be found righteous in the State also. But if any one transgresses, and does violence to the laws, or thinks to dictate to his rulers, such an one can win no praise from me. No, whomsoever the city may appoint, that man must be obeyed, in little things and great, in just things and unjust; and I should feel sure that one who thus obeys would be a good ruler no less than a good subject, and in the storm of spears would stand his ground where he was set, loyal and dauntless at his comrade's side.

But disobedience is the worst of evils. This it is that ruins cities; this makes homes desolate; by this, the ranks of allies are broken into headlong rout; but, of the lives whose course is fair, the greater part owes safety to obedience. Therefore we must support the cause of order, and in no wise suffer a woman to worst us. Better to fall from power, if we must, by a man's hand; then we should not be called weaker than a woman.

Leader:
To us, unless our years have stolen our wit, thou seemest to say wisely what thou sayest.

Haemon:
Father, the gods implant reason in men, the highest of all things that we call our own. Not mine the skill—far from me be the quest!—to say wherein thou speakest not aright; and yet another man, too, might have some useful thought. At least, it is my natural office to watch, on thy behalf, all that men say, or do, or find to blame. For the dread of thy frown forbids the citizen to speak such words as would offend thine ear; but I can hear these murmurs in the dark, these moanings of the city for this maiden; 'no woman,' they say, 'ever merited her doom less,—none ever was to die so

shamefully for deeds so glorious as hers; who, when her own brother had fallen in bloody strife, would not leave him unburied, to be devoured by carrion dogs, or by any bird:— deserves not *she* the meed of golden honour?'

Such is the darkling rumour that spreads in secret. For me, my father, no treasure is so precious as thy welfare. What, indeed, is a nobler ornament for children than a prospering sire's fair fame, or for sire than son's? Wear not, then, one mood only in thyself; think not that thy word, and thine alone, must be right. For if any man thinks that he alone is wise,—that in speech, or in mind, he hath no peer,—such a soul, when laid open, is ever found empty.

No, though a man be wise, 'tis no shame for him to learn many things, and to bend in season. Seest thou, beside the wintry torrent's course, how the trees that yield to it save every twig, while the stiff-necked perish root and branch? And even thus he who keeps the sheet of his sail taut, and never slackens it, upsets his boat, and finishes his voyage with keel uppermost.

Nay, forego thy wrath; permit thyself to change. For if I, a younger man, may offer my thought, it were far best, I ween, that men should be all-wise by nature; but, otherwise—and oft the scale inclines not so—'tis good also to learn from those who speak aright.

Leader:
Sire, 'tis meet that thou shouldest profit by his words, if he speaks aught in season, and thou, Haemon, by thy father's; for on both parts there hath been wise speech.

Creon:
Men of my age—are we indeed to be schooled, then, by men of his?

Haemon:
In nothing that is not right; but if I am young, thou shouldest look to my merits, not to my years.

Creon:
Is it a merit to honour the unruly?

Haemon:
  I could wish no one to show respect for evil-doers.

Creon:
  Then is not she tainted with that malady?

Haemon:
  Our Theban folk, with one voice denies it.

Creon:
  Shall Thebes prescribe to me how I must rule?

Haemon:
  See, there thou hast spoken like a youth indeed.

Creon:
  Am I to rule this land by other judgment than mine own?

Haemon:
  That is no city which belongs to one man.

Creon:
  Is not the city held to be the ruler's?

Haemon:
  Thou wouldst make a good monarch of a desert.

Creon:
  This boy, it seems, is the woman's champion.

Haemon:
  If thou art a woman; indeed, my care is for thee.

Creon:
  Shameless, at open feud with thy father!

Haemon:
  Nay, I see thee offending against justice.

Creon:
  Do I offend, when I respect mine own prerogatives?

Haemon:
> Thou dost not respect them, when thou tramplest on the gods' honours.

Creon:
> O dastard nature, yielding place to woman!

Haemon:
> Thou wilt never find me yield to baseness.

Creon:
> All thy words, at least, plead for that girl.

Haemon:
> And for thee, and for me, and for the gods below.

Creon:
> Thou canst never marry her, on this side of the grave.

Haemon:
> Then she must die, and in death destroy another.

Creon:
> How! doth thy boldness run to open threats?

Haemon:
> What threat is it, to combat vain resolves?

Creon:
> Thou shalt rue thy witless teaching of wisdom.

Haemon:
> Wert thou not my father, I would have called thee unwise.

Creon:
> Thou woman's slave, use not wheedling speech with me.

Haemon:
> Thou wouldest speak, and then hear no reply?

Creon:
> Sayest thou so? Now, by the heaven above us—be sure of

it—thou shalt smart for taunting me in this opprobrious strain. Bring forth that hated thing, that she may die forthwith in his presence—before his eyes—at her bridegroom's side!

Haemon:
No, not at my side—never think it—shall she perish; nor shalt thou ever set eyes more upon my face:—rave, then, with such friends as can endure thee.

(*Exit* Haemon.)

Leader:
The man is gone, O king, in angry haste; a youthful mind, when stung, is fierce.

Creon:
Let him do, or dream, more than man—good speed to him!—But he shall not save these two girls from their doom.

Leader:
Dost thou indeed purpose to slay both?

Creon:
Not her whose hands are pure: thou sayest well.

Leader:
And by what doom mean'st thou to slay the other?

Creon:
I will take her where the path is loneliest, and hide her, living, in a rocky vault, with so much food set forth as piety prescribes, that the city may avoid a public stain. And there, praying to Hades, the only god whom she worships, perchance she will obtain release from death; or else will learn, at last, though late, that it is lost labour to revere the dead.

(Creon *goes into the palace.*)

Chorus (*singing*):

strophe

Love, unconquered in the fight, Love, who makest havoc of

wealth, who keepest thy vigil on the soft cheek of a maiden; thou roamest over the sea, and among the homes of dwellers in the wilds; no immortal can escape thee, nor any among men whose life is for a day; and he to whom thou hast come is mad.

antistrophe

The just themselves have their minds warped by thee to wrong, for their ruin: 'tis thou that hast stirred up this present strife of kinsmen; victorious is the love-kindling light from the eyes of the fair bride; it is a power enthroned in sway beside the eternal laws; for there the goddess Aphrodite is working her unconquerable will.

(Antigone *is led out of the palace by two of* Creon's *attendants who are about to conduct her to her doom.*)

But now I also am carried beyond the bounds of loyalty, and can no more keep back the streaming tears, when I see Antigone thus passing to the bridal chamber where all are laid to rest.

(*The following lines between* Antigone *and the* Chorus *are chanted responsively.*)

Antigone:

strophe I

See me, citizens of my fatherland, setting forth on my last way, looking my last on the sunlight that is for me no more; no, Hades who gives sleep to all leads me living to Acheron's shore; who have had no portion in the chant that brings the bride, nor hath any song been mine for the crowning of bridals; whom the lord of the Dark Lake shall wed.

Chorus:

systema I

Glorious, therefore, and with praise, thou departest to that deep place of the dead: wasting sickness hath not smitten thee; thou hast not found the wages of the sword; no, mistress of thine own fate, and still alive, thou shalt pass to Hades, as no other of mortal kind hath passed.

Antigone:

antistrophe 1

I have heard in other days how dread a doom befell our Phrygian guest, the daughter of Tantalus, on the Sipylian heights; how, like clinging ivy, the growth of stone subdued her; and the rains fail not, as men tell, from her wasting form, nor fails the snow, while beneath her weeping lids the tears bedew her bosom; and most like to hers is the fate that brings me to my rest.

Chorus:

systema 2

Yet she was a goddess, thou knowest, and born of gods; we are mortals, and of mortal race. But 'tis great renown for a woman who hath perished that she should have shared the doom of the godlike, in her life, and afterward in death.

Antigone:

strophe 2

Ah, I am mocked! In the name of our fathers' gods, can ye not wail till I am gone,—must ye taunt me to my face, O my city, and ye, her wealthy sons? Ah, fount of Dirce, and thou holy ground of Thebe whose chariots are many; ye, at least, will bear me witness, in what sort, unwept of friends, and by what laws I pass to the rock-closed prison of my strange tomb, ah me unhappy! who have no home on the earth or in the shades, no home with the living or with the dead.

Chorus:

strophe 3

Thou hast rushed forward to the utmost verge of daring; and against that throne where Justice sits on high thou hast fallen, my daughter, with a grievous fall. But in this ordeal thou art paying, haply, for thy father's sin.

Antigone:

antistrophe 2

Thou hast touched on my bitterest thought,—awaking the evernew lament for my sire and for all the doom given to us, the famed house of Labdacus. Alas for the horrors of the mother's bed! alas for the wretched mother's slumber at the side of her own son,—and my sire! From what manner of parents did I take my miserable being! And to them I go thus, accursed, unwed, to share their home. Alas, my brother, ill-starred in thy marriage, in thy death thou hast undone my life!

Chorus:

antistrophe 3

Reverent action claims a certain praise for reverence; but an offence against power cannot be brooked by him who hath power in his keeping. Thy self-willed temper hath wrought thy ruin.

Antigone:

epode

Unwept, unfriended, without marriage-song, I am led forth in my sorrow on this journey that can be delayed no more. No longer, hapless one, may I behold yon day-star's sacred eye; but for my fate no tear is shed, no friend makes moan.

(Creon *enters from the palace.*)

Creon:

Know ye not that songs and wailings before death would never cease, if it profited to utter them? Away with her—away! And when ye have enclosed her, according to my word, in her vaulted grave, leave her alone, forlorn—whether she wishes to die, or to live a buried life in such a home. Our hands are clean as touching this maiden. But this is certain—she shall be deprived of her sojourn in the light.

Antigone:

Tomb, bridal-chamber, eternal prison in the caverned rock, whither I go to find mine own, those many who have perished, and whom Persephone hath received among the dead! Last of all shall I pass thither, and far most miserably of all, before the term of my life is spent. But I cherish good hope that my coming will be welcome to my father, and pleasant to thee, my mother, and welcome, brother, to thee; for, when ye died, with mine own hands I washed and dressed you, and poured drink-offerings at your graves; and now, Polyneices, 'tis for tending thy corpse that I win such recompense as this.

And yet I honoured thee, as the wise will deem, rightly. Never, had I been a mother of children, or if a husband had been mouldering in death, would I have taken this task upon me in the city's despite. What law, ye ask, is my warrant for that word? The husband lost, another might have been found, and child from another, to replace the first-born; but, father and mother hidden with Hades, no brother's life could ever bloom for me again. Such was the law whereby I held thee first in honour; but Creon deemed me guilty of error therein, and of outrage, ah brother mine! And now he leads me thus, a captive in his hands; no bridal bed, no bridal song hath been mine, no joy of marriage, no portion in the nurture of children; but thus, forlorn of friends, unhappy one, I go living to the vaults of death.

And what law of heaven have I transgressed? Why, hapless one, should I look to the gods any more,—what ally should I invoke,—when by piety I have earned the name of impious? Nay, then, if these things are pleasing to the gods, when I have suffered my doom, I shall come to know my sin; but if the sin is with my judges, I could wish them no fuller measure of evil than they, on their part, mete wrongfully to me.

Chorus:
Still the same tempest of the soul vexes this maiden with the same fierce gusts.

Creon:
Then for this shall her guards have cause to rue their slowness.

Antigone:
Ah me! that word hath come very near to death.

Creon:
I can cheer thee with no hope that this doom is not thus to be fulfilled.

Antigone:
O city of my fathers in the land of Thebe! O ye gods, eldest of our race!—they lead me hence—now, now—they tarry not! Behold me, princes of Thebes, the last daughter of the

house of your kings,—see what I suffer, and from whom, because I feared to cast away the fear of Heaven!

(Antigone is led away by the guards.)

Chorus *(singing)*:

strophe 1

Even thus endured Danae in her beauty to change the light of day for brass-bound walls; and in that chamber, secret as the grave, she was held close prisoner; yet was she of a proud lineage, O my daughter, and charged with the keeping of the seed of Zeus, that fell in the golden rain.

But dreadful is the mysterious power of fate; there is no deliverance from it by wealth or by war, by fenced city, or dark, sea-beaten ships.

antistrophe 1

And bonds tamed the son of Dryas, swift to wrath, that king of the Edonians; so paid he for his frenzied taunts, when, by the will of Dionysus, he was pent in a rocky prison. There the fierce exuberance of his madness slowly passed away. That man learned to know the god, whom in his frenzy he had provoked with mokeries; for he had sought to quell the god-possessed women, and the Bacchanalian fire; and he angered the Muses that love the flute.

strophe 2

And by the waters of the Dark Rocks, the waters of the twofold sea, are the shores of Bosporus, and Thracian Salmydessus; where Ares, neighbour to the city, saw the accurst, blinding wound dealt to the two sons of Phineus by his fierce wife,—the wound that brought darkness to those vengeance-craving orbs, smitten with her bloody hands, smitten with her shuttle for a dagger.

antistrophe 2

Pining in their misery, they bewailed their cruel doom, those sons of a mother hapless in her marriage; but she traced her descent from the ancient line of the Erechtheidae; and in far-distant caves she was nursed amid her father's storms, that child of Boreas, swift as a steed over the steep hills, a daughter of gods; yet upon her also the gray Fates bore hard, my daughter.

(Enter Teiresias, led by a Boy, on the spectators' right.)

Teiresias:
Princes of Thebes, we have come, with linked steps, both served by the eyes of one; for thus, by a guide's help, the blind must walk.

Creon:
And what, aged Teiresias, are thy tidings?

Teiresias:
I will tell thee; and do thou hearken to the seer.

Creon:
Indeed, it has not been my wont to slight thy counsel.

Teiresias:
Therefore didst thou steer our city's course aright.

Creon:
I have felt, and can attest, thy benefits.

Teiresias:
Mark that now, once more, thou standest on fate's fine edge.

Creon:
What means this? How I shudder at thy message!

Teiresias:
Thou wilt learn, when thou hearest the warnings of mine art. As I took my place on mine old seat of augury, where all birds have been wont to gather within my ken, I heard a strange voice among them; they were screaming with dire, feverish rage, that drowned their language in a jargon; and I knew that they were rending each other with their talons, murderously; the whirr of wings told no doubtful tale.

Forthwith, in fear, I essayed burnt-sacrifice on a duly kindled altar: but from my offerings the Fire-god showed no flame; a dank moisture, oozing from the thigh-flesh, trickled forth upon the embers, and smoked, and sputtered; the gall was scattered to the air; and the streaming thighs lay bared of the fat that had been wrapped round them.

Such was the failure of the rites by which I vainly asked a sign, as from this boy I learned; for he is my guide, as I am guide to others. And 'tis thy counsel that hath brought this sickness on our State. For the altars of our city and of our hearths have been tainted, one and all, by birds and dogs, with carrion from the hapless corpse, the son of Oedipus: and therefore the gods no more accept prayer and sacrifice at our hands, or the flame of meat-offering; nor doth any bird give a clear sign by its shrill cry, for they have tasted the fatness of a slain man's blood.

Think, then, on these things, my son. All men are liable to err; but when an error hath been made, that man is no longer witless or unblest who heals the ill into which he hath fallen, and remains not stubborn.

Self-will, we know, incurs the charge of folly. Nay, allow the claim of the dead; stab not the fallen; what prowess is it to slay the slain anew? I have sought thy good, and for thy good I speak: and never is it sweeter to learn from a good counsellor than when he counsels for thine own gain.

Creon:
Old man, ye all shoot your shafts at me, as archers at the butts;—ye must needs practise on me with seer-craft also;—aye, the seer-tribe hath long trafficked in me, and made me their merchandise. Gain your gains, drive your trade, if ye list, in the silver-gold of Sardis and the gold of India; but ye shall not hide that man in the grave,—no, though the eagles of Zeus should bear the carrion morsels to their Master's throne—no, not for dread of that defilement will I suffer his burial:—for well I know that no mortal can defile the gods.— But, aged Teiresias, the wisest fall with a shameful fall, when they clothe shameful thoughts in fair words, for lucre's sake.

Teiresias:
Alas! Doth any man know, doth any consider . . .

Creon:
Whereof? What general truth dost thou announce?

Teiresias:
How precious, above all wealth, is good counsel.

Creon:
>As folly, I think, is the worst mischief.

Teiresias:
>Yet thou art tainted with that distemper.

Creon:
>I would not answer the seer with a taunt.

Teiresias:
>But thou dost, in saying that I prophesy falsely.

Creon:
>Well, the prophet-tribe was ever fond of money.

Teiresias:
>And the race bred of tyrants loves base gain.

Creon:
>Knowest thou that thy speech is spoken of thy king?

Teiresias:
>I know it; for through me thou hast saved Thebes.

Creon:
>Thou art a wise seer; but thou lovest evil deeds.

Teiresias:
>Thou wilt rouse me to utter the dread secret in my soul.

Creon:
>Out with it!—Only speak it not for gain.

Teiresias:
>Indeed, methinks, I shall not,—as touching thee.

Creon:
>Know that thou shalt not trade on my resolve.

Teiresias:
>Then know thou—aye, know it well—that thou shalt not live through many more courses of the sun's swift chariot, ere

one begotten of thine own loins shall have been given by thee, a corpse for corpses; because thou hast thrust children of the sunlight to the shades, and ruthlessly lodged a living soul in the grave; but keepest in this world one who belongs to the gods infernal, a corpse unburied, unhonoured, all unhallowed. In such thou hast no part, nor have the gods above, but this is a violence done to them by thee. Therefore the avenging destroyers lie in wait for thee, the Furies of Hades and of the gods, that thou mayest be taken in these same ills.

And mark well if I speak these things as a hireling. A time not long to be delayed shall awaken the wailing of men and of women in thy house. And a tumult of hatred against thee stirs all the cities whose mangled sons had the burial-rite from dogs, or from wild beasts, or from some winged bird that bore a polluting breath to each city that contains the hearths of the dead.

Such arrows for thy heart—since thou provokest me—have I launched at thee, archer-like, in my anger,—sure arrows, of which thou shalt not escape the smart.—Boy, lead me home, that he may spend his rage on younger men, and learn to keep a tongue more temperate, and to bear within his breast a better mind than now he bears.

(The Boy leads Teiresias out.)

Leader of the Chorus:
The man hath gone, O King, with dread prophecies. And, since the hair on this head, once dark, hath been white, I know that he hath never been a false prophet to our city.

Creon:
I, too, know it well, and am troubled in soul. 'Tis dire to yield; but, by resistance, to smite my pride with ruin—this, too, is a dire choice.

Leader:
Son of Menoeceus, it behoves thee to take wise counsel.

Creon:
What should I do, then? Speak, and I will obey.

Leader:
Go thou, and free the maiden from her rocky chamber, and make a tomb for the unburied dead.

Creon:
And this is thy counsel? Thou wouldst have me yield?

Leader:
Yea, King, and with all speed; for swift harms from the gods cut short the folly of men.

Creon:
Ah me, 'tis hard, but I resign my cherished resolve,—I obey. We must not wage a vain war with destiny.

Leader:
Go, thou, and do these things; leave them not to others.

Creon:
Even as I am I'll go:—on, on, my servants, each and all of you,—take axes in your hands, and hasten to the ground that ye see yonder! Since our judgment hath taken this turn, I will be present to unloose her, as I myself bound her. My heart misgives me, 'tis best to keep the established laws, even to life's end.

(Creon *and his servants hasten out on the spectator's left.*)

Chorus (*singing*):

strophe I
O thou of many names, glory of the Cadmeian bride, offspring of loud-thundering Zeus! thou who watchest over famed Italia, and reignest, where all guests are welcomed, in the sheltered plain of Eleusinian Deo! O Bacchus, dweller in Thebe, mother-city of Bacchants, by the softly-gliding stream of Ismenus, on the soil where the fierce dragon's teeth were sown!

antistrophe I
Thou hast been seen where torch-flames glare through smoke, above the crests of the twin peaks, where move the Corycian nymphs, thy votaries, hard by Castalia's stream.
Thou comest from the ivy-mantled slopes of Nysa's

hills, and from the shore green with many-clustered vines, while thy name is lifted up on strains of more than mortal power, as thou visitest the ways of Thebe:

strophe 2

Thebe, of all cities, thou holdest first in honour, thou, and thy mother whom the lightning smote; and now, when all our people is captive to a violent plague, come thou with healing feet over the Parnassian height, or over the moaning strait!

antistrophe 2

O thou with whom the stars rejoice as they move, the stars whose breath is fire; O master of the voices of the night; son begotten of Zeus; appear, O king, with thine attendant Thyiads, who in nightlong frenzy dance before thee, the giver of good gifts, Iacchus!

(Enter Messenger, *on the spectators left.)*

Messenger:
Dwellers by the house of Cadmus and of Amphion, there is no estate of mortal life that I would ever praise or blame as settled. Fortune raises and Fortune humbles the lucky or unlucky from day to day, and no one can prophesy to men concerning those things which are established. For Creon was blest once, as I count bliss; he had saved this land of Cadmus from its foes; he was clothed with sole dominion in the land; he reigned, the glorious sire of princely children. And now all hath been lost. For when a man hath forfeited his pleasures, I count him not as living,—I hold him but a breathing corpse. Heap up riches in thy house, if thou wilt; live in kingly state; yet, if there be no gladness therewith, I would not give the shadow of a vapour for all the rest, compared with joy.

Leader of the Chorus:
And what is this new grief that thou hast to tell for our princes?

Messenger:
Death; and the living are guilty for the dead.

Leader:
And who is the slayer? Who the striken? Speak.

Messenger:
Haemon hath perished; his blood hath been shed by no stranger.

Leader:
By his father's hand, or by his own?

Messenger:
By his own, in wrath with his sire for the murder.

Leader:
O prophet, how true, then, hast thou proved thy word!

Messenger:
These things stand thus; ye must consider of the rest.

Leader:
Lo, I see the hapless Eurydice, Creon's wife, approaching; she comes from the house by chance, haply,—or because she knows the tidings of her son.

(Enter Eurydice from the palace.)

Eurydice:
People of Thebes, I heard your words as I was going forth, to salute the goddess Pallas with my prayers. Even as I was loosing the fastenings of the gate, to open it, the message of a household woe smote on mine ear: I sank back, terror-stricken, into the arms of my handmaids, and my senses fled. But say again what the tidings were; I shall hear them as one who is no stranger to sorrow.

Messenger:
Dear lady, I will witness of what I saw, and will leave no word of the truth untold. Why, indeed, should I soothe thee with words in which I must presently be found false? Truth is ever best.—I attended thy lord as his guide to the furthest part of the plain, where the body of Polyneices, torn by dogs, still lay unpitied. We prayed the goddess of the roads, and

Pluto, in mercy to restrain their wrath; we washed the dead with holy washing; and with freshly-plucked boughs we solemnly burned such relics as there were. We raised a high mound of his native earth; and then we turned away to enter the maiden's nuptial chamber with rocky couch, the caverned mansion of the bride of Death. And, from afar off, one of us heard a voice of loud wailing at that bride's unhallowed bower; and came to tell our master Creon.

And as the king drew nearer, doubtful sounds of a bitter cry floated around him; he groaned, and said in accents of anguish, 'Wretched that I am, can my foreboding be true? Am I going on the wofullest way that ever I went? My son's voice greets me.—Go, my servants,—haste ye nearer, and when ye have reached the tomb, pass through the gap, where the stones have been wrenched away, to the cell's very mouth,—and look, and see if 'tis Haemon's voice that I know, or if mine ear is cheated by the gods.'

This search, at our despairing master's word, we went to make; and in the furthest part of the tomb we descried *her* hanging by the neck, slung by a thread-wrought halter of fine linen; while *he* was embracing her with arms thrown around her waist,—bewailing the loss of his bride who is with the dead, and his father's deeds, and his own ill-starred love.

But his father, when he saw him, cried aloud with a dread cry and went in, and called to him with a voice of wailing:—'Unhappy, what a deed hast thou done! What thought hath come to thee? What manner of mischance hath marred thy reason? Come forth, my child! I pray thee—I implore!' But the boy glared at him with fierce eyes, spat in his face, and, without a word of answer, drew his cross-hilted sword:—as his father rushed forth in flight, he missed his aim;—then, hapless one, wroth with himself, he straightway leaned with all his weight against his sword, and drove it, half its length, into his side; and, while sense lingered, he clasped the maiden to his faint embrace, and, as he gasped, sent forth on her pale cheek the swift stream of the oozing blood.

Corpse enfolding corpse he lies; he hath won his nuptial rites, poor youth, not here, yet in the halls of Death; and he hath witnessed to mankind that, of all curses which cleave to man, ill counsel is the sovereign curse.

(Eurydice *retires into the house.*)

Leader:
What wouldst thou augur from this? The lady hath turned back, and is gone, without a word, good or evil.

Messenger:
I, too, am startled; yet I nourish the hope that, at these sore tidings of her son, she cannot deign to give her sorrow public vent, but in the privacy of the house will set her handmaids to mourn the household grief. For she is not untaught of discretion, that she should err.

Leader:
I know not; but to me, at least, a strained silence seems to portend peril, no less than vain abundance of lament.

Messenger:
Well, I will enter the house, and learn whether indeed she is not hiding some repressed purpose in the depths of a passionate heart. Yea, thou sayest well: excess of silence, too, may have a perilous meaning.

(*The* Messenger *goes into the palace. Enter* Creon, *on the spectators' left, with attendants, carrying the shrouded body of* Haemon *on a bier. The following lines between* Creon *and the* Chorus *are chanted responsively.*)

Chorus:
Lo, yonder the king himself draws near, bearing that which tells too clear a tale,—the work of no stranger's madness,—if we may say it,—but of his own misdeeds.

Creon:

strophe I

Woe for the sins of a darkened soul, stubborn sins, fraught with death! Ah, ye behold us, the sire who hath slain, the son who hath perished! Woe is me, for the wretched blindness of my counsels! Alas, my son, thou hast died in thy youth, by a timeless doom, woe is me!—thy spirit hath fled,—not by thy folly, but by mine own!

Chorus:

strophe 2

Ah me, how all too late thou seemest to see the right!

Creon:

Ah me, I have learned the bitter lesson! But then, methinks, oh then, some god smote me from above with crushing weight, and hurled me into ways of cruelty, woe is me,—overthrowing and trampling on my joy! Woe, woe, for the troublous toils of men!

(Enter Messenger *from the house.)*

Messenger:

Sire, thou hast come, methinks, as one whose hands are not empty, but who hath store laid up besides; thou bearest yonder burden with thee; and thou art soon to look upon the woes within thy house.

Creon:

And what worse ill is yet to follow upon ills?

Messenger:

Thy queen hath died, true mother of yon corpse—ah, hapless lady!—by blows newly dealt.

Creon:

antistrophe 1

Oh Hades, all-receiving, whom no sacrifice can appease! Hast thou, then, no mercy for me? O thou herald of evil, bitter tidings, what word dost thou utter? Alas, I was already as dead, and thou hast smitten me anew! What sayest thou, my son? What is this new message that thou bringest—woe, woe is me!—of a wife's doom,—of slaughter heaped on slaughter?

Chorus:

Thou canst behold: 'tis no longer hidden within.

(The doors of the palace are opened, and the corpse of Eurydice *is disclosed.)*

Creon:

antistrophe 2

Ah, me,—yonder I behold a new, a second woe! What destiny, ah what, can yet await me? I have but now raised my son in my arms,—and there, again, I see a corpse before me! Alas, alas, unhappy mother! Alas, my child!

Messenger:

There, at the altar, self-stabbed with a keen knife, she suffered her darkening eyes to close, when she had wailed for the noble fate of Megareus who died before, and then for his fate who lies there,—and when, with her last breath, she had invoked evil fortunes upon thee, the slayer of thy sons.

Creon:

strophe 3

Woe, woe! I thrill with dread. Is there none to strike me to the heart with two-edged sword?—O miserable that I am, and steeped in miserable anguish!

Messenger:

Yea, both this son's doom, and that other's, were laid to thy charge by her whose corpse thou seest.

Creon:

And what was the manner of the violent deed by which she passed away?

Messenger:

Her own hand struck her to the heart, when she had learned her son's sorely lamented fate.

Creon:

strophe 4

Ah me, this guilt can never be fixed on any other of mortal kind, for my acquittal! I, even I, was thy slayer, wretched that I am—I own the truth. Lead me away, O my servants, lead me hence with all speed, whose life is but as death!

Chorus:

Thy counsels are good, if there can be good with ills; briefest is best, when trouble is in our path.

Creon:

antistrophe 3

Oh, let it come, let it appear, that fairest of fates for me, that brings my last day,—aye, best fate of all! Oh, let it come, that I may never look upon to-morrow's light.

Chorus:

These things are in the future; present tasks claim our care: the ordering of the future rests where it should rest.

Creon:

All my desires, at least, were summed in that prayer.

Chorus:

Pray thou no more; for mortals have no escape from destined woe.

Creon:

antistrophe 4

Lead me away, I pray you; a rash, foolish man; who have slain thee, ah my son, unwittingly, and thee, too, my wife—unhappy that I am! I know not which way I should bend my gaze, or where I should seek support; for all is amiss with that which is in my hands,—and yonder, again, a crushing fate hath leapt upon my head.

(As Creon is being conducted into the palace, the Leader of the Chorus speaks the closing verses.)

Leader:

Wisdom is the supreme part of happiness; and reverence towards the gods must be inviolate. Great words of prideful men are ever punished with great blows, and, in old age, teach the chastened to be wise.

Comments and Questions

1. In Antigone's opening lines, we hear her ask Ismene whether or not Ismene knows of the edict that forbids the burial of Polyneices, and Creon goes to great lengths to determine whether or not Antigone knew of his proclamation before sentencing her for disobedience. In our society, we often state that "ignorance is no defense of the law." Would Creon have allowed a defense of ignorance and excused Antigone's acts if she had not been aware of the law? If so, at what point in the play would he excuse her? From the beginning? After the impassioned plea by Haemon?

2. Compare the motives of both Antigone and Ismene. Which one of the sisters sacrifices the most? Antigone tests Ismene by stating that Ismene will show herself to be "nobly bred" if she helps Antigone in the forbidden deed, but that Ismene will show herself to be "the base daughter of a noble line" if she fails to act. Antigone tells us that she herself will "not suffer aught so dreadful as an ignoble death" of Polyneices and that she will never be found false to him, but she also tells us that she does this for it is in keeping with the laws "which the gods have stablished in his honor." What if the gods had forbidden the burial of one who slays a brother? Would Antigone have risked her life at the hands of Creon if it meant that she would be denied a place in the hereafter? Ismene states that she does not dishonour the gods but that she has not the strength to disobey the State. Then how does she justify offering to share the guilt of Antigone? Can you see how she might be the martyr rather than Antigone? If she admits guilt without participating in the deed then she will also be subject to a public stoning, but, unlike Antigone, her death will be for a deed which she did not commit. If Antigone is correct, then Ismene will not have secured a place in the afterlife. What does the following line say of Antigone: "Nay, justice will not suffer thee to do that: thou didst not consent to the deed, nor did I give them part in it." Is she protecting Ismene or rejecting her?

3. Consider the depiction of the role of women in Greek society as evidenced by this drama. Ismene tells Antigone that they "were born women" and "should not strive with men." Does

Antigone consider herself to be striving with men? Does Eurydice offer any insight into the role of women in Greek Society?

4. Of which sister is Creon speaking when he says: "Lo, one of these maidens hath newly shown herself foolish, as the other hath been since her life began?" What purpose does Creon give for rejecting the pleas of both Ismene and Haemon to spare the life of Antigone? Is he correct in his statement that "disobedience is the worst of all evils" and that "whosoever the city may appoint, that man must be obeyed, in little things and great, in just things and unjust." Why is he finally persuaded to yield his earlier position?

5. What laws does Haemon break? How is the Chorus affected by the dialogue between Haemon and Creon? What is the role of the Leader during the exchange between father and son?

William Shakespeare

The Merchant of Venice

Dramatis Personae

Duke of Venice.
Prince of Morocco, *suitor to Portia.*
Prince of Arragon, *suitor to Portia.*
Antonio, *a merchant of Venice.*
Bassanio, *his kinsman and friend.*
Solanio, *friend to Antonio and Bassanio.*
Salarino, *friend to Antonio and Bassanio.*
Gratiano, *friend to Antonio and Bassanio.*
Lorenzo, *in love with Jessica.*
Shylock, *a rich Jew.*
Tubal, *a Jew, his friend.*
Launcelot Gobbo, *a clown, servant to Shylock.*
Old Gobbo, *father to Launcelot.*
Leonardo, *servant to Bassanio.*
Balthazar, *servant to Portia.*
Stephano, *servant to Portia.*
Portia, *a rich heiress.*
Nerissa, *her waiting-maid.*
Jessica, *daughter to Shylock.*

Magnificoes of Venice, Officers of the Court of Justice, Gaoler, Servants, *and other* Attendants.

SCENE.—*Partly at Venice, and partly at Belmont, the seat of Portia, on the Continent.*

(ACT I. SCENE I.—*Venice. A street. Enter* Antonio, Salarino, *and* Solanio.)

Antonio:
>In sooth, I know not why I am so sad:
>It wearies me; you say it wearies you;
>But how I caught it, found it, or came by it,
>What stuff 'tis made of, whereof it is born,
>I am to learn;
>And such a want-wit sadness makes of me,
>That I have much ado to know myself.

Salarino:
>Your mind is tossing on the ocean;
>There, where your argosies with portly sail,—
>Like signiors and rich burghers of the flood,
>Or, as it were, the pageants of the sea,—
>Do overpeer the petty traffickers,
>That curtsey to them, do them reverence,
>As they fly by them with their woven wings.

Solanio:
>Believe me, sir, had I such venture forth,
>The better part of my affections would
>Be with my hopes abroad. I should be still
>Plucking the grass, to know where sits the wind;
>Peering in maps for ports, and piers, and roads;
>And every object that might make me fear
>Misfortune to my ventures, out of doubt
>Would make me sad.

Salarino:
>   My wind, cooling my broth.
>Would blow me to an ague, when I thought
>What harm a wind too great might do at sea.
>I should not see the sandy hour-glass run,
>But I should think of shallows and of flats;
>And see my wealthy Andrew dockt in sand,
>Vailing her high-top lower than her ribs,
>To kiss her burial. Should I go to church,
>And see the holy edifice of stone,
>And not bethink me straight of dangerous rocks,
>Which touching but my gentle vessel's side,
>Would scatter all her spices on the stream;
>Enrobe the roaring waters with my silks;

>   And, in a word, but even now worth this,
>   And now worth nothing? Shall I have the thought
>   To think on this; and shall I lack the thought,
>   That such a thing bechanced would make me sad?
>   But tell not me; I know Antonio
>   Is sad to think upon his merchandise.

Antonio:
>   Believe me, no: I thank my fortune for it,
>   My ventures are not in one bottom trusted,
>   Nor to one place; nor is my whole estate
>   Upon the fortune of this present year:
>   Therefore my merchandise makes me not sad.

Salarino:
>   Why, then you are in love.

Antonio:
>   Fie, fie

Salarino:
>   Not in nove neither? Then let's say you're sad,
>   Because you are not merry: and 'twere as easy
>   For you to laugh, and leap, and say you are merry,
>   Because you are not sad. Now, by two-headed Janus,
>   Nature hath framed strange fellows in her time:
>   Some that will evermore peep through their eyes,
>   And laugh, like parrots, at a bag-piper;
>   And other of such vinegar aspect,
>   That they'll not show their teeth in way of smile,
>   Though Nestor swear the jest be laughable.

Solanio:
>   Here comes Bassanio, your most noble kinsman,
>   Gratiano, and Lorenzo. Fare ye well:
>   We leave you now with better company.

Salarino:
>   I would have stay'd till I had made you merry,
>   If worthier friends had not prevented me.

Antonio:
> Your worth is very dear in my regard.
> I take it, your own business calls on you,
> And you embrace th' occasion to depart.

> *(Enter Bassanio, Lorenzo, and Gratiano.)*

Salarino:
> Good morrow, my good lords.

Bassanio:
> Good signiors both, when shall we laugh? say, when?
> You grow exceeding strange: must it be so?

Salarino:
> We'll make our leisures to attend on yours.

> *(Exeunt Salarino and Solanio.)*

Lorenzo:
> My Lord Bassanio, since you have found Antonio,
> We two will leave you: but, at dinner-time,
> I pray you, have in mind where we must meet.

Bassanio:
> I will not fail you.

Gratiano:
> You look not well, Signior Antonio;
> You have too much respect upon the world:
> They lose it that do buy it with much care:
> Believe me, you are marvellously changed.

Antonio:
> I hold the world but as the world, Gratiano;
> A stage, where every man must play a part,
> And mine a sad one.

Gratiano:
> Let me play the fool:
> With mirth and laughter let old wrinkles come;
> And let my liver rather heat with wine

Than my heart cool with mortifying groans.
Why should a man, whose blood is warm within,
Sit like his grandsire cut in alabaster?
Sleep when he wakes? and creep into the jaundice
By being peevish? I tell thee what, Antonio,—
I love thee, and it is my love that speaks,—
There are a sort of men, whose visages
Do cream and mantle like a standing pond;
And do a wilful stillness entertain,
With purpose to be drest in an opinion
Of wisdom, gravity, profound conceit;
As who should say, 'I am Sir Oracle,
And when I ope my lips, let no dog bark!'
O my Antonio, I do know of these,
That therefore only are reputed wise
For saying nothing; when, I am very sure,
If they should speak, would almost damn those ears,
Which, hearing them, would call their brothers fools.
I'll tell thee more of this another time:
But fish not, with this melancholy bait,
For this fool-gudgeon, this opinion.—
Come, good Lorenzo.—Fare ye well awhile:
I'll end my exhortation after dinner.

Lorenzo:
Well, we will leave you, then, till dinner-time:
I must be one of these same dumb wise men,
For Gratiano never lets me speak.

Gratiano:
Well, keep me company but two years moe,
Thou shalt not know the sound of thine own tongue.

Antonio:
Farewell: I'll grow a talker for this gear.

Gratiano:
Thanks, i'faith; for silence is only commendable
In a neat's tongue dried, and a maid not vendible.

(*Exeunt* Gratiano *and* Lorenzo.)

Antonio:
>Is that any thing now?

Bassanio:
>Gratiano speaks an infinite deal of nothing, more than any man in all Venice. His reasons are as two grains of wheat hid in two bushels of chaff: you shall seek all day ere you find them; and when you have them, they are not worth the search.

Antonio:
>Well; tell me now, what lady is the same
>To whom you swore a secret pilgrimage,
>That you to-day promised to tell me of?

Bassanio:
>'Tis not unknown to you, Antonio,
>How much I have disabled mine estate,
>By something showing a more swelling port
>Than my faint means would grant continuance:
>Nor do I now make moan to be abridged
>From such a noble rate; but my chief care
>Is, to come fairly off from the great debts,
>Wherein my time, something too prodigal,
>Hath left me gaged. To you, Antonio,
>I owe the most, in money and in love;
>And from your love I have a warranty
>To unburden all my plots and purposes
>How to get clear of all the debts I owe.

Antonio:
>I pray you, good Bassanio, let me know it;
>And if it stand, as you yourself still do,
>Within the eye of honour, be assured
>My purse, my person, my extremest means,
>Lie all unlockt to your occasions.

Bassanio:
>In my school-days, when I had lost one shaft,
>I shot his fellow of the selfsame flight
>The selfsame way with more advised watch,
>To find the other forth; and by advent'ring both,

I oft found both: I urge this childhood proof,
Because what follows is pure innocence.
I owe you much; and, like a wilful youth,
That which I owe is lost: but if you please
To shoot another arrow that self way
Which you did shoot the first, I do not doubt,
As I will watch the aim, or to find both,
Or bring your latter hazard back again,
And thankfully rest debtor for the first.

Antonio:
You know me well; and herein spend but time
To wind about my love with circumstance;
And out of doubt you do me now more wrong
In making question of my uttermost,
Than if you had made waste of all I have:
Then do but say to me what I should do,
That in your knowledge may by me be done,
And I am prest unto it: therefore, speak.

Bassanio:
In Belmont is a lady richly left;
And she is fair, and, fairer than that word,
Of wondrous virtues: sometimes from her eyes
I did receive fair speechless messages:
Her name is Portia; nothing undervalued
To Cato's daughter, Brutus' Portia:
Nor is the wide world ignorant of her worth;
For the four winds blow in from every coast
Renowned suitors: and her sunny locks
Hang on her temples like a golden fleece;
Which makes her seat of Belmont Colchos' strond,
And many Jasons come in quest of her.
O my Antonio, had I but the means
To hold a rival place with one of them,
I have a mind presages me such thrift,
That I should questionless be fortunate!

Antonio:
Thou know'st that all my fortunes are at sea;
Neither have I money, nor commodity
To raise a present sum: therefore, go forth;

Try what my credit can in Venice do:
That shall be rackt, even to the uttermost,
To furnish thee to Belmont, to fair Portia.
Go, presently inquire, and so will I,
Where money is; and I no question make,
To have it of my trust, or for my sake.

(Exeunt.)

(SCENE II.—Belmont. A room in Portia's house. Enter Portia and Nerissa.)

Portia:
By my troth, Nerissa, my little body is aweary of this great world.

Nerissa:
You would be, sweet madam, if your miseries were in the same abundance as your good fortunes are: and yet, for aught I see, they are as sick that surfeit with too much, as they that starve with nothing. It is no mean happiness, therefore, to be seated in the mean: superfluity comes sooner by white hairs; but competency lives longer.

Portia:
Good sentences, and well pronounced.

Nerissa:
They would be better, if well follow'd.

Portia:
If to do were as easy as to know what were good to do, chapels had been churches, and poor men's cottages princes' palaces. It is a good divine that follows his own instructions: I can easier teach twenty what were good to be done, than be one of the twenty to follow mine own teaching. The brain may devise laws for the blood; but a hot temper leaps o'er a cold decree: such a hare is madness the youth, to skip o'er the meshes of good-counsel the cripple. But this reasoning is not in the fashion to choose me a husband:—O me, the word 'choose'! I may neither choose who I would, nor refuse who I dislike; so is the will of a living daughter curb'd by the will

of a dead father.—Is it not hard, Nerissa, that I cannot choose one, nor refuse none?

Nerissa:
Your father was ever virtuous; and holy men, at their death, have good inspirations: therefore, the lottery, that he hath devised in these three chests of gold, silver, and lead,—whereof who chooses his meaning chooses you,—will, no doubt, never be chosen by any rightly, but one who shall rightly love. But what warmth is there in your affection towards any of these princely suitors that are already come?

Portia:
I pray thee, over-name them; and as thou namest them, I will describe them; and, according to my description, level at my affection.

Nerissa:
First, there is the Neapolitan prince.

Portia:
Ay, that's a colt indeed, for he doth nothing but talk of his horse; and he makes it a great appropriation to his own good parts, that he can shoe him himself. I am much afeard my lady his mother play'd false with a smith.

Nerissa:
Then there is the County Palatine.

Portia:
He doth nothing but frown; as who should say, 'And you will not have me, choose:' he hears merry tales, and smiles not: I fear he will prove the weeping philosopher when he grows old, being so full of unmannerly sadness in his youth. I had rather be married to a Death's-head with a bone in his mouth than to either of these:—God defend me from these two!

Nerissa:
How say you by the French lord, Monsieur Le Bon?

Portia:
God made him, and therefore let him pass for a man. In

truth, I know it is a sin to be a mocker but, he!—why, he hath a horse better than the Neapolitan's; a better bad habit of frowning than the Count Palatine: he is every man in no man; if a throstle sing, he falls straight a-capering; he will fence with his own shadow: if I should marry him, I should marry twenty husbands. If he would despise me, I would forgive him; for if he love me to madness, I shall never requite him.

Nerissa:
What say you, then, to Falconbridge, the young baron of England?

Portia:
You know I say nothing to him: for he understands not me, nor I him: he hath neither Latin, French, nor Italian; and you will come into the court and swear that I have a poor pennyworth in the English. He is a proper man's picture; but, alas, who can converse with a dumb-show? How oddly he is suited! I think he bought his doublet in Italy, his round hose in France, his bonnet in Germany, and his behaviour every where.

Nerissa:
What think you of the Scottish lord, his neighbour?

Portia:
That he hath a neighbourly charity in him; for he borrow'd a box of the ear of the Englishman, and swore he would pay him again when he was able: I think the Frenchman became his surety, and seal'd under for another.

Nerissa:
How like you the young German, the Duke of Saxony's nephew?

Portia:
Very vilely in the morning, when he is sober; and most vilely in the afternoon, when he is drunk: when he is best, he is a little worse than a man; and when he is worst, he is little better than a beast. And the worst fall that ever fell, I hope I shall make shift to go without him.

Nerissa:
> If he should offer to choose, and choose the right casket, you should refuse to perform your father's will, if you should refuse to accept him.

Portia:
> Therefore, for fear of the worst, I pray thee, set a deep glass of Rhenish wine on the contrary casket; for, if the devil be within, and that temptation without, I know he will choose it. I will do any thing, Nerissa, ere I will be married to a sponge.

Nerissa:
> You need not fear, lady, the having any of these lords: they have acquainted me with their determinations; which is, indeed, to return to their home, and to trouble you with no more suit, unless you may be won by some other sort than your father's imposition, depending on the caskets.

Portia:
> If I live to be as old as Sibylla, I will die as chaste as Diana, unless I be obtain'd by the manner of my father's will. I am glad this parcel of wooers are so reasonable; for there is not one among them but I dote on his very absence; and I pray God grant them a fair departure.

Nerissa:
> Do you not remember, lady, in your father's time, a Venetian, a scholar and a soldier, that came hither in company of the Marquis of Montferrat?

Portia:
> Yes, yes, it was Bassanio: as I think, so was he call'd.

Nerissa:
> True, madam: he, of all the men that ever my foolish eyes lookt upon, was the best deserving a fair lady.

Portia:
> I remember him well; and I remember him worthy of thy praise.

(Enter a servant.)

How now! what news?

Servant:
The four strangers seek for you, madam, to take their leave: and there is a forerunner come from a fifth, the Prince of Morocco; who brings word, the prince his master will be here to-night.

Portia:
If I could bid the fifth welcome with so good a heart as I can bid the other four farewell, I should be glad of his approach: if he have the condition of a saint and the complexion of a devil, I had rather he should shrive me than wive me.
Come, Nerissa.—Sirrah, go before.—
Whiles we shut the gates upon one wooer, another knocks at the door.

(Exeunt.)

(SCENE III.—Venice. A public place. Enter Bassanio *with* Shylock *the Jew.)*

Shylock:
Three thousand ducats,—well.

Bassanio:
Ay, sir, for three months.

Shylock:
For three months,—well.

Bassanio:
For the which, as I told you, Antonio shall be bound.

Shylock:
Antonio shall become bound,—well.

Bassanio:
May you stead me? will you pleasure me? shall I know your answer?

Shylock:
Three thousand ducats for three months, and Antonio bound.

Bassanio:
Your answer to that.

Shylock:
Antonio is a good man.

Bassanio:
Have you heard any imputation to the contrary?

Shylock:
Ho, no, no, no, no;—my meaning, in saying he is a good man is to have you understand me that he is sufficient. Yet his means are in supposition: he hath an argosy bound to Tripolis, another to the Indies; I understand, moreover, upon the Rialto, he hath a third at Mexico, a fourth for England,— and other ventures he hath, squander'd abroad. But ships are but boards, sailors but men: there be land-rats and water-rats, water-thieves and land-thieves, I mean pirates; and then there is the peril of waters, winds, and rocks. The man is, notwithstanding, sufficient:—three thousand ducats:—I think I may take his bond.

Bassanio:
Be assured you may.

Shylock:
I will be assured I may; and, that I may be assured, I will bethink me. May I speak with Antonio?

Bassanio:
If it please you to dine with us.

Shylock:
Yes, to smell pork; to eat of the habitation which your prophet the Nazarite conjured the devil into. I will buy with you, sell with you, talk with you, walk with you, and so following; but I will not eat with you, drink with you, nor pray with you. What news on the Rialto?—Who is he comes here?

(Enter Antonio.)

Bassanio:
    This is Signior Antonio.

Shylock *(aside)*:
    How like a fawning publican he looks!
    I hate him for he is a Christian!
    But more, for that, in low simplicity,
    He lends out money gratis, and brings down
    The rate of usance here with us in Venice.
    If I can catch him once upon the hip,
    I will feed fat the ancient grudge I bear him.
    He hates our sacred nation; and he rails,
    Even there where merchants most do congregate,
    On me, my bargains, and my well-won thrift,
    Which he calls interest. Cursed be my tribe,
    If I forgive him!

Bassanio:
                Shylock, do you hear?

Shylock:
    I am debating of my present store;
    And, by the near guess of my memory,
    I cannot instantly raise up the gross
    Of full three thousand ducats. What of that?
    Tubal, a wealthy Hebrew of my tribe,
    Will furnish me. But soft! how many months
    Do you desire?—Rest you fair, good signior;
                              (To Antonio.*)*
    Your worship was the last man in our mouths.

Antonio:
    Shylock, although I neither lend nor borrow
    By taking nor by giving of excess,
    Yet, to supply the ripe wants of my friend,
    I'll break a custom.—Is he yet possest
    How much ye would?

Shylock:
                Ay, ay, three thousand ducats.

Antonio:
>And for three months.

Shylock:
>I had forgot,—three months, you told me so.
>Well, then, your bond; and let me see,—but hear you;
>Methought you said you neither lend nor borrow
>Upon advantage.

Antonio:
>>I do never use it.

Shylock:
>When Jacob grazed his uncle Laban's sheep,—
>This Jacob from our holy Abram was
>(As his wise mother wrought in his behalf)
>The third possessor; ay, he was the third,—

Antonio:
>And what of him? did he take interest?

Shylock:
>No, not take interest; not as you would say,
>Directly interest: mark what Jacob did.
>When Laban and himself were compromised
>That all the eanlings which were streakt and pied
>Should fall as Jacob's hire, the ewes, being rank,
>In th' end of autumn turned to the rams;
>And when the work of generation was
>Between these woolly breeders in the act,
>The skilful shepherd peel'd me certain wands,
>And, in the doing of the deed of kind,
>He stuck them up before the fulsome ewes,
>Who, then conceiving, did in eaning time
>Fall parti-colour'd lambs, and those were Jacob's.
>This was a way to thrive, and he was blest:
>And thrift is blessing, if men steal it not.

Antonio:
>This was a venture, sir, that Jacob served for;
>A thing not in his power to bring to pass,
>But sway'd and fashion'd by the hand of heaven.

Was this inserted to make interest good?
Or is your gold and silver ewes and rams?

Shylock:
I cannot tell: I make it breed as fast:—
But note me, signior.

Antonio:
Mark you this, Bassanio,
The devil can cite Scripture for his purpose.
An evil soul, producing holy witness,
Is like a villain with a smiling cheek;
A goodly apple rotten at the heart:
O, what a goodly outside falsehood hath!

Shylock:
Three thousand ducats,—'tis a good round sum.
Three months from twelve,—then, let me see, the rate—

Antonio:
Well, Shylock, shall we be beholden to you?

Shylock:
Signior Antonio, many a time and oft,
In the Rialto, you have rated me
About my moneys and my usances:
Still have I borne it with a patient shrug;
For sufferance is the badge of all our tribe:
You call me misbeliever, cut-throat dog,
And spit upon my Jewish gaberdine,
And all for use of that which is mine own.
Well, then, it now appears you need my help:
Go to, then; you come to me, and you say,
'Shylock, we would have moneys:'—you say so;
You, that did void your rheum upon my beard,
And foot me as you spurn a stranger cur
Over your threshold: moneys is your suit.
What should I say to you? Should I not say,
'Hath a dog money? is it possible
A cur can lend three thousand ducats?' or
Shall I bend low, and in a bondman's key,
With bated breath and whispering humbleness,

Say this,—
'Fair sir, you spit on me on Wednesday last;
You spurn'd me such a day; another time
You call'd me dog; and for these courtesies
I'll lend you thus much moneys'?

Antonio:
I am as like to call thee so again,
To spit on thee again, to spurn thee too.
If thou wilt lend this money, lend it not
As to thy friends—for when did friendship take
A breed for barren metal of his friend?—
But lend it rather to thine enemy;
Who if he break, thou mayst with better face
Exact the penalty.

Shylock:
Why, look you, how you storm!
I would be friends with you, and have your love,
Forget the shames that you have stain'd me with,
Supply your present wants, and take no doit
Of usance for my moneys,
And you'll not hear me: this is kind I offer.

Bassanio:
This were kindness.

Shylock:
This kindness will I show:—
Go with me to a notary, seal me there
Your single bond; and, in a merry sport,
If you repay me not on such a day,
In such a place, such sum or sums as are
Exprest in the condition, let the forfeit
Be nominated for an equal pound
Of your fair flesh, to be cut off and taken
In what part of your body pleaseth me.

Antonio:
Content, i'faith: I'll seal to such a bond,
And say there is much kindness in the Jew.

Bassanio:
>You shall not seal to such a bond for me:
>I'll rather dwell in my necessity.

Antonio:
>Why, fear not, man; I will not forfeit it:
>Within these two months, that's a month before
>This bond expires, I do expect return
>Of thrice three times the value of this bond.

Shylock:
>O father Abram, what these Christians are,
>Whose own hard dealings teaches them suspect
>The thoughts of others!—Pray you, tell me this;
>If he should break his day, what should I gain
>By the exaction of the forfeiture?
>A pound of man's flesh taken from a man
>Is not so estimable, profitable neither,
>As flesh of muttons, beefs, or goats. I say,
>To buy his favour, I extend this friendship:
>If he will take it, so; if not, adieu;
>And, for my love, I pray you wrong me not.

Antonio:
>Yes, Shylock, I will seal unto this bond.

Shylock:
>Then meet me forthwith at the notary's,—
>Give him direction for this merry bond;
>And I will go and purse the ducats straight;
>See to my house, left in the fearful guard
>Of an unthrifty knave; and presently
>I will be with you.

Antonio:
>>Hie thee, gentle Jew.

>(*Exit* Shylock.)

>The Hebrew will turn Christian: he grows kind.

Bassanio:
>I like not fair terms and a villain's mind.

Antonio:
>Come on: in this there can be no dismay;
>My ships come home a month before the day.

>>*(Exeunt.)*

(ACT II. SCENE I.—Belmont. A room in Portia's house. Enter the Prince of Morocco, a tawny Moor all in white, and three or four Followers accordingly, with Portia, Nerissa, and their Train. Flourish of cornets.)

Prince of Morocco:
>Mislike me not for my complexion,
>The shadow'd livery of the burnisht sun,
>To whom I am a neighbour and near bred.
>Bring me the fairest creature northward born,
>Where Phoebus' fire scarce thaws the icicles,
>And let us make incision for your love,
>To prove whose blood is reddest, his or mine.
>I tell thee, lady, this aspect of mine
>Hath fear'd the valiant: by my love, I swear
>The best-regarded virgins of our clime
>Hath loved it too: I would not change this hue,
>Except to steal your thoughts, my gentle queen.

Portia:
>In terms of choice I am not solely led
>By nice direction of a maiden's eyes;
>Besides, the lottery of my destiny
>Bars me the right of voluntary choosing:
>But, if my father had not scanted me,
>And hedg'd me by his will, to yield myself
>His wife who wins me by that means I told you,
>Yourself, renowned prince, then stood as fair
>As any comer I have lookt on yet
>For my affection.

Prince of Morocco:
>>Even for that I thank you:
>Therefore, I pray you, lead me to the caskets,
>To try my fortune. By this scimitar,
>That slew the Sophy and a Persian prince

>   That won three fields of Sultan Solyman,
>   I would outstare the sternest eyes that look,
>   Outbrave the heart most daring on the earth,
>   Pluck the young sucking-cubs from the she-bear,
>   Yea, mock the lion when he roars for prey,
>   To win thee, lady. But, alas the while!
>   If Hercules and Lichas play at dice
>   Which is the better man, the greater throw
>   May turn by fortune from the weaker hand:
>   So is Alcides beaten by his page;
>   And so may I, blind Fortune leading me,
>   Miss that which one unworthier may attain,
>   And die with grieving.

Portia:
>   You must take your chance,
>   And either not attempt to choose at all,
>   Or swear before you choose,—if you choose wrong,
>   Never to speak to lady afterward
>   In way of marriage: therefore be advised.

Prince of Morocco:
>   Nor will not. Come, bring me unto my chance.

Portia:
>   First, forward to the temple: after dinner
>   Your hazard shall be made.

Prince of Morocco:
>   Good fortune, then!
>   To make me blest or cursed'st among men.

>   *(Cornets, and exeunt.)*

(SCENE II.—Venice. A street. Enter Launcelot *the Clown, alone.)*

Launcelot Gobbo:
> Certainly my conscience will serve me to run from this Jew my master. The fiend is at mine elbow, and tempts me, saying to me, 'Gobbo, Launcelot Gobbo, good Launcelot,' or 'good Gobbo,' or 'good Launcelot Gobbo, use your legs, take the start, run away.' My conscience says, 'No; take heed,

honest Launcelot; take heed, honest Gobbo,' or, as aforesaid, 'honest Launcelot Gobbo; do not run; scorn running with thy heels.' Well, the most courageous fiend bids me pack: '*Via!*' says the fiend, 'away!' says the fiend; 'for the heavens, rouse up a brave mind,' says the fiend, 'and run.' Well, my conscience, hanging about the neck of my heart, says very wisely to me, 'My honest friend Launcelot, being an honest man's son,'—or rather an honest woman's son;—for, indeed, my father did something smack, something grow to,—he had a kind of taste;—well, my conscience says, 'Launcelot, budge not.' 'Budge,' says the fiend. 'Budge not,' says my conscience. 'Conscience,' say I, 'you counsel well; 'fiend,' say I, 'you counsel well:' to be ruled by my conscience, I should stay with the Jew my master, who—God bless the mark!—is a kind of devil; and, to run away from the Jew, I should be ruled by the fiend, who, saving your reverence, is the devil himself. Certainly the Jew is the very devil incarnal; and, in my conscience, my conscience is but a kind of hard conscience, to offer to counsel me to stay with the Jew. The fiend gives the more friendly counsel: I will run, fiend; my heels are at your command; I will run.

(Enter Old Gobbo *with a basket.)*

Old Gobbo:
Master young man, you, I pray you, which is the way to master Jew's?

Launcelot Gobbo *(aside)*:
O heavens, this is my true-begotten father! who, being more than sand-blind, high-gravel-blind, knows me not:—I will try confusions with him.

Old Gobbo:
Master young gentleman, I pray you, which is the way to master Jew's?

Launcelot Gobbo:
Turn up on your right hand at the next turning, but, at the next turning of all, on your left; marry, at the very next turning, turn of no hand, but turn down indirectly to the Jew's house.

Old Gobbo:
> By God's sonties, 'twill be a hard way to hit. Can you tell me whether one Launcelot, that dwells with him, dwell with him or no?

Launcelot Gobbo:
> Talk you of young Master Launcelot? *(Aside.)* Mark me now; now will I raise the waters.—Talk you of young Master Launcelot?

Old Gobbo:
> No master, sir, but a poor man's son: his father, though I say it, is an honest exceeding poor man, and, God be thankt, well to live.

Launcelot Gobbo:
> Well, let his father be what a' will, we talk of young Master Launcelot.

Old Gobbo:
> Your worship's friend, and Launcelot, sir.

Launcelot Gobbo:
> But, I pray you, *ergo,* old man, *ergo,* I beseech you, talk you of young Master Launcelot?

Old Gobbo:
> Of Launcelot, an't please your mastership.

Launcelot Gobbo:
> *Ergo,* Master Launcelot. Talk not of Master Launcelot, father; for the young gentleman—according to Fates and Destinies, and such odd sayings, the Sisters Three, and such branches of learning—is, indeed, deceased; or, as you would say in plain terms, gone to heaven.

Old Gobbo:
> Marry, God forbid! the boy was the very staff of my age, my very prop.

Launcelot Gobbo:
> Do I look like a cudgel or a hovel-post, a staff, or a prop?—Do you know me, father?

Old Gobbo:
>Alack the day, I know you not, young gentleman: but, I pray you, tell me, is my boy—God rest his soul!—alive or dead?

Launcelot Gobbo:
>Do you not know me, father?

Old Gobbo:
>Alack, sir, I am sand-blind; I know you not.

Launcelot Gobbo:
>Nay, indeed, if you had your eyes, you might fail of the knowing me: it is a wise father that knows his own child. Well, old man, I will tell you news of your son: give me your blessing *(kneels)*: truth will come to light; murder cannot be hid long,—a man's son may; but, in the end, truth will out.

Old Gobbo:
>Pray you, sir, stand up: I am sure you are not Launcelot, my boy.

Launcelot Gobbo:
>Pray you, let's have no more fooling about it, but give me your blessing: I am Launcelot, your boy that was, your son that is, your child that shall be.

Old Gobbo:
>I cannot think you are my son.

Launcelot Gobbo:
>I know not what I shall think of that: but I am Launcelot, the Jew's man; and I am sure Margery your wife is my mother.

Old Gobbo:
>Her name is Margery, indeed: I'll be sworn, if thou be Launcelot, thou art mine own flesh and blood. Lord worshipt might he be! what a beard hast thou got! thou hast got more hair on thy chin than Dobbin my fill-horse has on his tail.

Launcelot Gobbo *(rising):*
It should seem, then, that Dobbin's tail grows backward; I am sure he had more hair of his tail than I have of my face when I last saw him.

Old Gobbo:
Lord, how art thou changed! How dost thou and thy master agree? I have brought him a present. How 'gree you now?

Launcelot Gobbo:
Well, well: but, for mine own part, as I have set up my rest to run away, so I will not rest till I have run some ground. My master's a very Jew: give him a present! give him a halter: I am famisht in his service; you may tell every finger I have with my ribs. Father, I am glad you are come: give me your present to one Master Bassanio, who, indeed, gives rare new liveries: if I serve not him, I will run as far as God has any ground.—O rare fortune! here comes the man:—to him, father; for I am a Jew, if I serve the Jew any longer.

(Enter Bassanio, *with* Leonardo *and a* Follower *or two.)*

Bassanio:
You may do so;—but let it be so hasted, that supper be ready at the furthest by five of the clock. See these letters deliver'd; put the liveries to making; and desire Gratiano to come anon to my lodging.

(Exit a servant.)

Launcelot Gobbo:
To him, father.

Old Gobbo:
God bless your worship!

Bassanio:
Gramercy: wouldst thou aught with me?

Old Gobbo:
Here's my son, sir, a poor boy,—

Launcelot Gobbo:
> Not a poor boy, sir, but the rich Jew's man; that would, sir,—as my father shall specify,—

Old Gobbo:
> He hath a great infection, sir, as one would say, to serve,—

Launcelot Gobbo:
> Indeed, the short and the long is, I serve the Jew, and have a desire,—as my father shall specify,—

Old Gobbo:
> His master and he—saving your worship's reverence—are scarce cater-cousins,—

Launcelot Gobbo:
> To be brief, the very truth is, that the Jew having done me wrong, doth cause me,—as my father, being, I hope, an old man, shall frutify unto you,—

Old Gobbo:
> I have here a dish of doves that I would bestow upon your worship; and my suit is,—

Launcelot Gobbo:
> In very brief, the suit is impertinent to myself, as your worship shall know by this honest old man; and, though I say it, though old man, yet poor man, my father.

Bassanio:
> One speak for both.—What would you?

Launcelot Gobbo:
> Serve you, sir.

Old Gobbo:
> That is the very defect of the matter, sir.

Bassanio:
> I know thee well; thou hast obtain'd thy suit:
> Shylock thy master spoke with me this day,
> And hath preferr'd thee,—if it be preferment

To leave a rich Jew's service, to become
The follower of so poor a gentleman.

Launcelot Gobbo:
The old proverb is very well parted between my master Shylock and you, sir: you have the grace of God, sir, and he hath enough.

Bassanio:
Thou speak'st it well.—Go, father, with thy son.—
Take leave of thy old master, and inquire
My lodging out.—Give him a livery
More guarded than his fellows': see it done.

Launcelot Gobbo:
Father, in.—I cannot get a service, no;—I have ne'er a tongue in my head.—Well *(looking on his palm)*, if any man in Italy have a fairer table, which doth offer to swear upon a book, I shall have a good fortune!—Go to, here's a simple line of life! here's a small trifle of wives! alas, fifteen wives is nothing! eleven widows and nine maids is a simple coming-in for one man; and then to scape drowning thrice, and to be in peril of my life with the edge of a feather-bed,—here are simple scapes! Well, if Fortune be a woman, she's a good wench for this gear.—Father, come; I'll take my leave of the Jew in the twinkling of an eye.

(*Exeunt* Launcelot *and* Old Gobbo.)

Bassanio:
I pray thee, good Leonardo, think on this:
These things being bought and orderly bestow'd,
Return in haste, for I do feast to-night
My best-esteem'd acquaintance: hie thee, go.

Leonardo:
My best endeavours shall be done herein.

(*Enter* Gratiano.)

Gratiano:
Where's your master?

Leonardo:
    Yonder, sir, he walks.

(Exit.)

Gratiano:
    Signior Bassanio,—

Bassanio:
    Gratiano!

Gratiano:
    I have a suit to you.

Bassanio:
    You have obtain'd it.

Gratiano:
    You must not deny me: I must go with you to Belmont.

Bassanio:
    Why, then you must. But hear thee, Gratiano:
    Thou art too wild, too rude, and bold of voice,—
    Parts that become thee happily enough,
    And in such eyes as ours appear not faults;
    But where thou art not known, why, there they show
    Something too liberal. Prithee, take pain
    To allay with some cold drops of modesty
    Thy skipping spirit; lest, through thy wild behaviour,
    I be misconstred in the place I go to,
    And lose my hopes.

Gratiano:
    Signior Bassanio, hear me:
    If I do not put on a sober habit,
    Talk with respect, and swear but now and then,
    Wear prayer-books in my pocket, look demurely;
    Nay, more, while grace is saying, hood mine eyes
    Thus with my hat, and sigh, and say amen;
    Use all the observance of civility,
    Like one well studied in a sad ostent
    To please his grandam,—never trust me more.

Bassanio:
    Well, we shall see your bearing.

Gratiano:
    Nay, but I bar to-night: you shall not gauge me
    By what we do to-night.

Bassanio:
                    No, that were pity:
    I would entreat you rather to put on
    Your boldest suit of mirth, for we have friends
    That purpose merriment. But fare ye well:
    I have some business.

Gratiano:
    And I must to Lorenzo and the rest:
    But we will visit you at supper-time.

                                (Exeunt.)

(SCENE III.—The same. A room in Shylock's *house. Enter* Jessica *and* Launcelot.*)*

Jessica:
    I am sorry thou wilt leave my father so:
    Our house is hell: and thou, a merry devil,
    Didst rob it of some taste of tediousness.
    But fare thee well; there is a ducat for thee:
    And, Launcelot, soon at supper shalt thou see
    Lorenzo, who is thy new master's guest:
    Give him this letter; do it secretly;—
    And so farewell: I would not have my father
    See me in talk with thee.

Launcelot Gobbo:
    Adieu; tears exhibit my tongue. Most beautiful pagan, most sweet Jew! if a Christian did not play the knave and get thee, I am much deceived. But, adieu: these foolish drops do something drown my manly spirit: adieu.

Jessica:
    Farewell, good Launcelot.—

(Exit Launcelot.)

> Alack, what heinous sin is it in me
> To be ashamed to be my father's child!
> But though I am a daughter to his blood,
> I am not to his manners. O Lorenzo,
> If thou keep promise, I shall end this strife,—
> Become a Christian, and thy loving wife!

(Exeunt.)

(SCENE IV.—The same. A street. Enter Gratiano, Lorenzo, Salarino, *and* Solanio.*)*

Lorenzo:
> Nay, we will slink away in supper-time,
> Disguise us at my lodging, and return
> All in an hour.

Gratiano:
> We have not made good preparation.

Salarino:
> We have not spoke us yet of torch-bearers.

Solanio:
> 'Tis vile, unless it may be quaintly order'd,
> And better in my mind not undertook.

Lorenzo:
> 'Tis now but four o'clock: we have two hours
> To furnish us.

(Enter Launcelot, *with a letter.)*

> Friend Launcelot, what's the news?

Launcelot Gobbo:
> And it shall please you to break up this, it shall seem to signify.

Lorenzo:
> I know the hand: in faith, 'tis a fair hand;
> And whiter than the paper it writ on

Is the fair hand that writ.

Gratiano:
                        Love-news, in faith.

Launcelot Gobbo:
By your leave, sir.

Lorenzo:
Whither goest thou?

Launcelot Gobbo:
Marry, sir, to bid my old master the Jew to sup to-night with my new master the Christian.

Lorenzo:
Hold here, take this *(gives money)*:—tell gentle Jessica I will not fail her; speak it privately; go.—

                        (Exit Launcelot.*)*

Gentlemen, will you prepare you for this mask to-night?
I am provided of a torch-bearer.

Salarino:
Ay, marry, I'll be gone about it straight.

Solanio:
And so will I.

Lorenzo:
                Meet me and Gratiano
At Gratiano's lodging some hour hence.

Salarino:
'Tis good we do so.

                    (Exeunt Salarino *and* Solanio.*)*

Gratiano:
Was not that letter from fair Jessica?

Lorenzo:
>I must needs tell thee all. She hath directed
>How I shall take her from her father's house;
>What gold and jewels she is furnisht with;
>What page's suit she hath in readiness.
>If e'er the Jew her father come to heaven,
>It will be for his gentle daughter's sake:
>And never dare misfortune cross her foot,
>Unless she do it under this excuse,—
>That she is issue to a faithless Jew.
>Come, go with me: peruse this as thou goest:
>Fair Jessica shall be my torch-bearer.

(Exeunt.)

(SCENE V.—The same. Before Shylock's *house. Enter* Shylock *and* Launcelot.*)*

Shylock:
>Well, thou shalt see, thy eyes shall be thy judge,
>The difference of old Shylock and Bassanio:—
>What, Jessica!—thou shalt not gormandize,
>As thou hast done with me;—what, Jessica!—
>And sleep and snore, and rend apparel out;—
>Why, Jessica, I say!

Launcelot Gobbo:
>Why, Jessica!

Shylock:
>Who bids thee call? I do not bid thee call.

Launcelot Gobbo:
Your worship was wont to tell me that I could do nothing without bidding.

(Enter Jessica.*)*

Jessica:
>Call you? what is your will?

Shylock:
>I am bid forth to supper, Jessica:
>There are my keys.—But wherefore should I go?
>I am not bid for love; they flatter me:
>But yet I'll go in hate, to feed upon
>The prodigal Christian.—Jessica, my girl,
>Look to my house.—I am right loth to go:
>There is some ill a-brewing towards my rest,
>For I did dream of money-bags to-night.

Launcelot Gobbo:
>I beseech you, sir, go: my young master doth expect your reproach.

Shylock:
>So do I his.

Launcelot Gobbo:
>And they have conspired together,—I will not say you shall see a mask; but if you do, then it was not for nothing that my nose fell a-bleeding on Black-Monday last at six o'clock i' th' morning, falling out that year on Ash-Wednesday was four year, in th' afternoon.

Shylock:
>What, are there masks?—Hear you me, Jessica:
>Lock up my doors; and when you hear the drum,
>And the vile squealing of the wry-neckt fife,
>Clamber not you up to the casements then,
>Nor thrust your head into the public street,
>To gaze on Christian fools with varnisht faces;
>But stop my house's ears, I mean my casements:
>Let not the sound of shallow foppery enter
>My sober house.—By Jacob's staff, I swear
>I have no mind of feasting forth to-night:
>But I will go.—Go you before me, sirrah;
>Say I will come.

Launcelot Gobbo:
>>I will go before, sir.—
>Mistress, look out at window for all this;
>>There will come a Christian by

Will be worth a Jewess' eye.

(Exit.)

Shylock:
What says that fool of Hagar's offspring, ha?

Jessica:
His words were, 'Farewell, mistress;' nothing else.

Shylock:
The patch is kind enough; but a huge feeder,
Snail-slow in profit, and he sleeps by day
More than the wild-cat: drones hive not with me;
Therefore I part with him; and part with him
To one that I would have him help to waste
His borrow'd purse.—Well, Jessica, go in:
Perhaps I will return immediately:
Do as I bid you; shut doors after you:
Fast bind, fast find,—
A proverb never stale in thrifty mind.

(Exit.)

Jessica:
Farewell; and if my fortune be not crost,
I have a father, you a daughter, lost.

(Exit.)

(*Enter the Maskers* Gratiano *and* Salarino.)

Gratiano:
This is the pent-house under which Lorenzo
Desired us to make stand.

Salarino:
His hour is almost past.

Gratiano:
And it is marvel he out-dwells his hour,
For lovers ever run before the clock.

Salarino:
>O, ten times faster Venus' pigeons fly
>To seal love's bonds new-made than they are wont
>To keep obliged faith unforfeited!

Gratiano:
>That ever holds: who riseth from a feast
>With that keen appetite that he sits down?
>Where is the horse that doth untread again
>His tedious measures with the unbated fire
>That he did pace them first? All things that are,
>Are with more spirit chased than enjoy'd.
>How like a younker or a prodigal
>The scarfed bark puts from her native bay,
>Hugg'd and embraced by the strumpet wind!
>How like a prodigal doth she return,
>With over-weather'd ribs, and ragged sails,
>Lean, rent, and beggar'd by the strumpet wind!

Salarino:
>Here comes Lorenzo:—more of this hereafter.

(Enter Lorenzo.)

Lorenzo:
>Sweet friends, your patience for my long abode;
>Not I, but my affairs, have made you wait:
>When you shall please to play the thieves for wives,
>I'll watch as long for you then.—Approach;
>Here dwells my father Jew.—Ho! who's within?

(Enter Jessica, above, in boy's clothes.)

Jessica:
>Who are you? Tell me, for more certainty,
>Albeit I'll swear that I do know your tongue.

Lorenzo:
>Lorenzo, and thy love.

Jessica:
>Lorenzo, certain; and my love, indeed,—

For who love I so much? And now who knows
But you, Lorenzo, whether I am yours?

Lorenzo:
Heaven and thy thoughts are witness that thou art.

Jessica:
Here, catch this casket; it is worth the pains.
I am glad 'tis night, you do not look on me,
For I am much ashamed of my exchange:
But love is blind, and lovers cannot see
The pretty follies that themselves commit;
For if they could, Cupid himself would blush
To see me thus transformed to a boy.

Lorenzo:
Descend, for you must be my torch-bearer.

Jessica:
What, must I hold a candle to my shames?
They in themselves, good sooth, are too-too light.
Why, 'tis an office of discovery, love;
And I should be obscured.

Lorenzo:
So are you, sweet,
Even in the lovely garnish of a boy.
But come at once;
For the close night doth play the runaway,
And we are stay'd for at Bassanio's feast.

Jessica:
I will make fast the doors, and gild myself
With some moe ducats, and be with you straight.

(Exit above.)

Gratiano:
Now, by my hood, a Gentile, and no Jew.

Lorenzo:
Beshrew me but I love her heartily;

> For she is wise, if I can judge of her;
> And fair she is, if that mine eyes be true;
> And true she is, as she hath proved herself;
> And therefore, like herself, wise, fair, and true,
> Shall she be placed in my constant soul.

(Enter Jessica, below.)

> What, art thou come?—On, gentlemen; away!
> Our masking mates by this time for us stay.

(Exit with Jessica and Salarino.)

(Enter Antonio.)

Antonio:
> Who's there?

Gratiano:
> Signior Antonio!

Antonio:
> Fie, fie, Gratiano! where are all the rest?
> 'Tis nine o'clock; our friends all stay for you.
> No mask to-night: the wind is come about;
> Bassanio presently will go aboard:
> I have sent twenty out to seek for you.

Gratiano:
> I am glad on't: I desire no more delight
> Than to be under sail and gone to-night.

(Exeunt.)

(SCENE VI.—Belmont. A room in Portia's house. Enter Portia, with the Prince of Morocco, and their Trains. Flourish cornets.)

Portia:
> Go draw aside the curtains, and discover
> The several caskets to this noble prince.—
> Now make your choice.

Prince of Morocco:
>The first, of gold, which this inscription bears,—
>'Who chooseth me shall gain what many men desire;'
>The second, silver, which this promise carries,—
>'Who chooseth me shall get as much as he deserves;'
>This third, dull lead, with warning all as blunt,—
>'Who chooseth me must give and hazard all he hath.'—
>How shall I know if I do choose the right?

Portia:
>The one of them contains my picture, prince:
>If you choose that, then I am yours withal.

Prince of Morocco:
>Some god direct my judgement! Let me see;
>I will survey the inscriptions back again.
>What says this leaden casket?
>'Who chooseth me must give and hazard all he hath.'
>Must give,—for what? for lead? hazard for lead?
>This casket threatens: men that hazard all
>Do it in hope of fair advantages:
>A golden mind stoops not to shows of dross;
>I'll then nor give nor hazard aught for lead.
>What says the silver, with her virgin hue?
>'Who chooseth me shall get as much as he deserves.'
>As much as he deserves!—Pause there, Morocco,
>And weigh thy value with an even hand:
>If thou be'st rated by thy estimation,
>Thou dost deserve enough; and yet enough
>May not extend so far as to the lady:
>And yet to be afeard of my deserving,
>Were but a weak disabling of myself.
>As much as I deserve!—Why, that's the lady:
>I do in birth deserve her, and in fortunes,
>In graces, and in qualities of breeding;
>But more than these, in love I do deserve.
>What if I stray'd no further, but chose here?—
>Let's see once more this saying graved in gold:
>'Who chooseth me shall gain what many men desire.'
>Why, that's the lady; all the world desires her;
>From the four corners of the earth they come,
>To kiss this shrine, this mortal-breathing saint:

The Hyrcanian deserts and the vasty wilds
Of wide Arabia are as throughfares now
For princes to come view fair Portia:
The watery kingdom, whose ambitious head
Spits in the face of heaven, is no bar
To stop the foreign spirits; but they come,
As o'er a brook, to see fair Portia.
One of these three contains her heavenly picture.
Is't like that lead contains her? 'Twere damnation
To think so base a thought: it were too gross
To rib her cerecloth in the obscure grave.
Or shall I think in silver she's immured,
Being ten times undervalued to tried gold?
O sinful thought! Never so rich a gem
Was set in worse than gold. They have in England
A coin that bears the figure of an angel
Stamped in gold,—but that's insculpt upon;
But here an angel in a golden bed
Lies all within.—Deliver me the key:
Here do I choose, and thrive I as I may!

Portia:
There, take it, prince; and if my form lie there,
Then I am yours.

(He opens the golden casket.)

Prince of Morocco:
O hell! what have we here?
A carrion Death, within whose empty eye
There is a written scroll! I'll read the writing.

All that glisters is not gold,—
Often have you heard that told:
Many a man his life hath sold
But my outside to behold:
Gilded tombs do worms infold.
Had you been as wise as bold,
Young in limbs, in judgement old,
Your answer had not been inscroll'd:
Fare you well; your suit is cold.

Cold, indeed; and labour lost:
Then, farewell, heat; and welcome, frost!—
Portia, adieu. I have too grieved a heart
To take a tedious leave: thus losers part.

(Exit with his Train. Cornets.)

Portia:
A gentle riddance.—Draw the curtains, go.—
Let all of his complexion choose me so.

(Exeunt.)

(SCENE VII.—Venice. A street. Enter Salarino and Solanio.)

Salarino:
Why, man, I saw Bassanio under sail:
With him is Gratiano gone along;
And in their ship I am sure Lorenzo is not.

Solanio:
The villain Jew with outcries raised the duke;
Who went with him to search Bassanio's ship.

Salarino:
He came too late, the ship was under sail:
But there the duke was given to understand
That in a gondola were seen together
Lorenzo and his amorous Jessica:
Besides, Antonio certified the duke
They were not with Bassanio in his ship.

Solanio:
I never heard a passion so confused,
So strange, outrageous, and so variable,
As the dog Jew did utter in the streets:
'My daughter!—O my ducats!—O my daughter!
Fled with a Christian!—O my Christian ducats!—
Justice! the law! my ducats, and my daughter!
A sealed bag, two sealed bags of ducats,
Of double ducats, stol'n from me by my daughter!
And jewels,—two stones, two rich and precious stones,

Stol'n by my daughter!—Justice! find the girl!
She hath the stones upon her, and the ducats!'

Salarino:
Why, all the boys in Venice follow him,
Crying,—his stones, his daughter, and his ducats.

Solanio:
Let good Antonio look he keep his day,
Or he shall pay for this.

Salarino:
      Marry, well remember'd,
I reason'd with a Frenchman yesterday,
Who told me,—in the narrow seas that part
The French and English, there miscarried
A vessel of our country richly fraught:
I thought upon Antonio when he told me;
And wisht in silence that it were not his.

Solanio:
You were best to tell Antonio what you hear;
Yet do not suddenly, for it may grieve him.

Salarino:
A kinder gentleman treads not the earth.
I saw Bassanio and Antonio part:
Bassanio told him he would make some speed
Of his return: he answer'd, 'Do not so,—
Slubber not business for my sake, Bassanio,
But stay the very riping of the time;
And for the Jew's bond which he hath of me,
Let it not enter in your mind of love:
Be merry; and employ your chiefest thoughts
To courtship, and such fair ostents of love
As shall conveniently become you there:'
And even there, his eye being big with tears,
Turning his face, he put his hand behind him,
And with affection wondrous sensible
He wrung Bassanio's hand; and so they parted.

Solanio:
>I think he only loves the world for him.
>I pray thee, let us go and find him out,
>And quicken his embraced heaviness
>With some delight or other.

Salarino:
>>Do we so.

>>>(*Exeunt.*)

(*SCENE VIII.—Belmont. A room in* Portia's *house. Enter* Nerissa *and a* Servitor.)

Nerissa:
>Quick, quick, I pray thee; draw the curtain straight:
>The Prince of Arragon hath ta'en his oath,
>And comes to his election presently.

(*Enter* Prince of Arragon, *his* Train, *and* Portia. *Flourish cornets.*)

Portia:
>Behold, there stand the caskets, noble prince:
>If you choose that wherein I am contain'd,
>Straight shall our nuptial rites be solemnized:
>But if you fail, without more speech, my lord,
>You must be gone from hence immediately.

Prince of Arragon:
>I am enjoin'd by oath to observe three things:—
>First, never to unfold to any one
>Which casket 'twas I chose; next, if I fail
>Of the right casket, never in my life
>To woo a maid in way of marriage; lastly,
>If I do fail in fortune of my choice,
>Immediately to leave you and be gone.

Portia:
>To these injunctions every one doth swear
>That comes to hazard for my worthless self.

Prince of Arragon:
>And so have I address me. Fortune now
>To my heart's hope!—Gold, silver, and base lead.
>'Who chooseth me must give and hazard all he hath.'
>You shall look fairer, ere I give or hazard.
>What says the golden chest? ha! let me see:
>'Who chooseth me shall gain what many men desire.'
>What many men desire!—that many may be meant
>By the fool multitude, that choose by show,
>Not learning more than the fond eye doth teach;
>Which pries not to th' interior, but, like the martlet,
>Builds in the weather on the outward wall,
>Even in the force and road of casualty.
>I will not choose what many men desire,
>Because I will not jump with common spirits,
>And rank me with the barbarous multitudes.
>Why, then to thee, thou silver treasure-house;
>Tell me once more what title thou dost bear:
>'Who chooseth me shall get as much as he deserves:'
>And well said too; for who shall go about
>To cozen fortune, and be honourable
>Without the stamp of merit? Let none presume
>To wear an undeserved dignity.
>O, that estates, degrees, and offices,
>Were not derived corruptly! and that clear honour
>Were purchased by the merit of the wearer!
>How many then should cover that stand bare!
>How many be commanded that command!
>How much low peasantry would then be glean'd
>From the true seed of honour! and how much honour
>Pickt from the chaff and ruin of the times,
>To be new-varnisht! Well, but to my choice:
>'Who chooseth me shall get as much as he deserves.'
>I will assume desert.—Give me a key for this,
>And instantly unlock my fortunes here.

>*(He opens the silver casket.)*

Portia *(aside):*
>Too long a pause for that which you find here.

Prince of Arragon:
>What's here? the portrait of a blinking idiot,

Presenting me a schedule! I will read it.
How much unlike art thou to Portia!
How much unlike my hopes and my deservings!
'Who chooseth me shall have as much as he deserves.'
Did I deserve no more than a fool's head?
Is that my prize? are my deserts no better?

Portia:
To offend, and judge, are distinct offices,
And of opposed natures.

Prince of Arragon:
What is here?

The fire seven times tried this:
Seven times tried that judgement is,
That did never choose amiss.
Some there be that shadows kiss;
Such have but a shadow's blissd.
There be fools alive, I wis,
Silver'd o'er; and so was this.
Take what wife you will to bed,
I will ever be your head:
So be gone; you are sped.

Still more fool I shall appear
By the time I linger here:
With one fool's head I came to woo,
But I go away with two.—
Sweet, adieu. I'll keep my oath,
Patiently to bear my wroth.

(Exit with his Train.*)*

Portia:
Thus hath the candle singed the moth.
O, these deliberate fools! when they do choose,
They have the wisdom by their wit to lose.

Nerissa:
The ancient saying is no heresy,—
Hanging and wiving goes by destiny.

Portia:
　　Come, draw the curtain, Nerissa.

(Enter a Servant.)

Servant:
　　Where is my lady?

Portia:
　　　　　　Here: what would my lord?

Servant:
　　Madam, there is alighted at your gate
　　A young Venetian, one that comes before
　　To signify th' approaching of his lord;
　　From whom he bringeth sensible regreets,
　　To wit, besides commends and courteous breath,
　　Gifts of rich value. Yet I have not seen
　　So likely an ambassador of love:
　　A day in April never came so sweet,
　　To show how costly summer was at hand,
　　As this fore-spurrer comes before his lord.

Portia:
　　No more, I pray thee: I am half afeard
　　Thou wilt say anon he is some kin to thee,
　　Thou spend'st such high-day wit in praising him.—
　　Come, come, Nerissa; for I long to see
　　Quick Cupid's post that comes so mannerly.

Nerissa:
　　Bassanio, lord Love, if thy will it be!

(Exeunt.)

(ACT III. SCENE I.—Venice. A street. Enter Solanio *and* Salarino.*)*

Solanio:
　　Now, what news on the Rialto?

Salarino:
　　Why, yet it lives there uncheckt, that Antonio hath a ship of

rich lading wrackt on the narrow seas; the Goodwins, I think they call the place; a very dangerous flat and fatal, where the carcasses of many a tall ship lie buried, as they say, if my gossip Report be an honest woman of her word.

Solanio:
I would she were as lying a gossip in that as ever knapt ginger, or made her neighbours believe she wept for the death of a third husband. But it is true,—without any slips of prolixity, or crossing the plain highway of talk,—that the good Antonio, the honest Antonio,——O, that I had a title good enough to keep his name company!—

Salarino:
Come, the full stop.

Solanio:
Ha,—what sayest thou?—Why, the end is, he hath lost a ship.

Salarino:
I would it might prove the end of his losses.

Solanio:
Let me say amen betimes, lest the devil cross my prayer,— for here he comes in the likeness of a Jew.

(*Enter* Shylock.)

How now, Shylock! what news among the merchants?

Shylock:
You knew, none so well, none so well as you, of my daughter's flight.

Salarino:
That's certain: I, for my part, knew the tailor that made the wings she flew withal.

Solanio:
And Shylock, for his own part, knew the bird was fledged; and then it is the complexion of them all to leave the dam.

Shylock:
> She is damn'd for it.

Salarino:
> That's certain, if the devil may be her judge.

Shylock:
> My own flesh and blood to rebel!

Solanio:
> Out upon it, old carrion! rebels it at these years?

Shylock:
> I say my daughter is my flesh and blood.

Salarino:
> There is more difference between thy flesh and hers than between jet and ivory; more between your bloods than there is between red wine and rhenish.—But tell us, do you hear whether Antonio have had any loss at sea or no?

Shylock:
> There I have another bad match: a bankrout, a prodigal, who dare scarce show his head on the Rialto;—a beggar, that was used to come so smug upon the mart;—let him look to his bond; he was wont to call me usurer;—let him look to his bond: he was wont to lend money for a Christian courtesy:—let him look to his bond.

Salarino:
> Why, I am sure, if he forfeit, thou wilt not take his flesh: what's that good for?

Shylock:
> To bait fish withal: if it will feed nothing else, it will feed my revenge. He hath disgraced me, and hinder'd me half a million; laugh'd at my losses, mockt at my gains, scorn'd my nation, thwarted my bargains, cooled my friends, heated mine enemies: and what's his reason? I am a Jew. Hath not a Jew eyes? hath not a Jew hands, organs, dimensions, senses, affections, passions? fed with the same food, hurt with the same weapons, subject to the same diseases, heal'd

by the same means, warm'd and cool'd by the same winter and summer, as a Christian is? If you prick us, do we not bleed? if you tickle us, do we not laugh? if you poison us, do we not die? and if you wrong us, shall we not revenge? if we are like you in the rest, we will resemble you in that. If a Jew wrong a Christian, what is his humility? revenge: if a Christian wrong a Jew, what should his sufferance be by Christian example? why, revenge. The villainy you teach me, I will execute; and it shall go hard but I will better the instruction.

(Enter a Servant *from* Antonio.*)*

Servant:
Gentlemen, my master Antonio is at his house, and desires to speak with you both.

Salarino:
We have been up and down to seek him.

Solanio:
Here comes another of the tribe: a third cannot be matcht, unless the devil himself turn Jew.

(Exeunt Solanio, Salarino, *and* Servant. *Enter* Tubal.*)*

Shylock:
How now, Tubal! what news from Genoa? hast thou found my daughter?

Tubal:
I often came where I did hear of her, but cannot find her.

Shylock:
Why, there, there, there, there! a diamond gone, cost me two thousand ducats in Frankfort! The curse never fell upon our nation till now; I never felt it till now:—two thousand ducats in that; and other precious, precious jewels.—I would my daughter were dead at my foot, and the jewels in her ear! would she were hearsed at my foot, and the ducats in her coffin! No news of them?—Why, so:—and I know not what's spent in the search: why, thou, loss upon loss! the thief gone with so much, and so much to find the thief; and no

satisfaction, no revenge: nor no ill luck stirring but what lights on my shoulders; no sighs but of my breathing; no tears but of my shedding.

Tubal:
Yes, other men have ill luck too: Antonio, as I heard in Genoa,—

Shylock:
What, what, what? ill luck, ill luck?

Tubal:
Hath an argosy cast away, coming from Tripolis.

Shylock:
I thank God, I thank God!—Is't true, is't true?

Tubal:
I spoke with some of the sailors that escaped the wrack.

Shylock:
I thank thee, good Tubal:—good news, good news! ha, ha!—where? in Genoa?

Tubal:
Your daughter spent in Genoa, as I heard, one night fourscore ducats.

Shylock:
Thou stick'st a dagger in me:—I shall never see my gold again: fourscore ducats at a sitting! fourscore ducats!

Tubal:
There came divers of Antonio's creditors in my company to Venice, that swear he cannot choose but break.

Shylock:
I am very glad of it:—I'll plague him; I'll torture him:—I am glad on't.

Tubal:
One of them show'd me a ring that he had of your daughter for a monkey.

Shylock:
> Out upon her! Thou torturest me, Tubal: it was my turquoise; I had it of Leah when I was a bachelor: I would not have given it for a wilderness of monkeys.

Tubal:
> But Antonio is certainly undone.

Shylock:
> Nay, that's true, that's very true. Go, Tubal, fee me an officer; bespeak him a fortnight before. I will have the heart of him, if he forfeit; for, were he out of Venice, I can make what merchandise I will. Go, Tubal, and meet me at our synagogue; go, good Tubal; at our synagogue, Tubal.

(Exeunt.)

(SCENE II.—Belmont. A room in Portia's *house. Enter* Bassanio, Portia, Gratiano, Nerissa, *and all their* Train.*)*

Portia:
> I pray you, tarry: pause a day or two
> Before you hazard; for, in choosing wrong,
> I lose your company: therefore, forbear awhile.
> There's something tells me—but it is not love—
> I would not lose you; and you know yourself,
> Hate counsels not in such a quality.
> But lest you should not understand me well,—
> And yet a maiden hath no tongue but thought,—
> I would detain you here some month or two
> Before you venture for me. I could teach you
> How to choose right, but then I am forsworn;
> So will I never be: so may you miss me;
> But if you do, you'll make me wish a sin,
> That I had been forsworn. Beshrew your eyes,
> They have o'erlookt me, and divided me;
> One half of me is yours, the other half yours,—
> Mine own, I would say; but if mine, then yours,
> And so all yours! O, these naughty times
> Put bars between the owners and their rights!
> And so, though yours, not yours.—Prove it so,
> Let fortune go to hell for it,—not I.

> I speak too long; but 'tis to peize the time,
> To eke it, and to draw it out in length,
> To stay you from election.

Bassanio:
> Let me choose;
> For, as I am, I live upon the rack.

Portia:
> Upon the rack, Bassanio! then confess
> What treason there is mingled with your love.

Bassanio:
> None but that ugly treason of mistrust,
> Which makes me fear the enjoying of my love:
> There may as well be amity and league
> 'Tween snow and fire, as treason and my love.

Portia:
> Ay, but I fear you speak upon the rack,
> Where men enforced do speak any thing.

Bassanio:
> Promise me life, and I'll confess the truth.

Portia:
> Well then, confess, and live.

Bassanio:
> 'Confess,' and 'love,'
> Had been the very sum of my confession:
> O happy torment, when my torturer
> Doth teach me answers for deliverance!
> But let me to my fortune and the caskets.

Portia:
> Away, then! I am lockt in one of them:
> If you do love me, you will find me out.—
> Nerissa, and the rest, stand all aloof.—
> Let music sound while he doth make his choice;
> Then, if he lose, he makes a swan-like end,
> Fading in music: that the comparison

May stand more proper, my eye shall be the stream
And watery death-bed for him. He may win;
And what is music then? then music is
Even as the flourish when true subjects bow
To a new-crowned monarch: such it is
As are those dulcet sounds in break of day
That creep into the dreaming bridegroom's ear,
And summon him to marriage.—Now he goes,
With no less presence, but with much more love,
Than young Alcides, when he did redeem
The virgin tribute paid by howling Troy
To the sea-monster: I stand for sacrifice;
The rest aloof are the Dardanian wives,
With bleared visages, come forth to view
The issue of th' exploit. Go, Hercules!
Live thou, I live:—with much much more dismay
I view the fight than thou that makest the fray.

(*Hear music.—A Song, the whilst* Bassanio *comments on the caskets to himself.*)

Tell me where is fancy bred,
Or in the heart or in the head?
How begot, how nourished?
   Reply, reply.
It is engender'd in the eyes,
With gazing fed; and fancy dies
In the cradle where it lies.
   Let us all ring fancy's knell;
   I'll begin it,—Ding, dong, bell.
All. Ding, dong, bell.

Bassanio:
So may the outward shows be least themselves:
The world is still deceived with ornament.
In law, what plea so tainted and corrupt,
But, being season'd with a gracious voice,
Obscures the show of evil? In religion,
What damned error, but some sober brow
Will bless it, and approve it with a text,
Hiding the grossness with fair ornament?
There is no vice so simple, but assumes

Some mark of virtue on his outward parts:
How many cowards, whose hearts are all as false
As stairs of sand, wear yet upon their chins
The beards of Hercules and frowning Mars;
Who, inward searcht, have livers white as milk;
And these assume but valour's excrement
To render them redoubted! Look on beauty,
And you shall see 'tis purchased by the weight;
Which therein works a miracle in nature,
Making them lightest that wear most of it:
So are those crisped snaky golden locks,
Which make such wanton gambols with the wind,
Upon supposed fairness, often known
To be the dowry of a second head,
The skull that bred them in the sepulchre.
Thus ornament is but the guiled shore
To a most dangerous sea; the beauteous scarf
Veiling an Indian beauty; in a word,
The seeming truth which cunning times put on
To entrap the wisest. Therefore, thou gaudy gold,
Hard food for Midas, I will none of thee;
Nor none of thee, thou stale and common drudge
'Tween man and man: but thou, thou meagre lead,
Which rather threatenest than dost promise aught,
Thy paleness moves me more than eloquence;
And here choose I:—joy be the consequence!

Portia *(aside):*
How all the other passions fleet to air,—
As doubtful thoughts, and rash-embraced despair,
And shuddering fear, and green-eyed jealousy!
O love, be moderate; allay thy ecstasy;
In measure rain thy joy; scant this excess!
I feel too much thy blessing: make it less,
For fear I surfeit!

Bassanio:
What find I here?
(Opening the leaden casket.)
Fair Portia's counterfeit! What demi-god
Hath come so near creation? Move these eyes?
Or whether, riding on the balls of mine,

Seem they in motion? Here are sever'd lips,
Parted with sugar breath: so sweet a bar
Should sunder such sweet friends. Here in her hairs
The painter plays the spider; and hath woven
A golden mesh t'entrap the hearts of men,
Faster than gnats in cobwebs: but her eyes,—
How could he see to do them? having made one,
Methinks it should have power to steal both his,
And leave itself unfurnisht. Yet look, how far
The substance of my praise doth wrong this shadow
In underprizing it, so far this shadow
Doth limp behind the substance.—Here's the scroll,
The continent and summary of my fortune.

> You that choose not by the view,
> Chance as fair, and choose as true!
> Since this fortune falls to you,
> Be content, and seek no new.
> If you be well pleased with this,
> And hold your fortune for your bliss,
> Turn you where your lady is,
> And claim her with a loving kiss.

A gentle scroll.—Fair lady, by your leave;
                                    (Kissing her.)
I come by note, to give and to receive.
Like one of two contending in a prize,
That thinks he hath done well in people's eyes,
Hearing applause and universal shout,
Giddy in spirit, still gazing in a doubt
Whether those peals of praise be his or no;
So, thrice-fair lady, stand I, even so;
As doubtful whether what I see be true,
Until confirm'd, sign'd, ratified by you.

Portia:
You see me, Lord Bassanio, where I stand,
Such as I am: though for myself alone
I would not be ambitious in my wish,
To wish myself much better; yet for you
I would be trebled twenty times myself;
A thousand times more fair, ten thousand times more rich;

> That, only to stand high in your account,
> I might in virtues, beauties, livings, friends,
> Exceed account: but the full sum of me
> Is sum of nothing; which, to term in gross,
> Is an unlesson'd girl, unschool'd, unpractised:
> Happy in this, she is not yet so old
> But she may learn; happier than this,
> She is not bred so dull but she can learn;
> Happiest of all is that her gentle spirit
> Commits itself to yours to be directed,
> As from her lord, her governor, her king.
> Myself and what is mine to you and yours
> Is now converted: but now I was the lord
> Of this fair mansion, master of my servants,
> Queen o'er myself; and even now, but now,
> This house, these servants, and this same myself,
> Are yours, my lord: I give them with this ring;
> Which when you part from, lose, or give away,
> Let it presage the ruin of your love,
> And be my vantage to exclaim on you.

Bassanio:
> Madam, you have bereft me of all words,
> Only my blood speaks to you in my veins:
> And there is such confusion in my powers,
> As, after some oration fairly spoke
> By a beloved prince, there doth appear
> Among the buzzing pleased multitude;
> Where every something, being blent together,
> Turns to a wild of nothing, save of joy,
> Exprest and not exprest. But when this ring
> Parts from this finger, then parts life from hence:
> O, then be bold to say Bassanio's dead!

Nerissa:
> My lord and lady, it is now our time,
> That have stood by, and seen our wishes prosper,
> To cry, good joy:—good joy, my lord and lady!

Gratiano:
> My Lord Bassanio and my gentle lady,
> I wish you all the joy that you can wish;
> For I am sure you can wish none from me:

> And, when your honours mean to solemnize
> The bargain of your faith, I do beseech you,
> Even at that time I may be married too.

Bassanio:
> With all my heart, so thou canst get a wife.

Gratiano:
> I thank your lordship, you have got me one.
> My eyes, my lord, can look as swift as yours:
> You saw the mistress, I beheld the maid;
> You loved, I loved; for intermission
> No more pertains to me, my lord, than you.
> Your fortune stood upon the caskets there;
> And so did mine too, as the matter falls;
> For wooing here, until I sweat again,
> And swearing, till my very roof was dry
> With oaths of love, at last,—if promise last,—
> I got a promise of this fair one here,
> To have her love, provided that your fortune
> Achieved her mistress.

Portia:
>   Is this true, Nerissa?

Nerissa:
> Madam, it is, so you stand pleased withal.

Bassanio:
> And do you, Gratiano, mean good faith?

Gratiano:
> Yes, faith, my lord.

Bassanio:
> Our feast shall be much honour'd in your marriage.

Gratiano:
> We'll play with them the first boy for a thousand ducats.

Nerissa:
> What, and stake down?

Gratiano:
>No; we shall ne'er win at that sport, and stake down.—
>But who comes here? Lorenzo and his infidel?
>What, and my old Venetian friend Solanio?

>*(Enter Lorenzo, Jessica, and Solanio.)*

Bassanio:
>Lorenzo and Solanio, welcome hither;
>If that the youth of my new interest here
>Have power to bid you welcome.—By your leave,
>I bid my very friends and countrymen,
>Sweet Portia, welcome.

Portia:
>So do I, my lord;
>They are entirely welcome.

Lorenzo:
>I thank your honour.—For my part, my lord,
>My purpose was not to have seen you here;
>But meeting with Solanio by the way,
>He did entreat me, past all saying nay,
>To come with him along.

Solanio:
>I did, my lord;
>And I have reason for't. Signior Antonio
>Commends him to you.

>*(Gives Bassanio a letter.)*

Bassanio:
>Ere I ope this letter,
>I pray you, tell me how my good friend doth.

Solanio:
>Not sick, my lord, unless it be in mind;
>Not well, unless in mind: his letter there
>Will show you his estate.

>*(Bassanio reads the letter.)*

Gratiano:
>Nerissa, cheer yon stranger; bid her welcome.—
>Your hand, Solanio: what's the news from Venice?
>How doth that royal merchant, good Antonio?
>I know he will be glad of our success;
>We are the Jasons, we have won the fleece.

Solanio:
>I would you had won the fleece that he hath lost!

Portia:
>There are some shrewd contents in yon same paper,
>That steals the colour from Bassanio's cheek:
>Some dear friend dead; else nothing in the world
>Could turn so much the constitution
>Of any constant man. What, worse and worse!—
>With leave, Bassanio; I am half yourself,
>And I must freely have the half of any thing
>That this same paper brings you.

Bassanio:
>   O sweet Portia,
>Here are a few of the unpleasant'st words
>That ever blotted paper! Gentle lady,
>When I did first impart my love to you,
>I freely told you, all the wealth I had
>Ran in my veins,—I was a gentleman;
>And then I told you true: and yet, dear lady,
>Rating myself at nothing, you shall see
>How much I was a braggart. When I told you
>My state was nothing, I should then have told you
>That I was worse than nothing; for, indeed,
>I have engaged myself to a dear friend,
>Engaged my friend to his mere enemy,
>To feed my means. Here is a letter, lady,—
>The paper as the body of my friend,
>And every word in it a gaping wound,
>Issuing life-blood.—But is it true, Solanio?
>Have all his ventures fail'd? What, not one hit?
>From Tripolis, from Mexico, and England,
>From Lisbon, Barbary, and India?
>And not one vessel scape the dreadful touch

Of merchant-marring rocks?

Solanio:
                                    Not one, my lord.
Besides, it should appear, that if he had
The present money to discharge the Jew,
He would not take it. Never did I know
A creature, that did bear the shape of man,
So keen and greedy to confound a man;
He plies the duke at morning and at night;
And doth impeach the freedom of the state,
If they deny him justice: twenty merchants,
The duke himself, and the magnificoes
Of greatest port, have all persuaded with him;
But none can drive him from the envious plea
Of forfeiture, of justice, and his bond.

Jessica:
When I was with him, I have heard him swear,
To Tubal and to Chus, his countrymen,
That he would rather have Antonio's flesh
Than twenty times the value of the sum
That he did owe him: and I know, my lord,
If law, authority, and power deny not,
It will go hard with poor Antonio.

Portia:
Is it your dear friend that is thus in trouble?

Bassanio:
The dearest friend to me, the kindest man,
The best-condition'd and unwearied spirit
In doing courtesies; and one in whom
The ancient Roman honour more appears
Than any that draws breath in Italy.

Portia:
What sum owes he the Jew?

Bassanio:
For me three thousand ducats.

Portia:
What, no more?
Pay him six thousand, and deface the bond;
Double six thousand, and then treble that,
Before a friend of this description
Shall lose a hair through Bassanio's fault.
First go with me to church and call me wife,
And then away to Venice to your friend;
For never shall you lie by Portia's side
With an unquiet soul. You shall have gold
To pay the petty debt twenty times over:
When it is paid, bring your true friend along.
My maid Nerissa and myself meantime
Will live as maids and widows. Come, away!
For you shall hence upon your wedding-day:
Bid your friends welcome, show a merry cheer:
Since you are dear-bought, I will love you dear.—
But let me hear the letter of your friend.

Bassanio (*reads*):
Sweet Bassanio, my ships have all miscarried, my creditors grow cruel, my estate is very low, my bond to the Jew is forfeit; and since in paying it, it is impossible I should live, all debts are clear'd between you and I, if I might but see you at my death. Notwithstanding, use your pleasure: if your love do not persuade you to come, let not my letter.

Portia:
O love, dispatch all business, and be gone!

Bassanio:
Since I have your good leave to go away,
    I will make haste: but, till I come again,
No bed shall e'er be guilty of my stay,
    No rest be interposer 'twixt us twain.

(*Exeunt.*)

(SCENE III.—*Venice. A street. Enter* Shylock, Salarino, Antonio, *and* Gaoler.)

Shylock:
>Gaoler, look to him:—tell not me of mercy;—
>This is the fool that lent out money gratis:—
>Gaoler, look to him.

Antonio:
>>Hear me yet, good Shylock.

Shylock:
>I'll have my bond; speak not against my bond:
>I have sworn an oath that I will have my bond.
>Thou call'dst me dog before thou hadst a cause;
>But, since I am a dog, beware my fangs:
>The duke shall grant me justice.—I do wonder,
>Thou naughty gaoler, that thou art so fond
>To come abroad with him at his request.

Antonio:
>I pray thee, hear me speak.

Shylock:
>I'll have my bond; I will not hear thee speak:
>I'll have my bond; and therefore speak no more.
>I'll not be made a soft and dull-eyed fool,
>To shake the head, relent, and sigh, and yield
>To Christian intercessors. Follow not;
>I'll have no speaking: I will have my bond.

>>>>*(Exit.)*

Salarino:
>It is the most impenetrable cur
>That ever kept with men.

Antonio:
>>Let him alone:
>I'll follow him no more with bootless prayers.
>He seeks my life; his reason well I know:
>I oft deliver'd from his forfeitures
>Many that have at times made moan to me;
>Therefore he hates me.

Salarino:
                    I am sure the duke
    Will never grant this forfeiture to hold.

Antonio:
    The duke cannot deny the course of law;
    For the commodity that strangers have
    With us in Venice, if it be denied,
    Will much impeach the justice of the state;
    Since that the trade and profit of the city
    Consisteth of all nations. Therefore, go:
    These griefs and losses have so bated me,
    That I shall hardly spare a pound of flesh
    To-morrow to my bloody creditor.—
    Well, gaoler, on.—Pray God, Bassanio come
    To see me pay his debt,—and then I care not!

                                      (Exeunt.)

(SCENE IV.—Belmont. A room in Portia's *house. Enter* Portia, Nerissa, Lorenzo, Jessica, *and* Balthazar, *a man of* Portia's.*)*

Lorenzo:
    Madam, although I speak it in your presence,
    You have a noble and a true conceit
    Of god-like amity; which appears most strongly
    In bearing thus the absence of your lord.
    But if you knew to whom you show this honour,
    How true a gentleman you send relief,
    How dear a lover of my lord your husband,
    I know you would be prouder of the work
    Than customary bounty can enforce you.

Portia:
    I never did repent for doing good,
    Nor shall not now: for in companions
    That do converse and waste the time together,
    Whose souls do bear an egal yoke of love,
    There must be needs a like proportion
    Of lineaments, of manners, and of spirit;
    Which makes me think that this Antonio,
    Being the bosom lover of my lord,

Must needs be like my lord. If it be so,
How little is the cost I have bestow'd
In purchasing the semblance of my soul
From out the state of hellish cruelty!
This comes too near the praising of myself;
Therefore no more of it: hear other things.—
Lorenzo, I commit into your hands
The husbandry and manage of my house
Until my lord's return: for mine own part,
I have toward heaven breathed a secret vow
To live in prayer and contemplation,
Only attended by Nerissa here,
Until her husband and my lord's return:
There is a monastery two miles off;
And there will we abide. I do desire you
Not to deny this imposition;
The which my love and some necessity
Now lays upon you.

Lorenzo:
                      Madam, with all my heart;
I shall obey you in all fair commands.

Portia:
My people do already know my mind,
And will acknowledge you and Jessica
In place of Lord Bassanio and myself.
So fare you well, till we shall meet again.

Lorenzo:
Fair thoughts and happy hours attend on you!

Jessica:
I wish your ladyship all heart's content.

Portia:
I thank you for your wish, and am well pleased
To wish it back on you: fare you well, Jessica.

                    (*Exeunt* Jessica *and* Lorenzo.)

Now, Balthazar,

As I have ever found thee honest-true,
So let me find thee still. Take this same letter,
And use thou all the endeavour of a man
In speed to Padua: see thou render this
Into my cousin's hand, Doctor Bellario;
And, look, what notes and garments he doth give thee,
Bring them, I pray thee, with imagined speed
Unto the tranect, to the common ferry
Which trades to Venice. Waste no time in words,
But get thee gone: I shall be there before thee.

Balthazar:
Madam, I go with all convenient speed.

(Exit.)

Portia:
Come on, Nerissa; I have work in hand
That you yet know not of: we'll see our husbands
Before they think of us.

Nerissa:
Shall they see us?

Portia:
They shall, Nerissa; but in such a habit,
That they shall think we are accomplished
With that we lack. I'll hold thee any wager,
When we are both accoutred like young men,
I'll prove the prettier fellow of the two,
And wear my dagger with the braver grace;
And speak between the change of man and boy
With a reed voice; and turn two mincing steps
Into a manly stride; and speak of frays,
Like a fine-bragging youth; and tell quaint lies,
How honourable ladies sought my love,
Which I denying, they fell sick and died,—
I could not do withal;—then I'll repent,
And wish, for all that, that I had not kill'd them:
And twenty of these puny lies I'll tell;
That men shall swear I have discontinued school
Above twelvemonth:—I have within my mind

> A thousand raw tricks of these bragging Jacks,
> Which I will practise.

Nerissa:
> Why shall we turn to men?

Portia:
> Fie, what a question's that,
> If thou wert near a lewd interpreter!
> But come, I'll tell thee all my whole device
> When I am in my coach, which stays for us
> At the park-gate; and therefore haste away,
> For we must measure twenty miles to-day.

(Exeunt.)

(SCENE V.—The same. A garden. Enter Launcelot *and* Jessica.*)*

Launcelot:
> Yes, truly; for, look you, the sins of the father are to be laid upon the children: therefore, I promise ye, I fear you. I was always plain with you, and so now I speak my agitation of the matter: therefore be o'good cheer; for, truly, I think you are damn'd. There is but one hope in it that can do you any good; and that is but a kind of bastard hope neither.

Jessica:
> And what hope is that, I pray thee?

Launcelot:
> Marry, you may partly hope that your father got you not,— that you are not the Jew's daughter.

Jessica:
> That were a kind of bastard hope, indeed: so the sins of my mother should be visited upon me.

Launcelot:
> Truly, then, I fear you are damn'd both by father and mother: thus when I shun Scylla, your father, I fall into Charybdis, your mother: well, you are gone both ways.

Jessica:
I shall be saved by my husband; he hath made me a Christian.

Launcelot:
Truly, the more to blame he: we were Christians enow before; e'en as many as could well live, one by another. This making of Christians will raise the price of hogs: if we grow all to be pork-eaters, we shall not shortly have a rasher on the coals for money.

Jessica:
I'll tell my husband, Launcelot, what you say: here he comes.

(Enter Lorenzo.)

Lorenzo:
I shall grow jealous of you shortly, Launcelot, if you thus get my wife into corners.

Jessica:
Nay, you need not fear us, Lorenzo: Launcelot and I are out. He tells me flatly, there's no mercy for me in heaven, because I am a Jew's daughter: and he says, you are no good member of the commonwealth; for in converting Jews to Christians, you raise the price of pork.

Lorenzo:
I shall answer that better to the commonwealth than you can the getting up of the negro's belly: the Moor's with child by you, Launcelot.

Launcelot:
It is much that the Moor should be more than reason: but if she be less than an honest woman, she is indeed more than I took her for.

Lorenzo:
How every fool can play upon the word! I think the best grace of wit will shortly turn into silence, and discourse grow commendable in none only but parrots.—Go in, sirrah; bid them prepare for dinner.

Launcelot:
> That's done, sir; they have all stomachs.

Lorenzo:
> Goodly Lord, what a wit-snapper you are! then bid them prepare dinner.

Launcelot:
> That is done too, sir; only 'cover' is the word.

Lorenzo:
> Will you cover, then, sir?

Launcelot:
> Not so, sir, neither; I know my duty.

Lorenzo:
> Yet more quarrelling with occasion! Wilt thou show the whole wealth of thy wit in an instant? I pray thee, understand a plain man in his plain meaning: go to thy fellows, bid them cover the table, serve in the meat, and we will come in to dinner.

Launcelot:
> For the table, sir, it shall be served in; for the meat, sir, it shall be cover'd; for your coming in to dinner, sir, why, let it be as humours and conceits shall govern.

> *(Exit.)*

Lorenzo:
> O dear discretion, how his words are suited!
> The fool hath planted in his memory
> An army of good words; and I do know
> A many fools, that stand in better place,
> Garnisht like him, that for a tricksy word
> Defy the matter.—How cheer'st thou, Jessica?
> And now, good sweet, say thy opinion,—
> How dost thou like the Lord Bassanio's wife?

Jessica:
> Past all expressing. It is very meet
> The Lord Bassanio live an upright life;

> For, having such a blessing in his lady,
> He finds the joys of heaven here on earth;
> And if on earth he do not mean it, then
> In reason he should never come to heaven.
> Why, if two gods should play some heavenly match,
> And on the wager lay two earthly women,
> And Portia one, there must be something else
> Pawn'd with the other; for the poor rude world
> Hath not her fellow.

Lorenzo:
>   Even such a husband
> Hast thou of me as she is for a wife.

Jessica:
> Nay, but ask my opinion too of that.

Lorenzo:
> I will anon: first, let us go to dinner.

Jessica:
> Nay, let me praise you while I have a stomach.

Lorenzo:
> No, prithee, let it serve for table-talk;
> Then, howso'er thou speak'st, 'mong other things
> I shall digest it.

Jessica:
>   Well, I'll set you forth.

(Exeunt.)

(ACT IV. SCENE I.—Venice. A court of justice. Enter the Duke, *the* Magnificoes, Antonio, Bassanio, Gratiano, Solanio, Salarino, *and others.)*

Duke of Venice:
> What, is Antonio here?

Antonio:
> Ready, so please your Grace.

Duke of Venice:
>I am sorry for thee: thou art come to answer
>A stony adversary, an inhuman wretch
>Uncapable of pity, void and empty
>From any dram of mercy.

Antonio:
>>I have heard
>Your Grace hath ta'en great pains to qualify
>His rigorous course; but since he stands obdurate,
>And that no lawful means can carry me
>Out of his envy's reach, I do oppose
>My patience to his fury; and am arm'd
>To suffer, with a quietness of spirit,
>The very tyranny and rage of his.

Duke of Venice:
>Go one, and call the Jew into the court.

Solanio:
>He's ready at the door: he comes, my lord.

>>*(Enter* Shylock.*)*

Duke of Venice:
>Make room, and let him stand before our face.—
>Shylock, the world thinks, and I think so too,
>That thou but lead'st this fashin of thy malice
>To the last hour of act; and then 'tis thought
>Thou'lt show thy mercy and remorse more strange
>Than is thy strange apparent cruelty;
>And where thou now exact'st the penalty,—
>Which is a pound of this poor merchant's flesh,—
>Thou wilt not only loose the forfeiture,
>But, toucht with human gentleness and love,
>Forgive a moiety of the principal;
>Glancing an eye of pity on his losses,
>That have of late so huddled on his back,
>Enow to press a royal merchant down,
>And pluck commiseration of his state
>From brassy bosoms and rough hearts of flint,
>From stubborn Turks and Tartars, never train'd

To offices of tender courtesy.
We all expect a gentle answer, Jew.

Shylock:
    I have possest your Grace of what I purpose;
    And by our holy Sabbath have I sworn
    To have the due and forfeit of my bond:
    If you deny it, let the danger light
    Upon your charter and your city's freedom.
    You'll ask me, why I rather choose to have
    A weight of carrion-flesh than to receive
    Three thousand ducats: I'll not answer that;
    But say it is my humour: is it answer'd?
    What if my house be troubled with a rat,
    And I be pleased to give ten thousand ducats
    To have it baned! What, are you answer'd yet?
    Some men there are love not a gaping pig;
    Some, that are mad if they behold a cat;
    And others, when the bag-pipe sings i' th' nose,
    Cannot contain their urine: for affection,
    Mistress of passion, sways it to the mood
    Of what it likes or loathes. Now, for your answer:
    As there is no firm reason to be render'd,
    Why he cannot abide a gaping pig;
    Why he, a harmless necessary cat;
    Why he, a woollen bag-pipe,—but of force
    Must yield to such inevitable shame
    As to offend himself, being offended;
    So can I give no reason, nor I will not,
    More than a lodged hate and a certain loathing
    I bear Antonio, that I follow thus
    A losing suit against him. Are you answer'd?

Bassanio:
    This is no answer, thou unfeeling man,
    To excuse the current of thy cruelty.

Shylock:
    I am not bound to please thee with my answer.

Bassanio:
    Do all men kill the things they do not love?

Shylock:
>Hates any man the thing he would not kill?

Bassanio:
>Every offence is not a hate at first.

Shylock:
>What, would'st thou have a serpent sting thee twice?

Antonio:
>I pray you, think you question with the Jew:
>You may as well go stand upon the beach,
>And bid the main flood bate his usual height;
>You may as well use question with the wolf,
>Why he hath made the ewe bleat for the lamb;
>You may as well forbid the mountain pines
>To wag their high tops, and to make no noise,
>When they are fretten with the gusts of heaven;
>You may as well do any thing most hard,
>As seek to soften that,—than which what's harder?—
>His Jewish heart:—therefore, I do beseech you,
>Make no more offers, use no further means,
>But, with all brief and plain conveniency,
>Let me have judgement, and the Jew his will.

Bassanio:
>For thy three thousand ducats here is six.

Shylock:
>If every ducat in six thousand ducats
>Were in six parts, and every part a ducat,
>I would not draw them,—I would have my bond.

Duke of Venice:
>How shalt thou hope for mercy, rendering none?

Shylock:
>What judgement shall I dread, doing no wrong?
>You have among you many a purchased slave,
>Which, like your asses and your dogs and mules.
>You use in abject and in slavish parts
>Because you bought them:—shall I say to you,
>Let them be free, marry them to your heirs?

Why sweat they under burdens? let their beds
Be made as soft as yours, and let their palates
Be season'd with such viands? You will answer,
The slaves are ours:—so do I answer you:
The pound of flesh, which I demand of him,
Is dearly bought, 'tis mine, and I will have it.
If you deny me, fie upon your law!
There is no force in the decrees of Venice.
I stand for judgment: answer.—shall I have it?

Duke of Venice:
Upon my power I may dismiss this court,
Unless Bellario, a learned doctor,
Whom I have sent for to determine this,
Come here to-day.

Solanio:
My lord, here stays without
A messenger with letters from the doctor,
New come from Padua.

Duke of Venice:
Bring us the letters; call the messenger.

Bassanio:
Good cheer, Antonio! What, man, courage yet
The Jew shall have my flesh, blood, bones, and all,
Ere thou shalt lose for me one drop of blood.

Antonio:
I am a tainted wether of the flock,
Meetest for death: the weakest kind of fruit
Drops earliest to the ground; and so let me:
You cannot better be employ'd, Bassanio,
Than to live still, and write mine epitaph.

(*Enter* Nerissa, *dressed like a lawyer's clerk.*)

Duke of Venice:
Came you from Padua, from Bellario?

Nerissa:
    From both, my lord. Bellario greets your Grace.

                                               (Presents a letter.)

Bassanio:
    Why dost thou whet thy knife so earnestly?

Shylock:
    To cut the forfeiture from that bankrout there.

Gratiano:
    Not on thy sole, but on thy soul, harsh Jew,
    Thou makest thy knife keen; but no metal can,
    No, not the hangman's axe, bear half the keenness
    Of thy sharp envy. Can no prayers pierce thee?

Shylock:
    No, none that thou hast wit enough to make.

Gratiano:
    O, be thou damn'd, inexecrable dog!
    And for thy life let justice be accused.
    Thou almost makest me waver in my faith,
    To hold opinion with Pythagoras,
    That souls of animals infuse themselves
    Into the trunks of men: thy currish spirit
    Govern'd a wolf, who, hang'd for human slaughter,
    Even from the gallows did his fell soul fleet,
    And, whilst thou lay'st in thy unhallow'd dam,
    Infused itself in thee; for thy desires
    Are wolvish, bloody, starved, and ravenous.

Shylock:
    Till thou canst rail the seal from off my bond,
    Thou but offend'st thy lungs to speak so loud:
    Repair thy wit, good youth, or it will fall
    To cureless ruin.—I stand here for law.

Duke of Venice:
    This letter from Bellario doth command
    A young and learned doctor to our court.—
    Where is he?

Nerissa:
>He attendeth here hard by,
>To know your answer, whether you'll admit him.

Duke of Venice:
>With all my heart.—Some three or four of you
>Go give him courteous conduct to this place.—
>Meantime the court shall hear Bellario's letter.

Clerk *(reads):*
>Your Grace shall understand, that at the receipt of your letter I am very sick: but in the instant that your messenger came, in loving visitation was with me a young doctor of Rome; his name is Balthazar. I acquainted him with the cause in controversy between the Jew and Antonio the merchant: we turn'd o'er many books together: he is furnisht with my opinion; which, better'd with his own learning,—the greatness whereof I cannot enough commend,—comes with him, at my importunity, to fill up your Grace's request in my stead. I beseech you, let his lack of years be no impediment to let him lack a reverend estimation; for I never knew so young a body with so old a head. I leave him to your gracious acceptance, whose trial shall better publish his commendation.

Duke of Venice:
>You hear the learn'd Bellario, what he writes:
>And here, I take it, is the doctor come.

>*(Enter* Portia *for* Balthazar.*)*

>Give me your hand. Come you from old Bellario?

Portia:
>I did, my lord.

Duke of Venice:
>You are welcome: take your place.
>Are you acquainted with the difference
>That holds this present question in the court?

Portia:
> I am informed throughly of the cause.—
> Which is the merchant here, and which the Jew?

Duke of Venice:
> Antonio and old Shylock, both stand forth.

Portia:
> Is your name Shylock?

Shylock:
> > Shylock is my name.

Portia:
> Of a strange nature is the suit you follow;
> Yet in such rule, that the Venetian law
> Cannot impugn you as you do proceed.—
> You stand within his danger, do you not?

Antonio:
> Ay, so he says.

Portia:
> > Do you confess the bond?

Antonio:
> I do.

Portia:
> > Then must the Jew be merciful.

Shylock:
> On what compulsion must I? tell me that.

Portia:
> The quality of mercy is not strain'd,—
> It droppeth as the gentle rain from heaven
> Upon the place beneath: it is twice blest,—
> It blesseth him that gives, and him that takes:
> 'Tis mightiest in the mightiest: it becomes
> The throned monarch better than his crown;
> His sceptre shows the force of temporal power,

The attribute to awe and majesty,
Wherein doth sit the dread and fear of kings;
But mercy is above this sceptred sway,—
It is enthroned in the hearts of kings,
It is an attribute to God himself;
And earthly power doth then show likest God's
When mercy seasons justice. Therefore Jew,
Though justice be thy plea, consider this,—
That, in the course of justice, none of us
Should see salvation: we do pray for mercy;
And that same prayer doth teach us all to render
The deeds of mercy. I have spoke thus much
To mitigate the justice of thy plea;
Which if thou follow, this strict court of Venice
Must needs give sentence 'gainst the merchant there.

Shylock:

My deeds upon my head! I crave the law,
The penalty and forfeit of my bond.

Portia:

Is he not able to discharge the money?

Bassanio:

Yes, here I tender it for him in the court;
Yea, thrice the sum: if that will not suffice,
I will be bound to pay it ten times o'er,
On forfeit of my hands, my head, my heart:
If this will not suffice, it must appear
That malice bears down truth. And I beseech you,
Wrest once the law to your authority:
To do a great right, do a little wrong;
And curb this cruel devil of his will.

Portia:

It must not be; there is no power in Venice
Can alter a decree established:
'Twill be recorded for a precedent;
And many an error, by the same example,
Will rush into the state: it cannot be.

Shylock:
>A Daniel come to judgement! yea, a Daniel!—
>O wise young judge, how I do honour thee!

Portia:
>I pray you, let me look upon the bond.

Shylock:
>Here 'tis, most reverend doctor, here it is.

Portia:
>Shylock, there's thrice thy money offer'd thee.

Shylock:
>An oath, an oath, I have an oath in heaven:
>Shall I lay perjury upon my soul?
>No, not for Venice.

Portia:
>Why, this bond is forfeit;
>And lawfully by this the Jew may claim
>A pound of flesh, to be by him cut off
>Nearest the merchant's heart.—Be merciful:
>Take thrice thy money; bid me tear the bond.

Shylock:
>When it is paid according to the tenour.—
>It doth appear you are a worthy judge;
>You know the law, your exposition
>Hath been most sound: I charge you by the law,
>Whereof you are a well-deserving pillar,
>Proceed to judgement: by my soul I swear
>There is no power in the tongue of man
>To alter me: I stay here on my bond.

Antonio:
>Most heartily I do beseech the court
>To give the judgement.

Portia:
>Why then, thus it is:—
>You must prepare your bosom for his knife.

Shylock:
>O noble judge! O excellent young man!

Portia:
>For the intent and purpose of the law
>Hath full relation to the penalty,
>Which here appeareth due upon the bond.

Shylock:
>'Tis very true: O wise and upright judge!
>How much more elder art thou than thy looks!

Portia:
>Therefore lay bare your bosom.

Shylock:
>>   Ay, his breast:
>So says the bond:—doth it not, noble judge?—
>Nearest his heart: those are the very words.

Portia:
>It is so. Are there balance here to weigh
>The flesh?

Shylock:
>I have them ready.

Portia:
>Have by some surgeon, Shylock, on your charge,
>To stop his wounds, lest he do bleed to death.

Shylock:
>Is it so nominated in the bond?

Portia:
>It is not so exprest: but what of that?
>'Twere good you do so much for charity.

Shylock:
>I cannot find it; 'tis not in the bond.

Portia:
>You, merchant, have you any thing to say?

Antonio:
>But little: I am arm'd and well prepared.—
>Give me your hand, Bassanio: fare you well!
>Grieve not that I am fall'n to this for you;
>For herein Fortune shows herself more kind
>Than is her custom: it is still her use
>To let the wretched man outlive his wealth,
>To view with hollow eye and wrinkled brow
>An age of poverty; from which lingering penance
>Of such a misery doth she cut me off.
>Commend me to your honourable wife:
>Tell her the process of Antonio's end;
>Say how I loved you, speak me fair in death;
>And, when the tale is told, bid her be judge
>Whether Bassanio had not once a love.
>Repent but you that you shall lose your friend,
>And he repents not that he pays your debt;
>For, if the Jew do cut but deep enough,
>I'll pay it presently with all my heart.

Bassanio:
>Antonio, I am married to a wife
>Which is as dear to me as life itself;
>But life itself, my wife, and all the world,
>Are not with me esteem'd above thy life:
>I would lose all, ay, sacrifice them all
>Here to this devil, to deliver you.

Portia:
>Your wife would give you little thanks for that,
>If she were by, to hear you make the offer.

Gratiano:
>I have a wife, whom, I protest, I love:
>I would she were in heaven, so she could
>Entreat some power to change this currish Jew.

Nerissa:
>'Tis well you offer it behind her back;

> The wish would make else an unquiet house.

Shylock *(aside):*
> These be the Christian husbands! I have a daughter;
> Would any of the stock of Barabbas
> Had been her husband rather than a Christian!—
> We trifle time: I pray thee, pursue sentence.

Portia:
> A pound of that same merchant's flesh is thine:
> The court awards it, and the law doth give it.

Shylock:
> Most rightful judge!

Portia:
> And you must cut this flesh from off his breast:
> The law allows it, and the court awards it.

Shylock:
> Most learned judge!—A sentence! come, prepare!

Portia:
> Tarry a little; there is something else.
> This bond doth give thee here no jot of blood,—
> The words expressly are, 'a pound of flesh':
> Take then thy bond, take thou thy pound of flesh;
> But, in the cutting it, if thou dost shed
> One drop of Christian blood, thy lands and goods
> Are, by the laws of Venice, confiscate
> Unto the state of Venice.

Gratiano:
> O upright judge!—Mark, Jew:—O learned judge!

Shylock:
> Is that the law?

Portia:
> Thyself shalt see the act:
> For, as thou urgest justice, be assured
> Thou shalt have justice, more than thou desirest.

Gratiano:
>O learned judge!—Mark, Jew:—a learned judge!

Shylock:
>I take his offer, then;—pay the bond thrice,
>And let the Christian go.

Bassanio:
>>Here is the money.

Portia:
>Soft!
>The Jew shall have all justice;—soft! no haste:—
>He shall have nothing but the penalty.

Gratiano:
>O Jew! an upright judge, a learned judge!

Portia:
>Therefore prepare thee to cut off the flesh.
>Shed thou no blood; nor cut thou less nor more
>But just a pound of flesh: if thou cutt'st more
>Or less than a just pound,—be it but so much
>As makes it light or heavy in the substance,
>Or the division of the twentieth part
>Of one poor scruple, nay, if the scale do turn
>But in the estimation of a hair,—
>Thou diest, and all thy goods are confiscate.

Gratiano:
>A second Daniel, a Daniel, Jew!
>Now, infidel, I have you on the hip.

Portia:
>Why doth the Jew pause? take thy forfeiture.

Shylock:
>Give me my principal, and let me go.

Bassanio:
>I have it ready for thee; here it is.

Portia:
>He hath refused it in the open court:
>He shall have merely justice and his bond.

Gratiano:
>A Daniel, still say I, a second Daniel!—
>I thank thee, Jew, for teaching me that word.

Shylock:
>Shall I not have barely my principal?

Portia:
>Thou shalt have nothing but the forfeiture,
>To be so taken at thy peril, Jew.

Shylock:
>Why, then the devil give him good of it!
>I'll stay no longer question.

Portia:
>   Tarry, Jew:
>The law hath yet another hold on you.
>It is enacted in the laws of Venice,—
>If it be proved against an alien
>That by direct or indirect attempts
>He seek the life of any citizen,
>The party 'gainst the which he doth contrive
>Shall seize one half his goods; the other half
>Comes to the privy coffer of the state;
>And the offender's life lies in the mercy
>Of the duke only, 'gainst all other voice.
>In which predicament, I say, thou stand'st;
>For it appears, by manifest proceeding,
>That indirectly, and directly too,
>Thou hast contrived against the very life
>Of the defendant; and thou hast incurr'd
>The danger formerly by me rehearsed.
>Down, therefore, and beg mercy of the duke.

Gratiano:
>Beg that thou mayst have leave to hang thyself:
>And yet, thy wealth being forfeit to the state,
>Thou hast not left the value of a cord;

Therefore thou must be hang'd at the state's charge.

Duke of Venice:
That thou shalt see the difference of our spirits,
I pardon thee thy life before thou ask it:
For half thy wealth, it is Antonio's;
The other half comes to the general state,
Which humbleness may drive unto a fine.

Portia:
Ay, for the state,—not for Antonio.

Shylock:
Nay, take my life and all; pardon not that:
You take my house, when you do take the prop
That doth sustain my house; you take my life,
When you do take the means whereby I live.

Portia:
What mercy can you render him, Antonio?

Gratiano:
A halter gratis; nothing else, for God's sake.

Antonio:
So please my lord the duke and all the court
To quit the fine for one half of his goods,
I am content; so he will let me have
The other half in use, to render it,
Upon his death, unto the gentleman
That lately stole his daughter:
Two things provided more,—that, for this favour,
He presently become a Christian;
The other, that he do record a gift,
Here in the court, of all he dies possest,
Unto his son Lorenzo and his daughter.

Duke of Venice:
He shall do this; or else I do recant
The pardon that I late pronounced here.

Portia:
Art thou contented, Jew? what dost thou say?

Shylock:
I am content.

Portia:
Clerk, draw a deed of gift.

Shylock:
I pray you, give me leave to go from hence;
I am not well: send the deed after me,
And I will sign it.

Duke of Venice:
Get thee gone, but do it.

Gratiano:
In christening shalt thou have two godfathers:
Had I been judge, thou shouldst have had ten more,
To bring thee to the gallows, not the font.

(Exit Shylock.)

Duke of Venice:
Sir, I entreat you home with me to dinner.

Portia:
I humbly do desire your Grace of pardon:
I must away this night toward Padua,
And it is meet I presently set forth.

Duke of Venice:
I am sorry that your leisure serves you not.—
Antonio, gratify this gentleman;
For in my mind, you are much bound to him.

(Exeunt Duke and his Train.)

Bassanio:
Most worthy gentleman, I and my friend
Have by your wisdom been this day acquitted

Of grievous penalties; in lieu whereof
Three thousand ducats, due unto the Jew,
We freely cope your courteous pains withal.

Antonio:
And stand indebted, over and above,
In love and service to you evermore.

Portia:
He is well paid that is well satisfied;
And I, delivering you, am satisfied,
And therein do account myself well paid:
My mind was never yet more mercenary.
I pray you, know me when we meet again:
I wish you well, and so I take my leave.

Bassanio:
Dear sir, of force I must attempt you further:
Take some remembrance of us, as a tribute,
Not as a fee: grant me two things, I pray you,—
Not to deny me, and to pardon me.

Portia:
You press me far, and therefore I will yield.
                              (To Antonio.*)*
Give me your gloves, I'll wear them for your sake;
                              (To Bassanio.*)*
And, for your love, I'll take this ring from you:—
Do not draw back your hand; I'll take no more;
And you in love shall not deny me this.

Bassanio:
This ring, good sir,—alas, it is a trifle!
I will not shame myself to give you this.

Portia:
I will have nothing else but only this;
And now methinks I have a mind to it.

Bassanio:
There's more depends on this than on the value,
The dearest ring in Venice will I give you,

And find it out by proclamation:
Only for this, I pray you, pardon me.

Portia:
I see, sir, you are liberal in offers:
You taught me first to beg; and now methinks
You teach me how a beggar should be answer'd.

Bassanio:
Good sir, this ring was given me by my wife;
And, when she put it on, she made me vow
That I should neither sell nor give nor lose it.

Portia:
That 'scuse serves many men to save their gifts.
And if your wife be not a mad-woman,
And know how well I have deserved this ring,
She would not hold out enemy for ever
For giving it to me. Well, peace be with you!

(*Exeunt* Portia *and* Nerissa.)

Antonio:
My Lord Bassanio, let him have the ring:
Let his deservings, and my love withal,
Be valued 'gainst your wife's commandment.

Bassanio:
Go, Gratiano, run and overtake him;
Give him this ring; and bring him, if thou canst,
Unto Antonio's house:—away! make haste.

(*Exeunt* Gratiano.)

Come, you and I will thither presently;
And in the morning early will we both
Fly toward Belmont: come, Antonio.

(*Exeunt.*)

(SCENE II.—*The same. A street. Enter* Portia *and* Nerissa.)

Portia:
>Inquire the Jew's house out, give him this deed,
>And let him sign it: we'll away to-night,
>And be a day before our husbands home:
>This deed will be well welcome to Lorenzo.

>*(Enter Gratiano.)*

Gratiano:
>Fair sir, you are well o'erta'en:
>My Lord Bassanio, upon more advice,
>Hath sent you here this ring; and doth entreat
>Your company at dinner.

Portia:
>That cannot be:
>His ring I do accept most thankfully;
>And so, I pray you, tell him: furthermore,
>I pray you, show my youth old Shylock's house.

Gratiano:
>That will I do.

Nerissa:
>Sir, I would speak with you.—
>*(To Portia.)*
>I'll see if I can get my husband's ring,
>Which I did make him swear to keep for ever.

Portia *(to Nerissa)*:
>Thou mayst, I warrant. We shall have old swearing
>That they did give the rings away to men;
>But we'll outface them, and outswear them too.—
>Away! make haste: thou know'st where I will tarry.

Nerissa:
>Come, good sir, will you show me to this house?

>*(Exeunt.)*

(ACT V. SCENE I.—Belmont. Avenue to Portia's house. Enter Lorenzo and Jessica.)

Lorenzo:
    The moon shines bright:—in such a night as this,
    When the sweet wind did gently kiss the trees,
    And they did make no noise,—in such a night
    Troilus methinks mounted the Troyan walls,
    And sigh'd his soul toward the Grecian tents,
    Where Cressid lay that night.

Jessica:
                            In such a night,
    Did Thisbe fearfully o'ertrip the dew,
    And saw the lion's shadow ere himself,
    And ran dismay'd away.

Lorenzo:
                            In such a night
    Stood Dido with a willow in her hand
    Upon the wild sea-banks, and waft her love
    To come again to Carthage.

Jessica:
                            In such a night,
    Medea gather'd the enchanted herbs
    That did renew old Aeson.

Lorenzo:
                            In such a night
    Did Jessica steal from the wealthy Jew,
    And with an unthrift love did run from Venice
    As far as Belmont.

Jessica:
                            In such a night
    Did young Lorenzo swear he loved her well,
    Stealing her soul with many vows of faith,
    And ne'er a true one.

Lorenzo:
                            In such a night
    Did pretty Jessica, like a little shrew,
    Slander her love, and he forgave it her.

Jessica:
>I would out-night you, did no body come:
>But, hark, I hear the footing of a man.

>>*(Enter* Stephano.*)*

Lorenzo:
>Who comes so fast in silence of the night?

Stephano:
>A friend.

Lorenzo:
>A friend! what friend? your name, I pray you, friend?

Stephano:
>Stephano is my name; and I bring word
>My mistress will before the break of day
>Be here at Belmont: she doth stray about
>By holy crosses, where she kneels and prays
>For happy wedlock hours.

Lorenzo:
>>Who comes with her?

Stephano:
>None but a holy hermit and her maid.
>I pray you, is my master yet return'd?

Lorenzo:
>He is not, nor we have not heard from him.—
>But go we in, I pray thee, Jessica,
>And ceremoniously let us prepare
>Some welcome for the mistress of the house.

>>*(Enter* Launcelot.*)*

Launcelot Gobbo:
>Sola, sola! wo ha, ho! sola, sola!

Lorenzo:
>Who calls?

Launcelot Gobbo:
> Sola!—did you see Master Lorenzo? Master Lorenzo!—sola, sola!

Lorenzo:
> Leave hollowing, man:—here.

Launcelot Gobbo:
> Sola!—where? where?

Lorenzo:
> Here.

Launcelot Gobbo:
> Tell him there's a post come from my master, with his horn full of good news: my master will be here ere morning.

(Exit.)

Lorenzo:
> Sweet soul, let's in, and there expect their coming.
> And yet no matter:—why should we go in?—
> My friend Stephano, signify, I pray you,
> Within the house, your mistress is at hand;
> And bring your music forth into the air.

(Exit Stephano.)

> How sweet the moonlight sleeps upon this bank!
> Here will we sit, and let the sounds of music
> Creep in our ears: soft stillness and the night
> Become the touches of sweet harmony.
> Sit, Jessica. Look, how the floor of heaven
> Is thick inlaid with patines of bright gold:
> There's not the smallest orb which thou behold'st
> But in his motion like an angel sings,
> Still quiring to the young-eyed cherubins,—
> Such harmony is in immortal souls;
> But whilst this muddy vesture of decay
> Doth grossly close it in, we cannot hear it.

(Enter Musicians.)

> Come, ho, and wake Diana with a hymn!

With sweetest touches pierce your mistress' ear,
And draw her home with music.

(Music plays.)

Jessica:
I am never merry when I hear sweet music.

Lorenzo:
The reason is, your spirits are attentive:
For do but note a wild and wanton herd,
Or race of youthful and unhandled colts,
Fetching mad bounds, bellowing, and neighing loud,
Which is the hot condition of their blood;
If they but hear perchance a trumpet sound,
Or any air of music touch their ears,
You shall perceive them make a mutual stand,
Their savage eyes turn'd to a modest gaze,
By the sweet power of music: therefore the poet
Did feign that Orpheus drew trees, stones, and floods;
Since naught so stockish, hard, and full of rage,
But music for the time doth change his nature.
The man that hath no music in himself,
Nor is not moved with concord of sweet sounds,
Is fit for treasons, stratagems, and spoils;
The motions of his spirit are dull as night,
And his affections dark as Erebus:
Let no such man be trusted.—Mark the music.

(Enter Portia *and* Nerissa.*)*

Portia:
That light we see is burning in my hall.
How far that little candle throws his beams!
So shines a good deed in a naughty world.

Nerissa:
When the moon shone, we did not see the candle.

Portia:
So doth the greater glory dim the less:
A substitute shines brightly as a king,

Until a king be by; and then his state
Empties itself, as doth an inland brook
Into the main of waters.—Music! hark!

Nerissa:
It is your music, madam, of the house.

Portia:
Nothing is good, I see, without respect:
Methinks it sounds much sweeter than by day.

Nerissa:
Silence bestows that virtue on it, madam.

Portia:
The crow doth sing as sweetly as the lark,
When neither is attended; and I think
The nightingale, if she should sing by day,
When every goose is cackling, would be thought
No better a musician than the wren.
How many things by season season'd are
To their right praise and true perfection!—
Peace, ho! the moon sleeps with Endymion,
And would not be awaked.

(Music ceases.)

Lorenzo:
                    That is the voice,
Or I am much deceived, of Portia.

Portia:
He knows me, as the blind man knows the cuckoo,
By the bad voice.

Lorenzo:
                    Dear lady, welcome home.

Portia:
We have been praying for our husbands' health,
Which speed, we hope, the better for our words.
Are they return'd?

Lorenzo:
> Madam, they are not yet;
> But there is come a messenger before,
> To signify their coming.

Portia:
> Go in, Nerissa;
> Give orders to my servants that they take
> No note at all of our being absent hence;—
> Nor you, Lorenzo;—Jessica, nor you

(A tucket sounds.)

Lorenzo:
> Your husband is at hand; I hear his trumpet:
> We are no tell-tales, madam; fear you not.

Portia:
> This night methinks is but the daylight sick;
> It looks a little paler: 'tis a day,
> Such as the day is when the sun is hid.

(Enter Bassanio, Antonio, Gratiano, and their Followers.)

Bassanio:
> We should hold day with the Antipodes,
> If you would walk in absence of the sun.

Portia:
> Let me give light, but let me not be light;
> For a light wife doth make a heavy husband,
> And never be Bassanio so for me:
> But God sort all!—You're welcome home, my lord

Bassanio:
> I thank you, madam. Give welcome to my friend
> This is the man, this is Antonio,
> To whom I am so infinitely bound.

Portia:
> You should in all sense be much bound to him,
> For, as I hear, he was much bound for you.

Antonio:
    No more than I am well acquitted of.

Portia:
    Sir, you are very welcome to our house:
    It must appear in other ways than words,
    Therefore I scant this breathing courtesy.

Gratiano (*to* Nerissa):
    By yonder moon I swear you do me wrong;
    In faith, I gave it to the judge's clerk:
    Would he were gelt that had it, for my part,
    Since you do take it, love, so much at heart.

Portia:
    A quarrel, ho, already! what's the matter?

Gratiano:
    About a hoop of gold, a paltry ring
    That she did give to me; whose posy was
    For all the world like cutler's poetry
    Upon a knife, 'Love me, and leave me not.'

Nerissa:
    What talk you of the posy or the value?
    You swore to me, when I did give it you,
    That you would wear it till your hour of death;
    And that it should lie with you in your grave:
    Though not for me, yet for your vehement oaths,
    You should have been respective, and have kept it.
    Gave it a judge's clerk! no, God's my judge,
    The clerk will ne'er wear hair on's face that had it.

Gratiano:
    He will, and if he live to be a man.

Nerissa:
    Ay, if a woman live to be a man.

Gratiano:
    Now, by this hand, I gave it to a youth,—
    A kind of boy; a little scrubbed boy,

No higher than thyself, the judge's clerk;
A prating boy, that begg'd it as a fee:
I could not for my heart deny it him.

Portia:
You were to blame,—I must be plain with you,—
To part so slightly with your wife's first gift;
A thing stuck on with oaths upon your finger,
And so riveted with faith unto your flesh.
I gave my love a ring, and made him swear
Never to part with it; and here he stands,—
I dare be sworn for him, he would not leave it,
Nor pluck it from his finger, for the wealth
That the world masters. Now, in faith, Gratiano,
You give your wife too unkind a cause of grief:
An 'twere to me, I should be mad at it.

Bassanio *(aside)*:
Why, I were best to cut my left hand off,
And swear I lost the ring defending it.

Gratiano:
My Lord Bassanio gave his ring away
Unto the judge that begg'd it, and indeed
Deserved it too; and then the boy, his clerk,
That took some pains in writing, he begg'd mind:
And neither man nor master would take aught
But the two rings.

Portia:
What ring gave you, my lord?
Not that, I hope, which you received of me.

Bassanio:
If I could add a lie unto a fault,
I would deny it; but you see my finger
Hath not the ring upon it,—it is gone.

Portia:
Even so void is your false heart of truth.
By heaven, I will ne'er come in your bed
Until I see the ring.

Nerissa:
>Nor I in yours
Till I again see mine.

Bassanio:
>Sweet Portia,
If you did know to whom I gave the ring,
If you did know for whom I gave the ring,
And would conceive for what I gave the ring,
And how unwillingly I left the ring,
When naught would be accepted but the ring,
You would abate the strength of your displeasure.

Portia:
>If you had known the virtue of the ring,
Or half her worthiness that gave the ring,
Or your own honour to contain the ring,
You would not then have parted with the ring.
What man is there so much unreasonable,
If you had pleased to have defended it
With any terms of zeal, wanted the modesty
To urge the thing held as a ceremony?
Nerissa teaches me what to believe:
I'll die for't but some woman had the ring.

Bassanio:
>No, by my honour, madam, by my soul,
No woman had it, but a civil doctor,
Which did refuse three thousand ducats of me,
And begg'd the ring; the which I did deny him,
And suffer'd him to go displeased away;
Even he that did uphold the very life
Of my dear friend. What should I say, sweet lady?
I was enforced to send it after him:
I was beset with shame and courtesy;
My honour would not let ingratitude
So much besmear it. Pardon me, good lady;
For, by these blessed candles of the night,
Had you been there, I think, you would have begg'd
The ring of me to give the worthy doctor.

Portia:
>Let not that doctor e'er come near my house:
>Since he hath got the jewel that I loved,
>And that which you did swear to keep for me,
>I will become as liberal as you;
>I'll not deny him any thing I have,
>No, not my body nor my husband's bed:
>Know him I shall, I am well sure of it:
>Lie not a night from home; watch me like Argus:
>If you do not, if I be left alone,
>Now, by mine honour, which is yet mine own,
>I'll have that doctor for my bedfellow.

Nerissa:
>And I his clerk; therefore be well advised
>How you do leave me to mine own protection.

Gratiano:
>Well, do you so: let not me take him, then;
>For if I do, I'll mar the young clerk's pen.

Antonio:
>I am the unhappy subject of these quarrels.

Portia:
>Sir, grieve not you; you are welcome notwithstanding.

Bassanio:
>Portia, forgive me this enforced wrong;
>And, in the hearing of these many friends,
>I swear to thee, even by thine own fair eyes,
>Wherein I see myself.—

Portia:
>   Mark you but that!
>In both my eyes he doubly sees himself;
>In each eye, one:—swear by your double self,
>And there's an oath of credit.

Bassanio:
>   Nay, but hear me:
>Pardon this fault, and by my soul I swear

I never more will break an oath with thee.

Antonio:
I once did lend my body for his wealth;
Which, but for him that had your husband's ring,
Had quite miscarried: I dare be bound again,
My soul upon the forfeit, that your lord
Will never more break faith advisedly.

Portia:
Then you shall be his surety. Give him this;
And bid him keep it better than the other.

Antonio:
Here, Lord Bassanio; swear to keep this ring.

Bassanio:
By heaven, it is the same I gave the doctor!

Portia:
I had it of him: pardon me, Bassanio;
For, by this ring, the doctor lay with me.

Nerissa:
And pardon me, my gentle Gratiano;
For that same scrubbed boy, the doctor's clerk,
In lieu of this, last night did lie with me.

Gratiano:
Why, this is like the mending of highways
In summer, where the ways are fair enough:
What, are we cuckolds ere we have deserved it?

Portia:
Speak not so grossly.—You are all amazed:
Here is a letter, read it at your leisure;
It comes from Padua, from Bellario:
There you shall find that Portia was the doctor;
Nerissa there her clerk: Lorenzo here
Shall witness I set forth as soon as you,
And even but now return'd; I have not yet
Enter'd my house.—Antonio, you are welcome;
And I have better news in store for you

　　　　Than you expect: unseal this letter soon;
　　　　There you shall find three of your argosies
　　　　Are richly come to harbour suddenly:
　　　　You shall not know by what strange accident
　　　　I chanced on this letter.

Antonio:
　　　　　　　　　　　　I am dumb.

Bassanio:
　　　　Were you the doctor, and I knew you not?

Gratiano:
　　　　Were you the clerk that is to make me cuckold?

Nerissa:
　　　　Ay, but the clerk that never means to do it,
　　　　Unless he live until he be a man.

Bassanio:
　　　　Sweet doctor, you shall be my bedfellow:
　　　　When I am absent, then lie with my wife.

Antonio:
　　　　Sweet lady, you have given me life and living;
　　　　For here I read for certain that my ships
　　　　Are safely come to road.

Portia:
　　　　　　　　　　　How now, Lorenzo!
　　　　My clerk hath some good comforts too for you.

Nerissa:
　　　　Ay, and I'll give them him without a fee.—
　　　　There do I give to you and Jessica,
　　　　From the rich Jew, a special deed of gift,
　　　　After his death, of all he dies possest of.

Lorenzo:
　　　　Fair ladies, you drop manna in the way
　　　　Of starved people.

Portia:
>It is almost morning,
>And yet I am sure you are not satisfied
>Of these events at full. Let us go in;
>And charge us there upon inter'gatories,
>And we will answer all things faithfully.

Gratiano:
>Let it be so: the first inter'gatory
>That my Nerissa shall be sworn on is,
>Whether till the next night she had rather stay,
>Or go to bed now, being two hours to day:
>But were the day come, I should wish it dark,
>That I were crouching with the doctor's clerk.
>Well, while I live I'll fear no other thing
>So sore as keeping safe Nerissa's ring.

(Exeunt.)

Comments and Questions

In 1872, Mr. Esek Cowen of Troy, New York, published a burlesque fictional "appellate opinion" on *The Merchant of Venice* entitled *"Shylock v. Antonio"* in the *Albany Law Journal*. Consider the following statements from that article:

1. "The right to do a certain act confers the right to the necessary incidents of that act...Now, as no one can cut an exact pound of flesh to a grain, as no one can do it without drawing blood, it seems too plain for argument that the parties could have intended no such restrictions; and the court had no right to supply them." Consider the negotiations between Antonio and Shylock. Does Antonio fully understand the terms of the bond? Would the terms of the bond be illegal? If so, what would be the disposition of the case?

2. "[T]he tender at the trial was sufficient to cancel the bond if it ever possessed any validity." Remember that Portia states that the bond is valid and that Shylock can claim his pound of flesh. Why does she refuse to let Shylock accept the offer of three times the bond when Bassanio is willing to pay it? Why does she refuse to let Shylock accept just the principal? Why does she state: "He has refused it in the open court: He shall have merely justice and his bond"? What is the significance of the words "merely justice"? Is she equating justice with revenge? Is justice served by Portia's intervention in this case? Is she a dispassionate, disinterested party to the proceedings?

3. "The plaintiff was then pursuing a civil though somewhat bloody, remedy; and what right had the referee, without complaint, warrant, or the intervention of a grand jury, to change the plaintiff into a defendant, on a criminal charge and herself into a criminal judge?" Consider the procedural problems presented by Mr. Cowen. Do we concern ourselves with such technicalities when we read drama? Is the reader of a comedy such as *The Merchant of Venice* more willing to engage in Coleridge's "willing suspension of disbelief" than he would be when reading a tragedy? If so, why? Comedy is said to have amusing characters and to end in happiness, whereas tragedy is said to have fatal or disastrous results. Support an argument that *The Merchant of Venice* is a tragedy not a comedy, if not literally, at least symbolically.

4. Not only was the plaintiff "required to deposit himself for his daughter's benefit, but to embrace Christianity for his own." Is Jessica a likeable character who deserves to participate in her father's estate without his consent? Discuss the anti-Semitic aspects of the play. Some would argue that plays such as this should not be taught in grade schools, colleges and universities. Do you support that proposition? Either way, justify your position?

William Shakespeare

Measure for Measure

Dramatis Personae

Vincentio, *the Duke.*
Angelo, *the Deputy.*
Escalus, *an ancient Lord.*
Claudio, *a young Gentleman.*
Lucio, *a Fantastic.*
Two other like Gentlemen.
Provost.
Thomas, *a Friar.*
Peter, *a Friar.*
A Justice.
Varrius.
Elbow, *a simple Constable.*
Froth, *a foolish Gentleman.*
Pompey, *servant to Mistress Overdone.*
Abhorson, *an Executioner.*
Barnardine, *a dissolute Prisoner.*
Isabella, *sister to Claudio.*
Mariana, *betrothed to Angelo.*
Juliet, *beloved of Claudio.*
Francisca, *a Nun.*
Mistress Overdone, *a Bawd.*

Lords, Officers, Citizens, Boy, *and* Attendants.

SCENE.—*Vienna.*

(ACT I. SCENE I.—*An apartment in the* Duke's *palace. Enter* Duke, Escalus, Lords, & Attendants.)

Duke:
>Escalus,—

Escalus:
>My lord?

Duke:
>Of government the properties to unfold,
>Would seem in me t'affect speech and discourse;
>Since I am put to know that your own science
>Exceeds, in that, the lists of all advice
>My strength can give you: then no more remains
>But that to your sufficiency ...
>... as your worth is able,
>And let them work. The nature of our people,
>Our city's institutions, and the terms
>For common justice, you're as pregnant in
>As art and practice has enriched any
>That we remember. There is our commission,
>From which we would not have you warp.—Call hither,
>I say, bid come before us Angelo.

(Exit an Attendant.*)*

>What figure of us think you he will bear?
>For, you must know, we have with special soul
>Elected him our absence to supply;
>Lent him our terror, dress'd him with our love,
>And given his deputation all the organs
>Of our own power: what think you of it?

Escalus:
>If any in Vienna be of worth
>To undergo such ample grace and honour,
>It is Lord Angelo.

Duke:
>Look where he comes.

(Enter Angelo.*)*

Angelo:
>Always obedient to your grace's will,
>I come to know your pleasure.

Duke:
>   Angelo,
>There is a kind of character in thy life,
>That to th' observer doth thy history
>Fully unfold. Thyself and thy belongings
>Are not thine own so proper, as to waste
>Thyself upon thy virtues, they on thee.
>Heaven doth with us as we with torches do,
>Not light them for themselves; for if our virtues
>Did not go forth of us, 'twere all alike
>As if we had them not. Spirits are not finely touch'd
>But to fine issues; nor Nature never lends
>The smallest scruple of her excellence
>But, like a thrifty goddess, she determines
>Herself the glory of a creditor,
>Both thanks and use. But I do bend my speech
>To one that can my part in him advertise;
>Hold, therefore, Angelo:—
>In our remove be thou at full ourself;
>Mortality and mercy in Vienna
>Live in thy tongue and heart: old Escalus,
>Though first in question, is thy secondary:—
>Take thy commission.

Angelo:
>   Now, good my lord,
>Let there be some more test made of my metal,
>Before so noble and so great a figure
>Be stamp'd upon it.

Duke:
>   No more evasion:
>We have with a leaven'd and prepared choice
>Proceeded to you; therefore take your honours.
>Our haste from hence is of so quick condition,
>That it prefers itself and leaves unquestion'd
>Matters of needful value. We shall write to you,
>As time and our concernings shall importune,

How it goes with us; and do look to know
What doth befall you here. So, fare you well:
To th' hopeful execution do I leave you
Of your commissions.

Angelo:
                          Yet, give leave, my lord,
That we may bring you something on the way.

Duke:
    My haste may not admit it;
Nor need you, on mine honour, have to do
With any scruple: your scope is as mine own,
So to enforce or qualify the laws
As to your soul seems good. Give me your hand:
I'll privily away. I love the people,
But do not like to stage me to their eyes:
Though it do well, I do not relish well
Their loud applause and Aves vehement;
Nor do I think the man of safe discretion
That does affect it. Once more, fare you well.

Angelo:
    The heavens give safety to your purposes!—

Escalus:
    Lead forth and bring you back in happiness!

Duke:
    I thank you. Fare you well.

(Exit.)

Escalus:
    I shall desire you, sir, to give me leave
To have free speech with you; and it concerns me
To look into the bottom of my place:
A power I have, but of what strength and nature
I am not yet instructed.

Angelo:
    'Tis so with me. Let us withdraw together,

And we may soon our satisfaction have
Touching that point.

Escalus:
I'll wait upon your honour.

(Exeunt.)

(SCENE II.—A street. Enter Lucio *and two other* Gentlemen.*)*

Lucio:
If the duke, with the other dukes, come not to composition with the King of Hungary, why, then, all the dukes fall upon the king.

First Gentleman:
Heaven grant us its peace, but not the King of Hungary's!

Second Gentleman:
Amen.

Lucio:
Thou concludest like the sanctimonious pirate, that went to sea with the Ten Commandments, but scraped one out of the table.

Second Gentleman:
'Thou shalt not steal'?

Lucio:
Ay, that he razed.

First Gentleman:
Why, 'twas a commandment to command the captain and all the rest from their functions: they put forth to steal. There's not a soldier of us all, that, in the thanksgiving before meat, do relish the petition well that prays for peace.

Second Gentleman:
I never heard any soldier dislike it.

Lucio:
>I believe thee; for I think thou never wast where grace was said.

Second Gentleman:
>No? a dozen times at least.

First Gentleman:
>What, in metre?

Lucio:
>In any proportion or in any language.

First Gentleman:
>I think, or in any religion.

Lucio:
>Ay, why not? Grace is grace, despite of all controversy: as, for example,—thou thyself art a wicked villain, despite of all grace.

First Gentleman:
>Well, there went but a pair of shears between us.

Lucio:
>I grant; as there may between the lists and the velvet. Thou art the list.

First Gentleman:
>And thou the velvet: thou art good velvet; thou'rt a three-piled piece, I warrant thee: I had as lief be a list of an English kersey, as be piled, as thou art piled, for a French velvet. Do I speak feelingly now?

Lucio:
>I think thou dost; and, indeed, with most painful feeling of thy speech, I will, out of thine own confession, learn to begin thy health; but, whilst I live, forget to drink after thee.

First Gentleman:
>I think I have done myself wrong, have I not?

Second Gentleman:
    Yes, that thou hast, whether thou art tainted or free.

Lucio:
    Behold, behold, where Madam Mitigation comes!

First Gentleman:
    I have purchased as many diseases under her roof as come to—

Second Gentleman:
    To what, I pray?

First Gentleman:
    Judge.

Second Gentleman:
    To three thousand dolours a year.

First Gentleman:
    Ay, and more.

Lucio:
    A French crown more.

First Gentleman:
    Thou art always figuring diseases in me; but thou art full of error,—I am sound.

Lucio:
    Nay, not as one would say, healthy; but so sound as things that are hollow: thy bones are hollow; impiety has made a feast of thee.

(Enter Mistress Overdone.)

First Gentleman:
    How now! which of your hips has the most profound sciatica?

Mistress Overdone:
    Well, well; there's one yonder arrested and carried to prison was worth five thousand of you all.

Second Gentleman:
   Who's that, I pray thee?

Mistress Overdone:
   Marry, sir, that's Claudio, Signior Claudio.

First Gentleman:
   Claudio to prison! 'tis not so.

Mistress Overdone:
   Nay, but I know 'tis so: I saw him arrested; saw him carried away; and, which is more, within these three days his head to be chopp'd off.

Lucio:
   But, after all this fooling, I would not have it so. Art thou sure of this?

Mistress Overdone:
   I am too sure of it: and it is for getting Madam Julietta with child.

Lucio:
   Believe me, this may be: he promised to meet me two hours since, and he was ever precise in promise-keeping.

Second Gentleman:
   Besides, you know, it draws something near to the speech we had to such a purpose.

First Gentleman:
   But, most of all, agreeing with the proclamation.

Lucio:
   Away! let's go learn the truth of it.

   (Exeunt Lucio *and* Gentlemen.*)*

Mistress Overdone:
   Thus, what with the war, what with the sweat, what with the gallows, and what with poverty, I am custom-shrunk.

(Enter Pompey.)

How now! What's the news with you?

Pompey:
Yonder man is carried to prison.

Mistress Overdone:
Well: what has he done?

Pompey:
A woman.

Mistress Overdone:
But what's his offence?

Pompey:
Groping for trouts in a peculiar river.

Mistress Overdone:
What, is there a maid with child by him?

Pompey:
No, but there's a woman with maid by him. You have not heard of the proclamation, have you?

Mistress Overdone:
What proclamation, man?

Pompey:
All houses in the suburbs of Vienna must be pluck'd down.

Mistress Overdone:
And what shall become of those in the city?

Pompey:
They shall stand for seed: they had gone down too, but that a wise burgher put in for them.

Mistress Overdone:
But shall all our houses of resort in the suburbs be pull'd down?

Pompey:
>To the ground, mistress.

Mistress Overdone:
>Why, here's a change indeed in the commonwealth! What shall become of me?

Pompey:
>Come; fear not you: good counsellors lack no clients: though you change your place, you need not change your trade; I'll be your tapster still. Courage! there will be pity taken on you: you that have worn your eyes almost out in the service, you will be consider'd.

Mistress Overdone:
>What's to do here, Thomas Tapster? let's withdraw.

Pompey:
>Here comes Signior Claudio, led by the provost to prison; and there's Madam Juliet.

(Exeunt.)

(Enter Provost, Claudio, Juliet, and Officers.)

Claudio:
>Fellow, why dost thou show me thus to th' world?
>Bear me to prison, where I am committed.

Provost:
>I do it not in evil disposition,
>But from Lord Angelo by special charge.

Claudio:
>Thus can the demigod Authority
>Make us pay down for our offence by weight.—
>The words of heaven;—on whom it will, it will;
>On whom it will not, so; yet still 'tis just.

(Enter Lucio and two Gentlemen.)

Lucio:
>Why, how now, Claudio! whence comes this restraint?

Claudio:
>From too much liberty, my Lucio, liberty:
>As surfeit is the father of much fast,
>So every scope by the immoderate use
>Turns to restraint. Our natures do pursue,
>Like rats that ravin down their proper bane,
>A thirsty evil; and when we drink we die.

Lucio:
>If I could speak so wisely under an arrest, I would send for certain of my creditors: and yet, to say the truth, I had as lief have the foppery of freedom as the morality of imprisonment.—What's thy offence, Claudio?

Claudio:
>What but to speak of would offend again.

Lucio:
>What, is't murder?

Claudio:
>No.

Lucio:
>Lechery?

Claudio:
>Call it so.

Provost:
>Away, sir! you must go.

Claudio:
>One word, good friend.—Lucio, a word with you.

>>*(Takes him aside.)*

Lucio:
>A hundred, if they'll do you any good.—
>Is lechery so look'd after?

Claudio:
>Thus stands it with me:—upon a true contract
>I got possession of Julietta's bed:
>You know the lady; she is fast my wife,
>Save that we do the denunciation lack
>Of outward order: this we came not to,
>Only for propagation of a dower
>Remaining in the coffer of her friends;
>From whom we thought it meet to hide our love
>Till time had made them for us. But it chances
>The stealth of our most mutual entertainment
>With character too gross is writ on Juliet.

Lucio:
>With child, perhaps?

Claudio:
>   Unhappily, even so.
>And the new deputy now for the duke,—
>Whether it be the fault and glimpse of newness,
>Or whether that the body public be
>A horse whereon the governor doth ride,
>Who, newly in the seat, that it may know
>He can command, lets it straight feel the spur;
>Whether the tyranny be in his place,
>Or in his eminence that fills it up,
>I stagger in:—but this new governor
>Awakes me all the enrolled penalties
>Which have, like unscour'd armour, hung by the wall
>So long, that nineteen zodiacs have gone round,
>And none of them been worn; and, for a name,
>Now puts the drowsy and neglected act
>Freshly on me:—'tis surely for a name.

Lucio:
>I warrant it is: and thy head stands so tickle on thy shoulders, that a milkmaid, if she be in love, may sigh it off. Send after the duke, and appeal to him.

Claudio:
>I have done so, but he's not to be found.
>I prithee, Lucio, do me this kind service:—

This day my sister should the cloister enter.
And there receive her approbation:
Acquaint her with the danger of my state;
Implore her, in my voice, that she make friends
To the strict deputy; bid herself assay him:
I have great hope in that; for in her youth
There is a prone and speechless dialect,
Such as move men; beside, she hath prosperous art
When she will play with reason and discourse,
And well she can persuade.

Lucio:
I pray she may; as well for the encouragement of the like, which else would stand under grievous imposition, as for the enjoying of thy life, who I would be sorry should be thus foolishly lost at a game of tick-tack. I'll to her.

Claudio:
I thank you, good friend Lucio.

Lucio:
Within two hours.

Claudio:
                    Come, officer, away!

                                        (Exeunt.)

(SCENE III.—A monastery. Enter Duke *and* Friar Thomas.*)*

Duke:
No, holy father; throw away that thought;
Believe not that the dribbling dart of love
Can pierce a complete bosom. Why I desire thee
To give me secret harbour, hath a purpose
More grave and wrinkled than the aims and ends
Of burning youth.

Friar Thomas:
                May your grace speak of it?

Duke:
>My holy sir, none better knows than you
>How I have ever loved the life removed;
>And held in idle price to haunt assemblies,
>Where youth, and cost, and witless bravery keeps.
>I have deliver'd to Lord Angelo—
>A man of stricture and firm abstinence—
>My absolute power and place here in Vienna,
>And he supposes me travell'd to Poland;
>For so I have strew'd it in the common ear,
>And so it is received. Now, pious sir,
>You will demand of me why I do this?

Friar Thomas:
>Gladly, my lord.

Duke:
>We have strict statutes and most biting laws,—
>The needful bits and curbs to headstrong wills,—
>Which for this fourteen years we have let slip;
>Even like an o'ergrown lion in a cave,
>That goes not out to prey. Now, as fond fathers,
>Having bound up the threat'ning twigs of birch,
>Only to stick it in their children's sight
>For terror, not to use, in time the rod
>Becomes more mock'd than fear'd; so our decrees,
>Dead to infliction, to themselves are dead;
>And liberty plucks justice by the nose;
>The baby beats the nurse, and quite athwart
>Goes all decorum.

Friar Thomas:
>   It rested in your grace
>To unloose this tied-up justice when you pleased:
>And it in you more dreadful would have seem'd
>Than in Lord Angelo.

Duke:
>   I do fear, too dreadful:
>Sith 'twas my fault to give the people scope,
>'Twould be my tyranny to strike and gall them
>For what I bid them do: for we bid this be done,

When evil deeds have their permissive pass,
And not the punishment. Therefore, indeed, my father,
I have on Angelo imposed the office,
Who may, in th'ambush of my name, strike home;
And yet my nature never in the fight
To do it slander. And to behold his sway,
I will, as 'twere a brother of your order,
Visit both prince and people: therefore, I prithee,
Supply me with the habit, and instruct me
How I may formally in person bear me
Like a true friar. Moe reasons for this action
At our more leisure shall I render you;
Only, this one:—Lord Angelo is precise;
Stands at a guard with envy; scarce confesses
That his blood flows, or that his appetite
Is more to bread than stone: hence shall we see,
If power change purpose, what our seemers be.

(Exeunt.)

(SCENE IV.—A nunnery. Enter Isabella *and* Francisca, *a* Nun.*)*

Isabella:
And have you nuns no further privileges?

Francisca:
Are not these large enough?

Isabella:
Yes, truly: I speak not as desiring more;
But rather wishing a more strict restraint
Upon the sisterhood, the votarists of Saint Clare.

Lucio *(within)*:
Ho! Peace be in this place!

Isabella:
Who's that which calls?

Francisca:
It is a man's voice. Gentle Isabella,
Turn you the key, and know his business of him;

You may, I may not; you are yet unsworn.
When you have vow'd, you must not speak with men
But in the presence of the prioress:
Then, if you speak, you must not show your face;
Or, if you show your face, you must not speak.
He calls again; I pray you, answer him.

(Exit.)

Isabella:
Peace and prosperity! Who is't that calls?

(Enter Lucio.)

Lucio:
Hail, virgin, if you be, as those cheek-roses
Proclaim you are no less! Can you so stead me
As bring me to the sight of Isabella,
A novice of this place, and the fair sister
To her unhappy brother Claudio?

Isabella:
Why 'her unhappy brother'? let me ask;
The rather, for I now must make you know
I am that Isabella and his sister.

Lucio:
Gentle and fair, your brother kindly greets you:
Not to be weary with you, he's in prison.

Isabella:
Woe me! For what?

Lucio:
For that which, if myself might be his judge,
He should receive his punishment in thanks:
He hath got his friend with child.

Isabella:
Sir, make me not your story.

Lucio:
>   'Tis true.
> I would not—though 'tis my familiar sin
> With maids to seem the lapwing, and to jest,
> Tongue far from heart—play with all virgins so:
> I hold you as a thing ensky'd and sainted;
> By your renouncement, an immortal spirit;
> And to be talk'd with in sincerity,
> As with a saint.

Isabella:
> You do blaspheme the good in mocking me.

Lucio:
> Do not believe it. Fewness and truth, 'tis thus:—
> Your brother and his lover have embraced:
> As those that feed grow full; as blossoming-time,
> That from the seedness the bare fallow brings
> To teeming foison; even so her plenteous womb
> Expresseth his full tilth and husbandry.

Isabella:
> Some one with child by him?—My cousin Juliet?

Lucio:
> Is she your cousin?

Isabella:
> Adoptedly; as school-maids change their names
> By vain, though apt, affection.

Lucio:
>   She it is.

Isabella:
> O, let him marry her.

Lucio:
>   This is the point.
> The duke is very strangely gone from hence;
> Bore many gentlemen, myself being one,
> In hand, and hope of action: but we do learn

By those that know the very nerves of state,
His givings-out were of an infinite distance
From his true-meant design. Upon his place,
And with full line of his authority,
Governs Lord Angelo; a man whose blood
Is very snow-broth; one who never feels
The wanton stings and motions of the sense,
But doth rebate and blunt his natural edge
With profits of the mind, study and fast.
He—to give fear to use and liberty,
Which have for long run by the hideous law,
As mice by lions—hath pick'd out an act,
Under whose heavy sense your brother's life
Falls into forfeit: he arrests him on it;
And follows close the rigour of the statute,
To make him an example. All hope is gone,
Unless you have the grace by your fair prayer
To soften Angelo: and that's my pith
Of business 'twixt you and your poor brother.

Isabella:
    Doth he so seek his life?

Lucio:
                      Has censured him
    Already; and, as I hear, the provost hath
    A warrant for his execution.

Isabella:
    Alas, what poor ability's in me
    To do him good!

Lucio:
                  Assay the power you have.

Isabella:
    My power! Alas, I doubt,—

Lucio:
                    Our doubts are traitors
    And make us lose the good we oft might win
    By fearing to attempt. Go to Lord Angelo,

    And let him learn to know, when maidens sue,
    Men give like gods; but when they weep and kneel,
    All their petitions are as freely theirs
    As they themselves would owe them.

Isabella:
    I'll see what I can do.

Lucio:
                But speedily.

Isabella:
    I will about it straight;
    No longer staying but to give the mother
    Notice of my affair. I humbly thank you:
    Commend me to my brother: soon at night
    I'll send him certain word of my success.

Lucio:
    I take my leave of you.

Isabella:
                Good sir, adieu.

                        (Exeunt.)

(ACT II. SCENE I.—A hall in Angelo's house. Enter Angelo, Escalus, a Justice, Provost, Officers, and other Attendants.)

Angelo:
    We must not make a scarecrow of the law,
    Setting it up to fear the birds of prey,
    And let it keep one shape, till custom make it
    Their perch, and not their terror.

Escalus:
                        Ay, but yet
    Let us be keen, and rather cut a little,
    Than fall, and bruise to death. Alas, this gentleman,
    Whom I would save, had a most noble father!
    Let but your honour know,—
    Whom I believe to be most strait in virtue,—

That, in the working of your own affections,
Had time cohered with place, or place with wishing,
Or that the resolute acting of your blood
Could have attain'd th' effect of your own purpose,
Whether you had not sometime in your life
Err'd in this point which now you censure him,
And pull'd the law upon you.

Angelo:
'Tis one thing to be tempted, Escalus,
Another thing to fall. I not deny,
The jury, passing on the prisoner's life,
May in the sworn twelve have a thief or two
Guiltier than him they try. What's open made to justice,
That justice seizes: what know the laws
That thieves do pass on thieves? 'Tis very pregnant,
The jewel that we find, we stoop and take't,
Because we see it; but what we do not see
We tread upon, and never think of it.
You may not so extenuate his offence
For I have had such faults; but rather tell me,
When I, that censure him, do so offend,
Let mine own judgement pattern out my death,
And nothing come in partial. Sir, he must die.

Escalus:
Be it as your wisdom will.

Angelo:
Where is the provost?

Provost:
Here, if it like your honour.

Angelo:
See that Claudio
Be executed by nine to-morrow morning:
Bring him his confessor, let him be prepared;
For that's the utmost of his pilgrimage.

(Exit Provost.)

Escalus (*aside*):
> Well, heaven forgive him! and forgive us all!
> Some rise by sin, and some by virtue fall;
> Some run from brakes of vice, and answer none;
> And some condemned for a fault alone.

(Enter Elbow, *and* Officers *with* Froth *and* Pompey.*)*

Elbow:
> Come, bring them away: if these be good people in a commonweal that do nothing but use their abuses in common houses, I know no law: bring them away.

Angelo:
> How now, sir! What's your name? and what's the matter?

Elbow:
> If it please your honour, I am the poor duke's constable, and my name is Elbow: I do lean upon justice, sir, and do bring in here before your good honour two notorious benefactors.

Angelo:
> Benefactors! Well; what benefactors are they? are they not malefactors?

Elbow:
> If it please your honour, I know not well what they are: but precise villains they are, that I am sure of; and void of all profanation in the world that good Christians ought to have.

Escalus:
> This comes off well; here's a wise officer.

Angelo:
> Go to:—what quality are they of? Elbow is your name? why dost thou not speak, Elbow?

Pompey:
> He cannot, sir; he's out at elbow.

Angelo:
> What are you, sir?

Elbow:
> He, sir! a tapster, sir; parcel-bawd; one that serves a bad woman; whose house, sir, was, as they say, pluck'd down in the suburbs; and now she professes a hot-house, which, I think, is a very ill house too.

Escalus:
> How know you that?

Elbow:
> My wife, sir, whom I detest before heaven and your honour,—

Escalus:
> How! thy wife!

Elbow:
> Ay, sir;—whom, I thank heaven, is an honest woman,—

Escalus:
> Dost thou detest her therefore?

Elbow:
> I say, sir, I will detest myself also, as well as she, that this house, if it be not a bawd's house, it is pity of her life, for it is a naughty house.

Escalus:
> How dost thou know that, constable?

Elbow:
> Marry, sir, by my wife; who, if she had been a woman cardinally given, might have been accused in fornication, adultery, and all uncleanliness there.

Escalus:
> By the woman's means?

Elbow:
> Ay, sir, by Mistress Overdone's means: but as she spit in his face, so she defied him.

Pompey:
Sir, if it please your honour, this is not so.

Elbow:
Prove it before these varlets here, thou honourable man; prove it.

Escalus *(to Angelo)*:
Do you hear how he misplaces?

Pompey:
Sir, she came in great with child; and longing—saving your honour's reverence—for stew'd prunes. Sir, we had but two in the house, which at that very distant time stood, as it were, in a fruit-dish, a dish of some three-pence;—your honours have seen such dishes; they are not China dishes, but very good dishes,—

Escalus:
Go to, go to: no matter for the dish, sir.

Pompey:
No, indeed, sir, not of a pin; you are therein in the right:—but to the point. As I say, this Mistress Elbow, being, as I say, with child, and being great-bellied, and longing, as I said, for prunes; and having but two in the dish, as I said, Master Froth here, this very man, having eaten the rest, as I said, and, as I say, paying for them very honestly;—for, as you know, Master Froth, I could not give you three-pence again,—

Froth:
No, indeed.

Pompey:
Very well;—you being then, if you be remember'd, cracking the stones of the aforesaid prunes,—

Froth:
Ay, so I did indeed.

Pompey:
> Why, very well;—I telling you then, if you be remember'd, that such a one and such a one were past cure of the thing you wot of, unless they kept very good diet, as I told you,—

Froth:
> All this is true.

Pompey:
> Why, very well, then,—

Escalus:
> Come, you are a tedious fool: to the purpose. What was done to Elbow's wife, that he hath cause to complain of? Come me to what was done to her.

Pompey:
> Sir, your honour cannot come to that yet.

Escalus:
> No, sir, nor I mean it not.

Pompey:
> Sir, but you shall come to it, by your honour's leave. And, I beseech you, look into Master Froth here, sir; a man of fourscore pound a year; whose father died at Hallowmas:—was't not at Hallowmas, Master Froth?—

Froth:
> All-hallond eve.

Pompey:
> Why, very well; I hope here be truths. He, sir, sitting, as I say, in a lower chair, sir;—'twas in the Bunch of Grapes, where, indeed, you have a delight to sit, have you not?—

Froth:
> I have so; because it is an open room, and good for winter.

Pompey:
> Why, very well, then; I hope here be truths.

Angelo:
>This will last out a night in Russia,
>When nights are longest there: I'll take my leave,
>And leave you to the hearing of the cause;
>Hoping you'll find good cause to whip them all.

Escalus:
>I think no less. Good morrow to your lordship.

>>*(Exit Angelo.)*

>Now, sir, come on: what was done to Elbow's wife, once more?

Pompey:
>Once, sir! there was nothing done to her once.

Elbow:
>I beseech you, sir, ask him what this man did to my wife.

Pompey:
>I beseech your honour, ask me.

Escalus:
>Well, sir; what did this gentleman to her?

Pompey:
>I beseech you, sir, look in this gentleman's face.—Good Master Froth, look upon his honour; 'tis for a good purpose.—Doth your honour mark his face?

Escalus:
>Ay, sir, very well.

Pompey:
>Nay, I beseech you, mark it well.

Escalus:
>Well, I do so.

Pompey:
>Doth your honour see any harm in his face?

Escalus:
Why, no.

Pompey:
I'll be supposed upon a book, his face is the worst thing about him. Good, then; if his face be the worst thing about him, how could Master Froth do the constable's wife any harm? I would know that of your honour.

Escalus:
He's in the right.—Constable, what say you to it?

Elbow:
First, and it like you, the house is a respected house; next, this is a respected fellow; and his mistress is a respected woman.

Pompey:
By this hand, sir, his wife is a more respected person than any of us all.

Elbow:
Varlet, thou liest; thou liest, wicked varlet! the time is yet to come, that she was ever respected with man, woman, or child.

Pompey:
Sir, she was respected with him before he married with her.

Escalus:
Which is the wiser here? Justice or Iniquity?—Is this true?

Elbow:
O thou caitiff! O thou varlet! O thou wicked Hannibal! I respected with her before I was married to her!—If ever I was respected with her, or she with me, let not your worship think me the poor duke's officer.—Prove this, thou wicked Hannibal, or I'll have mine action of battery on thee.

Escalus:
If he took you a box o'th'ear, you might have your action of slander too.

Elbow:
> Marry, I thank your good worship for it.—What is't your worship's pleasure I shall do with this wicked caitiff?

Escalus:
> Truly, officer, because he hath some offences in him that thou wouldst discover if thou couldst, let him continue in his courses till thou know'st what they are.

Elbow:
> Marry, I thank your worship for it.—Thou seest, thou wicked varlet, now, what's come upon thee: thou art to continue now, thou varlet; thou art to continue.

Escalus *(to Froth):*
> Where were you born, friend?

Froth:
> Here in Vienna, sir.

Escalus:
> Are you of fourscore pounds a year?

Froth:
> Yes, an't please you, sir.

Escalus:
> So.—*(to* Pompey*)* What trade are you of, sir?

Pompey:
> A tapster; a poor widow's tapster.

Escalus:
> Your mistress' name?

Pompey:
> Mistress Overdone.

Escalus:
> Hath she had any more than one husband?

Pompey:
> Nine, sir; Overdone by the last.

Escalus:
> Nine!—Come hither to me, Master Froth. Master Froth, I would not have you acquainted with tapsters: they will draw you, Master Froth, and you will hang them. Get you gone, and let me hear no more of you.

Froth:
> I thank your worship. For mine own part, I never come into any room in a taphouse, but I am drawn in.

Escalus:
> Well, no more of it, Master Froth: farewell.

> *(Exit Froth.)*

> Come you hither to me, master tapster. What's your name, master tapster?

Pompey:
> Pompey.

Escalus:
> What else?

Pompey:
> Bum, sir.

Escalus:
> Troth, and your bum is the greatest thing about you; so that, in the beastliest sense, you are Pompey the Great. Pompey, you are partly a bawd, Pompey, howsoever you colour it in being a tapster. Are you not? come, tell me true: it shall be the better for you.

Pompey:
> Truly, sir, I am a poor fellow that would live.

Escalus:
> How would you live, Pompey? by being a bawd? What do you think of the trade, Pompey? is it a lawful trade?

Pompey:
If the law would allow it, sir.

Escalus:
But the law will not allow it, Pompey; nor it shall not be allow'd in Vienna.

Pompey:
Does your worship mean to geld and splay all the youth of the city?

Escalus:
No, Pompey.

Pompey:
Truly, sir, in my poor opinion, they will to't, then. If your worship will take order for the drabs and the knaves, you need not to fear the bawds.

Escalus:
There is pretty orders beginning, I can tell you: it is but heading and hanging.

Pompey:
If you head and hang all that offend that way but for ten year together, you'll be glad to give out a commission for more heads: if this law hold in Vienna ten year, I'll rent the fairest house in it after three-pence a bay: if you live to see this come to pass, say Pompey told you so.

Escalus:
Thank you, good Pompey; and, in requital of your prophecy, hark you:—I advise you, let me not find you before me again upon any complaint whatsoever; no, not for dwelling where you do: if I do, Pompey, I shall beat you to your tent, and prove a shrewd Caesar to you; in plain dealing, Pompey, I shall have you whipt: so, for this time, Pompey, fare you well.

Pompey:
I thank your worship for your good counsel. *(Aside.)*
But I shall follow it as the flesh and fortune shall better determine.

Whip me! No, no; let carman whip his jade:
The valiant's heart's not whipt out of his trade.

(Exit.)

Escalus:
Come hither to me, Master Elbow; come hither, master constable. How long have you been in this place of constable?

Elbow:
Seven year and a half, sir.

Escalus:
I thought, by your readiness in the office, you had continued in it some time. You say, seven years together?

Elbow:
And a half, sir.

Escalus:
Alas, it hath been great pains to you! They do you wrong to put you so oft upon't: are there not men in your ward sufficient to serve it?

Elbow:
Faith, sir, few of any wit in such matters: as they are chosen, they are glad to choose me for them; I do it for some piece of money, and go through with all.

Escalus:
Look you bring me in the names of some six or seven, the most sufficient of your parish.

Elbow:
To your worship's house, sir?

Escalus:
To my house. Fare you well.

(Exit Elbow.*)*

What's o'clock, think you?

Justice:
> Eleven, sir.

Escalus:
> I pray you home to dinner with me.

Justice:
> I humbly thank you.

Escalus:
> It grieves me for the death of Claudio;
> But there's no remedy.

Justice:
> Lord Angelo is severe.

Escalus:
> It is but needful:
> Mercy is not itself, that oft looks so;
> Pardon is still the nurse of second woe:
> But yet,—poor Claudio!—There is no remedy.—
> Come, sir.

(Exeunt.)

(SCENE II.—Another room in the same. Enter Provost *and a* Servant.*)*

Servant:
> He's hearing of a cause; he will come straight:
> I'll tell him of you.

Provost:
> Pray you, do.

(Exit Servant.*)*

> I'll know
> His pleasure; may be he will relent. Alas,
> He hath but as offended in a dream!
> All sects, all ages smack of this vice; and he
> To die for't!

(Enter Angelo.)

Angelo:
    Now, what's the matter, provost?

Provost:
    Is it your will Claudio shall die to-morrow?

Angelo:
    Did not I tell the yea? hadst thou not order?
    Why dost thou ask again?

Provost:
                 Lest I might be too rash:
    Under your good correction, I have seen,
    When, after execution, judgement hath
    Repented o'er his doom.

Angelo:
                 Go to; let that be mine:
    Do you your office, or give up your place,
    And you shall well be spared.

Provost:
                 I crave your honour's pardon.—
    What shall be done, sir, with the groaning Juliet?
    She's very near her hour.

Angelo:
                 Dispose of her
    To some more fitter place; and that with speed.

(Enter Servant.)

Servant:
    Here is the sister of the man condemn'd
    Desires access to you.

Angelo:
                 Hath he a sister?

Provost:
> Ay, my good lord; a very virtuous maid,
> And to be shortly of a sisterhood,
> If not already.

Angelo:
> Well, let her be admitted.

(Exit Servant.)

> See you the fornicatress be removed:
> Let her have needful, but not lavish, means;
> There shall be order for't.

(Enter Isabella and Lucio.)

Provost:
> 'Save your honour!

Angelo:
> Stay a little while. *(To Isabella.)* You're welcome: what's your will?

Isabella:
> I am a woeful suitor to your honour,
> Please but your honour hear me.

Angelo:
> Well; what's your suit?

Isabella:
> There is a vice that most I do abhor,
> And most desire should meet the blow of justice;
> For which I would not plead, but that I must;
> For which I must not plead, but that I am
> At war 'twixt *will* and *will not*.

Angelo:
> Well; the matter?

Isabella:
> I have a brother is condemn'd to die:
> I do beseech you, let it be his fault,
> And not my brother.

Provost *(aside):*
                    Heaven give thee moving graces!

Angelo:
    Condemn the fault, and not the actor of it?
    Why, every fault's condemn'd ere it be done:
    Mine were the very cipher of a function,
    To fine the faults, whose fine stands in record,
    And let go by the actor.

Isabella:
                    O just but severe law!
    I had a brother, then.—Heaven keep your honour!

Lucio *(aside to* Isabella*):*
    Give't not o'er so: to him again, entreat him;
    Kneel down before him, hang upon his gown:
    You are too cold; if you should need a pin,
    You could not with more tame a tongue desire it:
    To him, I say.

Isabella:
    Must he needs die?

Angelo:
                    Maiden, no remedy.

Isabella:
    Yes; I do think that you might pardon him,
    And neither heaven nor man grieve at the mercy.

Angelo:
    I will not do't.

Isabella:
                But can you, if you would?

Angelo:
    Look, what I will not, that I cannot do.

Isabella:
    But might you do't, and do the world no wrong.

> If so your heart were touch'd with that remorse
> As mine is to him.

Angelo:
> He's sentenced; 'tis too late.

Lucio *(aside to* Isabella*)*:
> You are too cold.

Isabella:
> Too late! why, no; I, that do speak a word,
> May call it back again. Well, believe this,
> No ceremony that to great ones 'longs,
> Not the king's crown nor the deputed sword,
> The marshal's truncheon nor the judge's robe,
> Become them with one half so good a grace
> As mercy does.
> If he had been as you, and you as he,
> You would have slipp'd like him; but he, like you,
> Would not have been so stern.

Angelo:
> Pray you, be gone.

Isabella:
> I would to heaven I had your potency,
> And you were Isabel! should it then be thus?
> No; I would tell what 'twere to be a judge,
> And what a prisoner.

Lucio *(aside to* Isabella*)*:
> Ay, touch him; there's the vein.

Angelo:
> Your brother is a forfeit of the law,
> And you but waste your words.

Isabella:
> Alas, alas!
> Why, all the souls that were were forfeit once;
> And He that might the vantage best have took
> Found out the remedy. How would you be,
> If He, which is the top of judgement, should

But judge you as you are? O, think on that;
And mercy then will breathe within your lips,
Like man new-made.

Angelo:
                        Be you content, fair maid;
It is the law, not I, condemn your brother:
Were he my kinsman, brother, or my son,
It should be thus with him:—he must die to-morrow.

Isabella:
To-morrow! O, that's sudden! Spare him, spare him!—
He's not prepared for death. Even for our kitchens
We kill the fowl of season: shall we serve heaven
With less respect than we do minister
To our gross selves? Good, good my lord, bethink you;
Who is it that hath died for this offence?
There's many have committed it.

Lucio (*aside to* Isabella):
                                      Ay, well said.

Angelo:
The law hath not been dead, though it hath slept:
Those many had not dared to do that evil,
If that the first that did th' edict infringe
Had answer'd for his deed: now 'tis awake,
Takes note of what is done; and, like a prophet,
Looks in a glass, that shows what future evils,—
Either new, or by remissness new-conceived,
And so in progress to be hatch'd and born,—
Are now to have no successive degrees,
But, ere they live, to end.

Isabella:
                        Yet show some pity.

Angelo:
I show it most of all when I show justice;
For then I pity those I do not know,
Which a dismiss'd offence would after gall;
And do him right that, answering one foul wrong,

Lives not to act another. Be satisfied;
Your brother dies to-morrow; be content.

Isabella:
So you must be the first that gives this sentence,
And he that suffers. O, it is excellent
To have a giant's strength; but it is tyrannous
To use it like a giant.

Lucio (*aside to* Isabella):
That's well said.

Isabella:
Could great men thunder
As Jove himself does, Jove would ne'er be quiet,
For every pelting, petty officer
Would use his heaven for thunder. Nothing but thunder!
Merciful Heaven,
Thou rather with thy sharp and sulphurous bolt
Splitt'st the unwedgeable and gnarled oak
Than the soft myrtle: but man, proud man,
Drest in a little brief authority,—
Most ignorant of what he's most assured,
His glassy essence,—like an angry ape,
Plays such fantastic tricks before high heaven
As make the angels weep; who, with our spleens,
Would all themselves laugh mortal.

Lucio (*aside to* Isabella):
O, to him, to him, wench! he will relent;
He's coming; I perceive't.

Provost (*aside*):
Pray heaven she win him!

Isabella:
We cannot weigh our brother with ourself:
Great men may jest with saints; 'tis wit in them,
But in the less foul profanation.

Lucio (*aside to* Isabella):
Thou'rt i'the right, girl; more o' that.

Isabella:
>That in the captain's but a choleric word,
>Which in the soldier is flat blasphemy.

Lucio *(aside to* Isabella*):*
>Art avised o' that? more on't.

Angelo:
>Why do you put these sayings upon me?

Isabella:
>Because authority, though it err like others,
>Hath yet a kind of medicine in itself,
>That skins the vice o'the top. Go to your bosom;
>Knock there, and ask your heart what it doth know
>That's like my brother's fault: if it confess
>A natural guiltiness such as is his,
>Let it not sound a thought upon your tongue
>Against my brother's life.

Angelo *(aside):*
>   She speaks, and 'tis
>Such sense, that my sense breeds with't.—Fare you well.

Isabella:
>Gentle my lord, turn back.

Angelo:
>I will bethink me: come again to-morrow.

Isabella:
>Hark how I'll bribe you: good my lord, turn back.

Angelo:
>How! bribe me!

Isabella:
>Ay, with such gifts that heaven shall share with you.

Lucio *(aside to* Isabella*):*
>You had marr'd all else.

Isabella:
>Not with fond shekels of the tested gold,
>Or stones, whose rates are either rich or poor
>As fancy values them; but with true prayers,
>That shall be up at heaven and enter there
>Ere sun-rise,—prayers from preserved souls,
>From fasting maids, whose minds are dedicate
>To nothing temporal.

Angelo:
>   Well; come to me to-morrow.

Lucio (*aside to* Isabella):
>Go to; 'tis well; away!

Isabella:
>Heaven keep your honour safe!

Angelo (*aside*):
>   Amen; for I
>Am that way going to temptation,
>Where prayers cross.

Isabella:
>   At what hour to-morrow
>Shall I attend your lordship?

Angelo:
>   At any time 'fore noon?

Isabella:
>Save you honour!

>   (*Exeunt* Isabella, Lucio, *and* Provost.)

Angelo:
>   From thee,—even from thy virtue!—
>What's this, what's this? Is this her fault or mine?
>The tempter or the tempted, who sins most, ha?
>Not she; nor doth she tempt: but it is I
>That, lying by the violet in the sun,
>Do as the carrion does, not as the flower,

Corrupt with virtuous season. Can it be
That modesty may more betray our sense
Than woman's lightness? Having waste ground enough,
Shall we desire to raze the sanctuary,
And pitch our evils there? O, fie, fie, fie!
What dost thou, or what art thou, Angelo?
Dost thou desire her foully for those things
That make her good? O, let her brother live:
Thieves for their robbery have authority
When judges steal themselves. What, do I love her,
That I desire to hear her speak again,
And feast upon her eyes? What is't I dream on?
O cunning enemy, that, to catch a saint
With saints dost bait thy hook! Most dangerous
Is that temptation that doth goad us on
To sin in loving virtue: never could the strumpet,
With all her double vigour, art and nature,
Once stir my temper; but this virtuous maid
Subdues me quite:—ever till now,
When men were fond, I smiled, and wonder'd how.

(Exit.)

(SCENE III.—A prison. Enter, severally, Duke *disguised as a friar, and* Provost.*)*

Duke:
Hail to you, provost!—so I think you are.

Provost:
I am the provost. What's your will, good friar?

Duke:
Bound by my charity and my blest order,
I come to visit the afflicted spirits
Here in the prison. Do me the common right
To let me see them, and to make me know
The nature of their crimes, that I may minister
To them accordingly.

Provost:
I would do more than that, if more were needful.

>   Look, here comes one,—a gentlewoman of mine,
>   Who, falling in the flaws of her own youth,
>   Hath blister'd her report: she is with child;
>   And he that got it, sentenced,—a young man
>   More fit to do another such offence
>   Than die for this.

(Enter Juliet.)

Duke:
> When must he die?

Provost:
> As I do think, to-morrow.—
> *(To Juliet.)*
> I have provided for you: stay awhile,
> And you shall be conducted.

Duke:
> Repent you, fair one, of the sin you carry?

Juliet:
> I do; and bear the shame most patiently.

Duke:
> I'll teach you how you shall arraign your conscience,
> And try your penitence, if it be sound,
> Or hollowly put on.

Juliet:
> I'll gladly learn.

Duke:
> Love you the man that wrong'd you?

Juliet:
> Yes, as I love the woman that wrong'd him.

Duke:
> So, then, it seems your most offenceful act
> Was mutually committed?

Juliet:
> Mutually.

Duke:
> Then was your sin of heavier kind than his.

Juliet:
> I do confess it, and repent it, father.

Duke:
> 'Tis meet so, daughter: but lest you do repent,
> As that the sin hath brought you to this shame,—
> Which sorrow is always toward ourselves, not heaven,
> Showing we would not spare heaven as we love it,
> But as we stand in fear,—

Juliet:
> I do repent me, as it is an evil,
> And take the shame with joy.

Duke:
> There rest.
> Your partner, as I hear, must die to-morrow,
> And I am going with instruction to him.
> Grace go with you! *Benedicite!*

(Exit.)

Juliet:
> Must die to-morrow! O injurious law,
> That respites me a life, whose very comfort
> Is still a dying horror!

Provost:
> 'Tis pity of him.

(Exeunt.)

(SCENE IV.—Angelo's *house.* Enter Angelo.)

Angelo:
> When I would pray and think, I think and pray

To several subjects. Heaven hath my empty words;
Whilst my invention, hearing not my tongue,
Anchors on Isabel: Heaven in my mouth,
As if I did but only chew his name;
And in my heart the strong and swelling evil
Of my conception. The state, whereon I studied,
Is like a good thing, being often read,
Grown sear'd and tedious; yea, my gravity,
Wherein—let no man hear me—I take pride,
Could I with boot change for an idle plume,
Which the air beats for vain. O place, O form,
How often dost thou with thy case, thy habit,
Wrench awe from fools, and tie the wiser souls
To thy false seeming! Blood, thou art blood:
Let's write good angel on the devil's horn,
'Tis not the devil's crest.

(Enter Servant.)

How now! who's there?

Servant:
One Isabel, a sister,
Desires access to you.

Angelo:
Teach her the way.

(Exit Servant.)

O heavens!
Why does my blood thus muster to my heart,
Making both it unable for itself,
And dispossessing all my other parts
Of necessary fitness?
So play the foolish throngs with one that swoons;
Come all to help him, and so stop the air
By which he should revive: and even so
The general, subject to a well-wish'd king,
Quit their own part, and in obsequious fondness
Crowd to his presence, where their untaught love
Must needs appear offence.

(Enter Isabella.)

How now, fair maid!

Isabella:
    I am come to know your pleasure.

Angelo:
    That you might know it, would much better please me
    Than to demand what 'tis. Your brother cannot live.

Isabella:
    Even so.—Heaven keep your honour! *(Retiring.)*

Angelo:
    Yet may he live awhile; and, it may be,
    As long as you or I: yet he must die.

Isabella:
    Under your sentence?

Angelo:
    Yea.

Isabella:
    When, I beseech you? that in his reprieve,
    Longer or shorter, he may be so fitted
    That his soul sicken not.

Angelo:
    Ha! fie, these filthy vices! It were as good
    To pardon him that hath from nature stol'n
    A man already made, as to remit
    Their saucy sweetness that do coin heaven's image
    In stamps that are forbid: 'tis all as easy
    Falsely to take away a life true made,
    As to put metal in restrained means
    To make a false one.

Isabella:
    'Tis set down so in heaven, but not in earth.

Angelo:
>Say you so? than I shall pose you quickly.
>Which had you rather,—that the most just law
>Now took your brother's life; or, to redeem him,
>Give up your body to such sweet uncleanness
>As she that he hath stain'd?

Isabella:
>>Sir, believe this,
>I had rather give my body than my soul.

Angelo:
>I talk not of your soul: our compell'd sins
>Stand more for number than accompt.

Isabella:
>>How say you?

Angelo:
>Nay, I'll not warrant that; for I can speak
>Against the thing I say. Answer to this:—
>I, now the voice of the recorded law,
>Pronounce a sentence on your brother's life:
>Might there not be a charity in sin
>To save this brother's life?

Isabella:
>>Please you to do't,
>I'll take it as a peril to my soul,
>It is no sin at all, but charity.

Angelo:
>Pleased you to do't at peril of your soul,
>Were equal poise of sin and charity.

Isabella:
>That I do beg his life, if it be sin,
>Heaven let me bear it! you granting of my suit,
>If that be sin, I'll make it my morn-prayer
>To have it added to the faults of mine,
>And nothing of your answer.

Angelo:
> > Nay, but hear me.
> Your sense pursues not mine: either you are ignorant,
> Or seem so, craftily; and that's not good.

Isabella:
> Let me be ignorant, and in nothing good,
> But graciously to know I am no better.

Angelo:
> Thus wisdom wishes to appear most bright
> When it doth tax itself; as these black masks
> Proclaim an enshield beauty ten times louder
> Than beauty could, display'd.—But mark me;
> To be received plain, I'll speak more gross:
> Your brother is to die.

Isabella:
> So.

Angelo:
> And his offence is so, as it appears,
> Accountant to the law upon that pain.

Isabella:
> True.

Angelo:
> Admit no other way to save his life,—
> As I subscribe not that, nor any other,
> But in the toss of question,—that you, his sister,
> Finding yourself desired of such a person,
> Whose credit with the judge, or own great place,
> Could fetch your brother from the manacles
> Of the all-bridling law; and that there were
> No earthly mean to save him, but that either
> You must lay down the treasures of your body
> To this supposed, or else to let him suffer;
> What would you do?

Isabella:
> As much for my poor brother as myself:

That is, were I under the terms of death,
Th'impression of keen whips I'ld wear as rubies,
And strip myself to death, as to a bed
That longing have been sick for, ere I'ld yield
My body up to shame.

Angelo:
                              Then must
Your brother die.

Isabella:
                              And 'twere the cheaper way:
Better it were a brother died at once,
Than that a sister, by redeeming him,
Should die for ever.

Angelo:
Were not you, then, as cruel as the sentence
That you have slander'd so?

Isabella:
Ignomy in ransom, and free pardon,
Are of two houses: lawful mercy
Is nothing kin to foul redemption.

Angelo:
You seem'd of late to make the law a tyrant;
And rather proved the sliding of your brother
A merriment than a vice.

Isabella:
O, pardon me, my lord; it oft falls out,
To have what we would have, we speak not what we mean:
I something do excuse the thing I hate,
For his advantage that I dearly love.

Angelo:
We are all frail.

Isabella:
                              Else let my brother die,
If not a feodary, but only he,

>Owe and succeed this weakness.

Angelo:
>Nay, women are frail too.

Isabella:
>Ay, as the glasses where they view themselves;
>Which are as easy broke as they make forms.
>Women!—Help heaven! men their creation mar
>In profiting by them. Nay, call us ten times frail;
>For we are soft as our complexions are,
>And credulous to false prints.

Angelo:
>I think it well:
>And from this testimony of your own sex,—
>Since, I suppose, we are made to be no stronger
>Than faults may shake our frames,—let me be bold;—
>I do arrest your words. Be that you are,
>That is, a woman; if you be more, you're none;
>If you be one,—as you are well exprest
>By all external warrants,—show it now,
>By putting on the destined livery.

Isabella:
>I have no tongue but one: gentle my lord,
>Let me entreat you speak the former language.

Angelo:
>Plainly conceive, I love you.

Isabella:
>My brother did love Juliet; and you tell me
>That he shall die for't.

Angelo:
>He shall not, Isabel, if you give me love.

Isabella:
>I know your virtue hath a licence in't,
>Which seems a little fouler than it is,
>To pluck on others.

Angelo:
>Believe me, on mine honour,
My words express my purpose.

Isabella:
>Ha! little honour to be much believed,
And most pernicious purpose!—Seeming, seeming!—
I will proclaim thee, Angelo; look for't:
Sign me a present pardon for my brother,
Or with an outstretch'd throat I'll tell the world
Aloud what man thou art.

Angelo:
>Who will believe thee, Isabel?
My unsoil'd name, th' austereness of my life,
My vouch against you, and my place i'the state,
Will so your accusation overweigh,
That you shall stifle in your own report,
And smell of calumny. I have begun;
And now I give my sensual race the rein:
Fit thy consent to my sharp appetite;
Lay by all nicety and prolixious blushes,
That banish what they sue for; redeem thy brother
By yielding up thy body to my will;
Or else he must not only die the death,
But thy unkindness shall his death draw out
To lingering sufferance. Answer me to-morrow,
Or, by the affection that now guides me most,
I'll prove a tyrant to him. As for you,
Say what you can, my false o'erweighs your true.

>>*(Exit.)*

Isabella:
>To whom should I complain? Did I tell this,
Who would believe me? O perilous mouths,
That bear in them one and the self-same tongue,
Either of condemnation or approof;
Bidding the law make court'sy to their will;
Hooking both right and wrong to the appetite,
To follow as it draws! I'll to my brother:
Though he hath fall'n by prompture of the blood,

Yet hath he in him such a mind of honour,
That, had he twenty heads to tender down
On twenty bloody blocks, he'ld yield them up,
Before his sister should her body stoop
To such abhorred pollution.
Then, Isabel, live chaste, and, brother, die:
More than our brother is our chastity.
I'll tell him yet of Angelo's request,
And fit his mind to death, for his soul's rest.

(Exit.)

(ACT III. SCENE I.—The prison. Enter Duke *disguised as before,* Claudio, *and* Provost.*)*

Duke:
So, then, you hope of pardon from Lord Angelo?

Claudio:
The miserable have no other medicine
But only hope:
I have hope to live, and am prepared to die.

Duke:
Be absolute for death; either death or life
Shall thereby be the sweeter. Reason thus with life:—
If I do lose thee, I do lose a thing
That none but fools would keep: a breath thou art,
Servile to all the skyey influences
That do this habitation, where thou keep'st,
Hourly afflict: merely, thou art death's fool;
For him thou labour'st by thy flight to shun,
And yet runn'st toward him still. Thou art not noble;
For all th'accommodations that thou bear'st
Are nursed by baseness. Thou'rt by no means valiant;
For thou dost fear the soft and tender fork
Of a poor worm. Thy best of rest is sleep,
And that thou oft provokest; yet grossly fear'st
Thy death, which is no more. Thou art not thyself;
For thou exists on many a thousand grains
That issue out of dust. Happy thou art not;
For what thou hast not, still thou strivest to get,

And what thou hast, forgett'st. Thou art not certain;
For thy complexion shifts to strange affects,
After the moon. If thou art rich, thou'rt poor;
For, like an ass whose back with ingots bows,
Thou bear'st thy heavy riches but a journey,
And death unloads thee. Friend has thou none;
For thine own bowels, which do call thee sire,
The mere effusions of thy proper loins,
Do curse the gout, serpigo, and the rheum,
For ending thee no sooner. Thou hast nor youth nor age,
But, as it were, an after-dinner's sleep,
Dreaming on both; for all thy blessed youth
Becomes as aged, and doth beg the alms
Of palsied eld; and when thou art old and rich,
Thou hast neither heat, affection, limb, nor beauty,
To make thy riches pleasant. What's yet in this
That bears the name of life? Yet in this life
Lie hid moe thousand deaths: yet death we fear,
That makes these odds all even.

Claudio:
                          I humbly thank you.
To sue to live, I find I seek to die;
And, seeking death, find life: let it come on.

Isabella *(within):*
What, ho! Peace here; grace and good company!

Provost:
Who's there? come in: the wish deserves a welcome.

Duke:
Dear sir, ere long I'll visit you again.

Claudio:
Most holy sir, I thank you.

(Enter Isabella.)

Isabella:
My business is a word or two with Claudio.

Provost:
>And very welcome.—Look, signior, here's your sister.

Duke:
>Provost, a word with you.

Provost:
>As many as you please.

Duke:
>Bring me to hear them speak, where I may be conceal'd.

>*(Exeunt Duke and Provost.)*

Claudio:
>Now, sister, what's the comfort?

Isabella:
>Why,
>As all comforts are; most good, most good indeed.
>Lord Angelo, having affairs to heaven,
>Intends you for his swift ambassador,
>Where you shall be an everlasting leiger:
>Therefore your best appointment make with speed;
>To-morrow you set on.

Claudio:
>Is there no remedy?

Isabella:
>None, but such remedy as, to save a head,
>To cleave a heart in twain.

Claudio:
>But is there any?

Isabella:
>Yes, brother, you may live:
>There is a devilish mercy in the judge,
>If you'll implore it, that will free your life,
>But fetter you till death.

Claudio:
> Perpetual durance?

Isabella:
> Ay, just; perpetual durance,—a restraint,
> Though all the world's vastidity you had,
> To a determined scope.

Claudio:
> But in what nature?

Isabella:
> In such a one as, you consenting to't,
> Would bark your honour from that trunk you bear,
> And leave you naked.

Claudio:
> Let me know the point.

Isabella:
> O, I do fear thee, Claudio; and I quake,
> Lest thou a feverous life shouldst entertain,
> And six or seven winters more respect
> Than a perpetual honour. Darest thou die?
> The sense of death is most in apprehension;
> And the poor beetle that we tread upon,
> In corporal sufferance finds a pang as great
> As when a giant dies.

Claudio:
> Why give you me this shame?
> Think you I can a resolution fetch
> From flowery tenderness? If I must die,
> I will encounter darkness as a bride,
> And hug it in mine arms.

Isabella:
> There spake my brother; there my father's grave
> Did utter forth a voice! Yes, thou must die:
> Thou art too noble to conserve a life
> In base appliances. This outward-sainted deputy—
> Whose settled visage and deliberate word

Nips youth i'the head, and follies doth emmew
As falcon doth the fowl—is yet a devil;
His filth within being cast, he would appear
A pond as deep as hell.

Claudio:
                            The priestly Angelo?

Isabella:
O, 'tis the cunning livery of hell,
The damned'st body to invest and cover
In priestly guards! Dost thou think, Claudio?—
If I would yield him my virginity,
Thou mightst be freed.

Claudio:
                            O heavens! it cannot be.

Isabella:
Yes, he would give't thee, from this rank offence,
So to offend him still. This night's the time
That I should do what I abhor to name,
Or else thou diest to-morrow.

Claudio:
                            Thou shalt not do't.

Isabella:
O, were it but my life,
I'd throw it down for your deliverance
As frankly as a pin.

Claudio:
                            Thanks, dear Isabel.

Isabella:
Be ready, Claudio, for your death to-morrow.

Claudio:
Yes.—Has he affections in him,
That thus can make him bite the law by the nose,
When he would force it? Sure, it is no sin;
Or of the deadly seven it is the least.

Isabella:
    Which is the least?

Claudio:
    If it were damnable, he being so wise,
    Why would he for the momentary trick
    Be perdurably fined?—O Isabel!

Isabella:
    What says my brother?

Claudio:
                         Death is a fearful thing.

Isabella:
    And shamed life a hateful.

Claudio:
    Ay, but to die, and go we know not where;
    To lie in cold obstruction, and to rot;
    This sensible warm motion to become
    A kneaded clod; and the delighted spirit
    To bathe in fiery floods, or to reside
    In thrilling region of thick-ribbed ice;
    To be imprison'd in the viewless winds,
    And blown with restless violence round about
    The pendent world; or to be worse than worst
    Of those that lawless and incertain thought
    Imagine howling!—'tis too horrible!
    The weariest and most loathed worldly life
    That age, ache, penury, and imprisonment
    Can lay on nature, is a paradise
    To what we fear of death.

Isabella:
    Alas, alas!

Claudio:
                Sweet sister, let me live:
    What sin you do to save a brother's life,
    Nature dispenses with the deed so far
    That it becomes a virtue.

Isabella:
>   O you beast!
> O faithless coward! O dishonest wretch!
> Wilt thou be made a man out of my vice?
> Is't not a kind of incest, to take life
> From thine own sister's shame? What should I think?
> Heaven shield my mother play'd my father fair?
> For such a warped slip of wilderness
> Ne'er issued from his blood. Take my defiance;
> Die, perish! Might but my bending down
> Reprieve thee from thy fate, it should proceed:
> I'll pray a thousand prayers for thy death,—
> No word to save thee.

Claudio:
> Nay, hear me, Isabel.

Isabella:
>   O, fie, fie, fie!
> Thy sin's not accidental, but a trade.
> Mercy to thee would prove itself a bawd:
> 'Tis best that thou diest quickly.

(Going.)

Claudio:
>   O, hear me, Isabella!

(Enter Duke.)

Duke:
> Vouchsafe a word, young sister, but one word.

Isabella:
> What is your will?

Duke:
> Might you dispense with your leisure, I would by and by have some speech with you: the satisfaction I would require is likewise your own benefit.

Isabella:
> I have no superfluous leisure; my stay must be stolen out of other affairs; but I will attend you awhile.

Duke:
> Son, I have overheard what hath pass'd between you and your sister. Angelo had never the purpose to corrupt her; only he hath made an assay of her virtue to practise his judgement with the disposition of natures: she, having the truth of honour in her, hath made him that gracious denial which he is most glad to receive. I am confessor to Angelo, and I know this to be true; therefore prepare yourself to death: do not satisfy your resolution with hopes that are fallible: to-morrow you must die; go to your knees, and make ready.

Claudio:
> Let me ask my sister pardon. I am so out of love with life, that I will sue to be rid of it.

Duke:
> Hold you there: farewell.

(Exit Claudio.)

> Provost, a word with you!

(Enter Provost.)

Provost:
> What's your will, father.

Duke:
> That now you are come, you will be gone. Leave me awhile with the maid: my mind promises with my habit no loss shall touch her by my company.

Provost:
> In good time.

(Exit.)

Duke:
> The hand that hath made you fair hath made you good: the goodness that is cheap in beauty makes beauty brief in goodness; but grace, being the soul of your complexion, shall keep the body of it ever fair. The assault that Angelo hath made to you, fortune hath convey'd to my understanding; and, but that frailty hath examples for his falling, I should wonder at Angelo. How will you do to content this substitute, and to save your brother?

Isabella:
> I am now going to resolve him, I had rather my brother die by the law than my son should be unlawfully born. But, O, how much is the good duke deceived in Angelo! If ever he return, and I can speak to him, I will open my lips in vain, or discover his government.

Duke:
> That shall not be much amiss: yet, as the matter now stands, he will avoid your accusation,—he made trial of you only. Therefore fasten your ear on my advisings: to the love I have in doing good a remedy presents itself. I do make myself believe that you may most uprighteously do a poor wrong'd lady a merited benefit; redeem your brother from the angry law; do no stain to your own gracious person; and much please the absent duke, if peradventure he shall ever return to have hearing of this business.

Isabella:
> Let me hear you speak further. I have spirit to do any thing that appears not foul in the truth of my spirit.

Duke:
> Virtue is bold, and goodness never fearful. Have you not heard speak of Mariana, the sister of Frederick the great soldier who miscarried at sea?

Isabella:
> I have heard of the lady, and good words went with her name.

Duke:
> She should this Angelo have married; was affianced to her by oath, and the nuptial appointed: between which time of the contract and limit of the solemnity, her brother Frederick was wrackt at sea, having in that perish'd vessel the dowry of his sister. But mark how heavily this befell to the poor gentlewoman: there she lost a noble and renown'd brother, in his love toward her ever most kind and natural; with him, the portion and sinew of her fortune, her marriage-dowry; with both, her combinate husband, this well-seeming Angelo.

Isabella:
> Can this be so? did Angelo so leave her?

Duke:
> Left her in her tears, and dried not one of them with his comfort; swallow'd his vows whole, pretending in her discoveries of dishonour: in few, bestow'd her on her own lamentation, which she yet wears for his sake; and he, a marble to her tears, is wash'd with them, but relents not.

Isabella:
> What a merit were it in death to take this poor maid from the world! What corruption in this life, that it will let this man live!—But how out of this can she avail?

Duke:
> It is a rupture that you may easily heal: and the cure of it not only saves your brother, but keeps you from dishonour in doing it.

Isabella:
> Show me how, good father.

Duke:
> This forenamed maid hath yet in her the continuance of her first affection: his unjust unkindness, that in all reason should have quench'd her love, hath, like an impediment in the current, made it more violent and unruly. Go you to Angelo; answer his requiring with a plausible obedience; agree with his demands to the point; only refer yourself to

his advantage,—first, that your stay with him may not be long; that the time may have all shadow and silence in it; and the place answer to convenience. This being granted in course—and now follows all—we shall advise this wrong'd maid to stead up your appointment, go in your place; if the encounter acknowledge itself hereafter, it may compel him to her recompense: and here, by this is your brother saved, your honour untainted, the poor Mariana advantaged, and the corrupt deputy scaled. The maid will I frame and make fit for his attempt. If you think well to carry this as you may, the doubleness of the benefit defends the deceit from reproof. What think you of it?

Isabella:
The image of it gives me content already; and I trust it will grow to a most prosperous perfection.

Duke:
It lies much in your holding up. Haste you speedily to Angelo: if for this night he entreat you to his bed, give him promise of satisfaction. I will presently to Saint Luke's: there, at the moated grange, resides this dejected Mariana. At that place call upon me; and dispatch with Angelo, that it may be quickly.

Isabella:
I thank you for this comfort. Fare you well, good father.

(*Exeunt.*)

(SCENE II.—*The street before the prison.* Enter Duke *disguised as before; to him,* Elbow *and* Officers *with* Pompey.)

Elbow:
Nay, if there be no remedy for it, but that you will needs buy and sell men and women like beasts, we shall have all the world drink brown and white bastard.

Duke:
O heavens! what stuff is here?

Pompey:
'Twas never merry world since, of two usuries, the merriest was put down, and the worser allowed by order of law a furr'd gown to keep him warm; and furr'd with fox and lamb-skins too, to signify, that craft, being richer than innocency, stands for the facing.

Elbow:
Come your way, sir.—'Bless you, good father friar.

Duke:
And you, good brother father. What offence hath this man made you, sir?

Elbow:
Marry, sir, he hath offended the law: and, sir, we take him to be a thief too, sir; for we have found upon him, sir, a strange picklock, which we have sent to the deputy.

Duke:
Fie, sirrah! a bawd, a wicked bawd!
The evil that thou causest to be done,
That is thy means to live. Do thou but think
What 'tis to cram a maw or clothe a back
From such a filthy vice: say to thyself,—
From their abominable and beastly touches
I drink, I eat, array myself, and live.
Canst thou believe thy living is a life,
So stinkingly depending? Go mend, go mend.

Pompey:
Indeed, it does stink in some sort, sir; but yet, sir, I would prove—

Duke:
Nay, if the devil have given thee proofs for sin,
Thou wilt prove his.—Take him to prison, officer:
Correction and instruction must both work
Ere this rude beast will profit.

Elbow:
He must before the deputy, sir; he has given him warning: the deputy cannot abide a whoremaster: if he be a

whoremonger, and comes before him, he were as good go a mile on his errand.

Duke:
That we were all, as some would seem to be,
From our faults, or faults from seeming, free!

Elbow:
His neck will come to your waist,—a cord, sir.

Pompey:
I spy comfort; I cry, bail! Here's a gentleman and a friend of mine.

(Enter Lucio.)

Lucio:
How now, noble Pompey! What, at the wheels of Cæsar! art thou led in triumph? What, is there none of Pygmalion's images, newly-made woman, to be had now, for putting the hand in the pocket and extracting it clutch'd? What reply, ha? What say'st thou to this tune, matter, and method? Is't not drown'd i'the last rain, ha? What say'st thou, Trot? Is the world as it was, man? Which is the way? Is it sad, and few words? or how? The trick of it?

Duke:
Still thus, and thus; still worse!

Lucio:
How doth my dear morsel, thy mistress? Procures she still, ha?

Pompey:
Troth, sir, she hath eaten up all her beef, and she is herself in the tub.

Lucio:
Why, 'tis good; it is the right of it; it must be so: ever your fresh whore and your powder'd bawd: an unshunn'd consequence; it must be so. Art going to prison, Pompey?

Pompey:
> Yes, faith, sir.

Lucio:
> Why, 'tis not amiss, Pompey. Farewell: go, say I sent thee thither. For debt, Pompey? or how?

Elbow:
> For being a bawd, for being a bawd.

Lucio:
> Well, then, imprison him: if imprisonment be the due of a bawd, why, 'tis his right: bawd is he doubtless, and of antiquity too; bawd-born.—Farewell, good Pompey. Commend me to the prison, Pompey: you will turn good husband now, Pompey; you will keep the house.

Pompey:
> I hope, sir, your good worship will be my bail.

Lucio:
> No, indeed, will I not, Pompey; it is not the wear. I will pray, Pompey, to increase your bondage: if you take it not patiently, why, your mettle is the more. Adieu, trusty Pompey.—Bless you, friar.

Duke:
> And you.

Lucio:
> Does Bridget paint still, Pompey, ha?

Elbow:
> Come your ways, sir; come.

Pompey:
> You will not bail me, then, sir?

Lucio:
> Then, Pompey, nor now.—What news abroad, friar, what news?

Elbow:
> Come your ways, sir; come.

Lucio:
> Go,—to kennel, Pompey, go.
>
> *(Exeunt* Elbow *and* Officers *with* Pompey.*)*
>
> What news, friar, of the duke?

Duke:
> I know none. Can you tell me of any?

Lucio:
> Some say he is with the Emperor of Russia; other some, he is in Rome: but where is he, think you?

Duke:
> I know not where; but wheresoever, I wish him well.

Lucio:
> It was a mad fantastical trick of him to steal from the state, and usurp the beggary he was never born to. Lord Angelo dukes it well in his absence; he puts transgression to't.

Duke:
> He does well in't.

Lucio:
> A little more lenity to lechery would do no harm in him: something too crabb'd that way, friar.

Duke:
> It is too general a vice, and severity must cure it.

Lucio:
> Yes, in good sooth, the vice is of a great kindred; it is well allied; but it is impossible to extirp it quite, friar, till eating and drinking be put down. They say this Angelo was not made by man and woman, after the downright way of creation: is it true, think you?

Duke:
How should he be made, then?

Lucio:
Some report a sea-maid spawn'd him; some, that he was begot between two stock-fishes. But it is certain that, when he makes water, his urine is congeal'd ice; that I know to be true: and he is a motion ungenerative; that's infallible.

Duke:
You are pleasant, sir, and speak apace.

Lucio:
Why, what a ruthless thing is this in him, for the rebellion of a codpiece to take away the life of a man! Would the duke that is absent have done this? Ere he would have hang'd a man for the getting a hundred bastards, he would have paid for the nursing a thousand: he had some feeling of the sport; he knew the service, and that instructed him to mercy.

Duke:
I never heard the absent duke much detected for women; he was not inclined that way.

Lucio:
O, sir, you are deceived.

Duke:
'Tis not possible.

Lucio:
Who, not the duke? yes, your beggar of fifty; and his use was to put a ducat in her clack-dish: the duke had crotchets in him. He would be drunk too; that let me inform you.

Duke:
You do him wrong, surely.

Lucio:
Sir, I was an inward of his. A sly fellow was the duke: and I believe I know the cause of his withdrawing.

Duke:
What, I prithee, might be the cause?

Lucio:
No,—pardon; 'tis a secret must be lockt within the teeth and the lips: but this I can let you understand,—the greater file of the subject held the duke to be wise.

Duke:
Wise! why, no question but he was.

Lucio:
A very superficial, ignorant, unweighing fellow.

Duke:
Either this is envy in you, folly, or mistaking: the very stream of his life and the business he hath helm'd must, upon a warranted need, give him a better proclamation. Let him be but testimonied in his own bringings-forth, and he shall appear to the envious a scholar, a statesman, and a soldier. Therefore you speak unskilfully; or if your knowledge be more, it is much darken'd in your malice.

Lucio:
Sir, I know him, and I love him.

Duke:
Love talks with better knowledge, and knowledge with dearer love.

Lucio:
Come, sir, I know what I know.

Duke:
I can hardly believe that, since you know not what you speak. But, if ever the duke return,—as our prayers are he may,—let me desire you to make your answer before him. If it be honest you have spoke, you have courage to maintain it: I am bound to call upon you; and, I pray you, your name?

Lucio:
Sir, my name is Lucio; well known to the duke.

Duke:
> He shall know you better, sir, if I may live to report you.

Lucio:
> I fear you not.

Duke:
> O, you hope the duke will return no more; or you imagine me too unhurtful an opposite. But, indeed, I can do you little harm; you'll forswear this again.

Lucio:
> I'll be hang'd first: thou art deceived in me, friar. But no more of this. Canst thou tell if Claudio die to-morrow or no?

Duke:
> Why should he die, sir?

Lucio:
> Why, for filling a bottle with a tun-dish. I would the duke we talk of were return'd again: this ungenitured agent will unpeople the province with continency; sparrows must not build in his house-eaves, because they are lecherous. The duke yet would have dark deeds darkly answer'd; he would never bring them to light: would he were return'd! Marry, this Claudio is condemn'd for untrussing. Farewell, good friar: I prithee, pray for me. The duke, I say to thee again, would eat mutton on Fridays. He's now past it; yet, and I say to thee, he would mouth with a beggar, though she smelt brown bread and garlick: say that I said so. Farewell.

(Exit.)

Duke:
> No might nor greatness in mortality
> Can censure scape; back-wounding calumny
> The whitest virtue strikes. What king so strong
> Can tie the gall up in the slanderous tongue?—
> But who comes here?

(Enter Escalus, Provost, and Officers with Mistress Overdone.)

Escalus:
Go; away with her to prison!

Mistress Overdone:
Good my lord, be good to me; your honour is accounted a merciful man; good my lord.

Escalus:
Double and treble admonition, and still forfeit in the same kind? This would make mercy swear and play the tyrant.

Provost:
A bawd of eleven years' continuance, may it please your honour.

Mistress Overdone:
My lord, this is one Lucio's information against me. Mistress Kate Keep-down was with child by him in the duke's time; he promised her marriage: his child is a year and a quarter old, come Philip and Jacob: I have kept it myself; and see how he goes about to abuse me!

Escalus:
That fellow is a fellow of much license:—let him be call'd before us.—Away with her to prison!—Go to; no more words.

(Exeunt Officers with Mistress Overdone.)

Provost, my brother Angelo will not be alter'd; Claudio must die to-morrow: let him be furnish'd with divines, and have all charitable preparation. If my brother wrought by my pity, it should not be so with him.

Provost:
So please you, this friar hath been with him, and advised him for the entertainment of death.

Escalus:
Good even, good father.

Duke:
Bliss and goodness on you!

Escalus:
> Of whence are you?

Duke:
> Not of this country, though my chance is now
> To use it for my time: I am a brother
> Of gracious order, late come from the See
> In special business from his holiness.

Escalus:
> What news abroad i'the world?

Duke:
> None, but that there is so great a fever on goodness, that the dissolution of it must cure it: novelty is only in request; and it is as dangerous to be aged in any kind of course, as it is virtuous to be constant in any undertaking: there is scarce truth enough alive to make societies secure; but security enough to make fellowships accurst:—much upon this riddle runs the wisdom of the world. This news is old enough, yet it is every day's news. I pray you, sir, of what disposition was the duke?

Escalus:
> One that, above all other strifes, contended especially to know himself.

Duke:
> What pleasure was he given to?

Escalus:
> Rather rejoicing to see another merry, than merry at any thing which profest to make him rejoice: a gentleman of all temperance. But leave we him to his events, with a prayer they may prove prosperous; and let me desire to know how you find Claudio prepared. I am made to understand that you have lent him visitation.

Duke:
> He professes to have received no sinister measure from his judge, but most willingly humbles himself to the determination of justice: yet had he framed to himself, by the instruction of his frailty, many deceiving promises of life;

which I, by my good leisure, have discredited to him, and now is he resolved to die.

Escalus:
You have paid the heavens your function, and the prisoner the very debt of your calling. I have labour'd for the poor gentleman to the extremest shore of my modesty: but my brother justice have I found so severe, that he hath forced me to tell him he is indeed Justice.

Duke:
If his own life answer the straitness of his proceeding, it shall become him well; wherein if he chance to fail, he hath sentenced himself.

Escalus:
I am going to visit the prisoner. Fare you well.

Duke:
Peace be with you!

(Exeunt Escalus and Provost.)

He who the sword of heaven will bear
Should be as holy as severe;
Pattern in himself to know,
Grace to stand, and virtue go;
More nor less to others paying
Than by self-offences weighing.
Shame to him whose cruel striking
Kills for faults of his own liking!
Twice treble shame on Angelo,
To weed my vice, and let his grow!
O, what may man within him hide,
Though angel on the outward side!
How may likeness wade in crimes,
Making practice on the times,
To draw with idle spiders' strings
Most ponderous and substantial things!
Craft against vice I must apply:
With Angelo to-night shall lie
His old betrothed but despised;

So disguise shall, by the disguised,
Pay with falsehood false exacting,
And perform an old contracting.

(Exit.)

(ACT IV. SCENE I.—The Moated Grange. Enter Mariana; *a* Boy *singing.)*

Song:
> Take, O take those lips away,
>   That so sweetly were forsworn;
> And those eyes, the break of day,
>   Lights that do mislead the morn:
> But my kisses bring again, bring again;
> Seals of love, but seal'd in vain, seal'd in vain.

Mariana:
Break off thy song, and haste thee quick away:
Here comes a man of comfort, whose advice
Hath often still'd my brawling discontent.

(Exit Boy.)

(Enter Duke *disguised as before.)*

I cry you mercy, sir; and well could wish
You had not found me here so musical:
Let me excuse me, and believe me so,—
My mirth it much displeased, but pleased my woe.

Duke:
'Tis good; though music oft hath such a charm
To make bad good, and good provoke to harm.—
I pray you, tell me, hath anybody inquired for me here to-day? much upon this time have I promised here to meet.

Mariana:
You have not been inquired after: I have sat here all day.

Duke:
I do constantly believe you.—The time is come even now. I

shall crave your forbearance a little: may be I will call upon
you anon, for some advantage to yourself.

Mariana:
I am always bound to you.

(Exit)

(Enter Isabella.)

Duke:
Very well met, and welcome.
What is the news from this good deputy?

Isabella:
He hath a garden circummured with brick,
Whose western side is with a vineyard back'd;
And to that vineyard is a planched gate,
That makes his opening with this bigger key:
This other doth command a little door
Which from the vineyard to the garden leads;
There have I made my promise
Upon the heavy middle of the night
To call upon him.

Duke:
But shall you on your knowledge find this way?

Isabella:
I have ta'en a due and wary note upon't:
With whispering and most guilty diligence,
In action all of precept, he did show me
The way twice o'er.

Duke:
Are there no other tokens
Between you 'greed concerning her observance?

Isabella:
No, none, but only a repair i'the dark;
And that I have possest him my most stay
Can be but brief; for I have made him know

> I have a servant comes with me along,
> That stays upon me; whose persuasion is
> I come about my brother.

Duke:
>   'Tis well borne up.
> I have not yet made known to Mariana
> A word of this.—What, ho! within! come forth!

(Enter Mariana.)

> I pray you, be acquainted with this maid;
> She comes to do you good.

Isabella:
>   I do desire the like.

Duke:
> Do you persuade yourself that I respect you?

Mariana:
> Good friar, I know you do, and have found it.

Duke:
> Take, then, this your companion by the hand,
> Who hath a story ready for your ear.
> I shall attend your leisure: but make haste;
> The vaporous night approaches.

Mariana:
>   Will't please you walk aside?

(Exeunt Mariana and Isabella.)

Duke:
> O place and greatness, millions of false eyes
> Are stuck upon thee! volumes of report
> Run with these false and most contrarious quests
> Upon thy doings! thousand escapes of wit
> Make thee the father of their idle dream,
> And rack thee in their fancies!

(Enter Mariana and Isabella.)

Welcome! How agreed?

Isabella:
She'll take the enterprise upon her, father,
If you advise it.

Duke:
It is not my consent,
But my entreaty too.

Isabella:
Little have you to say
When you depart from him, but, soft and low,
'Remember now my brother.'

Mariana:
Fear me not.

Duke:
Nor, gentle daughter, fear you not at all.
He is your husband on a pre-contract:
To bring you thus together, 'tis no sin,
Sith that the justice of your title to him
Doth flourish the deceit. Come, let us go:
Our corn's to reap, for yet our tilth's to sow.

(Exeunt.)

(SCENE II.—The prison. Enter Provost and Pompey.)

Provost:
Come hither, sirrah. Can you cut off a man's head?

Pompey:
If the man be a bachelor, sir, I can; but if he be a married man, he's his wife's head, and I can never cut off a woman's head.

Provost:
Come, sir, leave me your snatches, and yield me a direct

answer. To-morrow morning are to die Claudio and Barnardine. Here is in our prison a common executioner, who in his office lacks a helper: if you will take it on you to assist him, it shall redeem you from your gyves; if not, you shall have your full time of imprisonment, and your deliverance with an unpitied whipping, for you have been a notorious bawd.

Pompey:
Sir, I have been an unlawful bawd time out of mind; but yet I will be content to be a lawful hangman. I would be glad to receive some instruction from my fellow partner.

Provost:
What, ho, Abhorson! Where's Abhorson, there?

(Enter Abhorson.)

Abhorson:
Do you call, sir?

Provost:
Sirrah, here's a fellow will help you to-morrow in your execution. If you think it meet, compound with him by the year, and let him abide here with you; if not, use him for the present, and dismiss him. He cannot plead his estimation with you; he hath been a bawd.

Abhorson:
A bawd, sir! fie upon him! he will discredit our mystery.

Provost:
Go to, sir; you weigh equally; a feather will turn the scale.

(Exit.)

Pompey:
Pray, sir, by your good favour,—for surely, sir, a good favour you have, but that you have a hanging look,—do you call, sir, your occupation a mystery?

Abhorson:
   Ay, sir; a mystery.

Pompey:
   Painting, sir, I have heard say, is a mystery; and your whores, sir, being members of my occupation, using painting, do prove my occupation a mystery: but what mystery there should be in hanging, if I should be hang'd, I cannot imagine.

Abhorson:
   Sir, it is a mystery.

Pompey:
   Proof?

Abhorson:
   Every true man's apparel fits your thief: if it be too little for your thief, your true man thinks it big enough; if it be too big for your theif, your thief thinks it little enough: so every true man's apparel fits your thief.

   (Enter Provost.*)*

Provost:
   Are you agreed?

Pompey:
   Sir, I will serve him; for I do find your hangman is a more penitent trade than your bawd,—he doth oftener ask forgiveness.

Provost:
   You, sirrah, provide your block and your axe to-morrow four o'clock.

Abhorson:
   Come on, bawd; I will instruct thee in my trade; follow.

Pompey:
   I do desire to learn, sir: and I hope, if you have occasion to use me for your own turn, you shall find me yare; for, truly, sir, for your kindness I owe you a good turn.

Provost:
    Call hither Barnardine and Claudio:

(Exeunt Pompey *and* Abhorson.*)*

    Th'one has my pity; not a jot the other,
    Being a murderer, though he were my brother.

(Enter Claudio.*)*

    Look, here's the warrant, Claudio, for thy death:
    'Tis now dead midnight, and by eight to-morrow
    Thou must be made immortal. Where's Barnardine?

Claudio:
    As fast lockt up in sleep as guiltless labour,
    When it lies starkly in the traveller's bones:
    He will not wake.

Provost:
              Who can do good on him?
    Well, go, prepare thyself.

(Knocking within.)

    But, hark, what noise?—
    Heaven give your spirits comfort!

(Exit Claudio.*)*

    By and by!—
    I hope it is some pardon or reprieve
    For the most gentle Claudio.

(Enter Duke *disguised as before.)*

    Welcome, father.

Duke:
    The best and wholesom'st spirits of the night
    Envelop you, good provost! Who call'd here of late?

Provost:
    None, since the curfew rung.

Duke:
    Not Isabel?

Provost:
            No.

Duke:
                They will, then, ere't be long.

Provost:
    What comfort is for Claudio?

Duke:
    There's some in hope.

Provost:
                It is a bitter deputy.

Duke:
    Not so, not so; his life is parallel'd
    Even with the stroke and line of his great justice:
    He doth with holy abstinence subdue
    That in himself which he spurs on his power
    To qualify in others: were he meal'd with that
    Which he corrects, then were he tyrannous;
    But this being so, he's just.

(Knocking within.)

    Now are they come.

(Exit Provost.)

    This is a gentle provost: seldom, when
    The steeled gaoler is the friend of men.

(Knocking within.)

    How now! what noise? That spirit's possest with haste
    That wounds th'unresisting postern with these strokes.

(Enter Provost.)

Provost:
>There he must stay until the officer
>Arise to let him in: he is call'd up.

Duke:
>Have you no countermand for Claudio yet,
>But he must die to-morrow?

Provost:
>   None, sir, none.

Duke:
>As near the dawning, provost, as it is,
>You shall hear more ere morning.

Provost:
>   Happily
>You something know; yet I believe there comes
>No countermand; no such example have we:
>Besides, upon the very siege of justice
>Lord Angelo hath to the public ear
>Profest the contrary.
>   *(Enter a* Messenger.*)*
>
>This is his lordship's man.

Duke:
>And here comes Claudio's pardon.

Messenger *(giving a paper):*
>My lord hath sent you this note; and by me this further charge,—that you swerve not from the smallest article of it, neither in time, matter, or other circumstance. Good morrow; for, as I take it, it is almost day.

Provost:
>I shall obey him.

>   *(Exit* Messenger.*)*

Duke *(aside):*
>This is his pardon, purchased by such sin
>For which the pardoner himself is in.

Hence hath offence his quick celerity,
　　　When it is borne in high authority:
　　　When vice makes mercy, mercy's so extended,
　　　That for the fault's love is th' offender friended.—
　　　Now, sir, what news?

Provost:
　　　I told you: Lord Angelo, belike thinking me remiss in mine office, awakens me with this unwonted putting-on; methinks strangely, for he hath not used it before.

Duke:
　　　Pray you, let's hear.

Provost (reads):
　　　Whatsoever you may hear to the contrary, let Claudio be executed by four of the clock; and in the afternoon Barnardine: for my better satisfaction, let me have Claudio's head sent me by five. Let this be duly perform'd; with a thought that more depends on it than we must yet deliver. Thus fail not to do your office, as you will answer it at your peril.
　　　What say you to this, sir?

Duke:
　　　What is that Barnardine who is to be executed in th'afternoon?

Provost:
　　　A Bohemian born, but here nursed up and bred; one that is a prisoner nine years old.

Duke:
　　　How came it that the absent duke had not either deliver'd him to his liberty or executed him? I have heard it was ever his manner to do so.

Provost:
　　　His friends still wrought reprieves for him: and, indeed, his fact, till now in the government of Lord Angelo, came not to an undoubtful proof.

Duke:
> It is now apparent?

Provost:
> Most manifest, and not denied by himself.

Duke:
> Hath he borne himself penitently in prison? How seems he to be touch'd?

Provost:
> A man that apprehends death no more dreadfully but as a drunken sleep; careless, reckless, and fearless of what's past, present, or to come; insensible of mortality, and desperately mortal.

Duke:
> He wants advice.

Provost:
> He will hear none: he hath evermore had the liberty of the prison; give him leave to escape hence, he would not: drunk many times a day, if not many days entirely drunk. We have very oft awaked him, as if to carry him to execution, and show'd him a seeming warrant for it: it hath not moved him at all.

Duke:
> More of him anon. There is written in your brow, provost, honesty and constancy: if I read it not truly, my ancient skill beguiles me; but, in the boldness of my cunning, I will lay myself in hazard. Claudio, whom here you have warrant to execute, is no greater forfeit to the law than Angelo, who hath sentenced him. To make you understand this in a manifested effect, I crave but four days' respite; for the which you are to do me both a present and a dangerous courtesy.

Provost:
> Pray, sir, in what?

Duke:
> In the delaying death.

Provost:
> Alack, how may I do it,—having the hour limited, and an express command, under penalty, to deliver his head in the view of Angelo? I may make my case as Claudio's, to cross this in the smallest.

Duke:
> By the vow of mine order I warrant you, if my instructions may be your guide. Let this Barnardine be this morning executed, and his head borne to Angelo.

Provost:
> Angelo hath seen them both, and will discover the favour.

Duke:
> O, death's a great disguiser; and you may add to it. Shave the head and tie the beard; and say it was the desire of the penitent to be so bared before his death: you know the course is common. If any thing fall to you upon this, more than thanks and good fortune, by the saint whom I profess, I will plead against it with my life.

Provost:
> Pardon me, good father; it is against my oath.

Duke:
> Were you sworn to the duke, or to the deputy?

Provost:
> To him, and to his substitutes.

Duke:
> You will think you have made no offence, if the duke avouch the justice of your dealing?

Provost:
> But what likelihood is in that?

Duke:
> Not a resemblance, but a certainty. Yet since I see you fearful that neither my coat, integrity, nor persuasion can with ease attempt you, I will go further than I meant, to

pluck all fears out of you. Look you, sir, here is the hand and seal of the duke: you know the character, I doubt not; and the signet is not strange to you.

Provost:
I know them both.

Duke:
The contents of this is the return of the duke; you shall anon over-read it at your pleasure; where you shall find, within these two days he will be here. This is a thing that Angelo knows not; for he this very day receives letters of strange tenour; perchance of the duke's death; perchance entering into some monastery; but, by chance, nothing of what is writ. Look, th'unfolding star calls up the shepherd. Put not yourself into amazement how these things should be: all difficulties are but easy when they are known. Call your executioner, and off with Barnardine's head: I will give him a present shrift, and advise him for a better place. Yet you are amazed; but this shall absolutely resolve you. Come away; it is almost clear dawn.

(Exeunt.)

(SCENE III.—Another room in the same. Enter Pompey.*)*

Pompey:
I am as well acquainted here as I was in our house of profession: one would think it were Mistress Overdone's own house, for here be many of her old customers. First, here's young Master Rash; he's in for a commodity of brown paper and old ginger, nine-score and seventeen pounds; of which he made five marks, ready money; marry, then ginger was not much in request, for the old women were all dead. Then is there here one Master Caper, at the suit of Master Three-pile the mercer, for some four suits of peach-colour'd satin, which now peaches him a beggar. Then have we here young Dizzy, and young Master Deep-vow, and Master Copper-spur, and Master Starve-lackey, the rapier-and-dagger-man, and young Drop-heir that kill'd lusty Pudding, and Master Forthright the tilter, and brave Master Shoe-tie the great traveller, and wild Half-can that stabb'd Pots, and, I

think, forty more, all great doers in our trade, and are now 'for the Lord's sake.'

(Enter Abhorson.)

Abhorson:
Sirrah, bring Barnardine hither.

Pompey:
Master Barnardine! you must rise and be hang'd, Master Barnardine!

Abhorson:
What, ho, Barnardine!

Barnardine *(within)*:
A pox o' your throats! Who makes that noise there? Who are you?

Pompey:
Your friends, sir; the hangman. You must be so good, sir, to rise and be put to death.

Barnardine *(within)*:
Away, you rogue, away! I am sleepy.

Abhorson:
Tell him he must awake, and that quickly too.

Pompey:
Pray, Master Barnardine, awake till you are executed, and sleep afterwards.

Abhorson:
Go in to him, and fetch him out.

Pompey:
He is coming, sir, he is coming; I hear his straw rustle.

Abhorson:
Is the axe upon the block, sirrah?

Pompey:
Very ready, sir.

(Enter Barnardine.)

Barnardine:
How now, Abhorson! what's the news with you?

Abhorson:
Truly, sir, I would desire you to clap into your prayers; for, look you, the warrant's come.

Barnardine:
You rogue, I have been drinking all night; I am not fitted for't.

Pompey:
O, the better, sir; for he that drinks all night, and is hang'd betimes in the morning, may sleep the sounder all the next day.

Abhorson:
Look you, sir; here comes your ghostly father: do we jest now, think you?

(Enter Duke disguised as before.)

Duke:
Sir, induced by my charity, and hearing how hastily you are to depart, I am come to advise you, comfort you, and pray with you.

Barnardine:
Friar, not I: I have been drinking hard all night, and I will have more time to prepare me, or they shall beat out my brains with billets: I will not consent to die this day, that's certain.

Duke:
O, sir, you must: and therefore I beseech you
Look forward on the journey you shall go.

Barnardine:
>I swear I will not die to-day for any man's persuasion.

Duke:
>But hear you,—

Barnardine:
>Not a word: if you have anything to say to me, come to my ward; from thence will not I to-day.

>>*(Exit.)*

Duke:
>Unfit to live or die: O gravel heart!—
>After him, fellows; bring him to the block.

>>*(Exeunt* Abhorson *and* Pompey.*)*

>>*(Enter* Provost.*)*

Provost:
>Now, sir, how do you find the prisoner?

Duke:
>A creature unprepared, unmeet for death;
>And to transport him in the mind he is
>Were damnable.

Provost:
>>Here in the prison, father,
>There died this morning of a cruel fever
>One Ragozine, a most notorious pirate,
>A man of Claudio's years; his beard and head
>Just of his colour. What if we do omit
>This reprobate till he were well inclined;
>And satisfy the deputy with the visage
>Of Ragozine, more like to Claudio?

Duke:
>O, 'tis an accident that heaven provides!
>Dispatch it presently; the hour draws on
>Prefixt by Angelo: see this be done,

And sent according to command; whiles I
Persuade this rude wretch willingly to die.

Provost:
This shall be done, good father, presently.
But Barnardine must die this afternoon:
And how shall we continue Claudio,
To save me from the danger that might come
If he were known alive?

Duke:
Let this be done,—put them in secret holds,
Both Barnardine and Claudio:
Ere twice the sun hath made his journal greeting
To th'under generation, you shall find
Your safety manifested.

Provost:
I am your free dependant.

Duke:
                        Quick, dispatch,
And send the head to Angelo.

(Exit Provost.)

Now will I write letters to Angelo,—
The provost, he shall bear them,—whose contents
Shall witness to him I am near at home,
And that, by great injunctions, I am bound
To enter publicly: him I'll desire
To meet me at the consecrated fount,
A league below the city; and from thence,
By cold gradation and well-balanced form,
We shall proceed with Angelo.

(Enter Provost with Ragozine's head.)

Provost:
Here is the head; I'll carry it myself.

Duke:
Convenient is it. Make a swift return;

For I would commune with you of such things
That want no ear but yours.

Provost:
                      I'll make all speed.

                              (Exit.)

Isabella *(within):*
Peace, ho, be here!

Duke:
The tongue of Isabel. She's come to know
If yet her brother's pardon be come hither:
But I will keep her ignorant of her good,
To make her heavenly comforts of despair,
When it is least expected.

                      (Enter Isabella.)

Isabella:
                    Ho, by your leave!

Duke:
Good morning to you, fair and gracious daughter.

Isabella:
The better, given by so holy a man.
Hath yet the deputy sent my brother's pardon?

Duke:
He hath released him, Isabel, from the world:
His head is off, and sent to Angelo.

Isabella:
Nay, but it is not so.

Duke:
It is no other: show your wisdom, daughter,
In your close patience.

Isabella:
>O, I will to him and pluck out his eyes!

Duke:
>You shall not be admitted to his sight.

Isabella:
>Unhappy Claudio! wretched Isabel!
>Injurious world! most damned Angelo!

Duke:
>This nor hurts him nor profits you a jot;
>Forbear it therefore; give your cause to heaven.
>Mark what I say, which you shall find
>By every syllable a faithful verity:
>The duke comes home to-morrow;—nay, dry your eyes;
>One of our covent, and his confessor,
>Gives me this instance: already he hath carried
>Notice to Escalus and Angelo;
>Who do prepare to meet him at the gates,
>There to give up their power. If you can, pace your wisdom
>In that good path that I would wish it go;
>And you shall have your bosom on this wretch,
>Grace of the duke, revenges to your heart,
>And general honour.

Isabella:
>   I am directed by you.

Duke:
>This letter, then, to Friar Peter give;
>'Tis that he sent me of the duke's return:
>Say, by this token, I desire his company
>At Mariana's house to-night. Her cause and yours
>I'll perfect him withal; and he shall bring you
>Before the duke; and to the head of Angelo
>Accuse him home and home. For my poor self,
>I am combined by a sacred vow,
>And shall be absent. Wend you with this letter:
>Command these fretting waters from your eyes
>With a light heart; trust not my holy order,
>If I pervert your course.—Who's here?

(Enter Lucio.)

Lucio:
Good even, friar: where's the provost?

Duke:
Not within, sir.

Lucio:
O pretty Isabella, I am pale at mine heart to see thine eyes so red: thou must be patient. I am fain to dine and sup with water and bran; I dare not for my head fill my belly; one fruitful meal would set me to't. But they say the duke will be here to-morrow. By my troth, Isabel, I loved thy brother: if the old fantastical duke of dark corners had been at home, he had lived.

(Exit Isabella.)

Duke:
Sir, the duke is marvellous little beholding to your reports; but the best is, he lives not in them.

Lucio:
Friar, thou know'st not the duke so well as I do: he's a better woodman than thou takest him for.

Duke:
Well, you'll answer this one day. Fare ye well.

Lucio:
Nay, tarry; I'll go along with thee: I can tell thee pretty tales of the duke.

Duke:
You have told me too many of him already, sir, if they be true, if not true, none were enough.

Lucio:
I was once before him for getting a wench with child.

Duke:
Did you such a thing?

Lucio:
    Yes, marry, did I: but I was fain to forswear it; they would else have married me to the rotten medlar.

Duke:
    Sir, your company is fairer than honest. Rest you well.

Lucio:
    By my troth, I'll go with thee to the lane's end: if bawdy talk offend you, we'll have very little of it. Nay, friar, I am a kind of burr: I shall stick.

                                                (*Exeunt.*)

(SCENE IV.—Angelo's *house. Enter* Angelo *and* Escalus.)

Escalus:
    Every letter he hath writ hath disvouch'd other.

Angelo:
    In most uneven and distracted manner. His actions show much like to madness: pray heaven his wisdom be not tainted! And why meet him at the gates, and redeliver our authorities there?

Escalus:
    I guess not.

Angelo:
    And why should we proclaim it in an hour before his entering, that if any crave redress of injustice, they should exhibit their petitions in the street?

Escalus:
    He shows his reason for that;—to have a dispatch of complaints, and to deliver us from devices hereafter, which shall then have no power to stand against us.

Angelo:
    Well, I beseech you, let it be proclaim'd:
    Betimes i'the morn I'll call you at your house:
    Give notice to such men of sort and suit
    As are to meet him.

Escalus:
                    I shall, sir. Fare you well.

Angelo:
    Good night.
                                (Exit Escalus.*)*

    This deed unshapes me quite, makes me unpregnant,
    And dull to all proceedings. A deflower'd maid!
    And by an eminent body that enforced
    The law against it! But that her tender shame
    Will not proclaim against her maiden loss,
    How might she tongue me! Yet reason dares her no;
    For my authority bears a credent bulk,
    That no particular scandal once can touch
    But it confounds the breather. He should have lived,
    Save that his riotous youth, with dangerous sense,
    Might in the times come to have ta'en revenge,
    By so receiving a dishonour'd life
    With ransom of such shame. Would yet he had lived!
    Alack, when once our grace we have forgot,
    Nothing goes right,—we would, and we would not!

                                      (Exit.)

(SCENE V.—Fields without the town. Enter Duke *in his own habit, and* Friar Peter.*)*

Duke:
    These letters at fit time deliver me:
                                  (Giving letters.)
    The provost knows our purpose and our plot.
    The matter being afoot, keep your instruction,
    And hold you ever to our special drift;
    Though sometimes you do blench from this to that,
    As cause doth minister. Go call at Flavius' house,
    And tell him where I stay: give the like notice
    To Valentinus, Rowland, and to Crassus,
    And bid them bring the trumpets to the gate;
    But send me Flavius first.

Friar Peter:
>It shall be speeded well.

>>*(Exit.)*

>>*(Enter Varrius.)*

Duke:
>I thank thee, Varrius; thou hast made good haste:
>Come, we will walk. There's other of our friends
>Will greet us here anon, my gentle Varrius.

>>*(Exeunt.)*

(SCENE VI.—Street near the city-gate. Enter Isabella and Mariana.)

Isabella:
>To speak so indirectly I am loth:
>I would say the truth; but to accuse him so,
>That is your part: yet I am advised to do it;
>He says, to vailful purpose.

Mariana:
>>Be ruled by him.

Isabella:
>Besides, he tells me that, if peradventure
>He speak against me on the adverse side,
>I should not think it strange; for 'tis a physic
>That's bitter to sweet end.

Mariana:
>I would Friar Peter,—

Isabella:
>>O, peace! the friar is come.

>>*(Enter Friar Peter.)*

Friar Peter:
>Come, I have found you out a stand most fit,
>Where you may have such vantage on the duke,

He shall not pass you. Twice have the trumpets sounded;
The generous and gravest citizens
Have hent the gates, and very near upon
The duke is ent'ring: therefore, hence, away!

(Exeunt.)

(ACT V. SCENE I.—A public place near the city-gate. Mariana *veiled,* Isabella, *and* Friar Peter *at their stand. Enter at opposite doors,* Duke *in his own habit,* Varrius, Lords; Angelo, Escalus, Lucio, Provost, Officers, *and* Citizens.*)*

Duke:
My very worthy cousin, fairly met:—
Our old and faithful friend, we are glad to see you.

Angelo and Escalus:
Happy return be to your royal grace!

Duke:
Many and hearty thankings to you both.
We have made inquiry of you; and we hear
Such goodness of your justice, that our soul
Cannot but yield you forth to public thanks,
Forerunning more requital.

Angelo:
You make my bonds still greater.

Duke:
O, your desert speaks loud; and I should wrong it,
To lock it in the wards of covert bosom,
When it deserves, with characters of brass,
A forted residence 'gainst the tooth of time
And razure of oblivion. Give me your hand,
And let the subject see, to make them know
That outward courtesies would fain proclaim
Favours that keep within.—Come, Escalus;
You must walk by us on our other hand:—
And good supports are you.

(Friar Peter and Isabella come forward.)

Friar Peter:
>Now is your time: speak loud, and kneel before him.

Isabella:
>Justice, O royal duke! Vail your regard
>Upon a wrong'd, I would fain have said, a maid!
>O worthy prince, dishonour not your eye
>By throwing it on any other object
>Till you have heard me in my true complaint,
>And given me justice, justice, justice, justice!

Duke:
>Relate your wrongs; in what? by whom? be brief.
>Here is Lord Angelo shall give you justice.
>Reveal yourself to him.

Isabella:
>>O worthy duke,
>You bid me seek redemption of the devil:
>Hear me yourself; for that which I must speak
>Must either punish me, not being believed,
>Or wring redress from you: hear me, O, hear me, here!

Angelo:
>My lord, her wits, I fear me, are not firm:
>She hath been a suitor to me for her brother
>Cut off by course of justice,—

Isabella:
>>By course of justice!

Angelo:
>And she will speak most bitterly and strange.

Isabella:
>Most strange, but yet most truly, will I speak:
>That Angelo's forsworn; is it not strange?
>That Angelo's a murderer; is't not strange?
>That Angelo is an adulterous thief,
>An hypocrite, a virgin-violator;
>Is it not strange and strange?

Duke:
                      Nay, it is ten times strange.

Isabella:
    It is not truer he is Angelo
    Than this is all as true as it is strange:
    Nay, it is ten times true; for truth is truth
    To th'end of reck'ning.

Duke:
                      Away with her!—Poor soul,
    She speaks this in th'infirmity of sense.

Isabella:
    O prince, I conjure thee, as thou believest
    There is another comfort than this world,
    That thou neglect me not, with that opinion
    That I am touch'd with madness! Make not impossible
    That which but seems unlike: 'tis not impossible
    But one, the wicked'st caitiff on the ground,
    May seem as shy, as grave, as just, as absolute
    As Angelo; even so may Angelo,
    In all his dressings, characts, titles, forms,
    Be an arch-villian; believe it, royal prince:
    If he be less, he's nothing; but he's more,
    Had I more name for badness.

Duke:
                      By mine honesty,
    If she be mad,—as I believe no other,—
    Her madness hath the oddest frame of sense,
    Such a dependency of thing on thing,
    As e'er I heard in madness.

Isabella:
                      O gracious duke,
    Harp not on that; nor do not banish reason
    For inequality; but let your reason serve
    To make the truth appear where it seems hid,
    And hide the false seems true.

Duke:
                      Many that are not mad

>   Have, sure, more lack of reason.—What would you say?

Isabella:
>   I am the sister of one Claudio,
>   Condemn'd upon the act of fornication
>   To lose his head; condemn'd by Angelo:
>   I, in probation of a sisterhood,
>   Was sent to by my brother; one Lucio
>   As then the messenger,—

Lucio:
>   That's I, an't like your grace:
>   I came to her from Claudio, and desired her
>   To try her gracious fortune with Lord Angelo
>   For her poor brother's pardon.

Isabella:
>   That's he indeed.

Duke:
>   You were not bid to speak.

Lucio:
>   No, my good lord;
>   Nor wish'd to hold my peace.

Duke:
>   I wish you now, then;
>   Pray you, take note of it: and when you have
>   A business for yourself, pray heaven you then
>   Be perfect.

Lucio:
>   I warrant your honour.

Duke:
>   The warrant's for yourself; take heed to't.

Isabella:
>   This gentleman told somewhat of my tale,—

Lucio:
    Right.

Duke:
    It may be right; but you are i'the wrong
    To speak before your time.—Proceed

Isabella:
                              I went
    To this pernicious caitiff deputy,—

Duke:
    That's somewhat madly spoken.

Isabella:
                            Pardon it;
    The phrase is to the matter.

Duke:
    Mended again. The matter;—proceed.

Isabella:
    In brief,—to set the needless process by,
    How I persuaded, how I pray'd, and kneel'd,
    How he refell'd me, and how I replied,—
    For this was of much length,—the vile conclusion
    I now begin with grief and shame to utter;
    He would not, but by gift of my chaste body
    To his concupiscible intemperate lust,
    Release my brother; and, after much debatement,
    My sisterly remorse confutes mine honour,
    And I did yield to him; but the next morn betimes,
    His purpose surfeiting, he sends a warrant
    For my poor brother's head.

Duke:
                  This is most likely!

Isabella:
    O, that it were as like as it is true!

Duke:
>By heaven, fond wretch, thou know'st not what thou
>>speak'st.
>
>Or else thou art suborn'd against his honour
>In hateful practice. First, his integrity
>Stands without blemish. Next, it imports no reason
>That with such vehemency he should pursue
>Faults proper to himself: if he had so offended,
>He would have weigh'd thy brother by himself,
>And not have cut him off. Some one hath set you on:
>Confess the truth, and say by whose advice
>Thou camest here to complain.

Isabella:
>   And is this all?
>Then, O you blessed ministers above,
>Keep me in patience, and with ripen'd time
>Unfold the evil which is here wrapt up
>In countenance!—Heaven shield your grace from woe,
>As I, thus wrong'd, hence unbelieved go!

Duke:
>I know you'ld fain be gone.—An officer!
>To prison with her!—Shall we thus permit
>A blasting and a scandalous breath to fall
>On him so near us? This needs must be a practice.—
>Who knew of your intent and coming hither?

Isabella:
>One that I would were here, Friar Lodowick.

Duke:
>A ghostly father, belike.—Who knows that Lodowick?

Lucio:
>My lord, I know him; 'tis a meddling friar;
>I do not like the man: had he been lay, my lord,
>For certain words he spake against your grace
>In your retirement, I had swinged him soundly.

Duke:
>Words against me! this' a good friar, belike!

       And to set on this wretched woman here
       Against our substitute!—Let this friar be found.

Lucio:
       But yesternight, my lord, she and that friar,
       I saw them at the prison: a saucy friar,
       A very scurvy fellow.

Friar Peter:
                   Bless'd be your royal grace!
       I have stood by, my lord, and I have heard
       Your royal ear abused. First, hath this woman
       Most wrongfully accused your substitute,
       Who is as free from touch or soil with her
       As she from one ungot.

Duke:
                   We did believe no less.
       Know you that Friar Lodowick that she speaks of?

Friar Peter:
       I know him for a man divine and holy;
       Not scurvy, nor a temporary meddler,
       As he's reported by this gentleman;
       And, on my trust, a man that never yet
       Did, as he vouches, misreport your grace.

Lucio:
       My lord, most villainously; believe it.

Friar Peter:
       Well, he in time may come to clear himself;
       But at this instant he is sick, my lord,
       Of a strange fever. Upon his mere request,—
       Being come to knowledge that there was complaint
       Intended 'gainst Lord Angelo,—came I hither,
       To speak, as from his mouth, what he doth know
       Is true and false; and what he, with his oath
       And all probation, will make up full clear,
       Whensoever he's convented. First, for this woman,—
       To justify this worthy nobleman,
       So vulgarly and personally accused,—

>Her shall you hear disproved to her eyes,
>Till she herself confess it.

Duke:
>Good friar, let's hear it.

(Isabella is carried off guarded; and Mariana comes forward.)

>Do you not smile at this, Lord Angelo?—
>O heaven, the vanity of wretched fools!—
>Give us some seats.—Come, cousin Angelo;
>In this I'll be impartial; be you judge
>Of your own cause.—Is this the witness, friar?
>First, let her show her face, and after speak.

Mariana:
>Pardon, my lord; I will not show my face
>Until my husband bid me.

Duke:
>What, are you married?

Mariana:
>No, my lord.

Duke:
>Are you a maid?

Mariana:
>No, my lord.

Duke:
>A widow, then?

Mariana:
>Neither, my lord.

Duke:
>Why, you are nothing, then:—neither maid, widow, nor wife?

Lucio:
>My lord, she may be a punk; for many of them are neither maid, widow, nor wife.

Duke:
>Silence that fellow: I would he had some cause
>To prattle for himself.

Lucio:
>Well, my lord.

Mariana:
>My lord, I do confess I ne'er was married;
>And I confess, besides, I am no maid:
>I've known my husband: yet my husband knows not
>That ever he knew me.

Lucio:
>He was drunk, then, my lord: it can be no better.

Duke:
>For the benefit of silence, would thou wert so too!

Lucio:
>Well, my lord.

Duke:
>This is no witness for Lord Angelo.

Mariana:
>Now I come to't, my lord:
>She that accuses him of fornication,
>In self-same manner doth accuse my husband;
>And charges him, my lord, with such a time
>When I'll depose I had him in mine arms
>With all th'effect of love.

Angelo:
>Charges she moe than me?

Mariana:
>>Not that I know.

Duke:
    No? you say your husband.

Mariana:
    Why, just, my lord, and that is Angelo,
    Who thinks he knows that he ne'er knew my body,
    But knows he thinks that he knows Isabel's.

Angelo:
    This is a strange abuse.—Let's see thy face.

Mariana:
    My husband bids me; now I will unmask.
    This is that face, thou cruel Angelo,
                    (Unveiling.)
    Which once thou sworest was worth the looking on;
    This is the hand which, with a vow'd contract,
    Was fast belockt in thine; this is the body
    That took away the match from Isabel,
    And did supply thee at thy garden-house
    In her imagined person.

Duke:
              Know you this woman?

Lucio:
    Carnally, she says.

Duke:
              Sirrah, no more!

Lucio:
    Enough, my lord.

Angelo:
    My lord, I must confess I know this woman:
    And five years since there was some speech of marriage
    Betwixt myself and her; which was broke off,
    Partly for that her promised proportions
    Came short of composition; but in chief
    For that her reputation was disvalued
    In levity: since which time of five years

I never spake with her, saw her, nor heard from her,
Upon my faith and honour.

Mariana:
Noble prince,
As there comes light from heaven and words from breath,
As there is sense in truth and truth in virtue,
I am affianced this man's wife as strongly
As words could make up vows: and, my good lord,
But Tuesday night last gone, in's garden-house,
He knew me as a wife. As this is true,
Let me in safety raise me from my knees;
Or else for ever be confixed here,
A marble monument!

Angelo:
I did but smile till now;
Now, good my lord, give me the scope of justice;
My patience here is touch'd. I do perceive
These poor informal women are no more
But instruments of some more mightier member
That sets them on: let me have way, my lord,
To find this practice out.

Duke:
Ay, with my heart;
And punish them to your height of pleasure.—
Thou foolish friar; and thou pernicious woman,
Compact with her that's gone, think'st thou thy oaths,
Though they would swear down each particular saint,
Were testimonies against his worth and credit,
That's seal'd in approbation?—You, Lord Escalus,
Sit with my cousin; lend him your kind pains
To find out this abuse, whence 'tis derived.—
There is another friar that set them on;
Let him be sent for.

Friar Peter:
Would he were here, my lord! for he, indeed,
Hath set the women on to this complaint:
Your provost knows the place where he abides,
And he may fetch him.

Duke:
>Go do it instantly.

>>*(Exit Provost.)*

>And you, my noble and well-warranted cousin,
>Whom it concerns to hear this matter forth,
>Do with your injuries as seems you best,
>In any chastisement: I for a while will leave you;
>But stir not till you have well determined
>Upon these slanderers.

Escalus:
>My lord, we'll do it throughly.

>>*(Exit Duke.)*

>Signior Lucio, did not you say you knew that
>Friar Lodowick to be a dishonest person?

Lucio:
>*Cucullus non facit monachum:* honest in nothing but in his clothes; and one that hath spoke most villainous speeches of the duke.

Escalus:
>We shall entreat you to abide here till he come, and enforce them against him: we shall find this friar a notable fellow.

Lucio:
>As any in Vienna, on my word.

Escalus:
>Call that same Isabel here once again: I would speak with her.

>>*(Exit an Attendant.)*

>—Pray you, my lord, give me leave to question; you shall see how I'll handle her.

Lucio:
>Not better than he, by her own report.

Escalus:
>Say you?

Lucio:
>Marry, sir, I think, if you handled her privately, she would sooner confess: perchance, publicly, she'll be ashamed.

Escalus:
>I will go darkly to work with her.

Lucio:
>That's the way; for women are light at midnight.

>>*(Enter* Officers *with* Isabella.*)*

Escalus *(to Isabella):*
>Come on, mistress: here's a gentlewoman denies all that you have said.

Lucio:
>My lord, here comes the rascal I spoke of; here with the provost.

Escalus:
>In very good time:—speak not you to him till we call upon you.

Lucio:
>Mum.

>>*(Enter* Duke *disguised as a friar, and* Provost.*)*

Escalus:
>Come, sir: did you set these women on to slander Lord Angelo? they have confess'd you did.

Duke:
>'Tis false.

Escalus:
>How! know you where you are?

Duke:
>Respect to your great place! and let the devil

Be sometime honour'd for his burning throne!—
Where is the duke? 'tis he should hear me speak.

Escalus:
The duke's in us; and we will hear you speak:
Look you speak justly.

Duke:
Boldly, at least.—But, O, poor souls,
Come you to seek the lamb here of the fox?
Good night to your redress! Is the duke gone?
Then is your cause gone too. The duke's unjust,
Thus to retort your manifest appeal,
And put your trial in the villian's mouth
Which here you come to accuse.

Lucio:
This is the rascal; this is he I spoke of.

Escalus:
Why, thou unreverend and unhallow'd friar,
Is't not enough thou hast suborn'd these women
To accuse this worthy man, but, in foul mouth,
And in the witness of his proper ear,
To call him villain? and then to glance from him
To th'duke himself, to tax him with injustice?—
Take him hence; to th'rack with him!—We'll touse you
Joint by joint, but we will know his purpose.—
What, 'unjust'?

Duke:
              Be not so hot; the duke
Dare no more stretch this finger of mine than he
Dare rack his own: his subject am I not,
Nor here provincial. My business in this state
Made me a looker-on here in Vienna,
Where I have seen corruption boil and bubble
Till it o'er-run the stew; laws for all faults,
But faults so countenanced, that the strong statutes
Stand like forfeits in a barber's shop,
As much in mock as mark.

Escalus:
>Slander to th'state!—Away with him to prison!

Angelo:
>What can you vouch against him, Signior Lucio?
>Is this the man that you did tell us of?

Lucio:
>'Tis he, my lord.—Come hither, goodman baldpate: do you know me?

Duke:
>I remember you, sir, by the sound of your voice:
>I met you at the prison, in the absence of the duke.

Lucio:
>O, did you so? And do you remember what you said of the duke?

Duke:
>Most notedly, sir.

Lucio:
>Do you so, sir? And was the duke a fleshmonger, a fool, and a coward, as you then reported him to be?

Duke:
>You must, sir, change persons with me, ere you make that my report; you, indeed, spoke so of him; and much more, much worse.

Lucio:
>O thou damnable fellow! Did not I pluck thee by the nose for thy speeches?

Duke:
>I protest I love the duke as I love myself.

Angelo:
>Hark, how the villain would close now, after his treasonable abuses!

Escalus:
Such a fellow is not to be talk'd withal.—Away with him to prison!—Where is the provost?—Away with him to prison! lay bolts enough upon him: let him speak no more.—Away with those giglots too, and with the other confederate companion!

Duke *(to the Provost):*
Stay, sir; stay awhile;

Angelo:
What, resists he?—Help him, Lucio.

Lucio:
Come, sir; come, sir; come sir, foh, sir! Why, you bald-pated, lying rascal, you must be hooded, must you? Show your knave's visage, with a pox to you! show your sheep-biting face, and be hang'd an hour! Will't not off?

(Pulls off the friar's hood, and discovers the Duke.*)*

Duke:
Thou art the first knave that e'er madest a duke.—
First, provost, let me bail these gentle three.—
(To Lucio.*)* Sneak not away, sir; for the friar and you
Must have a word anon.—Lay hold on him.

Lucio:
This may prove worse than hanging.

Duke *(to Escalus):*
What you have spoke I pardon: sit you down:
We'll borrow place of him. *(To* Angelo.*)* Sir, by your leave.
Hast thou or word, or wit, or impudence,
That yet can do thee office? If thou hast,
Rely upon it till my tale be heard,
And hold no longer out.

Angelo:
     O my dread lord,
I should be guiltier than my guiltiness,
To think I can be undiscernible,

When I perceive your grace, like power divine,
Hath look'd upon my passes. Then, good prince,
No longer session hold upon my shame,
But let my trial be mine own confession:
Immediate sentence then, and sequent death,
Is all the grace I beg.

Duke:
                        Come hither, Mariana.—
Say, wast thou e'er contracted to this woman?

Angelo:
    I was, my lord.

Duke:
    Go take her hence, and marry her instantly.—
Do you the office, friar; which consummate,
Return him here again.—Go with him, provost.

(Exeunt Angelo, Mariana, Friar, Peter, and Provost.)

Escalus:
    My lord, I am more amazed at his dishonour
Than at the strangeness of it.

Duke:
                        Come hither, Isabel.
Your friar is now your prince: as I was then
Advertising and holy to your business,
Not changing heart with habit, I am still
Attorney'd at your service.

Isabella:
                        O, give me pardon,
That I, your vassal, have employ'd and pain'd
Your unknown sovereignty!

Duke:
                      You are pardon'd, Isabel:
And now, dear maid, be you as free to us.
Your brother's death, I know, sits at your heart;
And you may marvel why I obscured myself,

Labouring to save his life, and would not rather
Make rash remonstrance of my hidden power
Than let him so be lost. O most kind maid,
It was the swift celerity of his death,
Which I did think with slower foot came on,
That brain'd my purpose:—but peace be with him!
That life is better life, past fearing death,
Than that which lives to fear: make it your comfort,
So happy is your brother.

Isabella:
                    I do, my lord.

    (Enter Angelo, Mariana, Friar Peter, *and* Provost.*)*

Duke:
For this new-married man, approaching here,
Whose salt imagination yet hath wrong'd
Your well-defended honour, you must pardon
For Mariana's sake: but as he adjudged your brother,—
Being criminal, in double violation
Of sacred chastity, and of promise-breach
Thereon dependent, for your brother's life,—
The very mercy of the law cries out
Most audible, even from his proper tongue,
'An Angelo for Claudio, death for death!'
Haste still pays haste, and leisure answers leisure;
Like doth quit like, and *Measure* still *for Measure.*
Then, Angelo, thy fault thus manifested,—
Which, though thou wouldst deny, denies thee vantage,—
We do condemn thee to the very block
Where Claudio stoop'd to death, and with like haste.—
Away with him!

Mariana:
              O my most gracious lord,
I hope you will not mock me with a husband.

Duke:
It is your husband mock'd you with a husband.
Consenting to the safeguard of your honour,
I thought your marriage fit; else imputation,

        For that he knew you, might reproach your life,
        And choke your good to come; for his possessions,
        Although by confiscation they are ours,
        We do instate and widow you withal,
        To buy you a better husband.

Mariana:
                                    O my dear lord,
        I crave no other, nor no better man.

Duke:
        Never crave him; we are definitive.

Mariana:
        Gentle my liege,—   *(Kneeling.)*

Duke:
                        You do but lose your labour.—
        Away with him to death! *(To* Lucio.*)* Now, sir, to you.

Mariana:
        O my good lord!—Sweet Isabel, take my part;
        Lend me your knees, and all my life to come
        I'll lend you all my life to do you service.

Duke:
        Against all sense you do importune her:
        Should she kneel down in mercy of this fact,
        Her brother's ghost his paved bed would break,
        And take her hence in horror.

Mariana:
                                    Isabel,
        Sweet Isabel, do yet but kneel by me;
        Hold up your hands, say nothing,—I'll speak all.
        They say, best men are moulded out of faults;
        And, for the most, become much more the better
        For being a little bad: so may my husband.
        O Isabel, will you not lend a knee?

Duke:
        He dies for Claudio's death.

Isabella:
> Most bounteous sir,   *(Kneeling.)*
> Look, if it please you, on this man condemn'd,
> As if my brother lived: I partly think
> A due sincerity govern'd his deeds,
> Till he did look on me: since it is so,
> Let him not die. My brother had but justice,
> In that he did the thing for which he died:
> For Angelo,
> His act did not o'ertake his bad intent;
> And must be buried but as an intent
> That perish'd by the way: thoughts are no subjects,
> Intents but merely thoughts.

Mariana:
> Merely, my lord.

Duke:
> Your suit's unprofitable; stand up, I say.—
> I have bethought me of another fault.—
> Provost, how came it Claudio was beheaded
> At an unusual hour?

Provost:
> It was commanded so.

Duke:
> Had you a special warrant for the deed?

Provost:
> No, my good lord; it was by private message.

Duke:
> For which I do discharge you of your office:
> Give up your keys.

Provost:
> Pardon me, noble lord:
> I thought it was a fault, but knew it not;
> Yet did repent me, after more advice:
> For testimony whereof, one in the prison,
> That should by private order else have died,
> I have reserved alive.

Duke:
> What's he?

Provost:
> His name is Barnardine.

Duke:
> I would thou hadst done so by Claudio.—
> Go fetch him hither; let me look upon him.

> > (*Exit* Provost.)

Escalus:
> I am sorry, one so learned and so wise
> As you, Lord Angelo, have still appear'd,
> Should slip so grossly, both in the heat of blood,
> And lack of temper'd judgement afterward.

Angelo:
> I am sorry that such sorrow I procure:
> And so deep sticks it in my penitent heart,
> That I crave death more willingly than mercy;
> 'Tis my deserving, and I do entreat it.

(*Enter* Provost, *with* Barnardine, Claudio, *muffled, and* Juliet.)

Duke:
> Which is that Barnardine?

Provost:
> This, my lord.

Duke:
> There was a friar told me of this man.—
> Sirrah, thou art said to have a stubborn soul,
> That apprehends no further than this world,
> And squarest thy life according. Thou'rt condemn'd:
> But, for those earthly faults, I quit them all;
> And pray thee take this mercy to provide
> For better times to come.—Friar, advise him;
> I leave him to your hand.—What muffled fellow's that?

Provost:
>This is another prisoner that I saved,
>Who should have died when Claudio lost his head;
>As like almost to Claudio as himself.

>>*(Unmuffles Claudio.)*

Duke *(to Isabella):*
>If he be like your brother, for his sake
>Is he pardon'd; and, for your lovely sake,
>Give me your hand, and say you will be mine,
>He is my brother too: but fitter time for that.
>By this Lord Angelo perceives he's safe;
>Methinks I see a quick'ning in his eye.—
>Well, Angelo, your evil quits you well:
>Look that you love your wife; her worth worth yours.—
>I find an apt remission in myself;
>And yet here's one in place I cannot pardon.—

>*(to Lucio):*
>You, sirrah, that knew me for a fool, a coward,
>One all of luxury, an ass, a madman;
>Wherein have I so deserved of you,
>That you extole me thus?

Lucio:
>Faith, my lord, I spoke it but according to the trick. If you will hang me for it, you may; but I had rather it would please you I might be whipt.

Duke:
>Whipt first, sir, and hang'd after.—
>Proclaim it, provost, round about the city,
>If any woman wrong'd by this lewd fellow,—
>As I have heard him swear himself there's one
>Whom he begot with child,—let her appear,
>And he shall marry her: the nuptial finish'd,
>Let him be whipt and hang'd.

Lucio:
>I beseech your highness, do not marry me to a whore! Your highness said even now, I made you a duke: good my lord,

do not recompense me in making me a cuckold.

Duke:
> Upon mine honour, thou shalt marry her.
> Thy slanders I forgive; and therewithal
> Remit thy other forfeits.—Take him to prison;
> And see our pleasure herein executed.

Lucio:
> Marrying a punk, my lord, is pressing to death, whipping, and hanging.

Duke:
> Slandering a prince deserves it.—

(Exeunt Officers with Lucio.)

> She, Claudio, that you wrong'd, look you restore.—
> Joy to you, Mariana!—Love her, Angelo:
> I have confess'd her, and I know her virtue.—
> Thanks, good friend Escalus, for thy much goodness:
> There's more behind that is more gratulate.—
> Thanks, provost, for thy care and secrecy:
> We shall employ thee in a worthier place.—
> Forgive him, Angelo, that brought you home
> The head of Ragozine for Claudio's:
> Th'offence pardons itself.—Dear Isabel,
> I have a motion much imports your good;
> Whereto if you'll a willing ear incline,
> What's mine is yours, and what is yours is mine.—
> So, bring us to our palace; where we'll show
> What's yet behind, that's meet you all should know.

(Exeunt.)

Comments and Questions

1. Compare Antigone with Isabella. Like Antigone, Isabella is prepared to give up her life for her brother, but she will not yield her virginity. Would Antigone have sacrificed her virginity to Creon if Creon had sanctioned a legal burial of Polyneices? What is the role of Divine law in *Antigone* and *Measure for Measure*? Compare Claudio with George Barnwell paying particular attention to Claudio's appeal to Isabella to let him live, followed by his almost immediate begging of her pardon for his selfish request. Compare Isabella with Portia. Regardless of the outcome of each play, which woman uses rhetoric and persuasion to her best advantage? Compare and contrast the acts of Claudio with the acts of Juliet. Juliet takes more blame for the act of her pregnancy than she attributes to Claudio. Why is she not subjected to the same statute as Claudio?

2. Much of *Measure for Measure* is concerned with laws that are on the books but which have not been enforced for many years. Are such laws really laws? In our society what would happen if some of the statutes that had not been enforced for decades were suddenly enforced? Does the public deserve notice that old laws, once enforced, but now forgotten, are to be enforced again? Why does Duke Vincentio need to revive these statutes? Why does he leave the job to Angelo rather than enforce them himself?

3. As you read *Measure for Measure* consider the articulated purposes of punishment. For instance Claudio asks: "Fellow, why dost thou show me thus to th' world? Bear me to prison, where I am committed." Lucio tells Isabella that Lord Angelo chose her brother's act, "[t]o make him an example": and Angelo states that "[t]hose many had not dared to do that evil, [i]f that the first that did th' edict infringe [h]ad answer'd for his deed." Isabella argues that we should condemn the fault and not the actor of it. If we subscribe to her theory, how would we need to change our modern courts, both civil and criminal? Angelo also says that justice ensures that the condemned person does not live to commit another wrong. What theory of punishment does he favor?

4. There is much discussion throughout the play of the role of a judge and there is mention of the role of the jury. How do Angelo and Duke Vincentio differ on the role of a judge? Should a judge be in a position of judging others of a crime which he has himself committed? If not, then how should we school and choose our judges? Angelo argues that a jury of twelve may "have a thief or two." If a jury of our peers is guaranteed by our constitution, should that include people who have committed similar crimes to the accused?

5. Many of our statutes require an element of *mens rea*, that is a finding that the accused had a certain mental state, before being found guilty of the crimes of which he is charged. Isabella states that her brother "did the thing for which he died," whereas Angelo only had the intent. Should we punish thoughts without deeds? What about the fact that even if Angelo did not make love to Isabella, he did make love to Mariana believing she was Isabella? Did he commit the same crime as Claudio? Or did the fact that he thought Mariana was Isabella remove the intent to sleep with Mariana? If so, could the act still be punished under Isabella's theories of intention and carrying out a deed?

Philip Massinger

The Fatal Dowry

Dramatis Personæ

Rochfort, *ex-premier president of the parliament of Dijon.*
Charalois, *a noble gentleman, son to the deceased marshal.*
Romont, *a brave officer, friend to Charalois.*
Novall Senior, *premier president of the parliament of Dijon.*
Novall Junior, *his son, in love with Beaumelle.*
Du Croy, *president of the parliament of Dijon.*
Charmi, *an advocate.*
Beaumont, *secretary to Rochfort.*
Pontalier, *friend of Novall Junior.*
Malotin, *friend of Novall Junior.*
Liladam, *a parasite, dependent on Novall Junior.*
Aymer, *a singer, and keeper of a music-house, also dependent on Novall Junior.*
Advocates.
Three creditors.
A Priest.
Tailor.
Barber.
Perfumer.
Page.

Beaumelle, *daughter to Rochfort.*
Florimel, *servant to Beaumelle.*
Bellapert, *servant to Beaumelle and secret agent of Novall Junior.*

Presidents, Captains, Soldiers, Mourners, Gaoler, Bailiffs, Servants.

SCENE.—*Dijon.*

(ACT I. SCENE I.—A street before the Court of Justice. Enter Charlois *with a paper,* Romont, *and* Charmi.*)*

Charmi:
>Sir, I may move the court to serve your will;
>But therein shall both wrong you and myself.

Romont:
>Why think you so, sir?

Charmi:
>'Cause I am familiar
>With what will be their answer: they will say,
>'Tis against law; and argue me of ignorance,
>For offering them the motion.

Romont:
>You know not, sir,
>How, in this cause, they may dispense with law;
>And therefore frame not you their answer for them,
>But do your parts.

Charmi:
>I love the cause so well,
>As I could run the hazard of a check for't.

Romont:
>From whom?

Charmi:
>Some of the bench, that watch to give it,
>More than to do the office that they sit for:
>But give me, sir, my fee.

Romont:
>Now you are noble.

(Gives him his purse.)

Charmi:
> I shall deserve this better yet, in giving
> My lord some counsel, if he please to hear it,
> Than I shall do with pleading.

Romont:
> What may it be, sir?

Charmi:
> That it would please his lordship, as the presidents
> And counsellors of court come by, to stand
> Here, and but shew himself, and to some one
> Or two, make his request:—there is a minute,
> When a man's presence speaks in his own cause,
> More than the tongues of twenty advocates.

Romont:
> I have urged that.

(Enter Rochfort *and* Du Croy.*)*

Charmi:
> Their lordships here are coming,
> I must go get me a place. You'll find me in court,
> And at your service.

(Exit.)

Romont:
> Now, put on your spirits.

Du Croy:
> The ease that you prepare yourself, my lord,
> In giving up the place you hold in court,
> Will prove, I fear, a trouble in the state,
> And that no slight one.

Rochfort:
> Pray you, sir, no more.

Romont:
> Now, sir, lose not this offer'd means their looks,

Fix'd on you with a pitying earnestness,
Invite you to demand their furtherance
To your good purpose:—this such a dulness,
So foolish and untimely, as—

Du Croy:
You know him?

Rochfort:
I do; and much lament the sudden fall
Of his brave house. It is young Charalois,
Son to the marshal, from whom he inherits
His fame and virtues only.

Romont:
Ha! they name you.

Du Croy:
His father died in prison two days since.

Rochfort:
Yes, to the shame of this ungrateful state;
That such a master in the art of war,
So noble, and so highly meriting
From this forgetful country, should, for want
Of means to satisfy his creditors
The sums he took up for the general good,
Meet with an end so infamous.

Romont:
Dare you ever
Hope for like opportunity?

Du Croy:
My good lord!

(They salute him as they pass by.)

Rochfort:
My wish bring comfort to you!

Du Croy:
>The time calls us.

Rochfort:
>Good morrow, colonel!

>>*(Exeunt Rochfort and Du Croy.)*

Romont:
>This obstinate spleen,
>You think, becomes your sorrow, and sorts well
>With your black suits; but, grant me wit or judgment,
>And, by the freedom of an honest man,
>And a true friend to boot, I swear 'tis shameful.
>And therefore flatter not yourself with hope,
>Your sable habit, with the hat and cloak,
>No, though the ribands help, have power to work them
>To what you would: for those that had no eyes
>To see the great acts of your father, will not,
>From any fashion sorrow can put on,
>Be taught to know their duties.

Charalois:
>If they will not,
>They are too old to learn, and I too young
>To give them counsel; since, if they partake
>The understanding and the hearts of men,
>They will prevent my words and tears: if not,
>What can persuasion, though made eloquent
>With grief, work upon such as have changed natures
>With the most savage beast? Blest, blest be ever
>The memory of that happy age, when justice
>Had no guards to keep off wrong'd innocence
>From flying to her succours, and, in that,
>Assurance of redress! where now, Romont,
>The damn'd with more ease may ascend from hell,
>Than we arrive at her. One Cereberus there
>Forbids the passage, in our courts a thousand,
>As loud and fertile-headed; and the client
>That wants the sops to fill their ravenous throats,
>Must hope for no access: why should I, then,
>Attempt impossibilities; you, friend, being

Too well acquainted with my dearth of means
To make my entrance that way?

Romont:
Would I were not!
But, sir, you have a cause, a cause so just,
Of such necessity, not to be deferr'd,
As would compel a maid, whose foot was never
Set o'er her father's threshold, nor within
The house where she was born, ever spake word
Which was not usher'd with pure virgin blushes,
To drown the tempest of a pleader's tongue,
And force corruption to give back the hire
It took against her. Let examples move you.
You see men great in birth, esteem, and fortune,
Rather than lose a scruple of their right,
Fawn basely upon such, whose gowns put off,
They would disdain for servants.

Charalois:
And to these
Can I become a suitor?

Romont:
Without loss:
Would you consider, that, to gain their favours,
Our chastest dames put off their modesties,
Soldiers forget their honours, usurers
Make sacrifice of gold, poets of wit,
And men religious part with fame and goodness.
Be therefore won to use the means that may
Advance your pious ends.

Charalois:
You shall o'ercome.

Romont:
And you receive the glory. Pray you, now practise.

Charalois:
'Tis well.

(Enter Novall Senior, Advocates, Liladam, *and three* Creditors.*)*

(Tenders his petition.)

Not look on me!

Romont:
You must have patience—
Offer it again.

Charalois:
And be again contemn'd!

Novall Senior:
I know what's to be done.

1 Creditor:
And, that your lordship
Will please to do your knowledge, we offer first
Our thankful hearts here, as a bounteous earnest
To what we will add.

Novall Senior:
One word more of this,
I am your enemy. Am I a man
Your bribes can work on? ha?

Liladam:
Friends, you mistake

(Aside to Creditor.*)*

The way to win my lord; he must not hear this,
But I, as one in favour, in his sight
May hearken to you for my profit.—Sir!
Pray hear them.

Novall Senior:
It is well.

Liladam:
Observe him now.

Novall Senior:
Your cause being good, and your proceedings so,

Without corruption I am your friend;
Speak your desires.

2 Creditor:
Oh, they are charitable;
The marshal stood engaged unto us three
Two hundred thousand crowns, which, by his death,
We are defeated of: for which great loss
We aim at nothing but his rotten flesh;
Nor is that cruelty.

1 Creditor:
I have a son
That talks of nothing but of guns and armour,
And swears he'll be a soldier; 'tis an humour
I would divert him from; and I am told,
That if I minister to him, in his drink,
Powder made of this bankrupt marshal's bones,
Provided that the carcass rot above ground,
'Twill cure his foolish frenzy.

Novall Senior:
You shew in it
A father's care. I have a son myself,
A fashionable gentleman, and a peaceful;
And, but I am assured he's not so given,
He should take of it too.

Charalois:
Sir!

(Tenders his petition.)

Novall Senior:
What are you?

Charalois:
A gentleman.

Novall Senior:
So are many that rake dunghills.
If you have any suit, move it in court:

I take no papers in corners.

(Exit.)

Romont:
 Yes,
 As the matter may be carried—and whereby—
 To manage the conveyance—Follow him.

Liladam:
 You are rude: I say he shall not pass.

(Exeunt Charalois *and* Advocates.*)*

Romont:
 You say so!
 On what assurance?
 For the well cutting of his lordship's corns,
 Picking his toes, or any office else
 Nearer to baseness!

Liladam:
 Look upon me better;
 Are these the ensigns of so course a fellow?
 Be well advised.

Romont:
 Out, rogue! do not I know
 These glorious weeds spring from the sordid dunghill
 Of thy officious baseness? wert thou worthy
 Of any thing from me, but my contempt,
 I would do more than this,— *(Beats him.)*
  —more, you court-spider!

Liladam:
 But that this man is lawless, he should find
 That I am valiant.

1 Creditor:
 If your ears are fast,
 'Tis nothing. What's a blow or two? as much.

2 Creditor:
    These chastisements as useful are as frequent,
    To such as would grow rich.

Romont:
    Are they so, rascals?
    I will befriend you, then.

                            (Kicks them.)

1 Creditor:
    Bear witness, sirs!

Liladam:
    Truth, I have born my part already, friends:
    In the court you shall have more.

                                    (Exit.)

Romont:
    I know you for
    The worst of spirits, that strive to rob the tombs
    Of what is their inheritance, the dead:
    For usurers, bred by a riotous peace,
    That hold the charter of your wealth and freedom
    By being knaves and cuckolds; that ne'er pray,
    But when you fear the rich heirs will grow wise,
    To keep their lands out of your parchment toils;
    And then, the devil your father's call'd upon,
    To invent some ways of luxury ne'er thought on.
    Be gone, and quickly, or I'll leave no room
    Upon your foreheads for your horns to sprout on—
    Without a murmur, or I will undo you;
    For I will beat you honest.

1 Creditor:
    Thrift forbid!
    We will bear this, rather than hazard that.

                            (Exeunt Creditors.)

                            (Re-enter Charalois.)

Romont:
> I am somewhat eased in this yet.

Charalois:
> Only friend,
> To what vain purpose do I make my sorrow
> Wait on the triumph of their cruelty?
> Or teach their pride, from my humility,
> To think it has o'ercome? They are determined
> What they will do; and it may well become me,
> To rob them of the glory they expect
> From my submiss entreaties.

Romont:
> Think not so, sir:
> The difficulties that you encounter with
> Will crown the undertaking—heaven! you weep:
> And I could do so too, but that I know
> There's more expected from the son and friend
> Of him whose fatal loss now shakes our natures,
> Than sighs or tears, in which a village nurse,
> Or cunning strumpet, when her knave is hang'd,
> May overcome us. We are men, young lord,
> Let us not do like women. To the court,
> And there speak like your birth: wake sleeping justice,
> Or dare the axe. This is a way will sort
> With what you are: I call you not to that
> I will shrink from myself; I will deserve
> Your thanks, or suffer with you—O how bravely
> That sudden fire of anger shews in you!
> Give fuel to it. Since you are on a shelf
> Of extreme danger, suffer like yourself.

(Exeunt.)

(SCENE II.—The Court of Justice. Enter Rochfort, Novall Senior, Presidents, Charmi, Du Croy, Beaumont, Advocates, *three* Creditors, *and* Officers.*)*

Du Croy:
> Your lordships seated, may this meeting prove
> Prosperous to us, and to the general good
> Of Burgandy!

Novall Senior:
    Speak to the point.

Du Croy:
    Which is
    With honour to dispose the place and power
    Of premier president, which this reverend man,
    Grave Rochfort, whom for honour's sake I name,
    Is purposed to resign; a place, my lords,
    In which he hath with such integrity
    Perform'd the first and best parts of a judge,
    That, as his life transcends all fair examples
    Of such as were before him in Dijon,
    So it remains to those that shall succeed him,
    A precedent they may imitate, but not equal.

Rochfort:
    I may not sit to hear this.

Du Croy:
    Let the love
    And thankfulness we are bound to pay to goodness,
    In this o'ercome your modesty.

Rochfort:
    My thanks
    For this great favour shall prevent your trouble.
    The honourable trust that was imposed
    Upon my weakness, since you witness for me
    It was not ill discharged, I will not mention;
    Nor now, if age had not deprived me of
    The little strength I had to govern well
    The province that I undertook, forsake it.

Novall Senior:
    That we could lend you of our years!

Du Croy:
    Or strength!

Novall Senior:
    Or, as you are, persuade you to continue

The noble exercise of your knowing judgment!

Rochfort:
That may not be; nor can your lordship's goodness,
Since your employments have conferr'd upon me
Sufficient wealth, deny the use of it:
And, though old age, when one foot's in the grave,
In many, when all humours else are spent,
Feeds no affection in them, but desire
To add height to the mountain of their riches,
In me it is not so. I rest content
With the honours and estate I now possess:
And, that I may have liberty to use
What heaven, still blessing my poor industry,
Hath made me master of, I pray the court
To ease me of my burthen, that I may
Employ the small remainder of my life
In living well, and learning how to die so.

(Enter Romont *and* Charalois.*)*

Romont:
See, sir, our advocate.

Du Croy:
The court entreats
Your lordship will be pleased to name the man,
Which you would have your successor, and, in me,
All promise to confirm it.

Rochfort:
I embrace it
As an assurance of their favour to me,
And name my lord Novall.

Du Croy:
The court allows it.

Rochfort:
But there are suitors wait here, and their causes
May be of more necessity to be heard;
I therefore wish that mine may be deferr'd,
And theirs have hearing.

Du Croy:
>If your lordship please *(To* Novall Senior.*)*
>To take the place, we will proceed.

Charmi:
>The cause
>We come to offer to your lordship's censure,
>Is in itself so noble, that it needs not
>Or rhetoric in me that plead, or favour
>From your grave lordships, to determine of it;
>Since to the praise of your impartial justice
>(Which guilty, nay, condemn'd men, dare not scandal)
>It will erect a trophy of your mercy,
>Which married to that justice—

Novall Senior:
>Speak to the cause.

Charmi:
>I will, my lord. To say, the late dead marshal,
>The father of this young lord here, my client,
>Hath done his country great and faithful service,
>Might task me of impertinence, to repeat
>What your grave lordships cannot but remember,
>He, in his life, became indebted to
>These thrifty men, (I will not wrong their credits,
>By giving them the attributes they now merit,)
>And failing, by the fortune of the wars,
>Of means to free himself from his engagements,
>He was arrested, and, for want of bail,
>Imprison'd at their suit; and, not long after,
>With loss of liberty, ended his life.
>And, though it be a maxim in our laws,
>All suits die with the person, these men's malice
>In death finds matter for their hate to work on;
>Denying him the decent rites of burial,
>Which the sworn enemies of the Christian faith
>Grant freely to their slaves. May it therefore please
>Your lordships so to fashion your decree,
>That, what their cruelty doth forbid, your pity
>May give allowance to.

Novall Senior:
    How long have you, sir,
    Practised in court?

Charmi:
    Some twenty years, my lord.

Novall Senior:
    By your gross ignorance, it should appear,
    Not twenty days.

Charmi:
    I hope I have given no cause
    In this, my lord.

Novall Senior:
    How dare you move the court
    To the dispensing with an act, confirm'd
    By parliament, to the terror of all bankrupts?
    Go home; and with more care peruse the statutes:
    Or the next motion, savouring of this boldness,
    May force you, sir, to leap, against your will,
    Over the place you plead at.

Charmi:
    I foresaw this.

Romont:
    Why, does your lordship think the moving of
    A cause more honest than this court had ever
    The honour to determine, can deserve
    A check like this?

Novall Senior:
    Strange boldness!

Romont:
    'Tis fit freedom:
    Or, do you conclude an advocate cannot hold
    His credit with the judge, unless he study
    His face more than the cause for which he pleads?

Charmi:
>Forbear.

Romont:
>Or cannot you, that have the power
>To qualify the rigour of the laws
>When you are pleased, take a little from
>The strictness of your sour decrees, enacted
>In favour of the greedy creditors,
>Against the o'erthrown debtor?

Novall Senior:
>Sirrah! you that prate
>Thus saucily, what are you?

Romont:
>Why, I'll tell thee,
>Thou purple-colour'd man! I am one to whom
>Thou ow'st the means thou hast of sitting there,
>A corrupt elder.

Charmi:
>Forbear.

Romont:
>The nose thou wear'st is my gift; and those eyes,
>That meet no object so base as their master,
>Had been long since torn from that guilty head,
>And thou thyself slave to some needy Swiss,
>Had I not worn a sword, and used it better
>Than, in thy prayers, thou ever didst thy tongue.

Novall Senior:
>Shall such an insolence pass unpunish'd!

Charmi:
>Hear me.

Romont:
>Yet I, that, in my service done my country,
>Disdain to be put in the scale with thee,
>Confess myself unworthy to be valued

With the least part, nay, hair of the dead marshal;
Of whose so many glorious undertakings,
Make choice of any one, and that the meanest,
Perform'd against the subtle fox of France,
The politic Louis, or the more desperate Swiss,
And 'twill outweigh all the good purposes,
Though put in act, that ever gownman practised.

Novall Senior:
Away with him to prison!

Romont:
If that curses,
Urged justly, and breath'd forth so, ever fell
On those that did deserve them, let not mine
Be spent in vain now, that thou from this instant
Mayst, in thy fear that they will fall upon thee,
Be sensible of the plagues they shall bring with them.
And for denying of a little earth
To cover what remains of our great soldier,
May all your wives prove whores, your factors thieves,
And, while you live, your riotous heirs undo you!
And thou, the patron of their cruelty,
Of all thy lordships live not to be owner
Of so much dung as will conceal a dog,
Or, what is worse, thyself in! And thy years,
To th' end thou mayst be wretched, I wish many;
And, as thou hast denied the dead a grave,
May misery in thy life make thee desire one,
Which men and all the elements keep from thee!
—I have begun well; imitate, exceed.

(Aside to Charalois.*)*

Rochfort:
Good counsel, were it a praiseworthy deed.

(Exeunt Officers *with* Romont.*)*

Du Croy:
Remember what we are.

Charalois:
>Thus low my duty
>Answers your lordship's counsel. I will use,
>In the few words with which I am to trouble
>Your lordship's ears, the temper that you wish me;
>Not that I fear to speak my thoughts as loud,
>And with a liberty beyond Romont;
>But that I know, for me, that am made up
>Of all that's wretched, so to haste my end,
>Would seem to most rather a willingness
>To quit the burthen of a hopeless life,
>Than scorn of death, or duty to the dead.
>I, therefore, bring the tribute of my praise
>To your severity, and commend the justice
>That will not, for the many services
>That any man hath done the commonwealth,
>Wink at his least of ills. What though my father
>Writ man before he was so, and confirm'd it,
>By numbering that day no part of his life,
>In which he did not service to his country;
>Was he to be free, therefore, from the laws
>And ceremonious form in your decrees!
>Or else, because he did as much as man,
>In those three memorable overthrows
>At Granson, Morat, Nancy, where his master,
>The warlike Charalois, (with whose misfortunes I bear his
>   name,) lost treasure, men, and life,
>To be excused from payment of those sums
>Which (his own patrimony spent) his zeal
>To serve his country forced him to take up!

Novall Senior:
>The precedent were ill.

Charalois:
>And yet, my lord, this much,
>I know, you'll grant; after those great defeatures,
>Which in their dreadful ruins buried quick

(Re-enter Officers.)

>Courage and hope in all men but himself,

>   He forced the proud foe, in his height of conquest,
>   To yield unto an honourable peace;
>   And in it saved an hundred thousand lives,
>   To end his own, that was sure proof against
>   The scalding summer's heat, and winter's frost,
>   Ill airs, the cannon, and the enemy's sword,
>   In a most loathsome prison.

Du Croy:
>   'Twas his fault
>   To be so prodigal.

Novall Senior:
>   He had from the state
>   Sufficient entertainment for the army.

Charalois:
>   Sufficient, my lords! You sit at home,
>   And, though your fees are boundless at the bar,
>   Are thrifty in the charges of the war—
>   But your wills be obey'd. To these I turn,
>   To these soft-hearted men, that wisely know
>   They're only good men that pay what they owe.

2 Creditor:
>   And so they are.

1 Creditor:
>   It is the city doctrine;
>   We stand bound to maintain it.

Charalois:
>   Be constant in it;
>   And since you are as merciless in your natures,
>   As base and mercenary in your means
>   By which you get your wealth, I will not urge
>   The court to take away one scruple from
>   The right of their laws, or [wish] one good thought
>   In you, to mend your disposition with.
>   I know there is no music to your ears
>   So pleasing as the groans of men in prison;
>   And that the tears of widows, and the cries

Of famish'd orphans, are the feasts that take you.
That to be in your danger, with more care
Should be avoided than infectious air,
The loath'd embraces of diseased women,
A flatterer's poison, or the loss of honour.—
Yet rather than my father's reverend dust
Shall want a place in that fair monument,
In which our noble ancestors lie intomb'd,
Before the court I offer up myself
A prisoner for it. Load me with those irons
That have worn out his life; in my best strength
I'll run to the encounter of cold, hunger,
And choose my dwelling where no sun dares enter,
So he may be released.

1 Creditor:
What mean you, sir?

2 Advocate:
Only your fee again: there's so much said
Already in this cause, and said so well,
That, should I only offer to speak in it,
I should be or not heard, or laugh'd at for it.

1 Creditor:
'Tis the first money advocate e'er gave back,
Though he said nothing.

Rochfort:
Be advised, young lord,
And well considerate; you throw away
Your liberty and joys of life together:
Your bounty is employ'd upon a subject
That is not sensible of it, with which wise man
Never abused his goodness. The great virtues
Of your dead father vindicate themselves
From these men's malice, and break ope the prison,
Though it contain his body.

Novall Senior:
Let him alone:
If he love cords, in God's name let him wear them;
Provided these consent.

Charalois:
>I hope they are not
>So ignorant in any way of profit,
>As to neglect a possibility
>To get their own, by seeking it from that
>Which can return them nothing but ill fame,
>And curses, for their barbarous cruelties.

3 Creditor:
>What think you of the offer?

2 Creditor:
>Very well.

1 Creditor:
>Accept it by all means. Let's shut him up:
>He is well shaped, and has a villainous tongue,
>And, should he study that way of revenge,
>As I dare almost swear he loves a wench,
>We have no wives, nor never shall get daughters,
>That will hold out against him.

Du Croy:
>What's your answer?

2 Creditor:
>Speak you for all.

1 Creditor:
>Why, let our executions
>That lie upon the Father, be return'd
>Upon the son, and we release the body.

Novall Senior:
>The court must grant you that.

Charalois:
>I thank your lordships.
>They have in it confirm'd on me such glory
>As no time can take from me: I am ready,
>Come, lead me where you please. Captivity,
>That comes with honour, is true liberty.

(Exeunt Charalois, Charmi, Officers, *and* Creditors.*)*

Novall Senior:
    Strange rashness!

Rochfort:
    A brave resolution rather,
    Worthy a better fortune: but, however,
    It is not now to be disputed; therefore
    To my own cause. Already I have found
    Your lordships bountiful in your favours to me,
    And that should teach my modesty to end here,
    And press your loves no further.

Du Croy:
    There is nothing
    The court can grant, but with assurance you
    May ask it, and obtain it.

Rochfort:
    You encourage
    A bold petitioner, and 'tis not fit
    Your favours should be lost: besides, 't'as been
    A custom many years, at the surrendering
    The place I now give up, to grant the president
    One boon, that parted with it: and, to confirm
    Your grace towards me, against all such as may
    Detract my actions and life hereafter,
    I now prefer it to you.

Du Croy:
    Speak it freely.

Rochfort:
    I then desire the liberty of Romont,
    And that my lord Novall, whose private wrong
    Was equal to the injury that was done
    To the dignity of the court, will pardon it,
    And now sign his enlargement.

Novall Senior:
    Pray you demand

Rochfort:
>The moiety of my estate, or any thing
>Within my power, but this.

Rochfort:
>Am I denied then
>My first and last request?

Du Croy:
>It must not be.

2 President:
>I have a voice to give in it.

3 President:
>And I.
>And if persuasion will not work him to it,
>We will make known our power.

Novall Senior:
>You are too violent;
>You shall have my consent: but would you had
>Made trial of my love in any thing
>But this, you should have found then—but it skills not:
>You have what you desire.

Rochfort:
>I thank your lordships.

Du Croy:
>The court is up. Make way.

>>*(Exeunt all but* Rochfort *and* Beaumont.*)*

Rochfort:
>I follow you.
>Beaumont!

Beaumont:
>My lord.

Rochfort:
>You are a scholar, Beaumont;

And can search deeper into the intents of men,
Than those that are less knowing.—How appear'd
The piety and brave behaviour of
Young Charalois, to you?

Beaumont:
It is my wonder,
Since I want language to express it fully:
And sure the colonel—

Rochfort:
Fie! he was faulty.
What present money have I?

Beaumont:
There's no want
Of any sum a private man has use for.

Rochfort:
'Tis well:
I am strangely taken with this Charalois.
Methinks, from his example the whole age
Should learn to be good, and continue so.
Virtue works strangely with us; and his goodness
Rising above his fortune, seems to me,
Prince-like, to will, not ask, a courtesy.

(Exeunt.)

(ACT II. SCENE I.—A street before the Prison. Enter Pontalier, Malotin, *and* Beaumont.*)*

Malotin:
'Tis strange.

Beaumont:
Methinks so.

Pontalier:
In a man but young,
Yet old in judgment; theoric and practic
In all humanity, and, to increase the wonder,

Religious, yet a soldier; that he should
Yield his free-living youth a captive for
The freedom of his aged father's corpse,
And rather choose to want life's necessaries,
Liberty, hope of fortune, than it should
In death be kept from Christian ceremony.

Malotin:
Come, 'tis a golden precedent in a son,
To let strong nature have the better hand,
In such a case, of all affected reason.
What years sit on this Charalois?

Beaumont:
Twenty-eight:
For since the clock did strike him seventeen old,
Under his father's wing this son hath fought,
Served and commanded, and so aptly both,
That sometimes he appear'd his father's father,
And never less than 's son; the old man's virtues
So recent in him, as the world may swear,
Nought but a fair tree could such fair fruit bear.

Pontalier:
But wherefore lets he such a barbarous law,
And men more barbarous to execute it,
Prevail on his soft disposition,
That he had rather die alive for debt
Of the old man, in prison, than they should
Rob him of sepulture; considering
These monies borrow'd bought the lenders peace,
And all the means they enjoy, nor were diffused
In any impious or licentious path?

Beaumont:
True! for my part, were it my father's trunk,
The tyrannous ram-heads with their horns should gore it,
Or cast it to their curs, than they less currish,
Ere prey on me so with their lion-law,
Being in my free will, as in his, to shun it.

Pontalier:
>Alas! he knows himself in poverty lost:
>For, in this partial avaricious age,
>What price bears honour? virtue? long ago,
>It was but praised, and freezed; but now-a-days,
>'Tis colder far, and has nor love nor praise:
>The very praise now freezeth too; for nature
>Did make the heathen far more Christian then,
>Than knowledge us, less heathenish, Christian.

Malotin:
>This morning is the funeral?

Pontalier:
>Certainly,
>And from this prison,—'twas the son's request.
>That his dear father might interment have,
>See, the young son enter'd a lively grave!

Beaumont:
>They come:—observe their order.

(Solemn music. Enter the Funeral Procession. The coffin borne by four, preceded by a Priest. Captains, Lieutenants, Ensigns, *and* Soldiers; Mourners, Scutcheons, &c. *and very good order.* Romont *and* Charalois, *followed by the* Gaolers *and* Officers, *with* Creditors, *meet it.)*

Charalois:
>How like a silent stream shaded with night,
>And gliding softly, with our windy sighs,
>Moves the whole frame of this solemnity!
>Tears, sighs, and blacks filling the simile;
>Whilst I, the only murmur in this grove
>Of death, thus hollowly break forth. Vouchsafe
>>*(To the* Bearers, *who set down the coffin.)*
>To stay awhile.—Rest, rest in peace, dear earth!
>Thou that brought'st rest to their unthankful lives,
>Whose cruelty denied thee rest in death!
>Here stands thy poor exécutor, thy son,
>That makes his life prisoner to bail thy death;
>Who gladlier puts on this captivity,

Than virgins, long in love, their wedding weeds.
Of all that ever thou hast done good to,
These only have good memories; for they
Remember best forget not gratitude.
I thank you for this last and friendly love.
(To the Soldiers.)
And though this country, like a viperous mother,
Not only hath eat up ungratefully
All means of thee, her son, but last, thyself,
Leaving thy heir so bare and indigent,
He cannot raise thee a poor monument,
Such as a flatterer or a usurer hath;
Thy worth, in every honest breast, builds one,
Making their friendly hearts thy funeral stone.

Pontalier:
>Sir.

Charalois:
>Peace! O, peace! this scene is wholly mine.
>What! weep ye, soldiers? blanch not.—Romont weeps!—
>Ha! let me see!—my miracle is eased,
>The gaolers and the creditors do weep;
>Even they that make us weep, do weep themselves!
>Be these thy body's balm! these and thy virtue
>Keep thy fame ever odoriferous,
>Whilst the great, proud, rich, undeserving man,
>Alive, stinks in his vices, and, being vanish'd,
>The golden calf, that was an idol deck'd
>With marble pillars, jet, and porphyry,
>Shall quickly, both in bone and name, consume,
>Though rapt in lead, spice, searcloth, and perfume!

1 Creditor:
>Sir.

Charalois:
>What? away, for shame! you, profane rogues,
>Must not be mingled with these holy relics;
>This is a sacrifice:—our shower shall crown
>His sepulchre with olive, myrrh, and bays,
>The plants of peace, of sorrow, victory;

Your tears would spring but weeds.

1 Creditor:
Would they so!
We'll keep them to stop bottles then.

Romont:
No, keep them
For your own sins, you rogues, till you repent;
You'll die else, and be damn'd.

2 Creditor:
Damn'd!—ha! ha! ha!

Romont:
Laugh ye?

3 Creditor:
Yes, faith, sir; we would be very glad
To please you either way.

1 Creditor:
You are ne'er content,
Crying nor laughing.

Romont:
Both with a birth, ye rogues?

2 Creditor:
Our wives, sir, taught us.

Romont:
Look, look, you slaves! your thankless cruelty,
And savage manuers of unkind Dijon,
Exhaust these floods, and not his father's death.

1 Creditor:
'Slid, sir! what would you? you're so choleric!

2 Creditor:
Most soldiers are so, i'faith;—let him alone.
They have little else to live on. We've not had

A penny of him, have we?

3 Creditor:
'Slight! would you have our hearts?

1 Creditor:
We have nothing but his body here in durance,
For all our money.

Priest:
On.

Charalois:
One moment more,
But to bestow a few poor legacies,
All I have left in my dead father's rights,
And I have done. Captain, wear thou these spurs,
That yet ne'er made his horse run from a foe.
Lieutenant, thou this scarf; and may it tie
Thy valour and thy honesty together!
For so it did in him. Ensign, this cuirass,
Your general's necklace once. You, gentle bearers,
Divide this purse of gold; this other, strew
Among the poor; 'tis all I have. Romont—
Wear thou this medal of himself—hat, like
A hearty oak, grew'st close to this tall pine,
Even in the wildest wilderness of war,
Whereon foes broke their swords, and tired themselves:
Wounded and hack'd ye were, but never fell'd.
For me, my portion provide in heaven!—
My root is earth'd, and I, a desolate branch,
Left scatter'd in the highway of the world,
Trod under foot, that might have been a column
Mainly supporting our demolish'd house.
This would I wear as my inheritance—
And what hope can arise to me from it,
When I and it are both here prisoners!
Only may this, if ever we be free,
Keep, or redeem, me from all infamy.

A dirge to solemn music:
Fie! cease to wonder,

Though you hear Orpheus with his ivory lute,
　　Move trees and rocks,
Charm bulls, bears, and men more savage, to be mute;
　　Weak foolish singer, here is one
　　Would have transform'd thyself to stone.

1 Creditor:
No further; look to them at your own peril.

2 Creditor:
No, as they please: their master's a good man.—
I would they were at the Bermudas!

Gaoler:
You must no further.
The prison limits you, and the creditors
Exact the strictness.

Romont:
Out, you wolvish mongrels!
Whose brains should be knock'd out, like dogs in July,
Lest your infection poison a whole town.

Charalois:
They grudge our sorrow. Your ill wills, perforce,
Turn now to charity: they would not have us
Walk too far mourning; usurers' relief
Grieves, if the debtors have too much of grief.

　　　　　　　　　　　　(Exeunt.)

(SCENE II.—A room in Rochfort's *house. Enter* Beaumelle, Florimel, *and* Bellapert.)

Beaumelle:
I prithee tell me, Florimel, why do women marry?

Florimel:
Why truly, madam, I think, to lie with their husbands.

Bellapert:
You are a fool. She lies madam; women marry husbands, to lie with other men.

Florimel:
'Faith, even such a woman wilt thou make. By this light, madam, this wagtail will spoil you, if you take delight in her license.

Beaumelle:
'Tis true, Florimel; and thou wilt make me too good for a young lady. What an electuary found my father out for his daughter, when he compounded you two my women! for thou, Florimel, art even a grain too heavy, simply, for a waiting-gentlewoman—

Florimel:
And thou, Bellapert, a grain too light.

Bellapert:
Well, go thy ways, goody wisdom, whom nobody regards. I wonder whether be elder, thou or thy hood? You think, because you served my lady's mother, are thirty-two years old, which is a pip out, you know—

Florimel:
Well said, whirligig.

Bellapert:
You are deceived; I want a peg in the middle.—Out of these prerogatives, you think to be mother of the maids here, and mortify them with proverbs: go, go, govern the sweetmeats, and weigh the sugar, that the wenches steal none; say your prayers twice a day, and, as I take it, you have performed your function.

Florimel:
I may be even with you.

Bellapert:
Hark! the court's broke up. Go, help my old lord out of his caroch, and scratch his head till dinner time.

Florimel:
Well.

(Exit.)

Bellapert:
Fie, madam, how you walk! By my maindenhead, you look seven years older than you did this morning. Why, there can be nothing under the sun valuable to make you thus a minute.

Beaumelle:
Ah, my sweet Bellapert, thou cabinet
To all my counsels, thou dost know the cause
That makes thy lady wither thus in youth.

Bellapert:
Uds-light! enjoy your wishes: whilst I live,
One way or other you shall crown your will.
Would you have him your husband that you love,
And can it not be? he is your servant, though,
And may perform the office of a husband.

Beaumelle:
But there is honour, wench.

Bellapert:
Such a disease
There is indeed, for which ere I would die—

Beaumelle:
Prithee, distinguish me a maid and wife.

Bellapert:
'Faith, madam, one may bear any man's children, t'other must bear no man's.

Beaumelle:
What is a husband?

Bellapert:
Physic, that, tumbling in your belly, will make you sick in the stomach. The only distinction betwixt a husband and a servant is, the first will lie with you when he pleases; the last shall lie with you when you please. Pray tell me, lady, do

you love, to marry after, or would marry, to love after?

Beaumelle:
I would meet love and marriage both at once.

Bellapert:
Why then you are out of the fashion, and will be contemn'd: for I will assure you, there are few women in the world, but either they have married first, and love after; or love first, and married after. You must do as you may, not as you would; your father's will is the goal you must fly to. If a husband approach you, you would have further off, is he you love, the less near you? A husband in these days is but a cloak, to be oftener laid upon your bed, than in your bed.

Beaumelle:
Humph!

Bellapert:
Sometimes you may wear him on your shoulder; now and then under your arm; but seldom or never let him cover you, for 'tis not the fashion.

(*Enter* Novall Junior, Pontalier, Malotin, Liladam, *and* Aymer.)

Novall Junior:
Best day to nature's curiosity,
Star of Dijon, the lustre of all France!
Perpetual spring dwell on thy rosy cheeks,
Whose breath is perfume to our continent!—
See! Flora trimm'd in her varieties.

Bellapert:
O, divine lord!

Novall Junior:
No autumn nor no age ever approach
This heavenly piece; which nature having wrought,
She lost her needle, and did then despair
Ever to work so lively and so fair!

Liladam:
>Uds-light! my lord, one of the purls of your band is, without all discipline, fallen out of his rank.

Novall Junior:
>How! I would not for a thousand crowns she had seen't. Dear Liladam, reform it.

Bellapert:
>Oh lord *per se*, lord! quintessence of honour! she walks not under a weed that would deny thee any thing.

Beaumelle:
>Prithee peace, wench; thou dost but blow the fire,
>That flames too much already.

(Liladam *and* Aymer *trim* Novall, *while* Bellapert *dresses her lady.*)

Aymer:
>By gad, my lord, you have the divinest tailor in Christendom; he hath made you look like an angel in your cloth-of-tissue doublet.

Pontalier:
>This is a three-legg'd lord; there's a fresh assult. Oh! that men should spend time thus! See, see, how her blood drives to her heart, and straight vaults to her cheeks again!

Malotin:
>What are these?

Pontalier:
>One of them there, the lower, is a good, foolish, knavish, sociable gallimaufry of a man, and has much caught my lord with singing; he is master of a music-house. The other is his dressing block, upon whom my lord lays all his clothes and fashions ere he vouchsafes them his own person: you shall see him in the morning in the Galley-foist, at noon in the Bullion, in the evening in Quirpo, and all night in—

Malotin:
>A bawdyhouse.

Pontalier:
> If my lord deny, they deny; if he affirm, they affirm: they skip into my lord's cast skins some twice a year; and thus they flatter to eat, eat to live, and live to praise my lord.

Malotin:
> Good sir, tell me one thing.

Pontalier:
> What's that?

Malotin:
> Dare these men ever fight on any cause?

Pontalier:
> Oh, no! 'twould spoil their clothes, and put their bands out of order.

Novall Junior:
> Mistress, you hear the news? your father has resign'd his presidentship to my lord my father.

Malotin:
> And lord Charalois
> Undone for ever.

Pontalier:
> Troth, 'tis pity, sir.
> A braver hope of so assured a father,
> Did never comfort France.

Liladam:
> A good dumb mourner.

Aymer:
> A silent black.

Novall Junior:
> Oh, fie upon him, how he wears his clothes!
> As if he had come this Christmas from St. Omers,
> To see his friends, and return'd after Twelfth-tide.

Liladam:
His colonel looks finely like a drover—

Novall Junior:
That had a winter lain perdue in the rain.

Aymer:
What, he that wears a clout about his neck,
His cuffs in's pocket, and his heart in's mouth?

Novall Junior:
Now, out upon him!

Beaumelle:
Servant, tie my hand.

(Novall Junior kisses her hand.)

How your lips blush, in scorn that they should pay
Tribute to hands, when lips are in the way!

Novall Junior:
I thus recant; *(Kisses her.)*
   yet now your hand looks white,
Because your lips robb'd it of such a right.
Monsieur Aymer, I prithee sing the song
Devoted to my mistress.

Music,—and a song by Aymer:
A Dialogue between a Man and a Woman.

Man:	*Set, Phœbus, set; a fairer sun doth rise*
	From the bright radiance of my mistress' eyes
	Than ever thou begat'st: I dare not look;
	Each hair a golden line, each word a hook,
	The more I strive, the more still I am took.
Woman:	*Fair servant, come; the day these eyes do lend*
	To warm thy blood, thou dost so vainly spend,
	Come, strangle breath.
Man:	*What note so sweet as this,*
	That calls the spirits to a further bliss?
Woman:	*Yet this out-savours wine, and this perfume.*
Man:	*Let's die; I languish, I consume.*

(Enter Rochfort and Beaumont.)

Beaumont:
Romont will come, sir, straight.

Rochfort:
'Tis well.

Beaumelle:
My father!

Novall Junior:
My honourable lord.

Rochfort:
My lord Novall, this is a virtue in you;
So early up and ready before noon,
That are the map of dressing through all France!

Novall Junior:
I rise to say my prayers, sir; here's my saint.

Rochfort:
'Tis well and courtly:—you must give me leave,—
I have some private conference with my daughter;
Pray use my garden: you shall dine with me.

Liladam:
We'll wait on you.

Novall Junior:
Good morn unto your lordship!
Remember, what you have vow'd—
                              (Aside to Beaumelle.)

Beaumelle:
—Perform I must.

(Exeunt all but Rochfort and Beaumelle.)

Rochfort:
Why, how now, Beaumelle? thou look'st not well.
Thou art sad of late;—come, cheer thee, I have found

A wholesome remedy for these maiden fits;
A goodly oak whereon to twist my vine,
Till her fair branches grow up to the stars.
Be near at hand.—Success crown my intent!
My business fills my little time so full,
I cannot stand to talk; I know thy duty
Is handmaid to my will, especially
When it presents nothing but good and fit.

Beaumelle:
Sir, I am yours.—Oh! if my fears prove true,
Fate hath wrong'd love, and will destroy me too.

(Aside, and Exit.)

(Enter Romont *and* Gaoler.*)*

Romont:
Sent you for me, sir?

Rochfort:
Yes.

Romont:
Your lordship's pleasure?

Rochfort:
Keeper, this prisoner I will see forthcoming,
Upon my word.—Sit down, good colonel.

(Exit Gaoler.*)*

Why I did wish you hither, noble sir,
Is to advise you from this iron carriage,
Which, so affected, Romont, you will wear;
To pity, and to counsel you submit
With expedition to the great Novall:
Recant your stern contempt, and slight neglect
Of the whole court and him, and opportunely,
Or you will undergo a heavy censure
In public, very shortly.

Romont:
>Reverend sir,
>I have observed you, and do know you well;
>And am now more afraid you know not me,
>By wishing my submission to Novall,
>Than I can be of all the bellowing mouths
>That wait upon him to pronounce the censure,
>Could it determine me torments and shame.
>Submit, and crave forgiveness of a beast!—
>'Tis true, this boil of state wears purple tissue,
>Is high fed, proud; so is his lordship's horse,
>And bears as rich caparisons. I know
>This elephant carries on his back not only
>Towers, castles, but the ponderous republic,
>And never stoops for't; with his strong-breath'd trunk
>Snuffs others titles, lordships, offices,
>Wealth, bribes, and lives, under his ravenous jaws:
>What's this unto my freedom? I dare die;
>And therefore ask this camel, if these blessings
>(For so they would be understood by a man)
>But mollify one rudeness in his nature,
>Sweeten the eager relish of the law,
>At whose great helm he sits. Helps he the poor,
>In a just business? Nay, does he not cross
>Every deserved soldier and scholar,
>As if, when nature made him, she had made
>The general antipathy of all virtue?
>How savagely and blasphemously he spake
>Touching the general, the brave general dead!
>I must weep when I think on't.

Rochfort:
>Sir.

Romont:
>My lord,
>I am not stubborn; I can melt, you see,
>And prize a virtue better than my life:
>For though I be not learn'd, I ever loved
>That holy mother of all issues good,
>Whose white hand, for a sceptre, holds a file
>To polish roughest customs; and, in you,

She has her right: see! I am calm as sleep.
But when I think of the gross injuries,
The godless wrong done to my general dead,
I rave indeed, and could eat this Novall;
A soulless dromedary!

Rochfort:
Oh! be temperate.
Sir, though I would persuade, I'll not constrain:
Each man's opinion freely is his own
Concerning any thing, or any body;
Be it right or wrong, 'tis at the judge's peril.

(Re-enter Beaumont.*)*

Beaumont:
These men, sir, wait without; my lord is come too.

Rochfort:
Pay them those sums upon the table; take
Their full releases:—stay, I want a witness.
Let me entreat you, colonel, to walk in,
And stand but by to see this money paid;
It does concern you and your friend; it was
The better cause you were sent for, though said otherwise.
The deed shall make this my request more plain.

Romont:
I shall obey your pleasure, sir, though ignorant
To what it tends.

(Exeunt Romont *and* Beaumont.*)*

(Enter Charalois.*)*

Rochfort:
Worthiest sir,
You are most welcome. Fie, no more of this!
You have outwept a woman, noble Charalois.
No man but has or must bury a father.

Charalois:
>Grave sir, I buried sorrow for his death,
>In the grave with him. I did never think
>He was immortal—though I vow I grieve,
>And see no reason why the vicious,
>Virtuous, valiant, and unworthy man,
>Should die alike.

Rochfort:
>They do not.

Charalois:
>In the manner
>Of dying, sir, they do not; but all die,
>And therein differ not:—but I have done.
>I spied the lively picture of my father,
>Passing your gallery, and that cast this water
>Into mine eyes: See,—foolish that I am,
>To let it do so!

Rochfort:
>Sweet and gentle nature!
>How silken is this well, comparatively
>To other men! *(Aside.)* I have a suit to you, sir.

Charalois:
>Take it, 'tis granted.

Rochfort:
>What?

Charalois:
>Nothing, my lord.

Rochfort:
>Nothing is quickly granted.

Charalois:
>Faith, my lord,
>That nothing granted is even all I have,
>For, all know, I have nothing left to grant.

Rochfort:
>Sir, have you any suit to me? I'll grant
>You something, any thing.

Charalois:
>Nay, surely, I that can
>Give nothing, will but sue for that again.
>No man will grant me any thing I sue for,
>But begging nothing, every man will give it.

Rochfort:
>Sir!
>The love I bore your father, and the worth
>I see in you, so much resembling his,
>Made me thus send for you:—and tender here,

(Draws a curtain, and discovers a table with money and jewels upon it.)

>Whatever you will take, gold, jewels, both,
>All, to supply your wants, and free yourself.
>Where heavenly virtue in high-blooded veins
>Is lodged, and can agree, men should kneel down,
>Adore, and sacrifice all that they have;
>And well they may, it is so seldom seen.—
>Put off your wonder, and here freely take,
>Or send your servants: nor, sir, shall you use,
>In aught of this, a poor man's fee, or bribe
>Unjustly taken of the rich, but what's
>Directly gotten, and yet by the law.

Charalois:
>How ill, sir, it becomes those hairs to mock!

Rochfort:
>Mock! thunder strike me then!

Charalois:
>You do amaze me:
>But you shall wonder too. I will not take
>One single piece of this great heap. Why should I
>Borrow, that have no means to pay? nay, am
>A very bankrupt, even in flattering hope
>Of ever raising any. All my begging,
>Is Romont's liberty.

(Re-enter Romont *and* Beaumont, *with* Creditors.)

Rochfort:
>Here is your friend,
>Enfranchised ere you spake. I give him to you;
>And, Charalois, I give you to your friend,
>As free a man as he. Your father's debts
>Are taken off.

Charalois:
>How!

Romont:
>Sir, it is most true;
>I am the witness.

1 Creditor:
>Yes, faith, we are paid.

2 Creditor:
>Heaven bless his lordship! I did think him wiser.

3 Creditor:
>He a statesman! he an ass. Pay other men's debts!

1 Creditor:
>That he was never bound for.

Romont:
>One more such
>Would save the rest of pleaders.

Charalois:
>Honour'd Rochfort—
>Lie still, my tongue, and, blushes, scald my cheeks,
>That offer thanks in words, for such great deeds.

Rochfort:
>Call in my daughter. Still I have a suit to you,

>>>>>>>>>*(Exit* Beaumont.)

>Would you requite me.

Romont:
> With his life, I assure you.

Rochfort:
> Nay, would you make me now your debtor, sir—

(Re-enter Beaumont with Beaumelle.)

> This is my only child: what she appears,
> Your lordship well may see: her education
> Follows not any; for her mind, I know it
> To be far fairer than her shape, and hope
> It will continue so. If now her birth
> Be not too mean for Charalois, take her, take
> This virgin by the hand, and call her Wife,
> Endow'd with all my fortunes. Bless me so;
> Requite me thus, and make me happier,
> In joining my poor empty name to yours,
> Than if my state were multiplied tenfold.

Charalois:
> Is this the payment, sir, that you expect!
> Why, you precipitate me more in debt,
> That nothing but my life can ever pay.
> This beauty being your daughter, in which yours
> I must conceive necessity of her virtue,
> Without all dowry is a prince's aim:
> Then, as she is, for poor and worthless me
> How much too worthy! Waken me, Romont,
> That I may know I dream'd, and find this vanish'd.

Romont:
> Sure, I sleep not.

Rochfort:
> Your sentence—life or death.

Charalois:
> Fair Beaumelle, can you love me?

Beaumelle:
> Yes, my lord.

(Enter Novall Junior, Pontalier, Malotin, Liladam, *and* Aymer. *They all salute.)*

Charalois:
>You need not question me if I can you:
>You are the fairest virgin in Dijon,
>And Rochfort is your father.

Novall Junior:
>What's this change? *(Aside.)*

Rochfort:
>You meet my wishes, gentlemen.

Romont:
>What make
>These dogs in doublets here?

Beaumelle:
>A visitation, sir.

Charalois:
>Then thus, fair Beaumelle, I write my faith,
>Thus seal it in the sight of heaven and men!
>Your fingers tie my heart-strings with this touch,
>In true-love knots, which nought but death shall loose.
>And let these tears, an emblem of our loves,
>Like crystal rivers individually
>Flow into one another, make one source,
>Which never man distinguish, less divide!
>Breath marry breath, and kisses mingle souls,
>Two hearts and bodies here incorporate!
>And, though with little wooing I have won,
>My future life shall be a wooing time,
>And every day new as the bridal one.
>Oh, sir! I groan under your courtesies,
>More than my father's bones under his wrongs;
>You, Curtius like, have thrown into the gulf
>Of this his country's foul ingratitude,
>Your life and fortunes, to redeem their shames.

Rochfort:
>No more, my glory! come, let's in, and hasten
>This celebration.

Romont, Malotin, Pontalier, Beaumont:
>All fair bliss upon it!

>>*(Exeunt* Rochfort, Charalois, Romont, Beaumont, *and* Malotin.*)*

Novall Junior *(as Beaumelle is going out)*:
>Mistress!

Beaumelle:
>Oh, servant!—Virtue strengthen me!
>Thy presence blows round my affection's vane:—
>You will undo me, if you speak again.

>>*(Exit.)*

Liladam, Aymer:
>Here will be sport for you! this works.

>>*(Exeunt.)*

Novall Junior:
>Peace! peace!

Pontalier:
>One word, my lord Novall.

Novall Junior:
>What, thou wouldst money?—there!

Pontalier:
>No, I will none; I'll not be bought a slave,
>A pander, or a parasite, for all
>Your father's worth. Though you have saved my life,
>Rescued me often from my wants, I must not
>Wink at your follies: that will ruin you.
>You know my blunt way, and my love to truth—
>Forsake the pursuit of this lady's honour,

Now you do see her made another man's,
And such a man's, so good, so popular!
Or you will pluck a thousand mischiefs on you.
The benefits you have done me are not lost,
Nor cast away, they are purs'd here in my heart;
But let me pay you, sir, a fairer way,
Than to defend your vices, or to sooth them.

Novall Junior:
Ha, ha! what are my courses unto thee?—
Good cousin Pontalier, meddle with that
That shall concern thyself.

(Exit.)

Pontalier:
No more but scorn!
Move on then, stars, work your pernicious will:
Only the wise rule, and prevent your ill.

(Exit.)

(Here a passage over the stage, while the act is playing for the marriage of Charalois *with* Beaumelle, *&c.)*

(ACT III. SCENE I.—A room in Charalois' *house. Enter* Novall Junior, *and* Bellapert.*)*

Novall Junior:
Fly not to these excuses; thou hast been
False in thy promise—and, when I have said
Ungrateful, all is spoken.

Bellapert:
Good my lord,
But hear me only.

Novall Junior:
To what purpose, trifler?
Can any thing that thou canst say make void
The marriage, or those pleasures but a dream,
Which Charalois, oh Venus! hath enjoy'd?

Bellapert:
    I yet could say that you receive advantage
    In what you think a loss, would you vouchsafe me;
    That you were never in the way, till now,
    With safety to arrive at your desires;
    That pleasure makes love to you, unattended
    By danger or repentance.

Novall Junior:
    That I could
    But apprehend one reason how this might be!
    Hope would not then forsake me.

Bellapert:
    The enjoying
    Of what you most desire, I say the enjoying,
    Shall, in the full possession of your wishes,
    Confirm that I am faithful.

Novall Junior:
    Give some relish
    How this may appear possible.

Bellapert:
    I will,
    Relish and taste, and make the banquet easy.
    You say my lady's married,—I confess it;
    That Charalois hath enjoy'd her;—'tis most true:
    That, with her, he's already master of
    The best part of my old lord's state—still better.
    But, that the first or last should be your hinderance,
    I utterly deny; for, but observe me;
    While she went for, and was, I swear, a virgin,
    What courtesy could she, with her honour, give,
    Or you receive with safety!—take me with you:
    When I say courtesy, do not think I mean
    A kiss, the tying of her shoe or garter,
    An hour of private conference; those are trifles.
    In this word courtesy we, that are gamesters, point at
    The sport direct, where not alone the lover
    Brings his artillery, but uses it;
    Which word expounded to you, such a courtesy
    Do you expect, and sudden.

Novall Junior:
>But he tasted
>The first sweets, Bellapert.

Bellapert:
>He wrong'd you shrewdly!
>He toil'd to climb up to the phoenix' next,
>And in his prints leaves your ascent more easy.
>I do not know, you that are perfect critics
>In women's books, may talk of maindenheads—

Novall Junior:
>But for her marriage!

Bellapert:
>'Tis a fair protection
>'Gainst all arrests of fear or shame for ever.
>Such as are fair, and yet not foolish, study
>To have one at thirteen; but they are mad
>That stay till twenty. Then, sir, for the pleasure,
>To say adultery's sweeter, that is stale;
>This only—is not the contentment more,
>To say, This is my cuckold, than my rival?
>More I could say—but briefly, she doats on you;
>If it prove otherwise, spare not; poison me,
>With the next gold you give me.

(Enter Beaumelle.)

Beaumelle:
>How's this, servant!
>Courting my woman?

Bellapert:
>As an entrance to
>The favour of the mistress. You are together;
>And I am perfect in my cue.

(Going.)

Beaumelle:
>Stay, Bellapert.

Bellapert:
    In this I must not, with your leave, obey you.
    Your tailor and your tirewoman wait without,
    And stay my counsel and direction for
    Your next day's dressing. I have much to do,
    Nor will your ladyship, now time is precious,
    Continue idle; this choice lord will find
    So fit employment for you!

                              (Exit.)

Beaumelle:
    I shall grow angry.

Novall Junior:
    Not so; you have a jewel in her, madam.

                      (Re-enter Bellapert.)

Bellapert:
    I had forgot to tell your ladyship
    The closet is private, and your couch [there] ready;
    And, if you please that I shall lose the key,
    But say so, and 'tis done.

                              (Exit.)

Beaumelle:
    You come to chide me, servant, and bring with you
    Sufficient warrant. You will say, and truly,
    My father found too much obedience in me,
    By being won too soon; yet, if you please
    But to remember all my hopes and fortunes
    Had reference to his liking, you will grant,
    That though I did not well towards you, I yet
    Did wisely for myself.

Novall Junior:
    With too much fervour
    I have so long loved, and still love you, mistress,
    To esteem that an injury to me,
    Which was to you convenient:—that is past

My help, is past my cure. You yet may, lady,
In recompense of all my duteous service,
(Provided that your will answer your power,)
Become my creditress.

Beaumelle:
I understand you;
And for assurance the request you make
Shall not be long unanswered,—pray you sit;
And by what you shall hear, you'll easily find,
My passions are much fitter to desire,
Than to be sued to.

(They court.)

(Enter Romont and Florimel behind.)

Florimel:
Sir, it is not envy
At the start my fellow has got of me in
My lady's good opinion, that's the motive
Of this discovery; but the due payment
Of what I owe her honour.

Romont:
So I conceive it.

Florimel:
I have observed too much, nor shall my silence
Prevent the remedy:—Yonder they are;
I dare not be seen with you. You may do
What you think fit, which will be, I presume,
The office of a faithful and tried friend
To my young lord.

(Exit.)

Romont:
This is no vision: ha!

Novall Junior:
With the next opportunity?

Beaumelle:
>By this kiss,
>And this, and this.

Novall Junior:
>That you would ever swear thus!

Romont (*comes forward*):
>If I seem rude, your pardon, lady; yours
>I do not ask: come; do not dare to shew me
>A face of anger, or the least dislike:
>Put on, and suddenly, a milder look,
>I shall grow rough else.

Novall Junior:
>What have I done, sir,
>To draw this harsh unsavoury language from you?

Romont:
>Done, popinjay! why, dost thou think, that, if
>I e'er had dreamt that thou hadst done me wrong,
>Thou shouldst outlive it?

Beaumelle:
>This is something more
>Than my lord's friendship gives commission for.

Novall Junior:
>Your presence and the place make him presume
>Upon my patience.

Romont:
>As if thou e'er wert angry
>But with thy tailor! and yet that poor shred
>Can bring more to the making up of a man,
>Than can be hoped from thee: thou art his creature;
>And did he not, each morning, new create thee,
>Thou'dst stink, and be forgotten. I'll not change
>One syllable more with thee, until thou bring
>Some testimony, under good men's hands,
>Thou art a Christian: I suspect thee strongly,
>And will be satisfied; till which time, keep from me.—

The entertainment of your visitation,
Has made what I intended one, a business.

Novall Junior:
So! we shall meet.—Madam.

Romont:
Use that leg again
And I'll cut off the other.

Novall Junior:
Very good.

(Exit.)

Romont:
What a perfume the muskcat leaves behind him!
Do you admit him for a property,
To save you charges, lady?

Beaumelle:
'Tis not useless,
Now you are to succeed him.

Romont:
So I respect you,
Not for yourself, but in remembrance of
Who is your father, and whose wife you now are,
That I choose rather not to understand
Your nasty scoff, than—

Beaumelle:
What, you will not beat me
If I expound it to you! Here's a tyrant
Spares neither man nor woman!

Romont:
My intents,
Madam, deserve not this; nor do I stay
To be the whetstone of your wit: preserve it
To spend on such as know how to admire
Such colour'd stuff. In me, there now speaks to you,

As true a friend and servant to your honour,
And one that will with as much hazard guard it,
As ever man did goodness:—but then, lady,
You must endeavour not alone to be,
But to appear, worthy such love and service.

Beaumelle:
To what tends this?

Romont:
Why, to this purpose, lady.
I do desire you should prove such a wife
To Charalois (and such a one he merits)
As Cæsar, did he live, could not except at;
Not only innocent from crime, but free
From all taint and suspicion.

Beaumelle:
They are base
That judge me otherwise.

Romont:
But yet be careful:
Detraction's a bold monster, and fears not
To wound the fame of princes, if it find
But any blemish in their lives to work on.
But I'll be plainer with you: had the people
Been learn'd to speak but what even now I saw,
Their malice out of that would raise an engine
To overthrow your honour. In my sight,
With yonder painted fool I frighted from you,
You used familiarity beyond
A modest entertainment: you embraced him
With too much ardour for a stranger, and
Met him with kisses neither chaste nor comely.
But learn you to forget him, as I will
Your bounties to him; you will find it safer
Rather to be uncourtly than immodest.

Beaumelle:
This pretty rag about your neck shews well,
And, being coarse and little worth, it speaks you
As terrible as thrifty.

Romont:
>Madam!

Beaumelle:
>Yes:
>And this strong belt, in which you hang your honour,
>Will outlast twenty scarfs.

Romont:
>What mean you, lady?

Beaumelle:
>And [then] all else about you cap-a-pié,
>So uniform in spite of handsomeness,
>Shews such a bold contempt of comeliness,
>That 'tis not strange your laundress in the leaguer
>Grew mad with love of you.

Romont:
>Is my free counsel
>Answer'd with this ridiculous scorn?

Beaumelle:
>These objects
>Stole very much of my attention from me;
>Yet something I remember, to speak truth,
>Deliver'd gravely, but to little purpose,
>That almost would have made me swear some curate
>Had stolen into the person of Romont,
>And, in the praise of goodwife honesty,
>Had read an homily.

Romont:
>By this hand—

Beaumelle:
>And sword,
>I will make up your oath, it will want weight else.—
>You are angry with me, and poor I laugh at it.
>Do you come from the camp, which affords only
>The conversation of cast suburb shores,
>To set down, to a lady of my rank,
>Limits of entertainment?

Romont:
>Sure a legion
>Has possest this woman!

Beaumelle:
>One stamp more would do well: yet I desire not
>You should grow horn-mad till you have a wife.
>You are come to warm meat, and perhaps clean linen;
>Feed, wear it, and be thankful. For me, know,
>That though a thousand watches were set on me,
>And you the master-spy, I yet would use
>The liberty that best likes me. I will revel,
>Feast, kiss, embrace, perhaps grant larger favours;
>Yet such as live upon my means shall know
>They must not murmur at it. If my lord
>Be now grown yellow, and has chose out you
>To serve his jealousy this way, tell him this:
>You have something to inform him.

(Exit.)

Romont:
>And I will;
>Believe it, wicked one, I will. Hear, heaven,
>But, hearing, pardon me!—if these fruits grow
>Upon the tree of marriage, let me shun it,
>As a forbidden sweet. An heir, and rich,
>Young, beautiful, yet add to this—a wife,
>And I will rather choose a spittle sinner
>Carted an age before, though three parts rotten,
>And take it for a blessing, rather than
>Be fetter'd to the hellish slavery
>Of such an impudence.

(Enter Beaumont with writings.)

Beaumont:
>Colonel, good fortune
>To meet you thus! You look sad; but I'll tell you
>Something that shall remove it. O, how happy
>Is my lord Charalois in his fair bride!

Romont:
> A happy man, indeed!—pray you, in what?

Beaumont:
> I dare swear, you would think so good a lady
> A dower sufficient.

Romont:
> No doubt. But, on.

Beaumont:
> So fair, so chaste, so virtuous, so—indeed,
> All that is excellent!

Romont:
> Women have no cunning
> To gull the world!
>
> *(Aside.)*

Beaumont:
> Yet, to all these, my lord,
> Her father, gives the full addition of
> All he does now possess in Burgundy:
> These writings, to confirm it, are new seal'd,
> And I most fortunate to present him with them;
> I must go seek him out. Can you direct me?

Romont:
> You'll find him breaking a young horse.

Beaumont:
> I thank you.
>
> *(Exit.)*

Romont:
> I must do something worthy Charalois' friendship.
> If she were well inclined, to keep her so
> Deserved not thanks; and yet, to stay a woman
> Spurr'd headlong by hot lust to her own ruin,
> Is harder than to prop a falling tower
> With a deceiving reed.

(Enter Rochfort, *speaking to a Servant within.)*

Rochfort:
> Some one seek for me
> As soon as he returns.

Romont:
> Her father! ha!—
> How if I break this to him? sure it cannot
> Meet with an ill construction: his wisdom,
> Made powerful by the authority of a father,
> Will warrant and give privilege to his counsels.
> It shall be so.—My lord!

Rochfort:
> Your friend, Romont.
> Would you aught with me?

Romont:
> I stand so engaged
> To your so many favours, that I hold it
> A breach in thankfulness, should I not discover,
> Though with some imputation to myself,
> All doubts that may concern you.

Rochfort:
> The performance
> Will make this protestation worth my thanks.

Romont:
> Then, with your patience, lend me your attention:
> For what I must deliver, whisper'd only,
> You will with too much grief receive.

(Enter Beaumelle *and* Bellapert, *behind.)*

Beaumelle:
> See, wench!
> Upon my life, as I forespake, he's now
> Preferring his complaint; but be thou perfect,
> And we will fit him.

Bellapert:
>Fear not me; pox on him!
>A captain turn informer against kissing!
>Would he were hang'd up in his rusty armour!—
>But, if our fresh wits cannot turn the plots
>Of such a mouldy murrion on itself,
>Rich clothes, choice fare, and a true friend at a call,
>With all the pleasures the night yields, forsake us!

Rochfort:
>This in my daughter! do not wrong her.

Bellapert:
>Now
>Begin: the game's afoot, and we in distance.

Beaumelle *(comes forward):*
>'Tis thy fault, foolish girl! pin on my veil,
>I will not wear those jewels. Am I not
>Already match'd beyond my hopes? yet still
>You prune and set me forth, as if I were
>Again to please a suitor.

Bellapert:
>'Tis the course
>That our great ladies take.

Beaumelle:
>A weak excuse!
>Those that are better seen in what concerns
>A lady's honour and fair fame, condemn it.
>You wait well! in your absence, my lord's friend,
>The understanding, grave, and wise Romont—

Romont:
>Must I be still her sport?

Beaumelle:
>Reproved me for it;
>And he has travell'd to bring home a judgment
>Not to be contradicted. You will say
>My father, that owes more to years than he,

> Has brought me up to music, language, courtship,
> And I must use them: true; but not to offend,
> Or render me suspected.

Rochfort:
> Does your fine story
> Begin from this?

Beaumelle:
> I thought a parting kiss
> From young Novall would have displeased no more
> Than heretofore it hath done; but I find
> I must restrain such favours now; look, therefore,
> As you are careful to continue mine,
> That I no more be visited. I'll endure
> The strictest course of life that jealousy
> Can think secure enough, ere my behaviour
> Shall call my fame in question.

Romont:
> Ten disemblers
> Are in this subtle devil! You believe this?

Rochfort:
> So far, that if you trouble me again
> With a report like this, I shall not only
> Judge you malicious in your disposition,
> But study to repent what I have done
> To such a nature.

Romont:
> Why, 'tis exceeding well.

Rochfort:
> And for you, daughter, off with this, off with it!
> I have that confidence in your goodness, I,
> That I will not consent to have you live
> Like to a recluse in a cloister: Go,
> Call in the gallants, let them make you merry;
> Use all fit liberty.

Bellapert:
>Blessing upon you!
>If this new preacher with the sword and feather
>Could prove his doctrine for canonical,
>We should have a fine world.

>>*(Exit.)*

Rochfort:
>Sir, if you please
>To bear yourself as fits a gentleman,
>The house is at your service; but, if not,
>Though you seek company elsewhere, your absence
>Will not be much lamented.

>>*(Exit.)*

Romont:
>If this be
>The recompense of striving to preserve
>A wanton gigglet honest, very shortly
>'Twill make all mankind panders.—Do you smile,
>Good lady looseness! your whole sex is like you,
>And that man's mad that seeks to better any:
>What new change have you next?

Beaumelle:
>Oh, fear not you, sir;
>I'll shift into a thousand, but I will
>Convert your heresy.

Romont:
>What heresy? speak.

Beaumelle:
>Of keeping a lady that is married,
>From entertaining servants—

(Enter Novall Junior, Malotin, Liladam, Aymer, *and* Pontalier.*)*

>—O, you are welcome!
>Use any means to vex him,

And then with welcome follow me.
>   *(Aside to them, and exit.)*

Novall Junior:
> You are tired
> With your grave exhortations, colonel!

Liladam:
> How is it? faith, your lordship may do well
> To help him to some church preferment: 'tis
> The fashion now for men of all conditions,
> However they have lived, to end that way.

Aymer:
> That face would do well in a surplice.

Romont:
> Rogues,
> Be silent—or—

Pontalier:
> 'Sdeath! will you suffer this?

Romont:
> And you, the master-rogue, the coward rascal,
> I shall be with you suddenly.

Novall Junior:
> Pontalier,
> If I should strike him, I know I should kill him;
> And therefore I would have thee beat him, for
> He's good for nothing else.

Liladam:
> His back
> Appears to me, as it would tire a beadle;
> And then he has a knotted brow, would bruise
> A courtlike hand to touch it.

Aymer:
> He looks like
> A currier when his hides grow dear.

Pontalier:
>Take heed
>He curry not some of you.

Novall Junior:
>Gads me! he's angry.

Romont:
>I break no jests; but I can break my sword
>About your pates.

>*(Enter Charalois and Beaumont.)*

Liladam:
>Here's more.

Aymer:
>Come, let's be gone:
>We are beleaguer'd.

Novall Junior:
>Look, they bring up their troops.

Pontalier:
>Will you sit down
>With this disgrace? you are abused most grossly.

Liladam:
>I grant you, sir, we are; and you would have us
>Stay, and be more abused.

Novall Junior:
>My lord, I'm sorry
>Your house is so inhospitable, we must quit it.

>*(Exeunt all but Charalois and Romont.)*

Charalois:
>Prithee, Romont, what caused this uproar?

Romont:
>Nothing;
>They laugh'd, and used their scurvy wits upon me.

Charalois:
>Come, 'tis thy jealous nature: but I wonder
>That you, which are an honest man and worthy,
>Should foster this suspicion: no man laughs,
>No one can whisper, but thou apprehend'st
>His conference and his scorn reflect on thee:
>For my part, they should scoff their thin wits out,
>So I not heard them; beat me, not being there.
>Leave, leave these fits to conscious men, to such
>As are obnoxious to those foolish things
>As they can gibe at.

Romont:
>Well, sir.

Charalois:
>Thou art known
>Valiant without defect, rightly defined,
>Which is as fearing to do injury,
>As tender to endure it; not a brabbler,
>A swearer—

Romont:
>Pish, pish! what needs this, my lord?
>If I be known none such, how vainly you
>Do cast away good counsel! I have loved you,
>And yet must freely speak; so young a tutor
>Fits not so old a soldier as I am:
>And I must tell you, 'twas in your behalf
>I grew enraged thus, yet had rather die
>Than open the great cause a syllable further.

Charalois:
>In my behalf! Wherein hath Charalois
>Unfitly so demean'd himself, to give
>The least occasion to the loosest tongue
>To throw aspersions on him? or so weakly
>Protected his own honour, as it should
>Need a defence from any but himself?
>They are fools that judge me by my outward seeming.
>Why should my gentleness beget abuse?
>The lion is not angry that does sleep,

Nor every man a coward that can weep.
  For God's sake, speak the cause.

Romont:
  Not for the world.
  Oh! it will strike disease into your bones,
  Beyond the cure of physic; drink your blood,
  Rob you of all your rest, contract your sight,
  Leave you no eyes but to see misery,
  And of your own; nor speech, but to wish thus,
  Would I had perish'd in the prison's jaws,
  From whence I was redeem'd!—'twill wear you old,
  Before you have experience in that art
  That causes your affliction.

Charalois:
  Thou dost strike
  A deathful coldness to my heart's high heat,
  And shrink'st my liver like the calenture.
  Declare this foe of mine, and life's, that like
  A man I may encounter and subdue it.
  It shall not have one such effect in me,
  As thou denouncest: with a soldier's arm,
  If it be strength, I'll meet it; if a fault
  Belonging to my mind, I'll cut it off
  With mine own reason, as a scholar should.
  Speak, though it make me monstrous.

Romont:
  I will die first.
  Farewell; continue merry, and high heaven
  Keep your wife chaste!

Charalois:
  Hum! Stay, and take this wolf
  Out of my breast, that thou hast lodged there, or
  For ever lose me.

Romont:
  Lose not, sir, yourself,
  And I will venture:—so, the door is fast.
                              (Locks the door.)

Now, noble Charalois, collect yourself,
Summon your spirits, muster all your strength
That can belong to man; sift passion
From every vein, and whatsoe'er ensues,
Upbraid not me hereafter, as the cause of
Jealousy, discontent, slaughter, and ruin:
Make me not parent to sin.—You will know
This secret that I burn with?

Charalois:
Devil on't,
What should it be! Romont, I heard you wish
My wife's continuance of chastity.

Romont:
There was no hurt in that.

Charalois:
Why, do you know
A likelihood, or possibility,
Unto the contrary?

Romont:
I know it not, but doubt it; these the grounds:
The servant of your wife now, young Novall,
The son unto your father's enemy,
(Which aggravates presumption the more,)
I have been warn'd of, touching her:—nay, seen them
Tied heart to heart, one in another's arms,
Multiplying kisses, as if they meant
To pose arithmetic; or whose eyes would
Be first burnt out with gazing on the other's.
I saw their mouths engender, and their palms
Glew'd, as if love had lock'd them; their words flow
And melt each other's, like two circling flames,
Where chastity, like a phœnix, methought, burn'd,
But left the world nor ashes, nor an heir.—
Why stand you silent thus? what cold dull phlegm,
As if you had no drop of choler mix'd
In your whole constitution, thus prevails,
To fix you now thus stupid, hearing this?

Charalois:
> You did not see him on my couch within,
> Like George a-horseback, on her, nor a-bed?

Romont:
> No.

Charalois:
> Ha! ha!

Romont:
> Laugh you! even so did your wife,
> And her indulgent father.

Charalois:
> They were wise:
> Wouldst have me be a fool?

Romont:
> No, but a man.

Charalois:
> There is no dram of manhood to suspect,
> On such thin airy circumstance as this;
> Mere compliment and courtship. Was this tale
> The hideous monster which you so conceal'd?
> Away, thou curious-impertinent,
> And idle searcher of such lean, nice toys!
> Go, thou seditious sower of debate,
> Fly to such matches, where the bridegroom doubts
> He holds not worth enough to countervail
> The virtue and the beauty of his wife!
> Thou buzzing drone, that 'bout my ears dost hum,
> To strike thy rankling sting into my heart,
> Whose venom time nor medicine could assuage,
> Thus do I put thee off! and, confident
> In mine own innocency and desert,
> Dare not conceive her so unreasonable,
> To put Novall in balance against me;
> An upstart, craned up to the height he has.
> Hence, busybody! thou'rt no friend to me,
> That must be kept to a wife's injury.

Romont:
>Is't possible?—farewell, fine honest man!
>Sweet-temper'd lord, adieu! What apoplexy
>Hath knit sense up? is this Romont's reward?
>Bear witness, the great spirit of thy father,
>With what a healthful hope I did administer
>This potion, that hath wrought so virulently!
>I not accuse thy wife of act, but would
>Prevent her precipice to thy dishonour,
>Which now thy tardy sluggishness will admit.
>Would I had seen thee graved with thy great sire,
>Ere lived to have men's marginal fingers point
>At Charalois, as a lamented story!
>An emperor put away his wife for touching
>Another man; but thou wouldst have thine tasted,
>And keep her, I think—Phoh! I am a fire,
>To warm a dead man, that waste out myself.
>Bleed—What a plague, a vengeance, is't to me,
>If you will be a cuckold? here, I shew
>A sword's point to thee, this side you may shun,
>Or that, the peril; if you will run on,
>I cannot help it.

Charalois:
>Didst thou never see me
>Angry, Romont?

Romont:
>Yes, and pursue a foe
>Like lightning.

Charalois:
>Prithee, see me so no more:
>I can be so again. Put up thy sword,
>And take thyself away, lest I draw mine.

Romont:
>Come, fright your foes with this, sir! I'm your friend,
>And dare stand by you thus.

Charalois:
>Thou art not my friend,

Or being so, thou art mad; I must not buy
Thy friendship at this rate. Had I just cause,
Thou know'st I durst pursue such injury
Through fire, air, water, earth, nay, were they all
Shuffled again to chaos; but there's none.
Thy skill, Romont, consists in camps, not courts.
Farewell, uncivil man! let's meet no more:
Here our long web of friendship I untwist.
Shall I go whine, walk pale, and lock my wife,
For nothing, from her birth's free liberty,
That open'd mine to me? yes! if I do,
The name of cuckold then dog me with scorn!
I am a Frenchman, no Italian born.

(Exit.)

Romont:
A dull Dutch rather: fall and cool, my blood!
Boil not in zeal of thy friend's hurt so high,
That is so low and cold himself in't! Woman,
How strong art thou! how easily beguiled!
How thou dost rack us by the very horns!
Now wealth, I see, change manners and the man.
Something I must do mine own wrath to assuage,
And note my friendship to an after-age.

(Exit.)

(ACT IV. SCENE I.—A room in Novall's *house.)*

(Novall Junior *discovered seated before a looking-glass, with a* Barber *and* Perfumer *dressing his hair, while a* Tailor *adjusts a new suit which he wears.* Liladam, Aymer, *and a* Page *attending.)*

Novall Junior:
Mend this a little: pox! thou hast burnt me. Oh, fie upon't! O lard! he has made me smell for all the world like a flax, or a red-headed woman's chamber: Powder, powder, powder!

Perfumer:
Oh, sweet lord!

Page:
> That's his perfumer.

Tailor:
> Oh, dear lord!

Novall Junior:
> Monsieur Liladam, Aymer, how allow you the model of these clothes?

Aymer:
> Admirably, admirably; oh, sweet lord! assuredly it's pity the worms should eat thee.

Page:
> Here's a fine cell! a lord, a tailor, a perfumer, a barber, and a pair of monsieurs: three to three; as little wit in the one, as honesty in the other. 'Sfoot! I'll into the country again, learn to speak truth, drink ale, and converse with my father's tenants; here I hear nothing all day, but—*Upon my soul, as I am a gentleman, and an honest man!*
>
> *(Aside.)*

Aymer:
> I vow and affirm, your tailor must needs be an expert geometrician; he has the longitude, latitude, altitude, profundity, every dimension of your body, so exquisitely—here's a lace laid as directly as if truth were a tailor.

Page:
> That were a miracle.
>
> *(Aside.)*

Liladam:
> With a hair's-breadth's error, there's a shoulder-piece cut, and the base of a pickadille in *puncto*.

Aymer:
> You are right, monsieur; his vestaments sit as if they grew upon him, or art had wrought them on the same loom as nature framed his lordship; as if your tailor were deep read in astrology, and had taken measure of your honourable

body with a Jacob's staff, an ephimerides.

Tailor:
I am bound t'ye, gentlemen.

Page:
You are deceived; they'll be bound to you: you must remember to trust them none.
(Aside.)

Novall Junior:
Nay, 'faith, thou art a reasonable neat artificer, give the devil his due.

Page:
Ay, if he would but cut the coat according to the cloth still.
(Aside.)

Novall Junior:
I now want only my mistress' approbation, who is, indeed, the most polite, punctual, queen of dressing in all Burgandy—pah! and makes all other young ladies appear as if they came from board last week out of the country: is't not true, Liladam?

Liladam:
True, my lord! as if any thing your lordship could say could be otherwise than true.

Novall Junior:
Nay, o'my soul, 'tis so; what fouler object in the world, than to see a young, fair, handsome beauty unhandsomely dighted, and incongruently accoutred? or a hopeful chevalier unmethodically appointed in the external ornaments of nature? For, even as the index tells us the contents of stories, and directs to the particular chapters, even so does the outward habit and superficial order of garments (in man and woman) give us a taste of the spirit, and demonstratively point (as it were a manual note from the margin) all the internal quality and habiliment of the soul; and there cannot be a more evident, palpable, gross manifestation of poor, degenerate, dunghilly blood and breeding, than a rude,

unpolished, disordered, and slovenly outside.

Page:
An admirable lecture! oh, all you gallants, that hope to be saved by your clothes, edify, edify!
(Aside.)

Aymer:
By the Lard, sweet lard, thou deservest a pension o' the state.

Page:
O' the tailors: two such lords were able to spread tailors o'er the face of the whole kingdom.
(Aside.)

Novall Junior:
Pox o' this glass! it flatters.—I could find in my heart to break it.

Page:
O, save the glass, my lord, and break their heads;
They are the greater flatterers, I assure you.
(Aside.)

Aymer:
Flatters! detracts, impairs—yet, put it by,
Lest thou, dear lord, Narcissus like, should'st doat
Upon thyself, and die; and rob the world
Of nature's copy, that she works form by.

Liladam:
Oh that I were the infanta queen of Europe!
Who but thyself, sweet lord, should marry me?

Novall Junior:
I marry! were there a queen o' the world, not I.
Wedlock! no; padlock, horselock:—I wear spurs
(He capers.)
To keep it off my heels. Yet, my Aymer,
Like a free, wanton jennet in the meadows,
I look about, and neigh, take hedge and ditch,
Feed in my neighbour's pastures, pick my choice

Of all their fair-maned mares: but married once,
A man I staked or poun'd, and cannot graze
Beyond his own hedge.

(Enter Pontalier *and* Malotin.*)*

Pontalier:
I have waited, sir,
Three hours to speak wi'ye, and not take it well
Such magpies are admitted, whilst I dance
Attendance.

Liladam:
Magpies! what d'ye take me for?

Pontalier:
A long thing with a most unpromising face.

Aymer:
I'll never ask him what he takes me for.

Malotin:
Do not, sir,
For he'll go near to tell you.

Pontalier:
Art not thou
A barber-surgeon?

Barber:
Yes, sirrah; why?

Pontalier:
My lord is sorely troubled with two scabs.

Liladam, Aymer:
Hum—

Pontalier:
I prithee cure him of them.

Novall Junior:
Pish! no more,
Thy gall sure's overflown; these are my council,

And we were now in serious discourse.

Pontalier:
    Of perfume and apparel! Can you rise,
    And spend five hours in dressing-talk with these?

Novall Junior:
    Thou'ldst have me be a dog: up, stretch, and shake,
    And ready for all day.

Pontalier:
    Sir, would you be
    More curious in preserving of your honour trim,
    It were more manly. I am come to wake
    Your reputation from this lethargy
    You let it sleep in; to persuade, impórtune,
    Nay, to provoke you, sir, to call to account
    This colonel Romont, for the foul wrong
    Which, like a burthen, he hath laid upon you,
    And, like a drunken porter, you sleep under.
    'Tis all the town talks; and, believe it, sir,
    If your tough sense persist thus, you are undone,
    Utterly lost; you will be scorn'd and baffled
    By every lacquey: season now your youth
    With one brave thing, and it shall keep the odour
    Even to your death, beyond, and on your tomb
    Scent like sweet oils and frankincense. Sir, this life,
    Which once you saved, I ne'er since counted mine;
    I borrow'd it of you, and now will pay it:
    I tender you the service of my sword,
    To bear your challenge; if you'll write, your fate
    I'll make mine own; whate'er betide you, I,
    That have lived by you, by your side will die.

Novall Junior:
    Ha! ha! wouldst have me challenge poor Romont?—
    Fight with close breeches, thou mayst think I dare not:
    Do not mistake me, coz, I am very valiant;
    But valour shall not make me such an ass.
    What use is there of valour now-a-days?
    'Tis sure or to be kill'd, or to be hang'd.

Fight thou as thy mind moves thee, 'tis thy trade;
Thou hast nothing else to do. Fight with Romont!
No; I'll not fight, under a lord.

Pontalier:
Farewell, sir!
I pity you.
Such living lords walk, their dead honour's graves,
For no companions fit but fools and knaves
Come, Malotin.

(Exeunt Pontalier *and* Malotin.*)*

(Enter Romont.*)*

Liladam:
'Sfoot, Colbrand, the low giant!

Aymer:
He has brought a battle in his face, let's go.

Page:
Colbrand, d'ye call him? he'll make some of you
Smoke, I believe.

Romont:
By your leave, sirs!

Aymer:
Are you a consort?

Romont:
Do you take me for
A fiddler? you're deceived: look! I'll pay you.

(Kicks them.)

Page:
It seems he knows you one, he bum-fiddles you so.

Liladam:
>Was there ever so base a fellow?

Aymer:
>A rascal.

Liladam:
>A most uncivil groom.

Aymer:
>Offer to kick a gentleman in a nobleman's chamber! a pox o' your manners!

Liladam:
>Let him alone, let him alone: thou shalt lose thy aim, fellow; if we stir against thee, hang us.

Page:
>'Sfoot! I think they have the better on him though they be kick'd, they talk so.

Liladam:
>Let's leave the mad ape.
>
>   *(Going.)*

Novall Junior:
>Gentlemen!

Liladam:
>Nay, my lord, we will not offer to dishonour you so much as to stay by you, since he's alone.

Novall Junior:
>Hark you!

Aymer:
>We doubt the cause, and will not disparage you so much as to take your lordship's quarrel in hand. Plague on him, how he has crumpled our bands!

Page:
>I'll e'en away with them, for this soldier beats man, woman, and child.

(Exeunt all but Novall Junior *and* Romont.*)*

Novall Junior:
    What mean you, sir? My people!

Romont:
    Your boy's gone,
                              (Locks the door.)
    And your door's lock'd; yet for no hurt to you,
    But privacy. Call up your blood again:—
    Be not afraid, I do beseech you, sir;
    And, therefore, come, without more circumstance,
    Tell me how far the passages have gone
    'Twixt you and your fair mistress, Beaumelle.
    Tell me the truth, and by my hope of heaven,
    It never shall go further.

Novall Junior:
    Tell you! why, sir, are you my confessor?

Romont:
    I will be your confounder, if you do not.
                             (Draws a pocket dag.)
    Stir not, nor spend your voice.

Novall Junior:
    What will you do?

Romont:
    Nothing, but line your brain-pan, sir, with lead,
    If you not satisfy me suddenly:
    I am desperate of my life, and command yours.

Novall Junior:
    Hold! hold! I'll speak. I vow to heaven and you,
    She's yet untouch'd, more than her face and hands.
    I cannot call her innocent; for, I yield,
    On my solicitous wooing, she consented,
    Where time and place met opportunity,
    To grant me all requests.

Romont:
>But may I build
>On this assurance?

Novall Junior:
>As upon your faith.

Romont:
>Write this, sir; nay, you must.

Novall Junior:
>Pox of this gun!

Romont:
>Withal, sir, you must swear, and put your oath
>Under your hand, (shake not,) ne'er to frequent
>This lady's company, nor ever send
>Token, or message, or letter, to incline
>This, too much prone already, yielding lady.

Novall Junior:
>'Tis done, sir.

Romont:
>Let me see this first is right:
>
>*(Reading.)*
>And here you wish a sudden death may light
>Upon your body, and hell take your soul,
>If ever more you see her, but by chance;
>Much less allure her. Now, my lord, your hand.

Novall Junior:
>My hand to this!

Romont:
>Your heart else, I assure you.

Novall Junior:
>Nay, there 'tis.

Romont:
>So! keep this last article

Of your faith given, and, stead of threatenings, sir,
The service of my sword and life is yours.
But not a word of it:—'tis fairies' treasure,
Which but reveal'd, brings on the blabber's ruin.
Use your youth better, and this excellent form
Heaven hath bestow'd upon you. So, good morrow
To your lordship!

(Exit.)

Novall Junior:
Good devil to your rogueship! No man's safe—
I'll have a cannon planted in my chamber,
Against such roaring rogues.

(Enter Bellapert, *hastily.)*

Bellapert:
My lord, away!
The caroch stays: now have your wish, and judge
If I have been forgetful.

Novall Junior:
Hah!

Bellapert:
Do you stand
Humming and hahing now?

(Exit.)

Novall Junior:
Sweet wench, I come.
Hence, fear!
I swore—that's all one; my next oath I'll keep
That I did mean to break, and then 'tis quit.
No pain is due to lovers' perjury:
If Jove himself laugh at it, so will I.

(Exit.)

(SCENE II.—An outer room in Aymer's *house. Enter* Charalois *and* Beaumont.*)*

Beaumont:
>I grieve for the distaste, though I have manners
>Not to enquire the cause, fallen out between
>Your lordship and Romont.

Charalois:
>I love a friend,
>So long as he continues in the bounds
>Prescribed by friendship; but, when he usurps
>Too far on what is proper to myself,
>And puts the habit of a governor on,
>I must and will preserve my liberty.
>But speak of something else, this is a theme
>I take no pleasure in. What's this Aymer,
>Whose voice for song, and excellent knowledge in
>The chiefest parts of music, you bestow
>Such praises on?

Beaumont:
>He is a gentleman
>(For so his quality speaks him) well received
>Among our greatest gallants; but yet holds
>His main dependence from the young lord Novall.
>Some tricks and crotchets he has in his head,
>As all musicians have, and more of him
>I dare not author: but, when you have heard him,
>I may presume your lordship so will like him,
>That you'll hereafter be a friend to music.

Charalois:
>I never was an enemy to't, Beaumont,
>Nor yet do I subscribe to the opinion
>Of those old captains, that thought nothing musical
>But cries of yielding enemies, neighing of horses,
>Clashing of armour, loud shouts, drums, and trumpets:
>Nor, on the other side, in favour of it,
>Affirm the world was made by musical discord;
>Or that the happiness of our life consists
>In a well-varied note upon the lute:
>I love it to the worth of't, and no further.—
>But let us see this wonder.

Beaumont:
>He prevents
>My calling of him.

>>*(Enter* Aymer, *speaking to one within.)*

Aymer:
>Let the coach be brought
>To the back gate, and serve the banquet up.—
>My good lord Charalois! I think my house
>Much honour'd in your presence.

Charalois:
>To have means
>To know you better, sir, has brought me hither
>A willing visitant; and you'll crown my welcome
>In making me a witness to your skill,
>Which, crediting from others, I admire.

Aymer:
>Had I been one hour sooner made acquainted
>With your intent, my lord, you should have found me
>Better provided: now, such as it is,
>Pray you grace with your acceptance.

Beaumont:
>You are modest.

Aymer:
>Begin the last new air.

>>*(To the Musicians within.)*

Charalois:
>Shall we not see them?

Aymer:
>This little distance from the instruments,
>Will to your ears convey the harmony
>With more delight.

Charalois:
    I'll not contend.

Aymer:
    You are tedious.
                        (To the Musicians.)
    By this means shall I with one banquet please
    Two companies, those within and these gulls here.

Music, and a song:

        Citizens' Song *of the Courtier.*

Courtier, if thou needs wilt wive,
From this lesson learn to thrive;
If thou match a lady, that passes thee in birth and state,
Let her curious garments be
Twice above thine own degree;
This will draw great eyes upon her,
Get her servants, and thee honour.

        Courtier's Song *of the Citizens.*

Poor citizen, if thou wilt be
A happy husband, learn of me
To set thy wife first in thy shop;
A fair wife, a kind wife, a sweet wife, sets a poor man up.
What though thy shelves be ne'er so bare,
A woman still is current ware;
Each man will cheapen, foe and friend;
But, whilst thou art at t'other end,
Whate'er thou seest, or what dost hear,
Fool, have no eye to, nor an ear;
And after supper, for her sake,
When thou hast fed, snort, though thou wake:
What though the gallants call thee Mome!
Yet with thy lantern light her home;
Then look into the town, and tell
If no such tradesmen there do well.

Beaumelle [*within*]:
    Ha! ha! ha!

Charalois:
>How's this! it is my lady's laugh, most certain.
>When I first pleased her, in this merry language
>She gave me thanks.
>>*(Aside.)*

Beaumont:
>How like you this?

Charalois:
>'Tis rare—
>Yet I may be deceived, and should be sorry,
>Upon uncertain suppositions, rashly
>To write myself in the black list of those
>I have declaim'd against, and to Romont.
>>*(Aside.)*

Aymer:
>I would he were well off!—Perhaps your lordship
>Likes not these sad tunes? I have a new song,
>Set to a lighter note, may please you better;
>'Tis call'd *the Happy Husband.*

Charalois:
>Pray you, sing it.

Song by Aymer.

Beaumelle [*within*]:
>Ha! ha! 'tis such a groom!

Charalois:
>Do I hear this,
>And yet stand doubtful?

>>*(Rushes into the house.)*

Aymer:
>Stay him—I am undone,
>And they discover'd.

Beaumont:
    What's the matter?

Aymer:
    Ah!
    That women, when they're well pleased, cannot hold;
    But must laugh out.

(Re-enter Charalois, *with his sword drawn, pursuing* Novall Junior, Beaumelle, *and* Bellapert.*)*

Novall Junior:
    Help! save me! murder! murder!

Beaumelle:
    Undone, undone, for ever!

Charalois:
    Oh, my heart!
    Hold yet a little—do not hope to 'scape
    By flight, it is impossible. Though I might
    On all advantage take thy life, and justly;
    This sword, my father's sword, that ne'er was drawn
    But to a noble purpose, shall not now
    Do the office of a hangman. I reserve it
    To right mine honour, not for a revenge
    So poor, that though with thee it should cut off
    Thy family, with all that are allied
    To thee in lust or baseness, 'twere still short of
    All terms of satisfaction. Draw!

Novall Junior:
    I dare not:
    I have already done you too much wrong,
    To fight in such a cause.

Charalois:
    Why, darest thou neither
    Be honest coward, nor yet valiant knave,
    In such a cause! come, do not shame thyself:
    Such whose bloods wrongs, or wrong done to themselves
    Could never heat, are yet in the defence

> Of their whores, daring. Look on her again:
> You thought her worth the hazard of your soul,
> And yet stand doubtful, in her quarrel, to
> Venture your body.

Beaumont:
> No, he fears his clothes,
> More than his flesh.

Charalois:
> Keep from me! guard thy life,
> Or, as thou hast lived like a goat, thou shalt
> Die like a sheep.

Novall Junior:
> Since there's no remedy,
> Despair of safety now in me prove courage!

(They fight, Novall falls.)

Charalois:
> How soon weak wrong's o'erthrown!
> Lend me your hand:
> Bear this to the caroch—come, you have taught me
> To say, you must and shall?

(Exeunt Beaumont and Bellapert, with the body of Novall; followed by Beaumelle.)

> I wrong you not,
> You are but to keep him company in love.—

(Re-enter Beaumont.)

> Is't done? 'tis well. Raise officers, and take care
> All you can apprehend within the house
> May be forthcoming. Do I appear much moved?

Beaumont:
> No, sir.

Charalois:
>My griefs are now thus to be born;
>Hereafter I'll find time and place to mourn.

>>*(Exeunt.)*

(SCENE III.—A street. Enter Romont and Pontalier.)

Pontalier:
>I was bound to seek you, sir.

Romont:
>And, had you found me
>In any place but in the street, I should
>Have done,—not talk'd to you. Are you, the captain,
>The hopeful Pontalier, whom I have seen
>Do, in the field, such service as then made you
>Their envy that commanded, here, at home,
>To play the parasite to a gilded knave,
>And, it may be, the pander?

Pontalier:
>Without this,
>I come to call you to account for what
>Is past already. I, by your example
>Of thankfulness to the dead general,
>By whom you were raised, have practised to be so
>To my good lord Novall, by whom I live;
>Whose least disgrace that is or may be offer'd,
>With all the hazard of my life and fortunes
>I will make good on you, or any man
>That has a hand in't: and, since you allow me
>A gentleman and a soldier, there's no doubt
>You will except against me. You shall meet
>With a fair enemy: you understand
>The right I look for, and must have?

Romont:
>I do;
>And with the next day's sun you shall hear from me.

>>*(Exeunt.)*

(SCENE IV.—A room in Charalois' *house. Enter* Charalois *with a casket,* Beaumelle, *and* Beaumont.*)*

Charalois:
    Pray bear this to my father, at his leisure
    He may peruse it: but with your best language
    Entreat his instant presence. You have sworn
    Not to reveal what I have done.

Beaumont:
    Nor will I—but—

Charalois:
    Doubt me not; by heaven, I will do nothing
    But what may stand with honour. Pray you, leave me

        (Exit Beaumont.*)*

    To my own thoughts.—If this be to me, rise;

        *(*Beaumelle *kneels.)*

    I am not worth the looking on, but only
    To feed contempt and scorn; and that from you,
    Who, with the loss of your fair name, have caused it,
    Were too much cruelty.

Beaumelle:
    I dare not move you
    To hear me speak. I know my fault is far
    Beyond qualification or excuse;
    That 'tis not fit for me to hope, or you
    To think of mercy; only I presume
    To entreat you would be pleased to look upon
    My sorrow for it, and believe these tears
    Are the true children of my grief, and not
    A woman's cunning.

Charalois:
    Can you, Beaumelle,
    Having deceived so great a trust as mine,
    Though I were all credulity, hope again

To get belief? No, no; if you look on me
With pity, or dare practise any means
To make my sufferings less, or give just cause
To all the world to think what I must do
Was call'd upon by you, use other ways:
Deny what I have seen, or justify
What you have done; and, as you desperately
Made shipwreck of your faith, to be a shore,
Use the arms of such a one, and such defence,
And multiply the sin with impudence.
Stand boldly up, and tell me to my teeth,
That you have done but what is warranted
By great examples, in all places where
Women inhabit; urge your own deserts,
Or want of me in merit; tell me how
Your dower, from the low gulf of poverty,
Weighed up my fortunes to what they now are:
That I was purchased by your choice and practice,
To shelter you from shame, that you might sin
As boldly as securely: that poor men
Are married to those wives that bring them wealth,
One day their husbands, but observers ever.
That when, by this proud usage, you have blown
The fire of my just vengeance to the height,
I then may kill you, and yet say 'twas done
In heat of blood, and after die myself,
To witness my repentance.

Beaumelle:
    O my fate!
That never would consent that I should see
How worthy you were both of love and duty,
Before I lost you; and my misery made
The glass in which I now behold your virtue!
While I was good, I was a part of you,
And of two, by the virtuous harmony
Of our fair minds, made one; but, since I wander'd
In the forbidden labyrinth of lust,
What was inseparable is by me divided.—
With justice, therefore, you may cut me off,
And from your memory wash the remembrance
That e'er I was; like to some vicious purpose,

Which, in your better judgment, you repent of,
And study to forget.

Charalois:
O Beaumelle,
That you can speak so well, and do so ill!
But you had been too great a blessing, if
You had continued chaste: see, how you force me
To this, because mine honour will not yield
That I again should love you.

Beaumelle:
In this life
It is not fit you should: yet you shall find,
Though I was bold enough to be a strumpet,
I dare not yet live one. Let those famed matrons,
That are canonized worthy of our sex,
Transcend me in their sanctity of life;
I yet will equal them in dying nobly,
Ambitious of no honour after life,
But that, when I am dead, you will forgive me.

Charalois:
How pity steals upon me! should I hear her

(Knocking within.)

But ten words more, I were lost.—One knock, go in.

(Exit Beaumelle.)

That to be merciful should be a sin!

(Enter Rochfort.)

O, sir, most welcome! Let me take your cloak,
I must not be denied.—Here are your robes,
As you love justice, once more put them on.
There is a cause to be determined of,
That does require such an integrity
As you have ever used.—I'll put you to
The trial of your constancy and goodness:

And look that you, that have been eagle-eyed
In other men's affairs, prove not a mole
In what concerns yourself. Take you your seat;
I will be for you presently.

(Exit.)

Rochfort:
Angels guard me!
To what strange tragedy does this induction
Serve for a prologue?

(Re-enter Charalois, Beaumelle, *and* Beaumont, *with Servants bearing the body of* Novall Junior.*)*

Charalois:
So, set it down before
The judgment-seat— *(Exeunt Servants.)*
—and stand you at the bar:
(To Beaumelle.*)*
For me, I am the accuser.

Rochfort:
Novall slain!
And Beaumelle, my daughter, in the place
Of one to be arraign'd!

Charalois:
O, are you touch'd!
I find that I must take another course.
Fear nothing, I will only blind your eyes;

(He binds his eyes.)

For justice should do so, when 'tis to meet
An object that may sway her equal doom
From what it should be aim'd at.—Good, my lord,
A day of hearing.

Rochfort:
It is granted, speak—
You shall have justice.

Charalois:
>I then here accuse,
>Most equal judge, the prisoner, your fair daughter,
>For whom I owed so much to you; your daughter,
>So worthy in her own parts, and that worth
>Set forth by yours, to whose so rare perfections,
>Truth witness with me, in the place of service
>I almost paid idolatrous sacrifice,
>To be a false adultress.

Rochfort:
>With whom?

Charalois:
>With this Novall here dead.

Rochfort:
>Be well advised;
>And ere you say *adultress* again,
>Her fame depending on it, be most sure
>That she is one.

Charalois:
>I took them in the act:
>I know no proof beyond it.

Rochfort:
>O my heart!

Charalois:
>A judge should feel no passions.

Rochfort:
>Yet remember
>He is a man, and cannot put off nature.
>What answer makes the prisoner?

Beaumelle:
>I confess
>The fact I am charged with, and yield myself
>Most miserably guilty.

Rochfort:
>Heaven take mercy
>Upon your soul, then! it must leave your body.—
>Now free mine eyes; I dare unmoved look on her,

>>(Charalois *unbinds his eyes.*)

>And fortify my sentence with strong reasons.
>Since that the politic law provides that servants,
>To whose care we commit our goods, shall die
>If they abuse our trust, what can you look for,
>To whose charge this most hopeful lord gave up
>All he received from his brave ancestors,
>Or he could leave to his posterity,
>His honour, wicked woman! in whose safety
>All his life's joys and comforts were lock'd up,
>Which thy - - - - lust, a thief, hath now stolen from him;
>And therefore—

Charalois:
>Stay, just judge:—may not what's lost
>By her one fault, (for I am charitable,
>And charge her not with many,) be forgotten
>In her fair life hereafter?

Rochfort:
>Never, sir.
>The wrong that's done to the chaste married bed,
>Repentant tears can never expiate;
>And be assured,—to pardon such a sin,
>Is an offence as great as to commit it.

Charalois:
>I may not then forgive her?

Rochfort:
>Nor she hope it.
>Nor can she wish to live: no sun shall rise,
>But, ere it set, shall shew her ugly lust
>In a new shape, and every one more horrid.
>Nay, even those prayers which, with such humble fervour,
>She seems to send up yonder, are beat back,

And all suits which her penitence can proffer,
As soon as made, are with contempt thrown out
Of all the courts of mercy.

Charalois:
Let her die, then!

(He stabs her.)

Better prepared, I'm sure, I could not take her,
Nor she accuse her father, as a judge
Partial against her.

Beaumelle:
I approve his sentence,
And kiss the executioner. My lust
Is now run from me in that blood in which
It was begot and nourish'd.

(Dies.)

Rochfort:
Is she dead, then?

Charalois:
Yes, sir; this is her heart-blood, is it not?
I think it be.

Rochfort:
And you have kill'd her?

Charalois:
True,
And did it by your doom.

Rochfort:
But I pronounced it
As a judge only, and a friend to justice;
And, zealous in defence of your wrong'd honour,
Broke all the ties of nature, and cast off
The love and soft affection of a father.
I, in your cause, put on a scarlet robe
Of red-died cruelty; but in return,
You have advanced for me no flag of mercy.

I look'd on you as a wrong'd husband; but
You closed your eyes against me as a father.
O Beaumelle! my daughter!

Charalois:
This is madness.

Rochfort:
Keep from me!—Could not one good thought rise up,
To tell you that she was my age's comfort,
Begot by a weak man, and born a woman,
And could not, therefore, but partake of frailty?
Or wherefore did not thankfulness step forth,
To urge my many merits, which I may
Object unto you, since you prove ungrateful,
Flint-hearted Charalois!

Charalois:
Nature does prevail
Above your virtue.

Rochfort:
No; it gives me eyes
To pierce the heart of your design against me:
I find it now, it was my state was aim'd at.
A nobler match was sought for, and the hours
I lived grew tedious to you: my compassion
Tow'rds you hath render'd me most miserable,
And foolish charity undone myself.
But there's a heaven above, from whose just wreak
No mists of policy can hide offenders.

Novall Senior [*within*]:
Force ope the doors!

(*Enter* Novall Senior, *with* Officers.)

O monster! cannibal!
Lay hold on him. My son, my son!—O Rochfort,
'Twas you gave liberty to this bloody wolf,
To worry all our comforts:—but this is
No time to quarrel; now give your assistance
For the revenge—

Rochfort:
>Call it a fitter name,
>Justice for innocent blood.

Charalois:
>Though all conspire
>Against that life which I am weary of,
>A little longer yet I'll strive to keep it,
>To shew, in spite of malice and their laws,
>His plea must speed, that hath an honest cause.

>>*(Exeunt.)*

(ACT V. SCENE I.—A street. Enter Tailor, *and two* Bailiffs *with* Liladam.*)*

Liladam:
>Why, 'tis both most unconscionable and untimely,
>To arrest a gallant for his clothes, before
>He has worn them out: besides, you said you ask'd
>My name in my lord's bond but for form only,
>And now you'll lay me up for't! Do not think
>The taking measure of a customer
>By a brace of varlets, though I rather wait
>Never so patiently, will prove a fashion
>Which any courtier or inns-of-court-man
>Would follow willingly.

Tailor:
>There I believe you.
>But, sir, I must have present monies, or
>Assurance to secure me when I shall;
>Or I will see to your coming forth.

Liladam:
>Plague on't!
>You have provided for my entrance in;
>That coming forth you talk of, concerns me.
>What shall I do? you have done me a disgrace
>In the arrest, but more in giving cause
>To all the street to think I cannot stand
>Without these two supporters for my arms.

Pray you, let them loose me: for their satisfaction,
I will not run away.

Tailor:
For theirs, you will not;
But for your own, you would. Look to him, fellows.

Liladam:
Why, do you call them fellows? do not wrong
Your reputation so. As you are merely
A tailor, faithful, apt to believe in gallants,
You are a companion at a ten-crown supper,
For cloth of bodkin, and may, with one lark,
Eat up three manchets, and no man observe you,
Or call your trade in question for't. But, when
You study your debt-book, and hold correspondence
With officers of the hanger, and leave swordsmen,
The learn'd conclude, the tailor and the serjeant,
In the expression of a knave and thief,
To be synonyma. Look, therefore, to it,
And let us part in peace; I would be loth
You should undo yourself.

(*Enter* Novall Senior, *and* Pontalier.)

Tailor:
To let you go,
Were the next way. But see! here's your old lord;
Let him but give his word I shall be paid,
And you are free.

Liladam:
'Slid! I will put him to't.
I can be but denied: or—what say you?
His lordship owing me three times your debt,
If you arrest him at my suit, and let me
Go run before, to see the action enter'd:—
'Twould be a witty jest!

Tailor:
I must have earnest:
I cannot pay my debts so.

Pontalier:
    Can your lordship
    Imagine, while I live, and wear a sword,
    Your son's death shall be unrevenged?

Novall Senior:
    I know not
    One reason why you should not do like others:
    I am sure, of all the herd that fed upon him,
    I cannot see in any, now he's gone,
    In pity or in thankfulness, one true sign
    Of sorrow for him.

Pontalier:
    All his bounties yet,
    Fell not in such unthankful ground: 'tis true,
    He had weaknesses, but such as few are free from;
    And, though none sooth'd them less than I, (for now,
    To say that I foresaw the dangers that
    Would rise from cherishing them, were but untimely,)
    I yet could wish the justice that you seek for,
    In the revenge, had been trusted to me,
    And not the uncertain issue of the laws.
    It has robb'd me of a noble testimony
    Of what I durst do for him:—but, however,
    My forfeit life redeem'd by him, though dead,
    Shall do him service.

Novall Senior:
    As far as my grief
    Will give me leave, I thank you.

Liladam:
    O, my lord!
    Oh my good lord! deliver me from these Furies.

Pontalier:
    Arrested! this is one of them, whose base
    And abject flattery help'd to dig his grave:
    He is not worth your pity, nor my anger.
    Go to the basket, and repent.

Novall Senior:
>Away!
>I only know thee now to hate thee deadly:
>I will do nothing for thee.

Liladam:
>Nor you, captain?

Pontalier:
>No; to your trade again; put off this case:
>It may be, the discovering what you were,
>When your unfortunate master took you up,
>May move compassion in your creditor.
>Confess the truth.

>>(*Exeunt* Novall Senior *and* Pontalier.)

Liladam:
>And now I think on't better,
>I will. Brother, your hand; your hand, sweet brother:
>I'm of your sect, and my gallantry but a dream,
>Out of which these two fearful apparitions,
>Against my will, have waked me. This rich sword,
>Grew suddenly out of a tailor's bodkin;
>These hangers, from my vails and fees in hell;
>And where as now this beaver sits, full often
>A thrifty cap, composed of broad-cloth lists,
>Near-kin unto the cushion where I sat,
>Cross-legg'd, and yet ungarter'd, hath been seen:
>Our breakfasts, famous for the butter'd loaves,
>I have with joy been oft acquainted with;
>And therefore use a conscience, though it be
>Forbidden in our hall towards other men,
>To me, that, as I have been, will again
>Be of the brotherhood.

1 Bailiff:
>I know him now;
>He was a prentice to Le Robe at Orleans.

Liladam:
>And from thence brought by my young lord, now dead,

Unto Dijon, and with him, till this hour,
Have been received here for a complete monsieur:
Nor wonder at it; for but tithe our gallants,
Even those of the first rank, and you will find
In every ten, one, peradventure two,
That smell rank of the dancing-school or fiddle,
The pantofle or pressing-iron:—but hereafter
We'll talk of this. I will surrender up
My suits again, there cannot be much loss;
'Tis but the turning of the lace, with one
Addition more you know of, and what wants,
I will work out.

Tailor:
Then here our quarrel ends:
The gallant is turn'd tailor, and all friends.

(Exeunt.)

(SCENE II.—The Court of Justice. Enter Romont *and* Beaumont.*)*

Romont:
You have them ready?

Beaumont:
Yes, and they will speak
Their knowledge in this cause, when you think fit
To have them call'd upon.

Romont:
'Tis well; and something
I can add to their evidence, to prove
This brave revenge, which they would have call'd murder,
A noble justice.

Beaumont:
In this you express
(The breach by my lord's want if you new made up)
A faithful friend.

Romont:
That friendship's raised on sand,

       Which every sudden gust of discontent,
       Or flowing of our passions, can change,
       As if it ne'er had been:—but do you know
       Who are to sit on him?

Beaumont:
       Monsieur Du Croy,
       Assisted by Charmi.

Romont:
       The advocate
       That pleaded for the marshal's funeral,
       And was check'd for it by Novall?

Beaumont:
       The same.

Romont:
       How fortunes that?

Beaumont:
       Why, sir, my lord Novall,
       Being the accuser, cannot be the judge;
       Nor would grieved Rochfort but lord Charalois,
       However he might wrong him by his power,
       Should have an equal hearing.

Romont:
       By my hopes
       Of Charalois' acquittal, I lament
       That reverend old man's fortune.

Beaumont:
       Had you seen him,
       As, to my grief, I have, now promise patience,
       And, ere it was believed, though spake by him
       That never brake his word, enraged again
       So far as to make war upon those hairs,
       Which not a barbarous Scythian durst presume
       To touch, but with a superstitious fear,
       As something sacred;—and then curse his daughter,
       But with more frequent violence, himself,

As if he had been guilty of her fault,
By being incredulous of your report,
You would not only judge him worthy pity,
But suffer with him:—but here comes the prisoner;

(Enter Officers *with* Charalois.*)*

I dare not stay to do my duty to him;
Yet, rest assured, all possible means in me
To do him service, keeps you company.

(Exit.)

Romont:
It is not doubted.

Charalois:
Why, yet as I came hither,
The people, apt to mock calamity,
And tread on the oppress'd, made no horns at me,
Though they are too familiar I deserve them.
And, knowing too what blood my sword hath drunk,
In wreak of that disgrace, they yet forbear
To shake their heads, or to revile me for
A murder; they rather all put on,
As for great losses the old Romans used,
A general face of sorrow, waited on
By a sad murmur breaking through their silence:
And no eye but was readier with a tear
To witness 'twas shed for me, than I could
Discern a face made up with scorn against me.
Why should I, then, though, for unusual wrongs,
I chose unusual means to right those wrongs,
Condemn myself, as over-partial
In my own cause?—Romont!

Romont:
Best friend, well met!
By my heart's love to you, and join to that,
My thankfulness that still lives to the dead,
I look upon you now with more true joy,
Than when I saw you married.

Charalois:
>You have reason
>To give you warrant for't: my falling off
>From such a friendship, with the scorn that answered
>Your too prophetic counsel, may well move you
>To think your meeting me, going to my death,
>A fit encounter for that hate which justly
>I have deserved from you.

Romont:
>Shall I still, then,
>Speak truth, and be ill understood?

Charalois:
>You are not.
>I am conscious I have wrong'd you; and allow me,
>Only a moral man;—to look on you,
>Whom foolishly I have abused and injured,
>Must of necessity be more terrible to me,
>Than any death the judges can pronounce,
>From the tribunal which I am to plead at.

Romont:
>Passion transports you.

Charalois:
>For what I have done
>To my false lady, or Novall, I can
>Give some apparent cause; but touching you,
>In my defence, child-like, I can say nothing
>But, I am sorry for't; a poor satisfaction!
>And yet, mistake me not; for it is more
>Than I will speak, to have my pardon sign'd
>For all I stand accused of.

Romont:
>You much weaken
>The strength of your good cause, should you but think
>A man for doing well could entertain
>A pardon, were it offer'd: you have given
>To blind and slow-paced justice wings and eyes,
>To see and overtake impieties,

Which, from a cold proceeding, had received
Indulgence or protection.

Charalois:
Think you so?

Romont:
Upon my soul! nor should the blood you challenged,
And took to cure your honour, breed more scruple
In your soft conscience, than if your sword
Had been sheath'd in a tiger or she-bear,
That in their bowels would have made your tomb.
To injure innocence is more than murder:
But when inhuman lusts transform us, then
As beasts we are to suffer, not like men.
To be lamented. Nor did Charalois ever
Perform an act so worthy the applause
Of a full theatre of perfect men,
As he hath done in this. The glory got
By overthrowing outward enemies,
Since strength and fortune are main sharers in it,
We cannot, but by pieces, call our own:
But, when we conquer our intestine foes,
Our passions bred within us, and of those
The most rebellious tyrant, powerful love,
Our reason suffering us to like no longer
Than the fair object, being good, deserves it,
That's a true victory! which, were great men
Ambitious to achieve, by your example
Setting no price upon the breach of faith,
But loss of life, 'twould fright adultery
Out of their families, and make lust appear
As loathsome to us in the first consent,
As when 'tis waited on by punishment.

Charalois:
You have confirm'd me. Who would love a woman,
That might enjoy in such a man a friend!
You have made me know the justice of my cause,
And mark'd me out the way how to defend it.

Romont:
>Continue to that resolution constant,
>And you shall, in contempt of their worst malice,
>Come off with honour—here they come.

Charalois:
>I am ready.

(Enter Du Croy, Charmi, Rochfort, Novall Senior, Pontalier, *and* Beaumont.*)*

Novall Senior:
>See, equal judges, with what confidence
>The cruel murderer stands, as if he would
>Outface the court and justice!

Rochfort:
>But look on him,
>And you shall find, for still methinks I do,
>Though guilt hath died him black, something good in him,
>That may perhaps work with a wiser man
>Than I have been, again to set him free,
>And give him all he has.

Charmi:
>This is not well.
>I would you had lived so, my lord, that I
>Might rather have continued your poor servant,
>Than sit here as your judge.

Du Croy:
>I am sorry for you.

Rochfort:
>In no act of my life I have deserved
>This injury from the court, that any here,
>Should thus uncivilly usurp on what
>Is proper to me only.

Du Croy:
>What distaste
>Receives my lord?

Rochfort:
>You say you are sorry for him;
>A grief in which I must not have a partner.
>'Tis I alone am sorry, that when I raised
>The building of my life, for seventy years,
>Upon so sure a ground, that all the vices
>Practised to ruin man, though brought against me,
>Could never undermine, and no way left
>To send these gray hairs to the grave with sorrow,
>Virtue, that was my patroness, betray'd me.
>For, entering, nay, possessing this young man,
>It lent him such a powerful majesty
>To grace whate'er he undertook, that freely
>I gave myself up, with my liberty,
>To be at his disposing. Had his person,
>Lovely I must confess, or far-famed valour,
>Or any other seeming good, that yet
>Holds a near neighbourhood with ill, wrought on me,
>I might have born it better: but, when goodness
>And piety itself in her best figure
>Were bribed to my destruction, can you blame me,
>Though I forget to suffer like a man,
>Or rather act a woman?

Beaumont:
>Good, my lord!—

Novall Senior:
>You hinder our proceeding.

Charmi:
>And forget
>The parts of an accuser.

Beaumont:
>Pray you, remember
>To use the temper which to me you promised.

Rochfort:
>Angels themselves must break, Beaumont, that promise
>Beyond the strength and patience of angels.
>But I have done:—My good lord, pardon me,

A weak old man, and, pray you, add to that,
A miserable father; yet be careful
That your compassion of my age, nor his,
Move you to any thing that may disbecome
The place on which you sit.

Charmi:
Read the indictment.

Charalois:
It shall be needless; I myself, my lords,
Will be my own accuser, and confess
All they can charge me with, nor will I spare
To aggravate that guilt with circumstance,
They seek to load me with; only I pray,
That, as for them you will vouchsafe me hearing,
I may
Not be denied it for myself, when I
Shall urge by what unanswerable reasons
I was compell'd to what I did, which yet,
Till you have taught me better, I repent not.

Rochfort:
The motion's honest.

Charmi:
And 'tis freely granted.

Charalois:
Then I confess, my lords, that I stood bound,
When, with my friends, even hope itself had left me,
To this man's charity, for my liberty;
Nor did his bounty end there, but began:
For, after my enlargement, cherishing
The good he did, he made me master of
His only daughter, and his whole estate.
Great ties of thankfulness, I must acknowledge:
Could any one, fee'd by you, press this further?—
But yet consider, my most honour'd lords,
If to receive a favour make a servant,
And benefits are bonds to tie the taker
To the imperious will of him that gives,

There's none but slaves will receive courtesies,
Since they must fetter us to our dishonours.
Can it be call'd magnificence in a prince,
To pour down riches with a liberal hand
Upon a poor man's wants, if that must bind him
To play the soothing parasite to his vices?
Or any man, because he saved my hand,
Presume my head and heart are at his service?
Or, did I stand engaged to buy my freedom
(When my captivity was honourable)
By making myself here, and fame hereafter,
Bondslaves to men's scorn, and callumnious tongues?—
Had his fair daughter's mind been like her feature,
Or, for some little blemish, I had sought
For my content elsewhere, wasting on others
My body and her dower; my forehead then
Deserved the brand of base ingratitude:
But if obsequious usage, and fair warning
To keep her worth my love, could not preserve her
From being a whore, and yet no cunning one,
So to offend, and yet the fault kept from me,
What should I do? Let any free-born spirit
Determine truly, if that thankfulness,
Choice form, with the whole world given for a dowry,
Could strengthen so an honest man with patience,
As with a willing neck to undergo
The insupportable yoke of slave, or wittol.

Charmi:
What proof have you she did play false, besides
Your oath?

Charalois:
Her own confession to her father:
I ask him for a witness.

Rochfort:
'Tis most true.
I would not willingly blend my last words
With an untruth.

Charalois:
>And then to clear myself,
>That his great wealth was not the mark I shot at,
>But that I held it, when fair Beaumelle
>Fell from her virtue, like the fatal gold
>Which Brennus took from Delphos, whose possession
>Brought with it ruin to himself and army:
>Here's one in court, Beaumont, by whom I sent
>All grants and writings back which made it mine,
>Before his daughter died by his own sentence,
>As freely as, unask'd, he gave it to me.

Beaumont:
>They are here to be seen.

Charmi:
>Open the casket.
>—Peruse that deed of gift.
>>*(To* Du Croy.*)*

Romont:
>Half of the danger
>Already is discharged; the other part
>As bravely; and you are not only free,
>But crown'd with praise for ever!

Du Croy:
>'Tis apparent.

Charmi:
>Your state, my lord, again is yours.

Rochfort:
>Not mine;
>I am not of the world. If it can prosper,
>(And yet, being justly got, I'll not examine
>Why it should be so fatal,) do you bestow it
>On pious uses: I'll go seek a grave.
>And yet, for proof I die in peace, your pardon
>I ask; and, as you grant it me, may heaven,
>Your conscience, and these judges, free you from
>What you are charged with! So, farewell for ever!—

(Exit.)

Novall Senior:
>I'll be mine own guide. Passion nor example
>Shall be my leaders. I have lost a son,
>A son, grave judges; I require his blood
>From his accursed homicide.

Charmi:
>What reply you,
>In your defence, for this?

Charalois:
>I but attended
>Your lordship's pleasure.—For the fact, as of
>The former, I confess it; but with what
>Base wrongs I was unwillingly drawn to it,
>To my few words there are some other proofs,
>To witness this for truth. When I was married,
>For there I must begin, the slain Novall
>Was to my wife, in way of our French courtship,
>A most devoted servant; but yet aimed at
>Nothing but means to quench his wanton heat,
>His heart being never warm'd by lawful fires,
>As mine was, lords: and though, on these presumptions,
>Join'd to the hate between his house and mine,
>I might, with opportunity and ease,
>Have found a way for my revenge, I did not;
>But still he had the freedom as before,
>When all was mine: and, told that he abused it
>With some unseemly license, by my friend,
>My approved friend, Romont, I gave no credit
>To the reporter, but reproved him for it,
>As one uncourtly, and malicious to him.
>What could I more, my lords? Yet, after this,
>He did continue in his first pursuit,
>Hotter than ever, and at length obtain'd it;
>But, how it came to my most certain knowledge,
>For the dignity of the court, and my own honour,
>I dare not say.

Novall Senior:
>If all may be believed
>A passionate prisoner speaks, who is so foolish
>That durst be wicked, that will appear guilty?
>No, my grave lords; in his impunity,
>But give example unto jealous men
>To cut the throats they hate, and they will never
>Want matter or pretence for their bad ends.

Charmi:
>You must find other proofs, to strengthen these
>But mere presumptions.

Du Croy:
>Or we shall hardly
>Allow your innocence.

Charalois:
>All your attempts
>Shall fall on me like brittle shafts on armour,
>That break themselves; or waves against a rock,
>That leave no sign of their ridiculous fury,
>But foam and splinters: my innocence, like these
>Shall stand triumphant, and your malice serve
>But for a trumpet to proclaim my conquest.
>Nor shall you, though you do the worst fate can,
>Howe'er condemn, affright an honest man.

Romont:
>May it please the court, I may be heard?

Novall Senior:
>You come not
>To rail again? but do—you shall not find
>Another Rochfort.

Romont:
>In Novall I cannot;
>But I come furnished with what will stop
>The mouth of his conspiracy 'gainst the life
>Of innocent Charalois. Do you know this character?

Novall Senior:
    Yes, 'tis my son's.

Romont:
    May it please your lordships, read it:
    And you shall find there, with what vehemency
    He did solicit Beaumelle; how he got
    A promise from her to enjoy his wishes;
    How after, he abjured her company,
    And yet—but that 'tis fit I spare the dead—
    Like a damn'd villain, as soon as recorded,
    He brake that oath:—to make this manifest,
    Produce his bawds and her's.

    (Enter Officers with Aymer, Florimel, and Bellapert.)

Charmi:
    Have they ta'en their oaths?

Romont:
    They have, and, rather than endure the rack,
    Confess the time, the meeting, nay, the act;
    What would you more? only this matron made
    A free discovery to a good end;
    And therefore I sue to the court, she may not
    Be placed in the black list of the delinquents.

Pontalier:
    I see by this, Novall's revenge needs me,
    And I shall do—

    (Aside.)

Charmi:
    'Tis evident.

Novall Senior:
    That I
    Till now was never wretched: here's no place
    To curse him or my stars.

    (Exit.)

Charmi:
>Lord Charalois,
>The injuries you have sustain'd appear
>So worthy of the mercy of the court,
>That, notwithstanding you have gone beyond
>The letter of the law, they yet acquit you.

Pontalier:
>But, in Novall, I do condemn him—thus.

>>*(Stabs him.)*

Charalois:
>I am slain.

Romont:
>Can I look on? Oh, murderous wretch!
>Thy challenge now I answer. So! die with him.

>>*(Stabs* Pontalier.*)*

Charmi:
>A guard! disarm him.

Romont:
>I yield up my sword
>Unforced—Oh, Charalois!

Charalois:
>For shame, Romont,
>Mourn not for him that dies as he hath lived,
>Still constant and unmoved: what's fall'n upon me
>Is by heaven's will, because I made myself
>A judge in my own cause, without their warrant;
>But He that lets me know thus much in death,
>With all good men—forgive me!

>>*(Dies.)*

Pontalier:
>I receive
>The vengeance which my love, not built on virtue,

Has made me worthy, worthy of.

(Dies.)

Charmi:
We are taught
By this sad precedent, how just soev'er
Our reasons are to remedy our wrongs,
We are yet to leave them to their will and power
That, to that purpose, have authority.
For you, Romont, although, in your excuse,
You may plead what you did was in revenge
Of the dishonour done unto the court,
Yet, since from us you had not warrant for it,
We banish you the state: for these, they shall,
As they are found guilty or innocent,
Or be set free, or suffer punishment.

(Exeunt.)

Comments and Questions

1. Charmi argues to the court that it is a maxim of the laws that "[A]ll debts die with the person"; but he is chastised by the bench for arguing against the statutes of Dijon which allow creditors to reach the flesh of dead bankrupts. Our own laws provide that creditors can reach the estate of the deceased to the extent that the estate covers outstanding debt. What else besides money is there to reach? What about if body parts were being sold on the open market? Should the creditor be allowed to claim the debtor's body parts to cover the outstanding debt? What about if the creditor was in dire need of a kidney transplant—kidneys selling for $20,000, the exact amount of the debt owed to him by the debtor at his death? If the idea of violating the sanctity of death bothers you, how do you feel about

allowing people to enter into contracts which provide for body parts to be used as collateral to secure a debt?

2. Compare and contrast the taking of flesh in *The Fatal Dowry* with the taking of flesh in *The Merchant of Venice*. Do you think that Massinger was influenced by Shakespeare's earlier theme?

3. Compare the acts of Antigone with the acts of Charalois in the first part of *The Fatal Dowry* as they each strive to afford a proper burial for their loved ones. We see that Antigone defies the laws of the state whereas Charalois works within the laws to achieve his goal. Do you believe that Charalois, like Antigone, is motivated by Divine laws? If not, what laws or beliefs prompt his behavior?

4. Charalois appears *pro se* in his trial for the murders of Novall, Jr. and Beaumelle. Although Charalois went beyond the letter of the law, he is successful in his arguments to the Court, but he is ultimately thwarted by the passionate act of Pontalier. Does Charalois believe that Divine law intercepts at this point? If so, why? Does he seem to be alluding to the Greek notion of Hubris when he says that he should not have been a judge of his own cause?

5. Rochfort plays many roles in the drama—ex-premier president of the parliament of Dijon, defender and savior of Charalois, father to Beaumelle, judge of his daughter's sins, plaintiff in the murder suit against Charalois. At all times he is impeccably honest, fair and impartial, and he tells Du Croy, who is now judging Charalois, that even though Rochfort himself is sorry for Charalois, Du Croy cannot engage in such sentiment. He also cautions the Court not to be moved by compassion for his own old age or the youth of Charalois. Unlike Mrs. Hale and Mrs. Peters in *Trifles*, Rochfort believes in the complete impartiality and objectivity of judge and jury. How far do you think such impartiality should extend? *The Death of Ivan Ilyicth* by Tolstóy offers a rare look at a judge reflecting on this very topic.

George Lillo

The London Merchant, or The History of George Barnwell

Dramatis Personae

Men:
    Thorowgood
    Barnwell, *uncle to George*
    George Barnwell
    Trueman
    Blunt

Women:
    Maria [Thorowgood]
    Millwood
    Lucy

Officers *with their* Attendants, Keeper, *and* Footmen.

PROLOGUE

Spoken by George Barnwell.

> The Tragic Muse, sublime, delights to show
> Princes distrest and scenes of royal woe;
> In awful pomp, majestic, to relate
> The fall of nations or some hero's fate:
> That sceptered chiefs may by example know
> The strange vicissitude of things below;
> What dangers on security attend;
> How pride and cruelty in ruin end;
> Hence Providence supreme to know, and own

> Humanity adds glory to a throne.
>   In ev'ry former age and foreign tongue
> With native grandeur thus the goddess sung.
> Upon our stage, indeed, with wished success,
> You've sometimes seen her in a humbler dress—
> Great only in distress. When she complains
> In Southerne's, Rowe's, or Otway's moving strains,
> The brilliant drops that fall from each bright eye
> The absent pomp with brighter gems supply.
> Forgive us then, if we attempt to show,
> In artless strains, a tale of private woe.
> A London 'prentice ruined, is our theme,
> Drawn from the famed old song that bears his name.
> We hope your taste is not so high to scorn
> A [moral] tale, esteemed ere you were born;
> Which, for a century of rolling years,
> Has filled a thousand thousand eyes with tears.
> If thoughtless youth to warn, and shame the age
> From vice destructive, well becomes the stage;
> If this example innocence insure,
> Prevent our guilt, or by reflection cure;
> If Millwood's dreadful crimes and sad despair
> Commend the virtue of the good and fair:
> Though art be wanting, and our numbers fail,
> Indulge the attempt, in justice to the tale!

SCENE.—*London, and an adjacent village. Time: about 1587.*

> Learn to be wise from others' harm,
>   And you shall do full well.
>   Old Ballad of *The Lady's Fall*.

(ACT I. SCENE I—A room in Thorowgood's *house. Enter* Thorowgood *and* Trueman.*)*

Trueman:
Sir, the packet from Genoa is arrived.
(Gives letters.)

Thorowgood:
Heav'n be praised! The storm that threatened our royal mistress, pure religion, liberty and laws, is for a time

diverted: the haughty and revengeful Spaniard, disappointed of the loan on which he depended from Genoa, must now attend the slow return of wealth from his new world to supply his empty coffers ere he can execute his purposed invasion of our happy island; by which means time is gained to make such preparations on our part as may, heav'n concurring, prevent his malice, or turn the meditated mischief on himself.

Trueman:
He must be insensible, indeed, who is not affected when the safety of his country is concerned. Sir, may I know by what means—if I am too bold—

Thorowgood:
Your curiosity is laudable. And I gratify it with the greater pleasure, because from thence you may learn how honest merchants, as such, may sometimes contribute to the safety of their country, as they do at all times to its happiness; that if hereafter you should be tempted to any action that has the appearance of vice or meanness in it, upon reflecting upon the dignity of our profession you may, with honest scorn, reject whatever is unworthy of it.

Trueman:
Should Barnwell, or I, who have the benefit of your example, by our ill conduct bring any imputation on that honorable name, we must be left without excuse.

Thorowgood:
You compliment, young man.

(Trueman *bows respectfully.*)

Nay, I'm not offended. As the name of merchant never degrades the gentleman, so by no means does it exclude him; only take heed not to purchase the character of complaisant at the expense of your sincerity. But to answer your question. The bank of Genoa had agreed, at excessive interest and on good security, to advance the King of Spain a sum of money sufficient to equip his vast Armado; of which our peerless Elizabeth (more than in name the mother of her people) being well informed, sent Walsingham, her wise and faithful secretary, to consult the merchants of this loyal city, who all agreed to direct their several agents to influence, if possible, the Genoese to break their contract with the Spanish court. 'Tis done; the state and bank of Genoa, having maturely weighed and rightly judged of their true interest, prefer the friendship of the merchants of London to that of a monarch who proudly styles himself King of both Indies.

Trueman:
Happy success of prudent councils! What an expense of blood and treasure is here saved! Excellent queen! Oh, how unlike those princes who make the danger of foreign enemies a pretence to oppress their subjects by taxes great and grievous to be borne.

Thorowgood:
Not so our gracious queen, whose richest exchequer is her people's love, as their happiness her greatest glory.

Trueman:
On these terms to defend us is to make our protection a benefit worthy her who confers it, and well worth our acceptance.—Sir, have you any commands for me at this time?

Thorowgood:
Only look carefully over the files to see whether there are any tradesmen's bills unpaid; if there are, send and discharge 'em. We must not let artificers lose their time, so useful to the public and their families, in unnecessary attendance.

(Exit Trueman.*)*

(Enter Maria.*)*

—Well, Maria, have you given orders for the entertainment? I would have it in some measure worthy the guests. Let there be plenty, and of the best, that the courtiers may at least commend our hospitality.

Maria:
> Sir, I have endeavored not to wrong your well-known generosity by an ill-timed parsimony.

Thorowgood:
> Nay, 'twas a needless caution; I have no cause to doubt your prudence.

Maria:
> Sir, I find myself unfit for conversation; I should but increase the number of the company without adding to their satisfaction.

Thorowgood:
> Nay, my child, this melancholy must not be indulged.

Maria:
> Company will but increase it. I wish you would dispense with my absence; solitude best suits my present temper.

Thorowgood:
> You are not insensible that it is chiefly on your account these noble lords do me the honor so frequently to grace my board; should you be absent, the disappointment may make them repent their condescension and think their labor lost.

Maria:
> He that shall think his time or honor lost in visiting you can set no real value on your daughter's company, whose only merit is that she is yours. The man of quality who chooses to converse with a gentleman and merchant of your worth and character may confer honor by so doing, but he loses none.

Thorowgood:
> Come, come, Maria; I need not tell you that a young gentleman may prefer your conversation to mine, yet intend me no disrespect at all, for, though he may lose no honor in my company, 'tis very natural for him to expect more pleasure in yours. I remember the time when the company of the greatest and wisest man in the kingdom would have been insipid and tiresome to me if it had deprived me of an opportunity of enjoying your mother's.

Maria:
> Yours no doubt was as agreeable to her, for generous minds know no pleasure in society but where 'tis mutual.

Thorowgood:
> Thou know'st I have no heir, no child but thee; the fruits of many years' successful industry must all be thine. Now, it would give me pleasure great as my love to see on whom you would bestow it. I am daily solicited by men of the greatest rank and merit for leave to address you, but I have hitherto declined it, in hopes that by observation I should learn which way your inclination tends; for, as I know love to be essential to happiness in the marriage state, I had rather my approbation should confirm your choice than direct it.

Maria:
> What can I say? How shall I answer as I ought this tenderness, so uncommon even in the best of parents? But you are without example; yet had you been less indulgent, I had been most wretched. That I look on the crowd of courtiers that visit here with equal esteem but equal indifference, you have observed, and I must needs confess; yet had you asserted your authority, and insisted on a parent's right to be obeyed, I had submitted, and to my duty sacrificed my peace.

Thorowgood:
> From your perfect obedience in every other instance I feared as much, and therefore would leave you without a bias in an affair wherein your happiness is so immediately concerned.

Maria:
> Whether from a want of that just ambition that would become your daughter, or from some other cause, I know not, but I find high birth and titles don't recommend the man who owns them to my affections.

Thorowgood:
> I would not that they should, unless his merit recommends him more. A noble birth and fortune, though they make not a bad man good, yet they are a real advantage to a worthy one, and place his virtues in the fairest light.

Maria:
> I cannot answer for my inclinations, but they shall ever be submitted to your wisdom and authority; and, as you will not compel me to marry where I cannot love, love shall never make me act contrary to my duty. Sir, have I your permission to retire?

Thorowgood:
> I'll see you to your chamber.

> > > (*Exeunt.*)

(SCENE II.—*A room in* Millwood's *house.* Millwood *at her toilet.* Lucy, *waiting.*)

Millwood:
> How do I look today, Lucy?

Lucy:
> Oh, killingly, madam! A little more red, and you'll be irresistible! But why this more than ordinary care of your dress and complexion? What new conquest are you aiming at?

Millwood:
> A conquest would be new indeed!

Lucy:
> Not to you, who make 'em every day,—but to me—well! 'tis what I'm never to expect, unfortunate as I am. But your wit and beauty—

Millwood:
> First made me a wretch, and still continue me so. Men, however generous or sincere to one another, are all selfish hypocrites in their affairs with us. We are no otherwise esteemed or regarded by them but as we contribute to their satisfaction.

Lucy:
> You are certainly, madam, on the wrong side in this argument. Is not the expense all theirs? And I am sure it is

our own fault if we ha'n't our share of the pleasure.

Millwood:
We are but slaves to men.

Lucy:
Nay, 'tis they that are slaves most certainly; for we lay them under contribution.

Millwood:
Slaves have no property—no, not even in themselves. All is the victor's.

Lucy:
You are strangely arbitrary in your principles, madam.

Millwood:
I would have my conquests complete, like those of the Spaniards in the New World, who first plundered the natives of all the wealth they had, and then condemned the wretches to the mines for life to work for more.

Lucy:
Well, I shall never approve of your scheme of government; I should think it much more politic, as well as just, to find my subjects an easier employment.

Millwood:
It's a general maxim among the knowing part of mankind, that a woman without virtue, like a man without honor or honesty, is capable of any action, though never so vile; and yet what pains will they not take, what arts not use, to seduce us from our innocence, and make us contemptible and wicked, even in their own opinions! Then is it not just, the villains, to their cost, should find us so? But guilt makes them suspicious, and keeps them on their guard; therefore we can take advantage only of the young and innocent part of the sex, who, having never injured women, apprehend no injury from them.

Lucy:
Ay, they must be young indeed.

Millwood:
> Such a one, I think, I have found. As I've passed through the City, I have often observed him, receiving and paying considerable sums of money, from thence I conclude he is employed in affairs of consequence.

Lucy:
> Is he handsome?

Millwood:
> Ay, ay, the stripling is well made and has a good face.

Lucy:
> About—

Millwood:
> Eighteen.

Lucy:
> Innocent, handsome, and about eighteen. You'll be vastly happy. Why, if you manage well, you may keep him to yourself these two or three years.

Millwood:
> If I manage well, I shall have done with him much sooner. Having long had a design on him, and meeting him yesterday, I made a full stop, and, gazing wishfully on his face, asked him his name. He blushed, and bowing very low, answered: 'George Barnwell.' I begged his pardon for the freedom I had taken, and told him that he was the person I had long wished to see, and to whom I had an affair of importance to communicate at a proper time and place. He named a tavern; I talked of honor and reputation, and invited him to my house. He swallowed the bait, promised to come, and this is the time I expect him.
>
> *(Knocking at the door.)*
>
> Somebody knocks;—d'ye hear; I am at home to nobody today but him.
>
> *(Exit* Lucy.*)*

—Less affairs must give way to those of more consequence, and I am strangely mistaken if this does not prove of great importance to me and him too, before I have done with him. Now, after what manner shall I receive him? Let me consider—what manner of person am I to receive? He is young, innocent, and bashful; therefore I must take care not to put him out of countenance at first. But then, if I have any skill in physiognomy, he is amorous, and, with a little assistance, will soon get the better of his modesty.—I'll e'en trust to Nature, who does wonders in these matters. If to seem what one is not, in order to be the better liked for what one really is; if to speak one thing, and mean the direct contrary, be art in a woman—I know nothing of nature.

(Enter Barnwell, *bowing very low.* Lucy *at a distance.)*

Millwood:
Sir! the surprise and joy—

Barnwell:
Madam—

Millwood *(advancing)*:
This is such a favor—

Barnwell:
Pardon me, madam—

Millwood *(still advances)*:
So unhoped for—

(Barnwell salutes her, and retires in confusion.)

—to see you here. Excuse the confusion—

Barnwell:
I fear I am too bold.

Millwood:
Alas, sir! I may justly apprehend you think me so. Please, sir, to sit.—I am as much at a loss how to receive this honor as I ought, as I am surprised at your goodness in conferring it.

Barnwell:
 I thought you had expected me—I promised to come.

Millwood:
 That is the more surprising; few men are such religious observers of their word.

Barnwell:
 All who are honest are.

Millwood:
 To one another. But we simple women are seldom thought of consequence enough to gain a place in your remembrance.

 (Laying her hand on his, as by accident.)

Barnwell *(aside)*:
 Her disorder is so great, she don't perceive she has laid her hand on mine. Heavens! how she trembles! What can this mean?

Millwood:
 The interest I have in all that relates to you (the reason of which you shall know hereafter), excites my curiosity; and, were I sure you would pardon my presumption, I should desire to know your real sentiments on a very particular subject.

Barnwell:
 Madam, you may command my poor thoughts on any subject; I have none that I would conceal.

Millwood:
 You'll think me bold.

Barnwell:
 No, indeed.

Millwood:
 What then are your thoughts of love?

Barnwell:
> If you mean the love of women, I have not thought of it at all. My youth and circumstances make such thoughts improper in me yet. But if you mean the general love we owe to mankind, I think no one has more of it in his temper than myself. I don't know that person in the world whose happiness I don't wish and wouldn't promote, were it in my power. In an especial manner I love my uncle and my master, but, above all, my friend.

Millwood:
> You have a friend then whom you love?

Barnwell:
> As he does me, sincerely.

Millwood:
> He is, no doubt, often blessed with your company and conversation.

Barnwell:
> We live in one house, and both serve the same worthy merchant.

Millwood:
> Happy, happy youth! Whoe'er thou art, I envy thee, and so must all who see and know this youth. What have I lost, by being formed a woman! I hate my sex—myself. Had I been a man, I might, perhaps, have been as happy in your friendship, as he who now enjoys it; but, as it is—oh!

Barnwell (aside):
> I never observed women before, or this is sure the most beautiful of her sex!—You seem disordered, madam! May I know the cause?

Millwood:
> Do not ask me. I can never speak it, whatever is the cause. I wish for things impossible. I would be a servant, bound to the same master, to live in one house with you.

Barnwell *(aside)*:
> How strange, and yet how kind, her words and actions are! And the effect they have on me is as strange. I feel desires I never knew before. I must be gone, while I have power to go.

Millwood:
> You will not, sure, leave me so soon!

Barnwell:
> Indeed, I must.

Millwood:
> You cannot be so cruel! I have prepared a poor supper, at which I promised myself your company.

Barnwell:
> I am sorry I must refuse the honor that you designed me, but my duty to my master calls me hence. I never yet neglected his service; he is so gentle, and so good a master, that, should I wrong him, though he might forgive me, I never should forgive myself.

Millwood:
> Am I refused, by the first man, the second favor I ever stooped to ask? Go then, thou proud, hard-hearted youth! But know, you are the only man that could be found who would let me sue twice for greater favors.

Barnwell *(aside)*:
> What shall I do! How shall I go or stay!

Millwood:
> Yet do not, do not, leave me! I with my sex's pride would meet your scorn, but when I look upon you—when I behold those eyes—oh! spare my tongue, and let my blushes—(this flood of tears to that will force its way) declare—what woman's modesty should hide.

Barnwell *(aside)*:
> Oh, heavens! she loves me, worthless as I am; her looks, her words, her flowing tears confess it. And can I leave her,

then? Oh, never, never!—Madam, dry up your tears! You shall command me always; I will stay here forever, if you'd have me.

Lucy *(aside)*:
So! she has wheedled him out of his virtue of obedience already, and will strip him of all the rest, one after another, till she has left him as few as her ladyship or myself.

Millwood:
Now you are kind, indeed; but I mean not to detain you always. I would have you shake off all slavish obedience to your master, but you may serve him still.

Lucy *(aside)*:
'Serve him still'! Ay, or he'll have no opportunity of fingering his cash, and then he'll not serve your end, I'll be sworn.

(Enter Blunt.)

Blunt:
Madam, supper's on the table.

Millwood:
Come, sir, you'll excuse all defects. My thoughts were too much employed on my guest to observe the entertainment.

(Exeunt Millwood and Barnwell.)

Blunt:
[What! is] all this preparation, this elegant supper, variety of wines, and music, for the entertainment of that young fellow?

Lucy:
So it seems.

Blunt:
What! is our mistress turned fool at last? She's in love with him, I suppose.

Lucy:
> I suppose not; but she designs to make him in love with her if she can.

Blunt:
> What will she get by that? He seems under age, and can't be supposed to have much money.

Lucy:
> But his master has, and that's the same thing, as she'll manage it.

Blunt:
> I don't like this fooling with a handsome young fellow; while she's endeavoring to ensnare him, she may be caught herself.

Lucy:
> Nay, were she like me, that would certainly be the consequence, for I confess, there is something in youth and innocence that moves me mightily.

Blunt:
> Yes, so does the smoothness and plumpness of a partridge move a mighty desire in the hawk to be the destruction of it.

Lucy:
> Why, birds are their prey, as men are ours—though, as you observed, we are sometimes caught ourselves; but that, I dare say, will never be the case with our mistress.

Blunt:
> I wish it may prove so, for you know we all depend upon her. Should she trifle away her time with a young fellow that there's nothing to be got by, we must all starve.

Lucy:
> There's no danger of that, for I am sure she has no view in this affair but interest.

Blunt:
> Well, and what hopes are there of success in that?

Lucy:
> The most promising that can be. 'Tis true, the youth has his scruples; but she'll soon teach him to answer them by stifling his conscience. Oh, the lad is in a hopeful way, depend upon't.

(Exeunt.)

(Scene draws and discovers Barnwell *and* Millwood *at supper. An entertainment of music and singing. After which they come forward).*

Barnwell:
> What can I answer? All that I know is, that you are fair and I am miserable.

Millwood:
> We are both so, and yet the fault is in ourselves.

Barnwell:
> To ease our present anguish by plunging into guilt is to buy a moment's pleasure with an age of pain.

Millwood:
> I should have thought the joys of love as lasting as they are great; if ours prove otherwise, 'tis your inconstancy must make them so.

Barnwell:
> The law of heaven will not be reversed, and that requires us to govern our passions.

Millwood:
> To give us sense of beauty and desires, and yet forbid us to taste and be happy, is cruelty to nature. Have we passions only to torment us?

Barnwell:
> To hear you talk, though in the cause of vice; to gaze upon your beauty, press your hand, and see your snow-white bosom heave and fall, enflames my wishes: my pulse beats high; my senses all are in a hurry, and I am on the rack of wild desire. Yet, for a moment's guilty pleasure, shall I lose

my innocence, my peace of mind, and hopes of solid happiness?

Millwood:
Chimeras all! Come on with me and prove
No joys like woman kind, no heav'n like love.

Barnwell:
I would not, yet must on.—
Reluctant thus, the merchant quits his ease,
And trusts to ricks, and sands, and stormy seas;
In hopes some unknown golden coast to find,
Commits himself, though doubtful, to the wind;
Longs much for joys to come, yet mourns those left behind.

(ACT II. SCENE I.—*A room in* Thorowgood's *house. Enter* Barnwell.)

Barnwell:
How strange are all things round me! Like some thief, who treads forbidden ground and fain would lurk unseen, fearful I enter each apartment of this well-known house. To guilty love, as if that were too little, already have I added breach of trust.—A thief!—Can I know myself that wretched thing, and look my honest friend and injured master in the face? Though hypocrisy may a while conceal my guilt, at length it will be known, and public shame and ruin must ensue. In the meantime, what must be my life? Ever to speak a language foreign to my heart; hourly to add to the number of my crimes in order to conceal 'em! Sure, such was the condition of the grand apostate, when first he lost his purity; like me, disconsolate he wandered, and, while yet in heaven, bore all his future hell about him.

(*Enter* Trueman.)

Trueman:
Barnwell! Oh, how I rejoice to see you safe! so will our master and his gentle daughter, who during your absence often enquired after you.

Barnwell (*aside*):
Would he were gone! His officious love will pry into the secrets of my soul.

Trueman:
Unless you knew the pain the whole family has felt on your account, you can't conceive how much you are beloved. But why thus cold and silent? When my heart is full of joy for your return, why do you turn away? why thus avoid me? what have I done? how am I altered since you saw me last? Or rather, what have you done? and why are you thus changed, for I am still the same.

Barnwell *(aside)*:
What have I done, indeed!

Trueman:
Not speak!—nor look upon me!

Barnwell *(aside)*:
By my face he will discover all I would conceal; methinks already I begin to hate him.

Trueman:
I cannot bear this usage from a friend—one whom till now I ever found so loving—whom yet I love, though this unkindness strikes at the root of friendship, and might destroy it in any breast but mine.

Barnwell *(turning to him)*:
I am not well. Sleep has been a stranger to these eyes since you beheld them last.

Trueman:
Heavy they look indeed, and swoll'n with tears; now they o'erflow; rightly did my sympathizing heart forbode last night, when thou wast absent, something fatal to our peace.

Barnwell:
Your friendship engages you too far. My troubles, whate'er they are, are mine alone; you have no interest in them, nor ought your concern for me give you a moment's pain.

Trueman:
You speak as if you knew of friendship nothing but the name. Before I saw your grief I felt it. Since we parted last I

have slept no more than you, but pensive in my chamber sat alone and spent the tedious night in wishes for your safety and return; e'en now, though ignorant of the cause, your sorrow wounds me to the heart.

Barnwell:
'Twill not be always thus. Friendship and all engagements cease, as circumstances and occasions vary; and, since you once may hate me, perhaps it might be better for us both that now you loved me less.

Trueman:
Sure, I but dream! Without a cause would Barnwell use me thus? Ungenerous and ungrateful youth, farewell! I shall endeavor to follow your advice. *(Going.)* *(Aside.)* Yet stay; perhaps I am too rash, and angry when the cause demands compassion. Some unforeseen calamity may have befall'n him, too great to bear.

Barnwell *(aside)*:
What part am I reduced to act! 'Tis vile and base to move his temper thus—the best of friends and men!

Trueman:
I am to blame; prithee, forgive me, Barnwell! Try to compose your ruffled mind, and let me know the cause that thus transports you from yourself. My friendly counsel may restore your peace.

Barnwell:
All that is possible for man to do for man, your generous friendship may effect; but here even that's in vain.

Trueman:
Something dreadful is laboring in your breast. Oh, give it vent, and let me share your grief; 'twill ease your pain, should it admit no cure, and make it lighter by the part I bear.

Barnwell:
Vain supposition! My woes increase by being observed; should the cause be known, they would exceed all bounds.

Trueman:
So well I know thy honest heart, guilt cannot harbor there.

Barnwell *(aside)*:
Oh, torture insupportable!

Trueman:
Then why am I excluded? Have I a thought I would conceal from you?

Barnwell:
If still you urge me on this hated subject, I'll never enter more beneath this roof nor see your face again.

Trueman:
'Tis strange. But I have done, say but you hate me not!

Barnwell:
Hate you! I am not that monster yet.

Trueman:
Shall our friendship still continue?

Barnwell:
It's a blessing I never was worthy of, yet now must stand on terms, and but upon conditions can confirm it.

Trueman:
What are they?

Barnwell:
Never hereafter, though you should wonder at my conduct, desire to know more than I am willing to reveal.

Trueman:
'Tis hard; but upon any conditions, I must be your friend.

Barnwell:
Then, as much as one lost to himself can be another's, I am yours.

(Embracing.)

Trueman:
> Be ever so, and may heav'n restore your peace!

Barnwell:
> Will yesterday return? We have heard the glorious sun, that till then incessant rolled, once stopped his rapid course, and once went back: the dead have risen, and parched rocks poured forth a liquid stream to quench a people's thirst: the sea divided and formed walls of water, while a whole nation passed in safety through its sandy bosom: hungry lions have refused their prey, and men unhurt have walked amidst consuming flames; but never yet did time, once past, return.

Trueman:
> Though the continued chain of time has never once been broke, nor ever will, but uninterrupted must keep on its course, till lost in eternity it ends there where it first begun; yet, as heaven can repair whatever evils time can bring upon us, we ought never to despair. But business requires our attendance—business, the youth's best preservative from ill, as idleness his worst of snares. Will you go with me?

Barnwell:
> I'll take a little time to reflect on what has passed, and follow you.

> *(Exit* Trueman.*)*

> —I might have trusted Trueman and engaged him to apply to my uncle to repair the wrong I have done my master—but what of Millwood? must I expose her too? Ungenerous and base! Then heav'n requires it not. But heaven requires that I forsake her. What! never see her more! Does heaven require that? I hope I may see her, and heaven not be offended. Presumptuous hope—dearly already have I proved my frailty; should I once more tempt heav'n, I may be left to fall never to rise again. Yet shall I leave her, forever leave her, and not let her know the cause?—she who loves me with such a boundless passion. Can cruelty be duty? I judge of what she then must feel by what I now endure. The love of life and fear of shame, opposed by inclination strong as death or shame, like wind and tide in raging conflict met,

when neither can prevail, keep me in doubt. How then can I determine?

(Enter Thorowgood.*)*

Thorowgood:
Without a cause assigned, or notice given, to absent yourself last night was a fault, young man, and I came to chide you for it, but hope I am prevented. That modest blush, the confusion so visible in your face, speak grief and shame. When we have offended heaven, it requires no more; and shall man, who needs himself to be forgiven, be harder to appease? If my pardon or love be of moment to your peace, look up, secure of both.

Barnwell *(aside)*:
This goodness has o'ercome me.—O sir! you know not the nature and extent of my offence, and I should abuse your mistaken bounty to receive it. Though I had rather die than speak my shame; though racks could not have forced the guilty secret from my breast, your kindness has.

Thorowgood:
Enough, enough; whate'er it be, this concern shows you're convinced, and I am satisfied. *(Aside.)* How painful is the sense of guilt to an ingenuous mind—some youthful folly which it were prudent not to enquire into. When we consider the frail condition of humanity, it may raise our pity, not our wonder, that youth should go astray when reason, weak at the best opposed to inclination, scarce formed and wholly unassisted by experience, faintly contends, or willingly becomes the slave of sense. The state of youth is much to be deplored, and the more so because they see it not, being then to danger most exposed when they are least prepared for their defence.

Barnwell:
It will be known, and you recall your pardon and abhor me.

Thorowgood:
I never will. Yet be upon your guard in this gay, thoughtless season of your life; when the sense of pleasure's quick and passion high, the voluptuous appetites raging and fierce

demand the strongest curb; take heed of a relapse. When vice becomes habitual, the very power of leaving it is lost.

Barnwell:
Hear me on my knees confess—

Thorowgood:
Not a syllable more upon this subject; it were not mercy, but cruelty, to hear what must give you such torment to reveal.

Barnwell:
This generosity amazes and distracts me.

Thorowgood:
This remorse makes thee dearer to me than if thou hadst never offended. Whatever is your fault, of this I'm certain; 'twas harder for you to offend than me to pardon.

(*Exit* Thorowgood.)

Barnwell:
Villain! villain! villain! basely to wrong so excellent a man! Should I again return to folly?—detested thought!—But what of Millwood then?—Why, I renounce her—I give her up.—The struggle's over and virtue has prevailed. Reason may convince, but gratitude compels. This unlooked-for generosity has saved me from destruction.

(*Going.*)

(*Enter a* Footman.)

Footman:
Sir, two ladies from your uncle in the country desire to see you.

Barnwell (*aside*):
Who should they be?—Tell them I'll wait upon 'em.

(*Exit* Footman.)

—Methinks I dread to see 'em. Now everything alarms me.

Guilt, what a coward hast thou made me!

(Exit.)

(SCENE II.—*Another room in* Thorowgood's *house.* Millwood *and* Lucy *discovered. Enter* Footman.*)*

Footman:
Ladies, he'll wait upon you immediately.

Millwood:
'Tis very well. I thank you.

(Exit Footman.*)*

(Enter Barnwell.*)*

Barnwell *(aside)*:
Confusion!—Millwood!

Millwood:
That angry look tells me that here I'm an unwelcome guest. I feared as much—the unhappy are so everywhere.

Barnwell:
Will nothing but my utter ruin content you?

Millwood:
Unkind and cruel! Lost myself, your happiness is now my only care.

Barnwell:
How did you gain admission?

Millwood:
Saying we were desired by your uncle to visit and deliver a message to you, we were received by the family without suspicion, and with much respect conducted here.

Barnwell:
Why did you come at all?

Millwood:
>I never shall trouble you more; I'm come to take my leave forever. Such is the malice of my fate. I go hopeless, despairing ever to return. This hour is all I have left. One short hour is all I have to bestow on love and you, for whom I thought the longest life too short.

Barnwell:
>Then we are met to part forever?

Millwood:
>It must be so. Yet think not that time or absence shall ever put a period to my grief or make me love you less: though I must leave you, yet condemn me not!

Barnwell:
>Condemn you? No, I approve your resolution and rejoice to hear it; 'tis just, 'tis necessary. I have well weighed, and found it so.

Lucy (aside):
>I'm afraid the young man has more sense than she thought he had.

Barnwell:
>Before you came, I had determined never to see you more.

Millwood (aside):
>Confusion!

Lucy (aside):
>Ay! we are all out! This is a turn so unexpected that I shall make nothing of my part; they must e'en play the scene betwixt themselves.

Millwood:
>'Twas some relief to think, though absent, you would love me still; but to find, though Fortune had been indulgent, that you, more cruel and inconstant, had resolved to cast me off—this, as I never could expect, I have not learnt to bear.

Barnwell:
>I am sorry to hear you blame in me a resolution that so well becomes us both.

Millwood:
>I have a reason for what I do, but you have none.

Barnwell:
>Can we want a reason for parting, who have so many to wish we never had met?

Millwood:
>Look on me, Barnwell! Am I deformed or old, that satiety so soon succeeds enjoyment? Nay, look again; am I not she whom yesterday you thought the fairest and the kindest of her sex? whose hand, trembling with ecstasy, you pressed and moulded thus, while on my eyes you gazed with such delight, as if desire increased by being fed?

Barnwell:
>No more! let me repent my former follies, if possible, without rememb'ring what they were.

Millwood:
>Why?

Barnwell:
>Such is my frailty that 'tis dangerous.

Millwood:
>Where is the danger, since we are to part?

Barnwell:
>The thought of that already is too painful.

Millwood:
>If it be painful to part, then I may hope at least you do not hate me?

Barnwell:
>No—no—I never said I did.—O my heart!—

Millwood:
   Perhaps you pity me?

Barnwell:
   I do—I do—indeed, I do.

Millwood:
   You'll think upon me?

Barnwell:
   Doubt it not, while I can think at all!

Millwood:
   You may judge an embrace at parting too great a favor—though it would be the last?

   (He draws back.)

   A look shall then suffice—farewell, forever.

   (Exeunt Millwood and Lucy.)

Barnwell:
   If to resolve to suffer be to conquer, I have conquered. Painful victory!

   (Re-enter Millwood and Lucy.)

Millwood:
   One thing I had forgot; I never must return to my own house again. This I thought proper to let you know, lest your mind should change and you should seek in vain to find me there. Forgive me this second intrusion; I only came to give you this caution, and that perhaps was needless.

Barnwell:
   I hope it was; yet it is kind, and I must thank you for it.

Millwood *(to Lucy):*
   My friend, your arm.—Now I am gone forever.

   (Going.)

Barnwell:
   One thing more: sure, there's no danger in my knowing where you go? If you think otherwise—

Millwood *(weeping)*:
   Alas!

Lucy *(aside)*:
   We are right, I find; that's my cue.—Ah, dear sir, she's going she knows not whither; but go she must.

Barnwell:
   Humanity obliges me to wish you well. Why will you thus expose yourself to needless troubles?

Lucy:
   Nay, there's no help for it. She must quit the town immediately, and the kingdom as soon as possible; it was no small matter, you may be sure, that could make her resolve to leave you.

Millwood:
   No more, my friend, since he for whose dear sake alone I suffer, and am content to suffer, is kind and pities me. Whene'er I wander through [wilds] and deserts, benighted and forlorn, that thought shall give me comfort.

Barnwell:
   For my sake? Oh, tell me how! which way am I so cursed as to bring such ruin on thee?

Millwood:
   No matter; I am contented with my lot.

Barnwell:
   Leave me not in this incertainty!

Millwood:
   I have said too much.

Barnwell:
   How, how am I the cause of your undoing?

Millwood:
 To know it will but increase your troubles.

Barnwell:
 My troubles can't be greater than they are.

Lucy:
 Well, well, sir, if she won't satisfy you, I will.

Barnwell:
 I am bound to you beyond expression.

Millwood:
 Remember, sir, that I desired you not to hear it.

Barnwell:
 Begin, and ease my racking expectation!

Lucy:
 Why, you must know, my lady here was an only child; but her parents, dying while she was young, left her and her fortune (no inconsiderable one, I assure you) to the care of a gentleman who has a good estate of his own.

Millwood:
 Ay, ay, the barbarous man is rich enough—but what are riches when compared to love?

Lucy:
 For a while he performed the office of a faithful guardian, settled her in a house, hired her servants—but you have seen in what manner she lived; so I need say no more of that.

Millwood:
 How I shall live hereafter, heaven knows!

Lucy:
 All things went on as one could wish till, some time ago, his wife dying, he fell violently in love with his charge, and would fain have married her. Now, the man is neither old nor ugly, but a good, personable sort of a man; but I don't know how it was, she could never endure him. In short, her

ill usage so provoked him, that he brought in an account of his executorship, wherein he makes her debtor to him.

Millwood:
A trifle in itself, but more than enough to ruin me, whom, by his unjust account, he had stripped of all before.

Lucy:
Now, she having neither money nor friend, except me, who am as unfortunate as herself, he compelled her to pass his account, and give bond for the sum he demanded, but still provided handsomely for her and continued his courtship till, being informed by his spies (truly I suspect some in her own family) that you were entertained at her house and stayed with her all night, he came this morning raving and storming like a madman; talks no more of marriage—so there's no hopes of making up matters that way—but vows her ruin unless she'll allow him the same favor that he supposes she granted you.

Barnwell:
Must she be ruined or find her refuge in another's arms?

Millwood:
He gave me but an hour to resolve in. That's happily spent with you—and now I go.

Barnwell:
To be exposed to all the rigors of the various seasons, the summer's parching heat, and winter's cold; unhoused to wander friendless through the unhospitable world, in misery and want, attended with fear and danger, and pursued by malice and revenge—wouldst thou endure all this for me, and can I do nothing, nothing to prevent it?

Lucy:
'Tis really a pity there can be no way found out.

Barnwell (aside):
Oh, where are all my resolutions now? Like early vapors, or the morning dew, chased by the sun's warm beams, they're vanished and lost, as though they had never been.

Lucy:
> Now, I advised her, sir, to comply with the gentleman; that would not only put an end to her troubles, but make her fortune at once.

Barnwell:
> Tormenting fiend, away! I had rather perish, nay, see her perish, than have her saved by him; I will myself prevent her ruin, though with my own. A moment's patience; I'll return immediately.

(Exit Barnwell.)

Lucy:
> 'Twas well you came, or by what I can perceive you had lost him.

Millwood:
> That, I must confess, was a danger I did not foresee. I was only afraid he should have come without money. You know a house of entertainment like mine is not kept without expense.

Lucy:
> That's very true. But then, you should be reasonable in your demands; 'tis pity to discourage a young man.

Millwood:
> Leave that to me.

(Re-enter Barnwell with a bag of money.)

Barnwell:
> What am I about to do? Now you, who boast your reason all-sufficient, suppose yourselves in my condition, and determine for me whether it's right to let her suffer for my faults, or, by this small addition to my guilt, prevent the ill effects of what is past.

Lucy *(aside)*:
> These young sinners think everything in the ways of wickedness so strange. But I could tell him that this is nothing but what's very common; for one vice as naturally begets

another, as a father a son. But he'll find out that himself, if he lives long enough.

Barnwell:
Here, take this, and with it purchase your deliverance; return to your house, and live in peace and safety.

Millwood:
So I may hope to see you there again.

Barnwell:
Answer me not, but fly—lest, in the agonies of my remorse, I take again what is not mine to give, and abandon thee to want and misery!

Millwood:
Say but you'll come!

Barnwell:
You are my fate, my heaven, or my hell. Only leave me now; dispose of me hereafter as you please.

(*Exeunt* Millwood *and* Lucy.)

What have I done! Were my resolutions founded on reason and sincerely made, why then has heaven suffered me to fall? I sought not the occasion; and if my heart deceives me not, compassion and generosity were my motives. Is virtue inconsistent with itself, or are vice and virtue only empty names? Or do they depend on accidents, beyond our power to produce or to prevent—wherein we have no part, and yet must be determined by the event? But why should I attempt to reason? All is confusion, horror, and remorse. I find I am lost, cast down from all my late erected hopes, and plunged again in guilt, yet scarce know how or why:
    Such undistinguished horrors make my brain,
    Like hell, the seat of darkness and of pain.

(*Exit.*)

(*ACT III. SCENE I.—A room in* Thorowgood's *house. Enter* Thorowgood *and* Trueman.)

Thorowgood:
Methinks I would not have you only learn the method of merchandise and practise it hereafter, merely as a means of getting wealth; 'twill be well worth your pains to study it as a science, to see how it is founded in reason and the nature of things; how it promotes humanity, as it has opened and yet keeps up an intercourse between nations far remote from one another in situation, customs and religion; promoting arts, industry, peace and plenty; by mutual benefits diffusing mutual love from pole to pole.

Trueman:
Something of this I have considered, and hope, by your assistance, to extend my thoughts much farther. I have observed those countries where trade is promoted and encouraged do not make discoveries to destroy, but to improve, mankind; by love and friendship to tame the fierce and polish the most savage; to teach them the advantages of honest traffic by taking from them, with their own consent, their useless superfluities, and giving them in return what, from their ignorance in manual arts, their situation, or some other accident, they stand in need of.

Thorowgood:
'Tis justly observed. The populous East, luxuriant, abounds with glittering gems, bright pearls, aromatic spices, and health-restoring drugs. The late found western world's rich earth glows with unnumbered veins of gold and silver ore. On every climate and on every country heaven has bestowed some good peculiar to itself. It is the industrious merchant's business to collect the various blessings of each soil and climate, and, with the product of the whole, to enrich his native country.—Well! I have examined your accounts. They are not only just, as I have always found them, but regularly kept and fairly entered. I commend your diligence. Method in business is the surest guide. He who neglects it frequently stumbles, and always wanders perplexed, uncertain, and in danger. Are Barnwell's accounts ready for my inspection? He does not use to be the last on these occasions.

Trueman:
Upon receiving your orders he retired, I thought, in some

confusion. If you please, I'll go and hasten him. I hope he hasn't been guilty of any neglect.

Thorowgood:
I'm now going to the Exchange; let him know, at my return I expect to find him ready.

(Exeunt.)

(Enter Maria with a book; sits and reads.)

Maria:
How forcible is truth! The weakest mind, inspired with love of that, fixed and collected in itself, with indifference beholds the united force of earth and hell opposing. Such souls are raised above the sense of pain, or so supported that they regard it not. The martyr cheaply purchases his heaven: small are his sufferings, great is his reward. Not so the wretch who combats love with duty, when the mind, weakened and dissolved by the soft passion, feeble and hopeless, opposes its own desires. What is an hour, a day, a year of pain, to a whole life of tortures such as these?

(Enter Trueman.)

Trueman:
O Barnwell! O my friend, how art thou fallen!

Maria:
Ha! Barnwell! What of him? Speak!—say, what of Barnwell!

Trueman:
'Tis not to be concealed. I've news to tell of him that will afflict your generous father, yourself, and all who know him.

Maria:
Defend us, heaven!

Trueman:
I cannot speak it. See there.

(Gives a letter. Maria *reads.)*

'Trueman,

I know my absence will surprise my honored master and yourself, and the more when you shall understand that the reason of my withdrawing, is my having embezzled part of the cash with which I was entrusted. After this, 'tis needless to inform you that I intend never to return again. Though this might have been known by examining my accounts, yet, to prevent that unnecessary trouble, and to cut off all fruitless expectations of my return, I have left this from the lost

George Barnwell.'

Trueman:
Lost indeed! Yet how he should be guilty of what he there charges himself withal, raises my wonder equal to my grief. Never had youth a higher sense of virtue. Justly he thought, and as he thought he practised; never was life more regular than his—an understanding uncommon at his years—an open, generous manliness of temper—his manners easy, unaffected, and engaging.

Maria:
This and much more you might have said with truth. He was the delight of every eye and joy of every heart that knew him.

Trueman:
Since such he was, and was my friend, can I support his loss? See! the fairest and happiest maid this wealthy city boasts, kindly condescends to weep for thy unhappy fate, poor ruined Barnwell!

Maria:
Trueman, do you think a soul so delicate as his, so sensible of shame, can e'er submit to live a slave to vice?

Trueman:
Never, never! So well I know him, I'm sure this act of his, so contrary to his nature, must have been caused by some unavoidable necessity.

Maria:
> Is there no means yet to preserve him?

Trueman:
> Oh, that there were! But few men recover reputation lost—a merchant, never. Nor would he, I fear, though I should find him, ever be brought to look his injured master in the face.

Maria:
> I fear as much—and therefore would never have my father know it.

Trueman:
> That's impossible.

Maria:
> What's the sum?

Trueman:
> 'Tis considerable. I've marked it here, to show it, with the letter, to your father, at his return.

Maria:
> If I should supply the money, could you so dispose of that, and the account, as to conceal this unhappy mismanagement from my father?

Trueman:
> Nothing more easy. But can you intend it? Will you save a helpless wretch from ruin? Oh! 'twere an act worthy such exalted virtue as Maria's. Sure, heaven in mercy to my friend inspired the generous thought!

Maria:
> Doubt not but I would purchase so great a happiness at a much dearer price:—but how shall he be found?

Trueman:
> Trust to my diligence for that. In the meantime, I'll conceal his absence from your father, or find such excuses for it that the real cause shall never be suspected.

Maria:
> In attempting to save from shame one whom we hope may yet return to virtue, to heaven and you, the only witnesses of this action, I appeal, whether I do anything misbecoming my sex and character.

Trueman:
> Earth must approve the deed, and heaven, I doubt not, will reward it.

Maria:
> If heaven succeeds it, I am well rewarded. A virgin's fame is sullied by suspicion's lightest breath; and therefore as this must be a secret from my father and the world, for Barnwell's sake, for mine, let it be so to him!

> *(Exeunt.)*

(SCENE II.—A room in Millwood's *house. Enter* Lucy *and* Blunt.)

Lucy:
> Well! what do you think of Millwood's conduct now?

Blunt:
> I own it is surprising; I don't know which to admire most, her feigned or his real passion—though I have sometimes been afraid that her avarice would discover her. But his youth and want of experience make it the easier to impose on him.

Lucy:
> No, it is his love. To do him justice, notwithstanding his youth, he don't want understanding; but you men are much easier imposed on in these affairs than your vanity will allow you to believe. Let me see the wisest of you all as much in love with me as Barnwell is with Millwood, and I'll engage to make as great a fool of him.

Blunt:
> And all circumstances considered, to make as much money of him too?

Lucy:
> I can't answer for that. Her artifice in making him rob his master at first, and the various stratagems by which she has obliged him to continue that course, astonish even me, who know her so well.

Blunt:
> But then you are to consider that the money was his master's.

Lucy:
> There was the difficulty of it. Had it been his own, it had been nothing. Were the world his, she might have it for a smile. But those golden days are done; he's ruined, and Millwood's hopes of farther profits there are at an end.

Blunt:
> That's no more than we all expected.

Lucy:
> Being called by his master to make up his accounts, he was forced to quit his house and service, and wisely flies to Millwood for relief and entertainment.

Blunt:
> I have not heard of this before! How did she receive him?

Lucy:
> As you would expect. She wondered what he meant; was astonished at his impudence; and, with an air of modesty peculiar to herself, swore so heartily that she never saw him before, that she put me out of countenance.

Blunt:
> That's much, indeed! But how did Barnwell behave?

Lucy:
> He grieved, and, at length, enraged at this barbarous treatment, was preparing to be gone; when, making toward the door, he showed a sum of money which he had brought from his master's—the last he's ever like to have from thence.

Blunt:
> But then Millwood?

Lucy:
> Ay, she, with her usual address, returned to her old arts of lying, swearing, and dissembling—hung on his neck, wept, and swore 'twas meant in jest, till the amorous youth melted into tears, threw the money into her lap, and swore he had rather die than think her false.

Blunt:
> Strange infatuation!

Lucy:
> But what followed was stranger still. As doubts and fears, followed by reconcilement, ever increase love where the passion is sincere, so in him it caused so wild a transport of excessive fondness, such joy, such grief, such pleasure, and such anguish, that nature in him seemed sinking with the weight, and the charmed soul disposed to quit his breast for hers. Just then, when every passion with lawless anarchy prevailed, and reason was in the raging tempest lost, the cruel, artful Millwood prevailed upon the wretched youth to promise—what I tremble but to think on.

Blunt:
> I am amazed! What can it be?

Lucy:
> You will be more so, to hear it is to attempt the life of his nearest relation and best benefactor—

Blunt:
> His uncle! whom we have often heard him speak of as a gentleman of a large estate and fair character in the country where he lives.

Lucy:
> The same. She was no sooner possessed of the last dear purchase of his ruin, but her avarice, insatiate as the grave, demanded this horrid sacrifice. Barnwell's near relation and unsuspected virtue must give too easy means to seize the good man's treasure, whose blood must seal the dreadful

secret and prevent the terrors of her guilty fears.

Blunt:
Is it possible she could persuade him to do an act like that? He is, by nature, honest, grateful, compassionate, and generous; and though his love and her artful persuasions have wrought him to practise what he most abhors, yet we all can witness for him with what reluctance he has still complied! So many tears he shed o'er each offence, as might, if possible, sanctify theft, and make a merit of a crime.

Lucy:
'Tis true, at the naming the murder of his uncle he started into rage, and, breaking from her arms, where she till then had held him with well-dissembled love and false endearments, called her 'cruel, monster, devil,' and told her she was born for his destruction. She thought it not for her purpose to meet his rage with rage, but affected a most passionate fit of grief—railed at her fate and cursed her wayward stars, that still her wants should force her to press him to act such deeds as she must needs abhor as well as he: but told him necessity had no law, and love no bounds; that therefore he never truly loved, but meant, in her necessity, to forsake her; then kneeled, and swore that since, by his refusal, he had given her cause to doubt his love, she never would see him more, unless, to prove it true, he robbed his uncle to supply her wants, and murdered him to keep it from discovery.

Blunt:
I am astonished! What said he?

Lucy:
Speechless he stood; but in his face you might have read that various passions tore his very soul. Oft he, in anguish, threw his eyes towards heaven, and then as often bent their beams on her; then wept and groaned, and beat his troubled breast. At length, with horror, not to be expressed, he cried: 'Thou cursed fair! have I not given dreadful proofs of love? What drew me from my youthful innocence, to stain my then unspotted soul, but love? What caused me to rob my worthy gentle master, but cursed love? What makes me now a fugi-

tive from his service, loathed by myself, and scorned by all the world, but love? What fills my eyes with tears, my soul with torture never felt on this side death before? Why, love, love, love! And why, above all, do I resolve (for,' tearing his hair, he cried, 'I do resolve) to kill my uncle?'

Blunt:

Was she not moved? It makes me weep to hear the sad relation.

Lucy:

Yes—with joy, that she had gained her point. She gave him no time to cool, but urged him to attempt it instantly. He's now gone; if he performs it and escapes, there's more money for her; if not, he'll ne'er return, and then she's fairly rid of him.

Blunt:

'Tis time the world were rid of such a monster.

Lucy:

If we don't do our endeavors to prevent this murder, we are as bad as she.

Blunt:

I'm afraid it is too late.

Lucy:

Perhaps not.—Her barbarity to Barnwell makes me hate her. We have run too great a length with her already. I did not think her or myself so wicked as I find, upon reflection, we are.

Blunt:

'Tis true, we have all been too much so. But there is something so horrid in murder, that all other crimes seem nothing when compared to that. I would not be involved in the guilt of that for all the world.

Lucy:

Nor I, heaven knows; therefore, let us clear ourselves by doing all that is in our power to prevent it. I have just thought of a way that, to me, seems probable. Will you join with me to detect this curs'd design?

Blunt:
With all my heart. He who knows of a murder intended to be committed and does not discover it, in the eye of the law and reason is a murderer.

Lucy:
Let us lose no time; I'll acquaint you with the particulars as we go.

(Exeunt.)

(SCENE III.—A walk at some distance from a country seat. Enter Barnwell.)

Barnwell:
A dismal gloom obscures the face of day; either the sun has slipped behind a cloud, or journeys down the west of heaven with more than common speed, to avoid the sight of what I'm doomed to act. Since I set forth on this accursed design, where'er I tread, methinks, the solid earth trembles beneath my feet. Yonder limpid stream, whose hoary fall has made a natural cascade, as I passed by, in doleful accents seemed to murmur 'Murder.' The earth, the air, and water, seemed concerned—but that's not strange; the world is punished, and nature feels a shock when Providence permits a good man's fall! Just heaven! Then what should I be?—for him that was my father's only brother, and since his death has been to me a father, who took me up an infant, and an orphan; reared me with tenderest care, and still indulged me with most paternal fondness. Yet here I stand avowed his destined murderer. I stiffen with horror at my own impiety. 'Tis yet unperformed. What if I quit my bloody purpose, and fly the place!

(Going, then stops.)

But [whither], oh whither, shall I fly? My master's once friendly doors are ever shut against me; and without money Millwood will never see me more, and life is not to be endured without her. She's got such firm possession of my heart, and governs there with such despotic sway—ay, there's the cause of all my sin and sorrow! 'Tis more than love; 'tis the fever of the soul and madness of desire. In vain does nature, reason, conscience, all oppose it; the impetuous passion bears down all before it, and drives me on to lust, to theft, and murder. O conscience! feeble guide to virtue, thou only show'st us when we go astray, but wantest power to stop us in our course.—Ha, in yonder shady walk I see my uncle. He's alone. Now for my disguise!

(Plucks out a vizor.)

This is his hour of private meditation. Thus daily he prepares his soul for heaven—whilst I—but what have I to do with heaven? Ha! No struggles, conscience!
Hence, hence, remorse, and ev'ry thought that's good:
The storm that lust began must end in blood.

(Puts on the vizor, draws a pistol and exit.)

(SCENE IV.—A close walk in a wood. Enter Uncle.*)*

Uncle:
If I were superstitious, I should fear some danger lurked unseen, or death were nigh. A heavy melancholy clouds my spirits; my imagination is filled with gashly forms of dreary graves and bodies changed by death, when the pale, lengthened visage attracts each weeping eye, and fills the musing soul, at once, with grief and horror, pity and aversion. I will indulge the thought. The wise man prepares himself for death by making it familiar to his mind. When strong reflections hold the mirror near, and the living in the dead behold their future selves, how does each inordinate passion and desire cease, or sicken at the view! The mind scarce moves; the blood, curdling and chilled, creeps slowly through the veins—fixed, still, and motionless we stand—so like the solemn object of our thoughts, we are almost at present—what we must be hereafter, till curiosity awakes the soul and sets it on inquiry.

(Enter George Barnwell *at a distance.)*

—O Death, thou strange mysterious power, seen every day, yet never understood but by the incommunicative dead, what art thou? The extensive mind of man, that with a thought circles the earth's vast globe, sinks to the center, or ascends above the stars; that worlds exotic finds, or thinks it finds—thy thick clouds attempts to pass in vain: lost and bewildered in the horrid gloom, defeated she returns more doubtful than before, of nothing certain—but of labor lost.

(During this speech, Barnwell sometimes presents the pistol and draws it back again.)

Barnwell *(throwing down the pistol)*:
Oh, 'tis impossible!

(Uncle starts and attempts to draw his sword.)

Uncle:
A man so near me, armed and masked!

Barnwell:
Nay, then there's no retreat.

(Plucks a poniard from his bosom, and stabs him.)

Uncle:
Oh! I am slain! All-gracious heaven, regard the prayer of thy dying servant! Bless, with the choicest blessings, my dearest nephew; forgive my murderer, and take my fleeting soul to endless mercy!

(Barnwell throws off his mask, runs to him, and, kneeling by him, raises and chafes him.)

Barnwell:
Expiring saint! O murdered, martyred uncle! Lift up your dying eyes, and view your nephew in your murderer! Oh, do not look so tenderly upon me! Let indignation lighten from your eyes, and blast me ere you die!—By heaven, he weeps in pity of my woes. Tears,—tears, for blood! The murdered, in the agonies of death, weeps for his murderer.—Oh, speak your pious purpose—pronounce my

pardon then—and take me with you!—He would, but cannot.—Oh, why, with such fond affection, do you press my murdering hand?—What! will you kiss me?

(Barnwell *kisses his* uncle, *who groans and dies.*)

Life, that hovered on his lips but till he had sealed my pardon, in that kiss expired. He's gone forever—and oh! I follow.

(*Swoons away upon his* uncle's *dead body.*)

—Do I still live to press the suffering bosom of the earth? Do I still breathe, and taint with my infectious breath the wholesome air? Let heaven from its high throne, in justice or in mercy, now look down on that dear murdered saint and me the murderer, and, if his vengeance spares, let pity strike and end my wretched being!—Murder the worst of crimes, and parricide the worst of murders, and this the worst of parricides! Cain, who stands on record from the birth of time, and must to its last final period, as accursed, slew a brother favored above him. Detested Nero by another's hand dispatched a mother that he feared and hated. But I, with my own hand, have murdered a brother, mother, father, and a friend most loving and beloved. This execrable act of mine's without a parallel. Oh, may it ever stand alone—the last of murders, as it is the worst!
    The rich man thus, in torment and despair,
    Preferred his vain but charitable prayer.
    The fool, his own soul lost, would fain be wise
    For others' good; but heaven his suit denies.
    By laws and means well known we stand or fall,
    And one eternal rule remains for all.

(*Exit.*)

(*ACT IV. SCENE I.—A room in* Thorowgood's *house. Enter* Maria.)

Maria:
How falsely do they judge who censure or applaud, as we're afflicted or rewarded here! I know I am unhappy, yet cannot charge myself with any crime more than the common

frailties of our kind, that should provoke just heaven to mark me out for sufferings so uncommon and severe. Falsely to accuse ourselves, heaven must abhor; then it is just and right that innocence should suffer, for heaven must be just in all its ways. Perhaps by that we are kept from moral evils much worse than penal, or more improved in virtue; or may not the lesser ills that we sustain be made the means of greater good to others? Might all the joyless days and sleepless nights that I have passed but purchase peace for thee,

> Thou dear, dear cause of all my grief and pain,
> Small were the loss, and infinite the gain;
> Though to the grave in secret love I pine,
> So life and fame and happiness were thine.

(Enter Trueman.)

—What news of Barnwell?

Trueman:
None. I have sought him with the greatest diligence, but all in vain.

Maria:
Does my father yet suspect the cause of his absence?

Trueman:
All appeared so just and fair to him, it is not possible he ever should; but his absence will no longer be concealed. Your father's wise; and, though he seems to hearken to the friendly excuses I would make for Barnwell, yet I am afraid he regards 'em only as such, without suffering them to influence his judgment.

Maria:
How does the unhappy youth defeat all our designs to serve him! Yet I can never repent what we have done. Should he return, 'twill make his reconciliation with my father easier, and preserve him from future reproach from a malicious, unforgiving world.

(Enter Thorowgood and Lucy.)

Thorowgood:
> This woman here has given me a sad, and (bating some circumstances) too probable account of Barnwell's defection.

Lucy:
> I am sorry, sir, that my frank confession of my former unhappy course of life should cause you to suspect my truth on this occasion.

Thorowgood:
> It is not that; your confession has in it all the appearance of truth. (*To them*) Among many other particulars, she informs me that Barnwell has been influenced to break his trust, and wrong me at several times of considerable sums of money; now, as I know this to be false, I would fain doubt the whole of her relation, too dreadful to be willingly believed.

Maria:
> Sir, your pardon; I find myself on a sudden so indisposed that I must retire.—(*Aside.*) Providence opposes all attempts to save him. Poor ruined Barnwell! Wretched, lost Maria!

> > (*Exit* Maria.)

Thorowgood:
> How am I distressed on every side! Pity for that unhappy youth, fear for the life of a much valued friend—and then my child, the only joy and hope of my declining life! Her melancholy increases hourly, and gives me painful apprehensions of her loss. O Trueman! this person informs me that your friend, at the instigation of an impious woman, is gone to rob and murder his venerable uncle.

Trueman:
> Oh, execrable deed! I am blasted with the horror of the thought.

Lucy:
> This delay may ruin all.

Thorowgood:
> What to do or think I know not. That he ever wronged me, I

know is false; the rest may be so too—there's all my hope.

Trueman:
Trust not to that; rather suppose all true than lose a moment's time: even now the horrid deed may be a doing—dreadful imagination!—or it may be done, and we be vainly debating on the means to prevent what is already past.

Thorowgood *(aside)*:
This earnestness convinces me that he knows more than he has yet discovered.—What ho! without there! who waits?

(Enter a Servant.*)*

—Order the groom to saddle the swiftest horse and prepare to set out with speed! An affair of life and death demands his diligence.

(Exit Servant.*)*

Thorowgood *(to Lucy)*:
For you, whose behavior on this occasion I have no time to commend as it deserves, I must engage your farther assistance. Return and observe this Millwood till I come. I have your directions, and will follow you as soon as possible.

(Exit Lucy.*)*

—Trueman, you, I am sure, will not be idle on this occasion.

(Exit Thorowgood.*)*

Trueman:
He only who is a friend can judge of my distress.

(Exit.)

*(SCENE II.—*Millwood's *house. Enter* Millwood.*)*

Millwood:
I wish I knew the event of his design; the attempt without success would ruin him.—Well! what have I to apprehend

from that? I fear too much. The mischief being only intended, his friends, in pity of his youth, turn all their rage on me. I should have thought of that before. Suppose the deed done: then, and then only, I shall be secure. Or what if he returns without attempting it at all?

(*Enter* Barnwell, *bloody.*)

But he is here, and I have done him wrong; his bloody hands show he has done the deed, but show he wants the prudence to conceal it.

Barnwell:
Where shall I hide me? [whither] shall I fly to avoid the swift, unerring hand of Justice?

Millwood:
Dismiss your fears. Though thousands had pursued you to the door, yet being entered here, you are safe as innocence. I have such a cavern, by art so cunningly contrived, that the piercing eyes of Jealousy and Revenge may search in vain, nor find the entrance to the safe retreat. There will I hide you if any danger's near.

Barnwell:
Oh, hide me—from myself if it be possible; for while I bear my conscience in my bosom, though I were hid where man's eye never saw nor light e'er dawned, 'twere all in vain. For oh! that inmate—that impartial judge, will try, convict, and sentence me for murder, and execute me with never-ending torments. Behold these hands all crimsoned o'er with my dear uncle's blood! Here's a sight to make a statue start with horror, or turn a living man into a statue.

Millwood:
Ridiculous! Then it seems you are afraid of your own shadow, or, what's less than a shadow, your conscience.

Barnwell:
Though to man unknown I did the accursed act, what can we hide from heaven's all-seeing eye?

Millwood:
> No more of this stuff! What advantage have you made of his death? or what advantage may yet be made of it? Did you secure the keys of his treasure—those no doubt were about him. What gold, what jewels, or what else of value have you brought me?

Barnwell:
> Think you I added sacrilege to murder? Oh! had you seen him as his life flowed from him in a crimson flood, and heard him praying for me by the double name of nephew and of murderer! (alas, alas! he knew not then that his nephew was his murderer) how would you have wished, as I did, though you had a thousand years of life to come, to have given them all to have lengthened his one hour! But, being dead, I fled the sight of what my hands had done, nor could I, to have gained the empire of the world, have violated, by theft, his sacred corpse.

Millwood:
> Whining, preposterous, canting villain, to murder your uncle, rob him of life, nature's first, last, dear prerogative, after which there's no injury—then fear to take what he no longer wanted, and bring to me your penury and guilt! Do you think I'll hazard my reputation—nay, my life, to entertain you?

Barnwell:
> O Millwood! this from thee!—but I have done; if you hate me, if you wish me dead, then are you happy—for oh! 'tis sure my grief will quickly end me.

Millwood *(aside)*:
> In his madness he will discover all and involve me in his ruin. We are on a precipice from whence there's no retreat for both—then to preserve myself. *(Pauses.)* There is no other way,—'tis dreadful; but reflection comes too late when danger's pressing—and there's no room for choice. It must be done.
>
> *(Rings a bell.)*
>
> *(Enter a Servant.)*

—Fetch me an officer, and seize this villain: he has confessed himself a murderer; should I let him escape, I justly might be thought as bad as he.

(Exit Servant.)

Barnwell:
O Millwood! sure you do not, cannot mean it. Stop the messenger!—upon my knees I beg you'd call him back! 'Tis fit I die indeed, but not by you. I will this instant deliver myself into the hands of justice, indeed I will; for death is all I wish. But thy ingratitude so tears my wounded soul, 'tis worse ten thousand times than death with torture.

Millwood:
Call it what you will, I am willing to live, and live secure—which nothing but your death can warrant.

Barnwell:
If there be a pitch of wickedness that seats the author beyond the reach of vengeance, you must be secure. But what remains for me but a dismal dungeon, hard-galling fetters, an awful trial, and an ignominious death—justly to fall unpitied and abhorred?—after death to be suspended between heaven and earth, a dreadful spectacle, the warning and horror of a gaping crowd? This I could bear—nay, wish not to avoid, had it but come from any hand but thine.

(Enter Blunt, Officer and Attendants.)

Millwood:
Heaven defend me! Conceal a murderer? Here, sir; take this youth into your custody. I accuse him of murder, and will appear to make good my charge.

(They seize him.)

Barnwell:
To whom, of what, or how shall I complain? I'll not accuse her: the hand of heav'n is in it, and this the punishment of lust and parricide. Yet heav'n, that justly cuts me off, still suffers her to live, perhaps to punish others. Tremendous

mercy! so fiends are cursed with immortality, to be the executioners of heaven.—

> Be warned, ye youths, who see my sad despair.
> Avoid lewd women, false as they are fair;
> By reason guided, honest joys pursue;
> The fair, to honor and to virtue true,
> Just to herself, will ne'er be false to you.
> By my example learn to shun my fate;
> (How wretched is the man who's wise too late!)
> Ere innocence, and fame, and life, be lost,
> Here purchase wisdom cheaply, at my cost!

(Exeunt Barnwell, Officer *and* Attendants.*)*

Millwood:
Where's Lucy? Why is she absent at such a time?

Blunt:
Would I had been so too. Lucy will soon be here, and, I hope, to thy confusion, thou devil!

Millwood:
Insolent! This to me?

Blunt:
The worst that we know of the devil is that he first seduces to sin and then betrays to punishment.

(Exit Blunt.*)*

Millwood:
They disapprove of my conduct then, and mean to take this opportunity to set up for themselves. My ruin is resolved. I see my danger, but scorn both it and them; I was not born to fall by such weak instruments.

(Going.)

(Enter Thorowgood.*)*

Thorowgood:
Where is the scandal of her own sex and curse of ours?

Millwood:
What means this insolence? Who do you seek?

Thorowgood:
Millwood.

Millwood:
Well, you have found her then. I am Millwood.

Thorowgood:
Then you are the most impious wretch that e'er the sun beheld.

Millwood:
From your appearance I should have expected wisdom and moderation, but your manners belie your aspect. What is your business here? I know you not.

Thorowgood:
Hereafter you may know me better; I am Barnwell's master.

Millwood:
Then you are master to a villain—which, I think, is not much to your credit.

Thorowgood:
Had he been as much above thy arts as my credit is superior to thy malice, I need not have blushed to own him.

Millwood:
My arts? I don't understand you, sir. If he has done amiss, what's that to me? Was he my servant, or yours? You should have taught him better.

Thorowgood:
Why should I wonder to find such uncommon impudence in one arrived to such a height of wickedness? When innocence is banished, modesty soon follows.—Know, sorceress, I'm not ignorant of any of thy arts by which you first deceived the unwary youth: I know how, step by step, you've led him on, reluctant and unwilling, from crime to crime, to this last horrid act, which you contrived and, by

your cursed wiles, even forced him to commit.

Millwood *(aside)*:
Ha! Lucy has got the advantage and accused me first. Unless I can turn the accusation and fix it upon her and Blunt, I am lost.

Thorowgood:
Had I known your cruel design sooner, it had been prevented. To see you punished as the law directs is all that now remains. Poor satisfaction! for he, innocent as he is, compared to you, must suffer too. But heaven, who knows our frame and graciously distinguishes between frailty and presumption, will make a difference, though man cannot, who sees not the heart, but only judges by the outward action.

Millwood:
I find, sir, we are both unhappy in our servants. I was surprised at such ill treatment, without cause, from a gentleman of your appearance, and therefore too hastily returned it; for which I ask your pardon. I now perceive you have been so far imposed on as to think me engaged in a former correspondence with your servant, and, some way or other, accessary to his undoing.

Thorowgood:
I charge you as the cause, the sole cause, of all his guilt and all his suffering—of all he now endures, and must endure, till a violent and shameful death shall put a dreadful period to his life and miseries together.

Millwood:
'Tis very strange! but who's secure from scandal and detraction? So far from contributing to his ruin, I never spoke to him till since that fatal accident, which I lament as much as you. 'Tis true, I have a servant, on whose account he has of late frequented my house; if she has abused my good opinion of her, am I to blame? Hasn't Barnwell done the same by you?

Thorowgood:
I hear you; pray, go on!

Millwood:
I have been informed he had a violent passion for her, and she for him; but till now I always thought it innocent; I know her poor, and given to expensive pleasures: now who can tell but she may have influenced the amorous youth to commit this murder, to supply her extravagancies? It must be so. I now recollect a thousand circumstances that confirm it. I'll have her and a manservant that I suspect as an accomplice, secured immediately. I hope, sir, you will lay aside your ill-grounded suspicions of me, and join to punish the real contrivers of this bloody deed.

(Offers to go.)

Thorowgood:
Madam, you pass not this way; I see your design, but shall protect them from your malice.

Millwood:
I hope you will not use your influence, and the credit of your name, to screen such guilty wretches. Consider, sir, the wickedness of persuading a thoughtless youth to such a crime!

Thorowgood:
I do—and of betraying him when it was done.

Millwood:
That which you call betraying him, may convince you of my innocence. She who loves him, though she contrived the murder, would never have delivered him into the hands of justice, as I, struck with horror at his crimes, have done.

Thorowgood *(aside)*:
How should an unexperienced youth escape her snares? The powerful magic of her wit and form might betray the wisest to simple dotage, and fire the blood that age had froze long since. Even I, that with just prejudice came prepared, had, by her artful story, been deceived, but that my strong

conviction of her guilt makes even a doubt impossible.—Those whom subtilely you would accuse, you know are your accusers; and (which proves unanswerably their innocence and your guilt) they accused you before the deed was done, and did all that was in their power to prevent it.

Millwood:
Sir, you are very hard to be convinced; but I have such a proof which, when produced, will silence all objections.

(Exit Millwood.*)*

(Enter Lucy, Trueman, Blunt, Officers, *etc.)*

Lucy:
Gentlemen, pray place yourselves, some on one side of that door, and some on the other; watch her entrance, and act as your prudence shall direct you.—*(To* Thorowgood.*)* This way! and note her behavior. I have observed her; she's driven to the last extremity, and is forming some desperate resolution. I guess at her design.

(Re-enter Millwood *with a pistol.* Trueman *secures her.)*

Trueman:
Here thy power of doing mischief ends, deceitful, cruel, bloody woman!

Millwood:
Fool, hypocrite, villain—man! Thou canst not call me that.

Trueman:
To call thee woman were to wrong thy sex, thou devil!

Millwood:
That imaginary being is an emblem of thy cursed sex collected—a mirror, wherein each particular man may see his own likeness and that of all mankind.

Trueman:
Think not by aggravating the faults of others to extenuate thy own, of which the abuse of such uncommon perfections

of mind and body is not the least!

Millwood:
If such I had, well may I curse your barbarous sex, who robbed me of 'em ere I knew their worth; then left me, too late, to count their value by their loss. Another and another spoiler came, and all my gain was poverty and reproach. My soul disdained, and yet disdains, dependence and contempt. Riches, no matter by what means obtained, I saw, secured the worst of men from both. I found it therefore necessary to be rich, and to that end I summoned all my arts. You call 'em wicked; be it so! They were such as my conversation with your sex had furnished me withal.

Trueman:
Sure, none but the worst of men conversed with thee.

Millwood:
Men of all degrees and all professions I have known, yet found no difference but in their several capacities; all were alike wicked to the utmost of their power. In pride, contention, avarice, cruelty and revenge, the reverend priesthood were my unerring guides. From suburb-magistrates, who live by ruined reputations, as the unhospitable natives of Cornwall do by shipwrecks, I learned that to charge my innocent neighbors with my crimes, was to merit their protection; for to screen the guilty is the less scandalous when many are suspected, and detraction, like darkness and death, blackens all objects and levels all distinction. Such are your venal magistrates, who favor none but such as, by their office, they are sworn to punish. With them, not to be guilty is the worst of crimes, and large fees privately paid are every needful virtue.

Trueman:
Your practice has sufficiently discovered your contempt of laws, both human and divine; no wonder then that you should hate the officers of both.

Millwood:
I know you and I hate you all. I expect no mercy and I ask for none; I followed my inclinations, and that the best of you do every day. All actions seem alike natural and indifferent

to man and beast, who devour, or are devoured, as they meet with others weaker or stronger than themselves.

Trueman:
What pity it is, a mind so comprehensive, daring, and inquisitive, should be a stranger to religion's sweet and powerful charms!

Millwood:
I am not fool enough to be an atheist, though I have known enough of men's hypocrisy to make a thousand simple women so. Whatever religion is in itself, as practised by mankind it has caused the evils you say it was designed to cure. War, plague, and famine, has not destroyed so many of the human race as this pretended piety has done, and with such barbarous cruelty, as if the only way to honor heaven were to turn the present world into hell.

Trueman:
Truth is truth, though from an enemy and spoke in malice. You bloody, blind, and superstitious bigots, how will you answer this?

Millwood:
What are your laws, of which you make your boast, but the fool's wisdom and the coward's valor—the instrument and screen of all your villainies, by which you punish in others what you act yourselves, or would have acted had you been in their circumstances? The judge who condemns the poor man for being a thief had been a thief himself had he been poor. Thus you go on deceiving and being deceived, harassing, plaguing, and destroying one another: but women are your universal prey.

> Women, by whom you are, the source of joy,
> With cruel arts you labor to destroy;
> A thousand ways our ruin you pursue,
> Yet blame in us those arts first taught by you.
> O may, from hence, each violated maid,
> By flatt'ring, faithless, barb'rous man betrayed,
> When robbed of innocence and virgin fame,
> From your destruction raise a nobler name;
> To right their sex's wrongs devote their mind,

And future Millwoods prove, to plague mankind!

(Exeunt.)

(ACT V. SCENE I.— A room in a prison. Enter Thorowgood, Blunt and Lucy.)

Thorowgood:
I have recommended to Barnwell a reverend divine, whose judgment and integrity I am well acquainted with: nor has Millwood been neglected, but she, unhappy woman, still obstinate, refuses his assistance.

Lucy:
This pious charity to the afflicted well becomes your character; yet pardon me, sir, if I wonder you were not at their trial.

Thorowgood:
I knew it was impossible to save him, and I and my family bear so great a part in his distress, that to have been present would but have aggravated our sorrows without relieving his.

Blunt:
It was mournful, indeed. Barnwell's youth and modest deportment, as he passed, drew tears from every eye. When placed at the bar and arraigned before the reverend judges, with many tears and interrupting sobs he confessed and aggravated his offences, without accusing or once reflecting on Millwood, the shameless author of his ruin—who, dauntless and unconcerned, stood by his side, viewing with visible pride and contempt the vast assembly, who all with sympathizing sorrow wept for the wretched youth. Millwood, when called upon to answer, loudly insisted upon her innocence, and made an artful and a bold defence; but, finding all in vain, the impartial jury and the learned bench concurring to find her guilty, how did she curse herself, poor Barnwell, us, her judges, all mankind! But what could that avail? she was condemned, and is this day to suffer with him.

Thorowgood:
The time draws on; I am going to visit Barnwell, as you are Millwood.

Lucy:
We have not wronged her, yet I dread this interview. She's proud, impatient, wrathful, and unforgiving. To be the branded instruments of vengeance, to suffer in her shame and sympathise with her in all she suffers, is the tribute we must pay for our former ill-spent lives and long confederacy with her in wickedness.

Thorowgood:
Happy for you it ended when it did! What you have done against Millwood, I know proceeded from a just abhorrence of her crimes, free from interest, malice, or revenge. Proselytes to virtue should be encouraged. Pursue your purposed reformation, and know me hereafter for your friend.

Lucy:
This is a blessing as unhoped for as unmerited; but heaven, that snatched us from impending ruin, sure intends you as its instrument to secure us from apostasy.

Thorowgood:
With gratitude to impute your deliverance to heaven, is just. Many, less virtuously disposed than Barnwell was, have never fallen in the manner he has done; may not such owe their safety rather to Providence than to themselves? With pity and compassion let us judge him! Great were his faults, but strong was the temptation. Let his ruin learn us diffidence, humanity, and circumspection; for we, who wonder at his fate—perhaps, had we like him been tried, like him we had fallen too.

(Exeunt.)

(SCENE II.—*A dungeon. A table and lamp.* Barnwell, *reading. Enter* Thorowgood *at a distance.*)

Thorowgood:
There see the bitter fruits of passion's detested reign and sensual appetite indulged—severe reflections, penitence, and tears.

Barnwell:
My honored, injured master, whose goodness has covered me a thousand times with shame, forgive this last unwilling disrespect! indeed, I saw you not.

Thorowgood:
'Tis well; I hope you were better employed in viewing of yourself. Your journey's long, your time for preparation almost spent. I sent a reverend divine to teach you to improve it, and should be glad to hear of his success.

Barnwell:
The word of truth, which he recommended for my constant companion in this my sad retirement, has at length removed the doubts I labored under. From thence I've learned the infinite extent of heavenly mercy; that my offences, though great, are not unpardonable; and that 'tis not my interest only, but my duty, to believe and to rejoice in that hope: so shall heaven receive the glory, and future penitents the profit of my example.

Thorowgood:
Proceed!

Barnwell:
'Tis wonderful that words should charm despair, speak peace and pardon to a murderer's conscience; but truth and mercy flow in every sentence, attended with force and energy divine. How shall I describe my present state of mind? I hope in doubt, and trembling I rejoice; I feel my grief increase, even as my fears give way. Joy and gratitude now supply more tears than the horror and anguish of despair before.

Thorowgood:
These are the genuine signs of true repentance, the only preparatory, the certain way to everlasting peace.—Oh, the joy it gives to see a soul formed and prepared for heaven! For this the faithful minister devotes himself to meditation, abstinence, and prayer, shunning the vain delights of sensual joys, and daily dies that others may live forever. For this he turns the sacred volumes o'er, and spends his life in painful

search of truth. The love of riches and the lust of power, he looks upon with just contempt and detestation, who only counts for wealth the souls he wins, and whose highest ambition is to serve mankind. If the reward of all his pains be to preserve one soul from wandering, or turn one from the error of his ways, how does he then rejoice, and own his little labors overpaid!

Barnwell:
What do I owe for all your generous kindness? But though I cannot, heaven can and will reward you.

Thorowgood:
To see thee thus is joy too great for words. Farewell! heaven strengthen thee! Farewell!

Barnwell:
O sir, there's something I would say if my sad, swelling heart would give me leave.

Thorowgood:
Give it vent a while and try.

Barnwell:
I had a friend—'tis true I am unworthy, yet methinks your generous example might persuade—could I not see him once before I go from whence there's no return?

Thorowgood:
He's coming, and as much thy friend as ever. (*Aside*.) But I'll not anticipate his sorrow; too soon he'll see the sad effect of his contagious ruin. This torrent of domestic misery bears too hard upon me; I must retire to indulge a weakness I find impossible to overcome.—Much loved, and much lamented youth, farewell! Heaven strengthen thee! Eternally farewell!

Barnwell:
The best of masters and of men, farewell! While I live, let me not want your prayers!

Thorowgood:
Thou shalt not: thy peace being made with heaven, death's

already vanquished; bear a little longer the pains that attend this transitory life, and cease from pain forever.

(Exit Thorowgood.)

Barnwell:
Perhaps I shall. I find a power within that bears my soul above the fears of death, and, spite of conscious shame and guilt, gives me a taste of pleasure more than mortal.

(Enter Trueman and Keeper.)

Keeper: Sir, there's the prisoner.

(Exit Keeper.)

Barnwell:
Trueman—my friend, whom I so wished to see! yet now he's here I dare not look upon him.
(Weeps.)

Trueman:
O Barnwell! Barnwell!

Barnwell:
Mercy, mercy, gracious heaven! For death, but not for this, I was prepared.

Trueman:
What have I suffered since I saw you last! What pain hath absence given me! But oh! to see thee thus!

Barnwell:
I know it is dreadful! I feel the anguish of thy generous soul—but I was born to murder all who love me.

(Both weep.)

Trueman:
I came not to reproach you; I thought to bring you comfort. But I'm deceived, for I have none to give. I came to share thy sorrow, but cannot bear my own.

Barnwell:
> My sense of guilt, indeed, you cannot know: 'tis what the good and innocent, like you, can ne'er conceive. But other griefs at present I have none but what I feel for you. In your sorrow I read you love me still; but yet methinks 'tis strange, when I consider what I am.

Trueman:
> No more of that! I can remember nothing but thy virtues, thy honest, tender friendship, our former happy state, and present misery.—Oh, had you trusted me when first the fair seducer tempted you, all might have been prevented.

Barnwell:
> Alas, thou know'st not what a wretch I've been! Breach of friendship was my first and least offence: so far was I lost to goodness, so devoted to the author of my ruin, that, had she insisted on my murdering thee, I think—I should have done it.

Trueman:
> Prithee, aggravate thy faults no more!

Barnwell:
> I think I should!—thus good and generous as you are, I should have murdered you!

Trueman:
> We have not yet embraced, and may be interrupted. Come to my arms!

Barnwell:
> Never! never will I taste such joys on earth; never will I so soothe my just remorse. Are these honest arms and faithful bosom fit to embrace and to support a murderer? These iron fetters only shall clasp, and flinty pavement bear me
>
> *(Throwing himself on the ground.)*
>
> —even these too good for such a bloody monster.

Trueman:
>Shall fortune sever those whom friendship joined? Thy miseries cannot lay thee so low but love will find thee. Here will we offer to stern calamity, this place the altar, and ourselves the sacrifice! Our mutual groans shall echo to each other through the dreary vault; our sighs shall number the moments as they pass, and mingling tears communicate such anguish as words were never made to express.

Barnwell:
>Then be it so!
>
>>*(Rising.)*
>
>Since you propose an intercourse of woe, pour all your griefs into my breast, and in exchange take mine!
>
>>*(Embracing.)*
>
>Where's now the anguish that you promised? You've taken mine and make me no return. Sure, peace and comfort dwell within these arms, and sorrow can't approach me while I'm here! This too is the work of heaven, which, having before spoke peace and pardon to me, now sends thee to confirm it. Oh, take, take some of the joy that overflows my breast!

Trueman:
>I do, I do. Almighty Power, how hast thou made us capable to bear, at once, the extremes of pleasure and of pain!
>
>>*(Enter Keeper.)*

Keeper:
>Sir!

Trueman:
>I come.
>
>>*(Exit Keeper.)*

Barnwell:
>Must you leave me? Death would soon have parted us forever.

Trueman:
>O my Barnwell, there's yet another task behind; again your heart must bleed for others' woes.

Barnwell:
>To meet and part with you, I thought was all I had to do on earth! What is there more for me to do or suffer?

Trueman:
>I dread to tell thee; yet it must be known!—Maria—

Barnwell:
>Our master's fair and virtuous daughter?

Trueman:
>The same.

Barnwell:
>No misfortune, I hope, has reached that lovely maid! Preserve her, heaven, from every ill, to show mankind that goodness is your care!

Trueman:
>Thy, thy misfortunes, my unhappy friend, have reached her. Whatever you and I have felt, and more, if more be possible, she feels for you.

Barnwell (*aside*):
>I know he doth abhor a lie and would not trifle with his dying friend. This is, indeed, the bitterness of death!

Trueman:
>You must remember, for we all observed it, for some time past a heavy melancholy weighed her down. Disconsolate she seemed, and pined and languished from a cause unknown till, hearing of your dreadful fate, the long stifled flame blazed out: she wept, she wrung her hands, and tore her hair, and in the transport of her grief discovered her own lost state whilst she lamented yours.

Barnwell:
>Will all the pain I feel restore thy ease, lovely, unhappy maid?

(Weeping.)

Why did you not let me die and never know it?

Trueman:

It was impossible; she makes no secret of her passion for you, and is determined to see you ere you die. She waits for me to introduce her.

(Exit Trueman.)

Barnwell:

Vain, busy thoughts, be still! What avails it to think on what I might have been? I now am—what I've made myself.

(Enter Trueman with Maria.)

Trueman:

Madam, reluctant I lead you to this dismal scene. This is the seat of misery and guilt. Here awful justice reserves her public victims. This is the entrance to shameful death.

Maria:

To this sad place, then no improper guest, the abandoned, lost Maria brings despair—and see the subject and the cause of all this world of woe! Silent and motionless he stands, as if his soul had quitted her abode and the lifeless form alone was left behind—yet that so perfect that beauty and death, ever at enmity, now seem united there.

Barnwell:

I groan but murmur not. Just heaven, I am your own; do with me what you please.

Maria:

Why are your streaming eyes still fixed below, as though thou'dst give the greedy earth thy sorrows and rob me of my due? Were happiness within your power, you should bestow it where you pleased; but in your misery I must and will partake!

Barnwell:
> Oh! say not so, but fly, abhor, and leave me to my fate! Consider what you are—how vast your fortune, and how bright your fame; have pity on your youth, your beauty, and unequalled virtue, for which so many noble peers have sighed in vain! Bless with your charms some honorable lord! adorn with your beauty and by your example improve the English court, that justly claims such merit; so shall I quickly be to you—as though I had never been.

Maria:
> When I forget you, I must be so, indeed. Reason, choice, virtue, all forbid it. Let women like Millwood, if there are more such women, smile in prosperity and in adversity forsake! Be it the pride of virtue to repair, or to partake, the ruin such have made.

Trueman:
> Lovely, ill-fated maid! Was there ever such generous distress before? How must this pierce his grateful heart, and aggravate his woes!

Barnwell:
> Ere I knew guilt or shame, when fortune smiled, and when my youthful hopes were at the highest—if then to have raised my thoughts to you had been presumption in me, never to have been pardoned, think how much beneath yourself you condescend, to regard me now!

Maria:
> Let her blush who, proferring love, invades the freedom of your sex's choice, and meanly sues in hopes of a return! Your inevitable fate hath rendered hope impossible as vain. Then why should I fear to avow a passion so just and so disinterested?

Trueman:
> If any should take occasion from Millwood's crimes to libel the best and fairest part of the creation, here let them see their error! The most distant hopes of such a tender passion from so bright a maid might add to the happiness of the most happy, and make the greatest proud. Yet here 'tis

lavished in vain: though by the rich present the generous donor is undone, he on whom it is bestowed receives no benefit.

Barnwell:
So the aromatic spices of the East, which all the living covet and esteem, are, with unavailing kindness, wasted on the dead.

Maria:
Yes, fruitless is my love, and unavailing all my sighs and tears. Can they save thee from approaching death—from such a death? Oh, terrible idea! What is her misery and distress, who sees the first, last object of her love, for whom alone she'd live—for whom she'd die a thousand, thousand deaths, if it were possible—expiring in her arms? Yet she is happy when compared to me. Were millions of worlds mine, I'd gladly give them in exchange for her condition. The most consummate woe is light to mine. The last of curses to other miserable maids is all I ask for my relief, and that's denied me.

Trueman:
Time and reflection cure all ills.

Maria:
All but this; his dreadful catastrophe, virtue herself abhors. To give a holiday to suburb slaves, and passing entertain the savage herd who, elbowing each other for a sight, pursue and press upon him like his fate! A mind with piety and resolution armed may smile on death. But public ignominy, everlasting shame,—shame, the death of souls—to die a thousand times, and yet survive even death itself, in never-dying infamy—is this to be endured? Can I, who live in him, and must, each hour of my devoted life, feel all these woes renewed—can I endure this?

Trueman:
Grief has so impaired her spirits, she pants as in the agonies of death.

Barnwell:
>Preserve her, heaven, and restore her peace; nor let her death be added to my crimes!

>>*(Bell tolls.)*

>I am summoned to my fate.

>>*(Enter Keeper and Officers.)*

Keeper:
>Sir, the officers attend you; Millwood is already summoned.

Barnwell:
>Tell 'em I'm ready.—And now, my friend, farewell!

>>*(Embracing.)*

>Support and comfort the best you can this mourning fair. No more! Forget not to pray for me!—

>>*(Turning to Maria.)*

>Would you, bright excellence, permit me the honor of a chaste embrace, the last happiness this world could give were mine.

>>*(She inclines toward him; they embrace.)*

>Exalted goodness! Oh, turn your eyes from earth and me to heaven, where virtue like yours is ever heard. Pray for the peace of my departing soul! Early my race of wickedness began, and soon reached the summit. Ere nature has finished her work and stamped me man—just at the time that others begin to stray—my course is finished. Though short my span of life, and few my days, yet count my crimes for years, and I have lived whole ages. Thus justice, in compassion to mankind, cuts off a wretch like me, by one such example to secure thousands from future ruin. Justice and mercy are in heaven the same: its utmost severity is mercy to the whole, thereby to cure man's folly and presumption, which else would render even infinite mercy vain and ineffectual.

>   If any youth, like you, in future times,
>   Shall mourn my fate, though he abhor my crimes;
>   Or tender maid, like you, my tale shall hear,
>   And to my sorrows give a pitying tear;
>   To each such melting eye and throbbing heart
>   Would gracious heaven this benefit impart—
>   Never to know my guilt nor feel my pain.
>   Then must you own, you ought not to complain;
>   Since you nor weep, nor shall I die, in vain.

(*Exeunt* Barnwell *and* Officers [*and* Trueman *and* Maria].)

(SCENE.—*The Last. The place of execution. The gallows and ladders at the farther end of the stage. A crowd of spectators.*)

(*Blunt and Lucy.*)

Lucy:
Heavens! What a throng!

Blunt:
How terrible is death when thus prepared!

Lucy:
Support them, heaven; thou only canst support them; all other help is vain.

Officer (*within*):
Make way there; make way, and give the prisoners room!

Lucy:
They are here; observe them well. How humble and composed young Barnwell seems! But Millwood looks wild, ruffled with passion, confounded and amazed.

(*Enter* Barnwell, Millwood, Officers *and* Executioner.)

Barnwell:
See, Millwood, see, our journey's at an end. Life, like a tale that's told, is past away; that short, but dark and unknown passage, death, is all the space 'tween us and endless joys, or woes eternal.

Millwood:
> Is this the end of all my flattering hopes? Were youth and beauty given me for a curse, and wisdom only to insure my ruin? They were, they were. Heaven, thou hast done thy worst. Or if thou hast in store some untried plague, somewhat that's worse than shame, despair and death, unpitied death, confirmed despair and soul-confounding shame—something that men and angels can't describe, and only fiends, who bear it, can conceive—now, pour it now on this devoted head, that I may feel the worst thou canst inflict and bid defiance to thy utmost power.

Barnwell:
> Yet ere we pass the dreadful gulf of death, yet ere you're plunged in everlasting woe, oh, bend your stubborn knees and harder heart, humbly to deprecate the wrath divine. Who knows but heaven, in your dying moments, may bestow that grace and mercy which your life despised?

Millwood:
> Why name you mercy to a wretch like me? Mercy's beyond my hope, almost beyond my wish. I can't repent, nor ask to be forgiven.

Barnwell:
> Oh, think what 'tis to be for ever, ever miserable; nor with vain pride oppose a power that's able to destroy you.

Millwood:
> That will destroy me: I feel it will. A deluge of wrath is pouring on my soul. Chains, darkness, wheels, racks, sharp stinging scorpions, molten lead, and seas of sulphur are light to what I feel.

Barnwell:
> Oh, add not to your vast account despair—a sin more injurious to heaven than all you've yet committed.

Millwood:
> Oh! I have sinned beyond the reach of mercy.

Barnwell:
> Oh, say not so: 'tis blasphemy to think it. As yon bright roof is higher than the earth, so and much more does heaven's goodness pass our apprehension. Oh, what created being shall presume to circumscribe mercy, that knows no bounds?

Millwood:
> This yields no hope. Though mercy may be boundless, yet 'tis free: and I was doomed, before the world began, to endless pains, and thou to joys eternal.

Barnwell:
> O gracious heaven! extend thy pity to her: let thy rich mercy flow in plenteous streams to chase her fears and heal her wounded soul.

Millwood:
> It will not be. Your prayers are lost in air, or else returned perhaps with double blessings to your bosom; but me they help not.

Barnwell:
> Yet hear me, Millwood!

Millwood:
> Away! I will not hear thee: I tell thee, youth, I am by heaven devoted a dreadful instance of its power to punish.

> (Barnwell *seems to pray.*)

> If thou wilt pray, pray for thyself, not me.—How doth his fervent soul mount with his words, and both ascend to heaven! that heaven, whose gates are shut with adamantine bars against my prayers, had I the will to pray. I cannot bear it—sure, 'tis the worst of torments to behold others enjoy that bliss that we must never taste.

Officer:
> The utmost limit of your time's expired.

Millwood:
> Incompassed with horror, whither must I go? I would not live—nor die. That I could cease to be!—or ne'er had been!

Barnwell:
>Since peace and comfort are denied her here, may she find mercy where she least expects it, and this be all her hell. From our example may all be taught to fly the first approach of vice; but, if o'ertaken
>>By strong temptation, weakness, or surprise,
>>Lament their guilt, and by repentance rise;
>>Th' impenitent alone die unforgiven;
>>To sin's like man, and to forgive like heaven.

(Barnwell and Millwood are conducted toward the gallows.)

(Enter Trueman.)

Lucy:
>Heart-breaking sight! O wretched, wretched Milllwood!

Trueman:
>How is she disposed to meet her fate?

Blunt:
>Who can describe unutterable woe?

Lucy:
>She goes to death encompassed with horror—loathing life, and yet afraid to die; no tongue can tell her anguish and despair.

Trueman:
>Heaven be better to her than her fears! may she prove a warning to others, a monument of mercy in herself!

Lucy:
>Oh, sorrow insupportable! break, break, my heart!

Trueman:
>In vain
>With bleeding hearts and weeping eyes we show
>A human, gen'rous sense of others' woe,
>Unless we mark what drew their ruin on,
>And, by avoiding that—prevent our own.

(Exeunt.)

Comments and Questions

1. In his dedication to *The London Merchant* Lillo states that the purpose of tragedy is "the exciting of the passions in order to the correcting such of them as are criminal, either in their nature, or through their excess." Aristotle used the word *catharsis* to describe the effect of tragedy believing that watching a play caused a kind of purging of unhealthy impulses and feelings. If we subscribe to the catharsis theory, how could literature in general, and tragic plays in particular, be used to reduce our existing prison population?

2. Literary characters are said to be of a "static" or "dynamic" nature. Static characters experience little or no change as the work progresses whereas dynamic characters are changed and shaped by dramatic events. Compare and contrast Millwood and George Barnwell. Are they static or dynamic characters? Remember that George Barnwell begged Millwood to hide him—first from Justice, then from himself so that he could escape his conscience. How would the play differ if Millwood had successfully hidden Barnwell? Are we misled into believing that Barnwell is a dynamic character by the fact that he appears to be repentant at the end of the play? Is he only "changed" because he is finally trapped and contained within the prison? If he were freed, would his conscience be sufficient to punish him for past wrongs and to prevent him from committing future crimes?

3. Throughout *The London Merchant*, Barnwell's friend Trueman, his employer Thorowgood, his employer's daughter Maria, and even his murdered Uncle Barnwell, act the way character witnesses would act in a criminal trial. How does the reading of literature allow us to come to understand the protagonist better than we are able to come to know the criminal in the dock?

4. It is important to note that Lillo eschewed both the subject and the style of the earlier Elizabethan playwrights, preferring to write *The London Merchant* mostly in prose rather than in verse and choosing as his subject the actions and morals of middle class people rather than the lives of kings and princes. The style would have been more accessible to

the middle class and the subject was to serve his didactic purpose. Although the merchants and their families would be considered middle-class, there are still differences in the social standing of Maria, Millwood, and Lucy. Compare and contrast these three characters.

5. In speaking of Barnwell, Thorowgood makes the following speech: "With pity and compassion let us judge him! Great were his faults, but strong was the temptation. Let his ruin learn us diffidence, humanity and circumspection; for we who wonder at his fate—perhaps, had we like him been tried, like him we had fallen too." Do you agree with the sentiment expressed in this speech by Thorowgood? Does reading literature like *The London Merchant* help us to understand the human condition? If it does, how might reading literature affect the judicial process?

Susan Glaspell

Trifles

Characters

County Attorney
Mrs. Peters
Sheriff
Mrs. Hale
Hale

SETTING:
> The kitchen in the now-abandoned farmhouse of John Wright, a gloomy kitchen, and left without having been put in order—the walls covered with a faded wall paper. Downstage right is a door leading to the parlor. On the right wall above this door is a built-in kitchen cupboard with shelves in the upper portion and drawers below. In the rear wall at right, up two steps is a door opening onto stairs leading to the second floor. In the rear wall at left is a door to the shed and from there to the outside. Between these two doors is an old-fashioned black iron stove. Running along the left wall from the shed door is an old iron sink and sink shelf, in which is set a hand pump. Downstage of the sink is an uncurtained window. Near the window is an old wooden rocker: Center stage is an unpainted wooden kitchen table with straight chairs on either side. There is a small chair downstage right. Unwashed pans under the sink, a loaf of bread outside the breadbox, a dish towel on the table—other signs of incompleted work. At the rear the shed door opens and the Sheriff comes in followed by the County Attorney and Hale. The Sheriff and Hale are men in middle life, the County Attorney is a young man; all are much bundled up and go at once to the stove. They are followed by the two women—

the Sheriff's *wife,* Mrs. Peters, *first; she is a slight wiry woman, a thin nervous face.* Mrs. Hale *is larger and would ordinarily be called more comfortable looking, but she is disturbed now and looks fearfully about as she enters. The women have come in slowly, and stand close together near the door:*

County Attorney *(at stove rubbing his hands):*
This feels good. Come up to the fire, ladies.

Mrs. Peters *(after taking a step forward):*
I'm not—cold.

Sheriff *(unbuttoning his overcoat and stepping away from the stove to right of table as if to mark the beginning of official business):*
Now, Mr. Hale, before we move things about, you explain to Mr. Henderson just what you saw when you came here yesterday morning.

County Attorney *(crossing down to left of the table):*
By the way, has anything been moved? Are things just as you left them yesterday?

Sheriff *(looking about):*
It's just the same. When it dropped below zero last night I thought I'd better send Frank out this morning to make a fire for us—*(Sits right of center table.)* no use getting pneumonia with a big case on, but I told him not to touch anything except the stove—and you know Frank.

County Attorney:
Somebody should have been left here yesterday.

Sheriff:
Oh—yesterday. When I had to send Frank to Morris Center for that man who went crazy—I want you to know I had my hands full yesterday. I knew you could get back from Omaha by today and as long as I went over everything here myself—

County Attorney:
Well, Mr. Hale, tell just what happened when you came here yesterday morning.

Hale *(crossing down to above table)*:
Harry and I had started to town with a load of potatoes. We came along the road from my place and as I got here I said, "I'm going to see if I can't get John Wright to go in with me on a party telephone." I spoke to Wright about it once before and he put me off, saying folks talked too much anyway, and all he asked was peace and quiet—I guess you know about how much he talked himself; but I thought maybe if I went to the house and talked about it before his wife, though I said to Harry that I didn't know as what his wife wanted made much difference to John—

County Attorney:
Let's talk about that later, Mr. Hale. I do want to talk about that, but tell me now just what happened when you got to the house.

Hale:
I didn't hear or see anything; I knocked at the door, and still it was all quiet inside. I knew they must be up, it was past eight o'clock. So I knocked again, and I thought I heard somebody say, "Come in." I wasn't sure, I'm not sure yet, but I opened the door—this door *(Indicating the door by which the two women are still standing.)* and there in that rocker— *(Pointing to it.)* sat Mrs. Wright. *(They all look at the rocker downstage left.)*

County Attorney:
What—was she doing?

Hale:
She was rockin' back and forth. She had her apron in her hand and was kind of—pleating it.

County Attorney:
And how did she—look?

Hale:
Well, she looked queer.

County Attorney:
How do you mean—queer?

Hale:
> Well, as if she didn't know what she was going to do next. And kind of done up.

County Attorney (*takes out notebook and pencil and sits left of center table*)**:**
> How did she seem to feel about your coming?

Hale:
> Why, I don't think she minded—one way or other. She didn't pay much attention. I said, "How do, Mrs. Wright, it's cold, ain't it?" And she said, "Is it?" —and went on kind of pleating at her apron. Well, I was surprised; she didn't ask me to come up to the stove, or to set down, but just sat there, not even looking at me, so I said, "I want to see John." And then she—laughed. I guess you would call it a laugh. I thought of Harry and the team outside, so I said a little sharp: "Can't I see John?" "No," she says, kind o' dull like. "Ain't he home?" says I. "Yes," says she, "he's home." "Then why can't I see him?" I asked her, out of patience. "'Cause he's dead," says she. *"Dead?"* says I. She just nodded her head, not getting a big excited, but rockin' back and forth. "Why—where is he?" says I, not knowing what to say. She just pointed upstairs—like that. (*Himself pointing to the room above.*) I started for the stairs, with the idea of going up there. I walked from there to here—then I says, "Why, what did he die of?" "He died of a rope round his neck," says she, and just went on pleatin' at her apron. Well, I went out and called Harry. I thought I might—need help. We went upstairs and there he was lyin'—

County Attorney:
> I think I'd rather have you go into that upstairs, where you can point it all out. Just go on now with the rest of the story.

Hale:
> Well, my first thought was to get that rope off. It looked. (*Stops, his face twitches.*) . . . but Harry, he went up to him, and he said, "No, he's dead all right, and we'd better not touch anything." So we went back downstairs. She was still sitting that same way. "Has anybody been notified?" I asked. "No," says she, unconcerned. "Who did this, Mrs. Wright?"

said Harry. He said it business-like—and she stopped pleatin' of her apron. "I don't know," she says. "You don't *know?*" says Harry. "No," says she. "Weren't you sleepin' in the bed with him?" says Harry. "Yes," says she, "but I was on the inside." "Somebody slipped a rope round his neck and strangled him and you didn't wake up?" says Harry. "I didn't wake up," she said after him. We must 'a' looked as if we didn't see how that could be, for after a minute she said, "I sleep sound." Harry was going to ask her more questions but I said maybe we ought to let her tell her story first to the coroner, or the sheriff, so Harry went fast as he could to Rivers' place, where there's a telephone.

County Attorney:
And what did Mrs. Wright do when she knew that you had gone for the coroner?

Hale:
She moved from the rocker to that chair over there *(Pointing to a small chair in the downstage right corner.)* and just sat there with her hands held together and looking down. I got a feeling that I ought to make some conversation, so I said I had come in to see if John wanted to put in a telephone, and at that she started to laugh, and then she stopped and looked at me—scared.

(The County Attorney, *who has had his notebook out, makes a note.)*

I dunno, maybe it wasn't scared. I wouldn't like to say it was. Soon Harry got back, and then Dr. Lloyd came, and you, Mr. Peters, and so I guess that's all I know that you don't.

County Attorney *(rising and looking around)*:
I guess we'll go upstairs first—and then out to the barn and around there. *(To the* Sheriff.*)* You're convinced that there was nothing important here—nothing that would point to any motive?

Sheriff:
Nothing here but kitchen things.

(The County Attorney, after again looking around the kitchen, opens the door of a cupboard closet in right wall. He brings a small chair from right—gets up on it and looks on a shelf. Pulls his hand away, sticky.)

County Attorney:
   Here's a nice mess.

   (The women draw nearer upstage center.)

Mrs. Peters *(to the other woman)*:
   Oh, her fruit; it did freeze. *(To the Lawyer.)* She worried about that when it turned so cold. She said the fire'd go out and her jars would break.

Sheriff *(rises)*:
   Well, can you beat the woman! Held for murder and worryin' about her preserves.

County Attorney *(getting down from chair)*:
   I guess before we're through she may have something more serious than preserves to worry about. *(Crosses down right center.)*

Hale:
   Well, women are used to worrying over trifles.

   (The two women move a little closer together.)

County Attorney *(with the gallantry of a young politician)*:
   And yet, for all their worries, what would we do without the ladies?

(The women do not unbend. He goes below the center table to the sink, takes a dipperful of water from the pail and pouring it into a basin, washes his hands. While he is doing this the Sheriff and Hale cross to cupboard, which they inspect. The County Attorney starts to wipe his hands on the roller towel, turns it for a cleaner place.)

   Dirty towels! *(Kicks his foot against the pans under the sink.)* Not much of a housekeeper, would you say, ladies?

Mrs. Hale *(stiffly)*:
   There's a great deal of work to be done on a farm.

County Attorney:
> To be sure. And yet *(With a little bow to her.)* I know there are some Dickson County farmhouses which do not have such roller towels. *(He gives it a pull to expose its full length again.)*

Mrs. Hale:
> Those towels get dirty awful quick. Men's hands aren't always as clean as they might be.

County Attorney:
> Ah, loyal to your sex, I see. But you and Mrs. Wright were neighbors. I suppose you were friends, too.

Mrs. Hale *(shaking her head)*:
> I've not seen much of her of late years. I've not been in this house—it's more than a year.

County Attorney *(crossing to women upstage center)*:
> And why was that? You didn't like her?

Mrs. Hale:
> I liked her all well enough. Farmers' wives have their hands full, Mr. Henderson. And then—

County Attorney:
> Yes—?

Mrs. Hale *(looking about)*:
> It never seemed a very cheerful place.

County Attorney:
> No—it's not cheerful. I shouldn't say she had the homemaking instinct.

Mrs. Hale:
> Well, I don't know as Wright had, either.

County Attorney:
> You mean that they didn't get on very well?

Mrs. Hale:
> No, I don't mean anything. But I don't think a place'd be any

cheerfuller for John Wright's being in it.

County Attorney:
I'd like to talk more of that a little later. I want to get the lay of things upstairs now. *(He goes past the women to upstage right where steps lead to a stair door.)*

Sheriff:
I suppose anything Mrs. Peters does'll be all right. She was to take in some clothes for her, you know, and a few little things. We left in such a hurry yesterday.

County Attorney:
Yes, but I would like to see what you take, Mrs. Peters, and keep an eye out for anything that might be of use to us.

Mrs. Peters:
Yes, Mr. Henderson.

(The men leave by upstage right door to stairs. The women listen to the men's steps on the stairs, then look about the kitchen.)

Mrs. Hale *(crossing left to sink)*:
I'd hate to have men coming into my kitchen, snooping around and criticizing. *(She arranges the pans under sink which the* Lawyer *had shoved out of place.)*

Mrs. Peters:
Of course, it's no more than their duty. *(Crosses to cupboard upstage right.)*

Mrs. Hale:
Duty's all right, but I guess that deputy sheriff that came out to make the fire might have got a little of this on. *(Gives the roller towel a pull.)* Wish I'd thought of that sooner. Seems mean to talk about her for not having things slicked up when she had to come away in such a hurry. *(Crosses right to* Mrs. Peters *at cupboard.)*

Mrs. Peters *(who has been looking through cupboard, lifts one end of a towel that covers a pan)*:
She had bread set. *(Stands still.)*

Mrs. Hale *(eyes fixed on a loaf of bread beside the breadbox, which is on a low shelf of the cupboard)*:
She was going to put this in there. *(Picks up loaf, then abruptly drops it. In a manner of returning to familiar things.)* It's a shame about her fruit. I wonder if it's all gone. *(Gets up on the chair and looks.)* I think there's some here that's all right, Mrs. Peters. Yes—here; *(Holding it toward the window.)* this is cherries, too. *(Looking again.)* I declare I believe that's the only one. *(Gets down, jar in her hand. Goes to the sink and wipes it off on the outside.)* She'll feel awful bad after all her hard work in the hot weather. I remember the afternoon I put up my cherries last summer.

(She puts the jar on the big kitchen table, center of the room. With a sigh, is about to sit down in the rocking chair. Before she is seated realizes what chair it is; with a slow look at it, steps back. The chair which she has touched rocks back and forth. Mrs. Peters moves to center table and they both watch the chair rock for a moment or two.)

Mrs. Peters *(shaking off the mood which the empty rocking chair has evoked. Now in a businesslike manner she speaks)*:
Well, I must get those things from the front room closet. *(She goes to the door at the right, but after looking into the other room, steps back.)* You coming with me, Mrs. Hale? You could help me carry them. *(They go in the other room; reappear;* Mrs. Peters *carrying a dress, petticoat and skirt,* Mrs. Hale *following with a pair of shoes.)* My, it's cold in there. *(She puts the clothes on the big table, and hurries to the stove.)*

Mrs. Hale *(right of center table examining the skirt)*:
Wright was close. I think maybe that's why she kept so much to herself. She didn't even belong to the Ladies' Aid. I suppose she felt she couldn't do her part, and then you don't enjoy things when you feel shabby. I heard she used to wear pretty clothes and be lively, when she was Minnie Foster, one of the town girls singing in the choir. But that—oh, that was thirty years ago. This all you was to take in?

Mrs. Peters:
She said she wanted an apron. Funny thing to want, for there isn't much to get you dirty in jail, goodness knows. But I suppose just to make her feel more natural. *(Crosses to*

cupboard.) She said they was in the top drawer in this cupboard. Yes, here. And then her little shawl that always hung behind the door. *(Opens stair door and looks.)* Yes, here it is. *(Quickly shuts door leading upstairs.)*

Mrs. Hale *(abruptly moving toward her)*:
Mrs. Peters?

Mrs. Peters:
Yes, Mrs. Hale? *(At upstage right door.)*

Mrs. Hale:
Do you think she did it?

Mrs. Peters *(in a frightened voice)*:
Oh, I don't know.

Mrs. Hale:
Well, I don't think she did. Asking for an apron and her litle shawl. Worrying about her fruit.

Mrs. Peters *(starts to speak, glances up, where footsteps are heard in the room above. In a low voice)*:
Mr. Peters says it looks bad for her. Mr. Henderson is awful sarcastic in a speech and he'll make fun of her sayin' she didn't wake up.

Mrs. Hale:
Well, I guess John Wright didn't wake when they was slipping that rope under his neck.

Mrs. Peters *(crossing slowly to table and placing shawl and apron on table with other clothing)*:
No, it's strange. It must have been done awful crafty and still. They say it was such a—funny way to kill a man, rigging it all up like that.

Mrs. Hale *(crossing to left of* Mrs. Peters *at table)*:
That's just what Mr. Hale said. There was a gun in the house. He says that's what he can't understand.

Mrs. Peters:
> Mr. Henderson said coming out that what was needed for the case was a motive; something to show anger, or—sudden feeling.

Mrs. Hale (*who is standing by the table*):
> Well, I don't see any signs of anger around here. (*She puts her hand on the dish towel which lies on the table, stands looking down at table, one-half of which is clean, the other half messy.*) It's wiped to here. (*Makes a move as if to finish work, then turns and looks at loaf of bread outside the breadbox. Drops towel. In that voice of coming back to familiar things.*) Wonder how they are finding things upstairs. (*Crossing below table to downstage right.*) I hope she had it a little more red-up up there. You know, it seems kind of *sneaking*. Locking her up in town and then coming out here and trying to get her own house to turn against her!

Mrs. Peters:
> But, Mrs. Hale, the law is the law.

Mrs. Hale:
> I s'pose 'tis. (*Unbuttoning her coat.*) Better loosen up your things, Mrs. Peters. You won't feel them when you go out.

(Mrs. Peters *takes off her fur tippet, goes to hang it on chair back left of table, stands looking at the work basket on floor near downstage left window.*)

Mrs. Peters:
> She was piecing a quilt.

(*She brings the large sewing basket to the center table and they look at the bright pieces,* Mrs. Hale *above the table and* Mrs. Peters *left of it.*)

Mrs. Hale:
> It's a log cabin pattern. Pretty, isn't it? I wonder if she was goin' to quilt it or just knot it?

(*Footsteps have been heard coming down the stairs. The* Sheriff *enters followed by* Hale *and the* County Attorney.)

Sheriff:
> They wonder if she was going to quilt it or just knot it!

(The men laugh, the women look abashed.)

County Attorney *(rubbing his hands over the stove)*:
> Frank's fire didn't do much up there, did it? Well, let's go out to the barn and get that cleared up.

(The men go outside by upstage left door.)

Mrs. Hale *(resentfully)*:
> I don't know as there's anything so strange, our takin' up our time with little things while we're waiting for them to get the evidence. *(She sits in chair right of table smoothing out a block with decision.)* I don't see as it's anything to laugh about.

Mrs. Peters *(apologetically)*:
> Of course they've got awful important things on their minds. *(Pulls up a chair and joins* Mrs. Hale *at the left of the table.)*

Mrs. Hale *(examining another block)*:
> Mrs. Peters, look at this one. Here, this is the one she was working on, and look at the sewing! All the rest of it has been so nice and even. And look at this! It's all over the place! Why, it looks as if she didn't know what she was about!

(After she has said this they look at each other, then start to glance back at the door: After an instant Mrs. Hale *has pulled at a knot and ripped the sewing.)*

Mrs. Peters:
> Oh, what are you doing, Mrs. Hale?

Mrs. Hale *(mildly)*:
> Just putting out a stich or two that's not sewed very good. *(Threading a needle.)* Bad sewing always made me fidgety.

Mrs. Peters *(with a glance at door, nervously)*:
> I don't think we ought to touch things.

Mrs. Hale:
I'll just finish up this end. *(Suddenly stopping and leaning forward.)* Mrs. Peters?

Mrs. Peters:
Yes, Mrs. Hale?

Mrs. Hale:
What do you suppose she was so nervous about?

Mrs. Peters:
Oh—I don't know. I don't know as she was nervous. I sometimes sew awful queer when I'm just tired. *(Mrs. Hale starts to say something, looks at Mrs. Peters, then goes on sewing.)* Well, I must get these things wrapped up. They may be through sooner than we think. *(Putting apron and other things together.)* I wonder where I can find a piece of paper, and string. *(Rises.)*

Mrs. Hale:
In that cupboard, maybe.

Mrs. Peters *(crosses right looking in cupboard)*:
Why, here's a bird-cage. *(Holds it up.)* Did she have a bird, Mrs. Hale?

Mrs. Hale:
Why, I don't know whether she did or not—I've not been here for so long. There was a man around last year selling canaries cheap, but I don't know as she took one; maybe she did. She used to sing real pretty herself.

Mrs. Peters *(glancing around)*:
Seems funny to think of a bird here. But she must have had one, or why would she have a cage? I wonder what happened to it?

Mrs. Hale:
I s'pose maybe the cat got it.

Mrs. Peters:
No, she didn't have a cat. She's got that feeling some people have about cats—being afraid of them. My cat got in her

room and she was real upset and asked me to take it out.

Mrs. Hale:
My sister Bessie was like that. Queer, ain't it?

Mrs. Peters *(examining the cage)*:
Why, look at this door. It's broke. One hinge is pulled apart. *(Takes a step down to* Mrs. Hale's *right.)*

Mrs. Hale *(looking too)*:
Looks as if someone must have been rough with it.

Mrs. Peters:
Why, yes. *(She brings the cage forward and puts it on the table.)*

Mrs. Hale *(glancing toward upstage left door)*:
I wish if they're going to find any evidence they'd be about it. I don't like this place.

Mrs. Peters:
But I'm awful glad you came with me, Mrs. Hale. It would be lonesome for me sitting here alone.

Mrs. Hale:
It would, wouldn't it? *(Dropping her sewing.)* But I tell you what I do wish, Mrs. Peters. I wish I had come over sometimes when *she* was here. I—*(Looking around the room.)*—wish I had.

Mrs. Peters:
But of course you were awful busy, Mrs. Hale—your house and your children.

Mrs. Hale *(rises and crosses left)*:
I could've come. I stayed away because it weren't cheerful—and that's why I ought to have come. I—*(Looking out left window.)*—I've never liked this place. Maybe because it's down in a hollow and you don't see the road. I dunno what it is, but it's a lonesome place and always was. I wish I had come over to see Minnie Foster sometimes. I can see now—*(Shakes her head.)*

Mrs. Peters *(left of table and above it)*:
> Well, you mustn't reproach yourself, Mrs. Hale. Somehow we just don't see how it is with other folks until—something turns up.

Mrs. Hale:
> Not having children makes less work—but it makes a quiet house, and Wright out to work all day, and no company when he did come in. *(Turning from window.)* Did you know John Wright, Mrs. Peters?

Mrs. Peters:
> Not to know him; I've seen him in town. They say he was a good man.

Mrs. Hale:
> Yes—good; he didn't drink, and kept his word as well as most, I guess, and paid his debts. But he was a hard man, Mrs. Peters. Just to pass the time of day with him—*(Shivers.)* Like a raw wind that gets to the bone. *(Pauses, her eye falling on the cage.)* I should think she would 'a' wanted a bird. But what do you suppose went with it?

Mrs. Peters:
> I don't know, unless it got sick and died.

(She reaches over and swings the broken door; swings it again, both women watch it.)

Mrs. Hale:
> You weren't raised round here, were you?

(Mrs. Peters shakes her head.)

> You didn't know—her?

Mrs. Peters:
> Not till they brought her yesterday.

Mrs. Hale:
> She—come to think of it, she was kind of like a bird herself—real sweet and pretty, but kind of timid and—fluttery. How—she—did—change. *(Silence; then as if struck by a happy*

thought and relieved to get back to everyday things. Crosses right above Mrs. Peters *to cupboard, replaces small chair used to stand on to its original place downstage right.)* Tell you what, Mrs. Peters, why don't you take the quilt in with you? It might take up her mind.

Mrs. Peters:
Why, I think that's a real nice idea, Mrs. Hale. There couldn't possibly be any objection to it, could there? Now, just what would I take? I wonder if her patches are in here—and her things.
(They look in the sewing basket.)

Mrs. Hale *(crosses to right of table)*:
Here's some red. I expect this has got sewing things in it. *(Brings out a fancy box.)* What a pretty box. Looks like something somebody would give you. Maybe her scissors are in here. *(Opens box. Suddenly puts her hand to her nose.)* Why—(Mrs. Peters *bends nearer; then turns her face away.)* There's something wrapped up in this piece of silk.

Mrs. Peters:
Why, this isn't her scissors.

Mrs. Hale *(lifting the silk)*:
Oh, Mrs. Peters—it's—(Mrs. Peters *bends closer.)*

Mrs. Peters:
It's the bird.

Mrs. Hale:
But, Mrs. Peters—look at it! Its neck! Look at its neck! It's all—other side *to*.

Mrs. Peters:
Somebody—wrung—its—neck.

(Their eyes meet. A look of growing comprehension, of horror. Steps are heard outside. Mrs. Hale *slips box under quilt pieces, and sinks into her chair. Enter* Sheriff *and* County Attorney. Mrs. Peters *steps downstage left and stands looking out of window.)*

County Attorney *(as one turning from serious things to little pleasantries)*:
We'll, ladies, have you decided whether she was going to quilt it or knot it? *(Crosses to center above table.)*

Mrs. Peters:
We think she was going to—knot it.

(Sheriff crosses to right of stove, lifts stove lid and glances at fire, then stands warming hands at stove.)

County Attorney:
Well, that's interesting, I'm sure. *(Seeing the bird-cage.)* Has the bird flown?

Mrs. Hale *(putting more quilt pieces over the box)*:
We think the—cat got it.

County Attorney *(preoccupied)*:
Is there a cat?

(Mrs. Hale glances in a quick covert way at Mrs. Peters.)

Mrs. Peters *(turning from window takes a step in)*:
Well, not *now*. They're superstitious, you know. They leave.

County Attorney *(to Sheriff Peters, continuing an interrupted conversation)*:
No sign at all of anyone having come from the outside. Their own rope. Now let's go up again and go over it piece by piece. *(They start upstairs.)* It would have to have been someone who knew just the—

(Mrs. Peters sits down left of the table. The two women sit there not looking at one another, but as if peering into something and at the same time holding back. When they talk now it is in the manner of feeling their way over strange ground, as if afraid of what they are saying, but as if they cannot help saying it.)

Mrs. Hale *(hesitatively and in a hushed voice)*:
She liked the bird. She was going to bury it in that pretty box.

Mrs. Peters *(in a whisper)*:
>   When I was a girl—my kitten—there was a boy took a hatchet, and before my eyes—and before I could get there— *(Covers her face an instant.)* If they hadn't held me back I would have—*(Catches herself, looks upstairs where steps are heard, falters weakly)*—hurt him.

Mrs. Hale *(with a slow look around her)*:
>   I wonder how it would seem never to have had any children around. *(Pause.)* No, Wright wouldn't like the bird—a thing that sang. She used to sing. He killed that, too.

Mrs. Peters *(moving uneasily)*:
>   We don't know who killed the bird.

Mrs. Hale:
>   I knew John Wright.

Mrs. Peters:
>   It was an awful thing was done in this house that night, Mrs. Hale. Killing a man while he slept, slipping a rope around his neck that choked the life out of him.

Mrs. Hale:
>   His neck. Choked the life out of him. *(Her hand goes out and rests on the birdcage.)*

Mrs. Peters *(with rising voice)*:
>   We don't know who killed him. We don't *know*.

Mrs. Hale *(her own feeling not interrupted)*:
>   If there'd been years and years of nothing, then a bird to sing to you, it would be awful—still, after the bird was still.

Mrs. Peters *(something within her speaking)*:
>   I know what stillness is. When we homesteaded in Dakota, and my first baby died—after he was two years old, and me with no other then—

Mrs. Hale *(moving)*:
>   How soon do you suppose they'll be through looking for the evidence?

Mrs. Peters:
> I know what stillness is. *(Pulling herself back.)* The law has got to punish crime, Mrs. Hale.

Mrs. Hale *(not as if answering that)*:
> I wish you'd seen Minnie Foster when she wore a white dress with blue ribbons and stood up there in the choir and sang. *(A look around the room.)* Oh, I *wish* I'd come over here once in a while! That was a crime! That was a crime! Who's going to punish that?

Mrs. Peters *(looking upstairs)*:
> We mustn't—take on.

Mrs. Hale:
> I might have known she needed help! I know how things can be—for women. I tell you, it's queer, Mrs. Peters. We live close together and we live far apart. We all go through the same things—it's all just a different kind of same thing. *(Brushes her eyes, noticing the jar of fruit, reaches out for it.)* If I was you I wouldn't tell her her fruit was gone. Tell her it *ain't*. Tell her it's all right. Take this in to prove it to her. She—she may never know whether it was broke or not.

Mrs. Peters *(takes the jar, looks about for something to wrap it in; takes petticoat from the clothes brought from the other room, very nervously begins winding this around the jar. In a false voice)*:
> My, it's a good thing the men couldn't hear us. Wouldn't they just laugh! Getting all stirred up over a little thing like a—dead canary. As if that could have anything to do with—with—wouldn't they *laugh!* *(The men are heard coming downstairs.)*

Mrs. Hale *(under her breath)*:
> Maybe they would—maybe they wouldn't.

County Attorney:
> No, Peters, it's all perfectly clear except a reason for doing it. But you know juries when it comes to women. If there was some definite thing.

(Crosses slowly to above table. Sheriff *crosses downstage right* Mrs. Hale

and Mrs. Peters *remain seated at either side of table.)*

> Something to show—something to make a story about—a thing that would connect up with this strange way of doing it—

(The women's eyes meet for an instant. Enter Hale *from outer door.)*

Hale *(remaining upstage left by door)*:
> Well, I've got the team around. Pretty cold out there.

County Attorney:
> I'm going to stay awhile by myself. *(To the* Sheriff.*)* You can send Frank out for me, can't you? I want to go over everything. I'm not satisfied we can't do better.

Sheriff:
> Do you want to see what Mrs. Peters is going to take in? *(The* Lawyer *picks up the apron, laughs.)*

County Attorney:
> Oh, I guess they're not very dangerous things the ladies have picked out. *(Moves a few things about, disturbing the quilt pieces which cover the box. Steps back.)* No, Mrs. Peters doesn't need supervising. For that matter a sheriff's wife is married to the law. Ever think of it that way, Mrs. Peters?

Mrs. Peters:
> Not—just that way.

Sheriff *(chuckling)*:
> Married to the law. *(Moves to downstage right door to the other room.)* I just want you to come in here a minute, George. We ought to take a look at these windows.

County Attorney *(scoffingly)*:
> Oh, windows!

Sheriff:
> We'll be right out, Mr. Hale.

(Hale *goes outside. The* Sheriff *follows the* County Attorney *into the other room. Then* Mrs. Hale *rises, hands tight together, looking intensely at* Mrs. Peters, *whose eyes make a slow turn, finally meeting* Mrs. Hale's. *A moment* Mrs. Hale *holds her, then her own eyes point the way to where the box is concealed. Suddenly* Mrs. Peters *throws back quilt pieces and tries to put the box in the bag she is carrying. It is too big. She opens box, starts to take bird out, cannot touch it, goes to pieces, stands there helpless. Sound of a knob turning in the other room.* Mrs. Hale *snatches the box and puts it in the pocket of her big coat. Enter* County Attorney *and* Sheriff, *who remains downstage right.)*

County Attorney (*crosses to upstage left door facetiously*):
Well, Henry, at least we found out that she was not going to quilt it. She was going to—what is it you call it, ladies.

Mrs. Hale (*standing center below table facing front, her hand against her pocket*):
We call it—knot it, Mr. Henderson.

Curtain.

Comments and Questions

1. The short story entitled "A Jury of Her Peers" written by Susan Glaspell is included in the anthology *Law in Literature: Legal Themes in Short Stories.* The dramatic version of that story is entitled *Trifles,* and it is included in this anthology not only because it is an excellent illustration of a law-related one-act play, but also because it provides a wonderful opportunity to see one story through two different genres. Which title do you think suits this play best? Was it necessary to name the play and the short story differently? Which work do you think was completed first? Actually *Trifles* was published in 1916 while "A Jury of Her Peers" first appeared in 1917, suggesting that the author preferred the later title herself. If you go back and read the short story, you will notice how closely the play resembles the earlier work. Try taking a short story and turning it into a play. It

should become apparent that the more an author engages the reader in dialogue, the more the work lends itself to a dramatic reading, both in actuality and in the imagination of the reader. Which genre do you prefer and why?

2. There is an expectation in the law that jurors are able to step aside from their prejudices, their biases, their life-experiences, and so pass judgment on a case with a degree of objectivity which might be unrealistic. Does the empathy, sympathy, understanding, and sensitivity that Mrs. Hale and Mrs. Peters exhibit in *Trifles* mar or enhance their judgment of Mrs. Wright? Although Mrs. Wright only has a jury of two, we can see in this story the kind of conformity that takes place during the jury decision-making process. Notice how Mrs. Hale works a subtle but magnificant change in the position of Mrs. Peters. What is it that finally convinces Mrs. Peters not to reveal the evidence that the two women find?

3. What are the male characters in the play trying to discover? What are the ironies involved in their purported purpose, the way in which they treat the women, and the activities that the women are engaged in?

4. In considering Mrs. Wright's motivation for the strangling of her husband, it helps to consider some of the factors found in the battered women's syndrome—elements of a psychological rather than a physical nature—economic depravity, emotional sterility, harm to the woman's pets. Would Mrs. Wright be able to use the battered women's syndrome as a defense if this case were tried today? Do you imagine that "the battered woman's syndrome" was an expression coined at the time that Susan Glaspell wrote *Trifles*?

5. Although Mr. Wright is not presented as a "live" character within the play, a picture of him is drawn for us from the dialogue of the other players. Do you like or dislike him? Make arguments for and against him based on the evidence provided by the text.

Lou Rivers

This Piece of Land

Characters

The Singer
Rosa
Perry
Sister Waters
The Deacon
Miss Nancy
Leroy
Mr. Charlie
Mr. Morgan

All characters are Black except one, Mr. Charlie.

SETTING:
    Time: 1932. One summer day.
    Place: A small farm in South Carolina.
        Center left is a one-story wooden shack obliquely facing downstage. The shack is above the yard and contains several steps leading from the yard up to its long porch and center door flanked by two windows. The porch holds many potted plants, a bench for sitting, and other household items. Upstage, a curved skydrop runs the full length of the stage giving the scene depth and providing right and left exits. A tree down right helps to define the acting area in front of the house and makes for a third exit to the road beyond the scene. There's an element of mysticism about the scene, the grounds not being clearly defined as separate from the sky.

The curtain rises on a quiet scene, just before dawn. The Singer's *silhouette slowly fades in across the sky. He sings and plays his guitar to the night fading into dawn.*

Singer *(Slow and lamenting)*:
"Mornin comes afore the noon.
... Then evenin comes ...
And night's too soon ...
Spring of year is like the morn ...
... And so life goes ...
When a man is born.

Autumn comes,
And winter chills.
The baby laughs ...
The young man thrills.
Day starts low;
The noon runs high.
Seasons begin
And seasons die ..."

(Singer *makes a horizontal crossing against the sky and disappears beyond the house. A lamp light appears in one of the windows and moves across to the next window. Soon* Rosa *enters from the house. She stands on the porch looking up and about her when* Perry, *carrying a farming tool, enters from the house; he stands on the porch beside* Rosa. *Presently he crosses and exits up stage beyond the skydrop.* Rosa *waves to him, stands there thinking, returns into the house. Soon the light moves from the window to the next; increases in intensity; shimmers; then goes out. The lights fade up to late morning. The* Deacon, Miss Nancy, *and* Sister Waters, *fanning herself, enter slowly and heavily, bringing a vase, quilts, and other items.* Rosa *comes to the porch.*)

Sister Waters:
Good morning, Sister Rosa.

(Rosa *returns greetings as* Sister Waters *puts her vase on the top step. Sympathetically.*)

I tried to sell your things, but nobody was able to buy them.

Miss Nancy *(Putting her items down on the top step)*:
And I tried every house on Main Street, Sister. Folks ain't got no use for them now.

The Deacon *(He puts his items on the top step)*:
I even tried the white folks' churches, Sister, But Sister, as Nancy said there's so little money stirrin nowadays. We did our best. (Rosa *looks down on the items then looks searchingly towards the horizon.*)

Rosa:
M-m-m-m-m. *(Presently.)* Thank you all for tryin. *(Picks up the vase, studies it.)* I remember Misses Walker wanted to buy this.

Miss Nancy:
I especially asked Misses Walker.

Rosa:
Once she offered me one hundred dollars for this vase...said it was genuine antique.

Miss Nancy:
She said she'd bought herself another one. (Rosa *fondles the quilt.*)

The Deacon:
We did our best, Sister.

Rosa:
I'm sure you all did.

The Deacon:
And as you know, we couldn't begin to pay what you is askin for them.

Rosa *(Nods)*:
I understand. Thank you all for tryin.

Miss Nancy:
We wish we could do more to help.

Rosa:
> Just pray, dear friends, that I don't falter. I've put my trust in Jesus and—well, thank you all for what you all tried to do.

Sister Waters (*Crosses to* Rosa):
> I pray for you. (*Rosa squeezes her hand.*)

Rosa:
> God bless you. Just remember—I don't want Perry to learn a word about this. (*They nod.*) Now don't let me keep you. I know you all have your own chores to do.

(*They nod in agreement and slowly and heavily exit. Rosa studies the articles then takes them into the house. When she comes back to the porch she hears* Leroy, *who is off, singing: "O Mary Don't You Weep." He enters from the opposite direction carrying his coat thrown across his arm.*)

Leroy:
> Hey, Mamma!

Rosa (*Without exuberance*):
> Hey, Leroy.

Leroy (*Sits on top step. Silence, as he looks about him.*):
> Phew! It must be at least ninety in the shade today. (*Takes his polka dot handkerchief from his hip pocket and wipes his brow.*) We sure nuff could use some rain, huh?

Rosa:
> Guess the Lord seen no reason yet to give it. (*Sits on the bench and takes her pipe and tobacco from her apron pocket. She fills her pipe.* Leroy *obliquely studies her.*)

Leroy:
> I know one thing for sure though, if this dry spell don't end off soon, not nary a farmer around here is gonna git a thing to yield this year but tomatoes.

Rosa:
> It haint been too bad . . . I guess . . . for the tomatoes. Perry says we ought to get a right good yield.

Leroy:
> Maybe so! But it sure aint much good when the market is already over-run with tomatoes, and George Junior says he heard Mr. Medina aint giving but thirty cents now.

Rosa:
> Thirty cents.

Leroy:
> Yes, mam, thirty cents!

Rosa:
> Lord, hush! Perry mightyn as well feed his tomatoes to the swine! What's they offerin in the big market?

Leroy:
> I don't know for sure, Mamma, but George Junior told Clarence Brown they is all offerin thirty cents.

Rosa:
> M-m-m-m. *(Lights her pipe and smokes.)*

Leroy *(Mops his brow)*:
> Phew! This sure is a hot one, huh? Where's papa?

Rosa:
> Out on the farm—pickin the last of the tomatoes . . . He'll be headin in toreckly for something to eat!

> *(Silence.)*

Leroy:
> You feelin all right, Mama?

Rosa:
> No worse then usual.

> *(Silence.)*

Leroy:
> Sadie told me you all finally heard from Carmen! . . . We thought we oughta write them and ask them to help out a bit.

Rosa:
> Taint no use to write them.

Leroy:
> I reckon not. Sadie said Carmen wrote she still wish it was some way she could come back home for a while.

Rosa (*Smoking her pipe*):
> That's what she writ . . . For a while at least she said. Said Thomas hadn't yet got no steady work.

Leroy:
> Can't say that sound too good, do it? He's been outta work for a long time.

Rosa:
> Perry said that, too—Both me and him has heared everywheres is as mean as hit can be—It's the depression they calls it.

Leroy:
> Is papa gonna send for them to come home?

Rosa:
> What for? . . . And with what? . . . Aint no money here. Might as well starve out there as to comin back home to starve down here. (*Silence.*) How's your younguns?

Leroy:
> All right. Booker Washington was kinda puny for a day or so—cuttin his teeth. I reckon—he's all right now, huh? Sadie said you sent a message you wanted to see me.

Rosa:
> I do! It's on business . . . I want when you go to town this afternoon to fetch Mr. Morgan out here to see me.

Leroy:
> You mean Mr. J.P. Morgan on West Bread Street?

Rosa:
> I do!

Leroy *(Anxious)*:
> Now, what for, Mamma? Didn't you just go to town last week to see Mr. Morgan?

Rosa:
> I did! Yes, I did. And I went the week before, and he knows it's for business.

Leroy:
> But, Mamma, why? Why you wanta—

Rosa *(Puffing on her pipe)*:
> I wants to see the man on business, Leroy. That's all I'm sayin.

Leroy: Mr. Morgan is a busy man—

Rosa: You just go fetch him and leave the rest to me and him.

(Silence.)

Leroy *(Troubled)*:
> Lord knows, Sadie and me tried everything we knowed to get hold of some money.

Rosa:
> Payment on the mortgage is due this month. Them bank folks done writ the second letter they don't aim to wait no longer.

Leroy:
> Mamma, now twont it be better if you and papa just give up all this strugglin and go on and let Mr. Charlie pay off the mortgage—

Rosa:
> No! It can't never be better!!

Leroy:
> He did it for the others, Mamma!

Rosa:
> This piece of land is Perry's. Hit can't never mean to Mr. Charlie what it means to Perry. And I don't mind tellin you, Leroy, the whole notion of him losing it is about to heave the heart out of his chest.

Leroy:
> It aint like you and papa was givin up the land for keeps. Mr. Charlie could pay off the mortgage like he did for Alex and the others, and each year you and papa could pay back a little of whatever you could. I don't see no harm in it.

Rosa:
> Twon't but a fool who thinks Alex and them others is ever gonna own their lands again.

Leroy:
> I don't know about that, Mamma—Alex said—

Rosa:
> Well, I do! Every year Alex, Bo-Sam, and them others don't pay nothing back but the interest on their lands, and the main loans keeps waitin right there for them to pay hit off, and they'll never be able to pay it off. Poor old Mr. Maxwell died and his widow and poor six children had to move offern that farm less in a month, the old lady being too weak to sharecrop—

Leroy:
> Well, I sure don't see how you and papa aim to beat that mortgage!

Rosa:
> We'll beat it. I got a plan.

Leroy (*Studies his mother*):
> Got somethin to do with Mr. Morgan?

Rosa:
> Never you mind! You jest fetch Mr. Morgan. After all, Perry mortgaged this farm for gettin me to doctors—and to the hospital—

Leroy:
> Papa don't grudge you nothin he's done for you—

Rosa:
> —And I don't aim to see him lose this land after all the hard work he done put in it—not on my account—especially when all the doctors and hospital aint done me no good!

Leroy:
> You's doing all right, Mamma! The doctors told you—It takes time. Don't expect to get well as quick as you want to! There's time for everything, Mamma!

Rosa:
> Hush, boy! Hush, Leroy! Now you know papa wouldn't like to hear you talk like that, huh? He's done everything—

Leroy (*Concerned*):
> Mamma—

Rosa:
> Do you hear me, Leroy?

Leroy (*Nods*):
> Yes, mam!

Rosa:
> If God chose it to be this way—then it'll have to be, I guess—But I don't aim for Perry to lose both me and the land, not at the same time. (*Rises.*) Here comes Perry now—drippin with sweat, poor man!

Perry (*Entering*):
> Thought I saw Mr. Charlie's car headin this way! (*Looks to the road.*) Musta made a stop! Hey, boy! What's brung you over here afore eatin time? (*Chuckles.*) Lookin for a handout, eh?

Leroy:
> No, Papa! Mamma told Sadie last night she wanted to see me.

Rosa (*Crosses on porch to fetch a towel; throws towel to* Perry):
> Want him to run an errand in town for me.

Perry (*Sits. Sighs, mops his brow*):
> This sure is a hot one, eh?

Leroy:
> I told mamma it must be at least ninety degress under the shade.

Perry:
> One of them mean critters is down there at the furnace all right. (*Bites a piece of tobacco.*) How's my grandboys?

Leroy:
> All right. Booker Washington is cuttin his bottom teeth now—and is gittin harder for Sadie to handle.

Perry (*Chuckles*):
> Little rascal! (*Spits.*) Saw Al Ehlers at prayer meetin last night and he says the mens is meetin over at his place tomorrow night—about men's day in the church—and about that idea of the cooperative the preacher spoke about last Sunday—Wants to be sure you git over there.

Leroy:
> Yea, I know. I seen Al in town day afore yesterday, and he told me then about the meetin. You aimin to go?

Perry:
> Depends on how Rosa here is feelin—

Rosa:
> I'll be all right. Don't stay here and watch over me. Go on over there and figure out when you all can get to puttin them steps up on the church. Sure don't look good—all these months the church has went without steps. (*Deliberately.*) I don't know how you all would manage to take a de-

ceased body into the church. *(The two men react quietly.)* I spoke to Al about that myself.

Leroy:
Stop by for me, and we'll go together.

Perry:
I'll head over there after supper.

Mr. Charlie *(Off. Calling in the distance)*:
Hey there, Perry! Perry—

Perry:
I knowed I saw his car headin this way. *(Rises and calls.)* Come on up, Mr. Charlie! Mr. Charlie, come on up!

Rosa *(Straining to see)*:
Lord, look at that man! He's go come up here wid all his lies! Sure as I'm born, that man is gonna hang up in hell by the point of his tongue.

Perry:
I told the misses and boy here I thought I seed your car comin up the road.

Mr. Charlie *(Off)*:
Stopped off at Buddy's place!

Rosa:
Don't you talk too long, Perry. I got your vittles in there nice and hot!

(Mr. Charlie enters. He wears a soiled white linen suit. He mops his brow.)

Mr. Charlie:
I'm willin to bet you all anything old Mayor Jenkins is down there firin the furnace today. This is a mean one, and you've gotta have a mean critter at the furnace.

Perry:
> As hot as it is, Mr. Charlie, that furnace must be gittin help from the devil hisself.

> *(Both* Mr. Charlie *and* Perry *laugh.)*

Mr. Charlie:
> We's got to git some rain soon or we is gonna parch away like them magnolia leaves. *(He points to a tree.)*

Perry:
> Sit down, Mr. Charlie.

Mr. Charlie *(Sitting)*:
> Phew! *(Mops his brow.)* Rosa, how's that overall misery of yours?

Rosa *(Sits)*:
> I don't complain none, Mr. Charlie. The good Lord knows how much I can bear.

Mr. Charlie:
> Now aint that said jest like a Christian? Rosa, I tell you, I do believe the good Lord is purifyin you for his kingdom. I tell my wife all the time if there's a true-true Christian anywheres around these parts, it's you.

Rosa:
> I tries to be, Mr. Charlie. I tries my level best.

Mr. Charlie:
> And by golly you do succeed. I wouldn't want you prayin agin me, by golly, I'll tell you that!

Rosa:
> You needn't worry about that. If I can't pray for you, Mr. Charlie, I won't pray against you.

Mr. Charlie *(Laughs)*:
> That ought to put my mind at ease, eh, Perry? *(Perry laughs.)* I sure don't want you people prayin agin me like you all got to prayin agin Mayor Jenkins.

Leroy *(Chuckles)*:
Mayor Jenkins was a wicked man, Mr. Charlie.

Mr. Charlie:
Maybe so . . . but twon't natcherel . . . the way he hauled off and went . . . when you all got to prayin! Twon't natcherel. *(Licks his cigar.)* Well, Perry, you ready to do business wid me?

Perry:
What business, Mr. Charlie?

Mr. Charlie:
About this here farm. Now you know what I mean—You and me don't aim to start playin cat and mouse wid each other at this late date, do we? You might as well do business wid me. I saw Leonard over at the bank this mornin and he said taint no question about foreclosin on you.

Perry:
They can't foreclose if I make my payments, Mr. Charlie?

Mr. Charlie *(Still licking his cigar)*:
That's all dependin, aint it, if you's able to make them payments? You aint made none in two months accordin to Leonard. I'm saying, let me make them for you like I did for the other boys. They aint regrettin it none, is they? At least I aint heard no complaints. You'd have a much longer time payin it off to me than you'd have payin it off to the bank. *(Strikes a match to light his cigar.)*

Perry:
I told Mr. Leonard last week I'll make up the payment at the end of the month.

Mr. Charlie:
That's what he said you said, but then I asked him—how is it you gonna do it? Seeing as the dry season didn't yield you people out here nothin. *(Strikes another match.)*

Rosa:
We got enough tomatoes to make the payments, Mr. Charlie.

Perry:
> That's right! We got quite a good yield. I reckon with them at sixty-five cents a bushel, we'll be able to pay the bank up to three months on that loan—at least.

Mr. Charlie:
> That's only three months! Right after, the fourth and the fifth is coming up. What you aim to do about them?

Perry:
> Until I start farmin again, I was thinkin of gittin a job in town like my boy here to sort of help out.

Mr. Charlie (*Lights his cigar and puffs at it rapidly*):
> Perry, I didn't reckon to hear you talk no foolery. There aint no jobs in town, boy, and I'm here to tell you. Why there's more men hangin around town trying to git a job—then there is flies on Lyon's Bakershop's screen door. I don't know whether you people know it or not, but we is having one hell of a depression in the country.

Perry:
> Mr. Charlie, I can always make it if I have to.

Mr. Charlie:
> You's a farmer, and you aint good at nothin else but farming—Aint Alex and the others told you yet—the big market aint givin but fifteen cents for tomatoes now?

Perry:
> Mr. Medina told me sixty-five cents a bushel when I spoke with him the last time.

Mr. Charlie:
> That was two weeks ago; the market is overrun now with tomatoes. They aint givin but fifteen cents a bushel to nobody! The white farmers as well as you people out here is gettin the *same* thing.

Perry:
> Fifteen cents?

Rosa:
> We'll give em to the hogs before we sell em for that! (Mr. Charlie *and* Rosa *stare at each other.*)

Mr. Charlie *(Presently)*:
> I know how you people out here feel. I feel the same way myself. It's a damn shame that, after all, I'm stuck with over one-hundred bushels of tomatoes. I paid my croppers sixty-five cents a bushel each last one of them, and now I gotta sell em for much less in the market. Taint no profit in doin that kind of business. Is there? Besides that, hit don't say nothin about the haulin cost from here to Charleston.

Perry:
> If I can't get at least sixty-five cents a bushel for my tomatoes, I don't see how I can raise the money for the bank.

Mr. Charlie:
> That's why I'm makin you my offer! You a good man, Perry!

> *(Silence.)*

Leroy:
> Mr. Charlie, if papa was to sign up with you—

Rosa:
> Perry never said he was signin up with nobody, Leroy!

Leroy:
> I was only—

Rosa:
> —With nobody, Leroy!!

Mr. Charlie *(Presently)*:
> Leroy, what was you gonna ask me?

Leroy:
> I was gonna ask you, sir, how much would you give papa for his tomatoes?

Mr. Charlie:
>Well—now—Leroy—I'll have to see. *(Takes his pad and pencil from his pocket.)*

Leroy:
>The same as you gave the others—sixty-five cents a bushel?

Mr. Charlie:
>Well, now that all depends! *(Begins figuring.)*

Leroy *(Strains to see* Mr. Charlie's *figuring)*:
>Depends on what, Mr. Charlie?

Mr. Charlie:
>On how many bushels I could take from your pa! I've got more tomatoes now than I know what do with! Perry, I tell you what I'll do. For at least fifty bushels, I'll give you sixty-five cents a bushel and pay you cash. How's that? For the remaindin bushels, I'll give you credit at thirty cents a bushel. You can't beat that nowheres around here.

Leroy:
>Seems fair enough to me, Papa!

Mr. Charlie:
>Damn sight better than what the bank would do! Besides I oughta git a little somethin out of the deal myself—at least gas money for haulin. I'll keep the innerest the same as the bank's now got it! Perry, what you say to that? Come on, boy, I aint got all day. *(Perry looks to Rosa who shakes her head. Mr. Charlie sees it.)*

Perry:
>I can't make up my mind right yet, Mr. Charlie—

Mr. Charlie *(Annoyed)*:
>Whatcha got to make up your mind about? *(Perry looks to Rosa.)*

Perry *(Presently)*:
>I'll have to let you know.

Mr. Charlie:
>Sharecroppin aint the worse thing could happen to *you*. I'm good to my croppers! Ask Alex or any of the other boys.

Perry:
>I aint sayin you aint, Mr. Charlie—It's just that—*(He looks to Rosa again. Turns to Mr. Charlie.)* I've got to have more time to think through what I've gotta do.

Mr. Charlie:
>More time! Jesus Christ—Man—You mean to tell me you aim to let a deal like this go by in search of a buyer? Where's your business sense, Perry? Time keeps movin, boy, and opportunity knocks at a new door each new second.

Rosa:
>Even God Himself allows us time, Mr. Charlie—

Mr. Charlie:
>I'll be damn! *(Looks from Perry to Rosa, who stares him down.)* All right, Perry! Take as long as you like—but don't let me get off to Charleston before you make up your mind—and I aim to roll my trucks startin next week.

Perry:
>All right, Mr. Charlie! I'll let you know by then!

Mr. Charlie:
>Good! *(Wipes his neck. Takes a fresh cigar and begins to lick it.)* You all take care of Rosa, here, and Rosa, you pray Perry do the right thing by us all. (Rosa *nods.*) Oh, by the way, I hear you fellows are havin a church meetin tomorrow night over at Al Ehler's house. Well, I'm sendin you all a case of Amy's home brew over there. I already told Al about it, and I paid Amy for it, and she'll keep it cool in the well till time you all's meetin. I want all of you fellows over there to think right good of me—and when you all pray, don't pray agin me!

Perry *(Chuckles)*:
>We don't aim to do much prayin over there, Mr. Charlie—just talk about our men's day program at the church.

Mr. Charlie:
> All right, Perry—but just in case you all do, take care! So long, Rosa! You pray good for all of us! *(Starts, but returns.)* By the way, Perry, I heard some of you boys been talkin about formin a cooperative—It taint none of my business, but I guess you all know that's communist talk—and against our American government way of life . . . A few men in town got to whisperin about it. *(A pause.)* Just thought I'd tell you. Your preacher mightn of knowed it when he suggested it. Well, until you all make up your minds, I'll mosey on along. Gotta lots of chores fore sunset. *(He exits.)*

>   *(Silence.)*

Leroy:
> Papa, if I was you—

Rosa:
> You aint your papa! *(More silence.)* Perry, aint you ready for your vittles?

Perry:
> Yeah—Rosa. Go on in and fix it.

Rosa *(Rises)*:
> You stayin, Leroy?

Leroy:
> No, Mamma. Sadie and the boys is waitin for me.

Rosa:
> Tell the boys I send love to em.

Leroy:
> All right . . . I guess Mr. Charlie sure nuff believes we all got together and prayed against Mayor Jenkins.

Rosa:
> That man is scared cause he knows he's a devil! And as sure as I was born a woman, he aims to git a holt of this land, but he won't do it. I swear on my life he won't git this piece of land!

Perry:
>Go on! Don't get yourself fretful!

Rosa:
>Hit don't need nobody prayin for or against him and his kind. They all done made homes for themselves in hell a long time ago right next to Mayor Jenkins—

Perry:
>Fix me somethin to eat.

Rosa:
>Leroy! You don't forget to do what I told you.

Leroy:
>No, Mama, I wont.

Rosa:
>And when you see Cousin Julia and Gus in town, you tell them I said they oughta come out to see me soon if they aim to.

Leroy:
>All right, Mamma, I'll tell em!

(Rosa *exits into the house. Presently* Leroy *rises and stretches lazily. He studies* Perry.)

Leroy:
>You all right, Papa?

Perry (*Nods*):
>It's poor Rosa! It's so hard keepin the truth from her.

Leroy:
>Papa, she ain't worried about herself. She's worried about you losin this land. (Perry *raises his hand to silence* Leroy. *They both look towards the door.*)

Perry:
>You mosey on along. I'm all right, son.

Leroy:
> See you, Papa!

Perry:
> Yea, boy! I'll eat and then take some time out to stroll over to Clarence and the others. See what's happenin about these tomatoes.

Leroy:
> Yeah, Papa, do that! And if I was you, I'd give some real hard thinkin on what Mr. Charlie is offerin you. After all, mamma don't understand everything. *(After a pause, he exits.)*

(Perry sits there thinking. He rises, looks up to the skies. Rosa calls him. He wearily exits into the house. The Singer's silhouette appears on the horizon as a bent farmer hoeing the ground. He sings:)

Singer:
> "This is the land promised to me—
> Forty acres to set me free.
> This is the land—
> This is the land—
> This piece of land
> Belongs to me!
> Work hard, my children, eat the dust.
> Work long, my children, and you must—
> Break ground, my children with your hand—
> But hold on—Hold on to your land!"

(The light fades into an hour later. Perry enters from the house picking his teeth. He crosses and stands looking up at the sky. The Singer's silhouette becomes Perry's shadow reaching across the sky. He sings:)

Singer:
> "Mornin comes afore the noon . . .
> . . . Then evenin comes . . .
> And night's too soon . . .
> End of morn is when he's born,
> And so death comes
> With the sun at morn.
> Laughter cries . . .

And weepin fills the empty quest
A black man makes
Of him that's low
And God on high,
Reasons for why . . .
He was born to die." *(Exits.)*

(Perry bites a piece of tobacco and crosses to exit by the way of the road. The lights fade down to a sunset. Rosa *enters from the house with a small pail of water to wet her potted plants as the* Singer *appears on the horizon. When she comes to a dying plant, she pulls it from the soil and turns it over in her hand and clutches it hard against her bosom. She looks to the horizon to see the silhouette of the* Singer *who watches. Finally she throws the plant to the ground and exits into the house. The* Singer *moves slowly across the horizon.* Leroy *and* Mr. Morgan *enter from the road.* Mr. Morgan *fans himself with a paper-card fan. He stands at the foot of the steps while* Leroy *enters upon the porch and calls.)*

Leroy *(Knocking and calling)*:
　　Mamma! Mamma, it's me, Leroy with Mr. Morgan.

Rosa *(From the house)*:
　　Comin!

Leroy:
　　Come on up, Mr. Morgan. Have a seat.

Mr. Morgan:
　　In a minute, Mr. Tucker! I get a wiff of cool breeze right here.

Leroy *(Knocking)*:
　　Mamma, come on. You know, Mr. Morgan is a busy man.

Rosa:
　　Yes, I'm coming. *(Enters.* Leroy *senses something is wrong.)*

Leroy:
　　What's wrong, Mamma?

Mr. Morgan:
　　Hydo, Misses Tucker?

Rosa:
> Right fair in the middlin, Mr. Morgan, thank you. How is Misses Morgan, and your offsprings?

Mr. Morgan:
> They're all fine, thank you.

Rosa:
> That's a blessin, I'm sure. Come up, Mr. Morgan, and have a seat. I believe it's cooler here on the porch.

Mr. Morgan:
> No, Misses Tucker, if you don't mind I rather stand right here. I don't know where that breeze is comin from, but right along here I'm gettin a real coolin-off feelin.

Rosa:
> Well, then, now you just stay right there, and Leroy will fetch you a chair from the house. Go on, Leroy, get Mr. Morgan a chair.

Leroy *(Concerned)*:
> Mamma, your eyes is wet from cryin. What you been cryin about, huh?

Rosa:
> Go on, and do as your ma tells you. (Leroy *goes into the house.*) I hear tell the folks in town is havin it mighty hard—just as hard as we is out here on the farms.

Mr. Morgan:
> It's the depression, Misses Tucker. The worse one this country's ever had—and accordin to the newspapers, it's headin even for worser times.

Rosa *(Sighs)*:
> Lord, I jest don't understand it.

Leroy *(Returning with chair)*:
> You don't understand what, Mamma?

Rosa:
> Well, I don't understand for one thing how this country of ours got itself into this mess in the first place. I jes don't understand why there is so much hungriness and misery about us when there is so much food you can't even sell.

Mr. Morgan:
> Misses Tucker, that's the way it goes with economics. And like the newspapers point it out—in this country one time we have a boom, and the next time we have a bust. You see, at this time, we're havin a bust.

Leroy:
> Mamma—

Rosa:
> Leroy, give Mr. Morgan the chair. (Leroy *crosses down to give the chair to* Mr. Morgan.)

Mr. Morgan:
> Thank you kindly, Misses Tucker. (*He sits.* Leroy *returns to the steps below* Rosa.)

Leroy:
> Mamma, if you is painin at all, tell me the truth!

Rosa (*Looks down at* Leroy *affectionately*):
> Son, Mamma is painin every blessed hour of the day.

Leroy:
> Mamma, do papa know it? Have you told papa? Is that why you've been cryin cause you's painin?

Rosa (*Touches his head*):
> Mamma is all right!

Leroy:
> But you've been cryin, Mamma . . . and that's not like you!

Rosa:
>After a while, you get used to livin with pains. It's the questions, son, that keeps turnin over in your mind you jest can't seem to get no answer to.

Leroy:
>What's the question, Mamma? Ask me the question! I'll answer the question, Mamma. What's the question you keep turnin over in your mind? Is that why you sent for Mr. Morgan?

Rosa (*She gently places her hand across* Leroy's *mouth*):
>Only God knows the answer, son. (*She moves away from* Leroy.)

Mr. Morgan:
>Misses Tucker, I don't *think* it's our Christian place to ever ask some kinds of questions. We then come mighty close to blasphemy.

Rosa:
>The good Book says God's got a reason of some kind for *everything* . . . a reason for all of us being here . . . a reason for some of us being white, and some of us being black.

Leroy:
>Mamma, stop talkin like that! You aint yourself! You want me to call the doctor?

Rosa:
>Why don't He see fit to let the reasons be made clear to us. Hit don't make no sense—Me being born, you, Perry, Leroy here . . . all of us strugglin to live, strugglin to hold on to a little somethin we can call our very own—and then without havin nary a word to say about it, we have to give it up and go away and be jedged.

Leroy:
>Mamma, you want me to call Pap?—I'm goin—You don't sound right to me.

Rosa:
> No! *(Stops Leroy.)* Aint no doctor can do me no good except Doctor Jesus! *(To the alarmed Leroy.)* Oh, you gotta ask if you is a honest woman. Why, God Almighty, did you see fittin to put hatred and malice in the hearts of your children . . . to put this livin things within me . . . *(Holds her abdomen.)* that don't serve no aim but to sap the usefulness outta me!

Leroy *(More alarmed)*:
> Mamma, what you talkin about?

Rosa *(To God)*:
> Why, God, *why?* *(To Leroy.)* Hit don't make no sense! And all the pushin and shovin and folks starvin and tearin the hearts out of one another. Why?! Didn't Jesus die on the cross to put an end to it all?

(Long silence. She looks down at the frightened Leroy and to the uncomfortable Mr. Morgan.)

Mr. Morgan:
> Them's mighty powerful and frightenin questions you is askin of God, Misses Tucker!

Rosa:
> Mighty powerful questions, but you gotta ask them if you is honest, Mr. Morgan.

Leroy:
> Mamma, I'm gonna call Papa!

Rosa:
> He aint on the place, Leroy! He went over to see Clarence and the others about what they aim to do with their tomatoes. He oughta be gettin back soon. You set down there and hush a while whilst I talk business with Mr. Morgan. *(She goes down to the ground to look over the land.)*

(Leroy sits on the top step anxious about Rosa. Mr. Morgan rises when Rosa comes down. Rosa finally takes a deep sigh and turns to Mr. Morgan.)

Rosa:
   Sit down, Mr. Morgan. *(He sits.)* Did you figure out the full amount as I told you to?

Mr. Morgan:
   Misses Tucker, there's plenty of time for us to figure out these things. Aint no sense in hurryin them on.

Rosa:
   I told you I wanted all that information figured out by the time I sent for you.

Leroy *(Rises)*:
   Mamma—

Rosa *(Waves* Leroy *quiet)*:
   How much you gonna charge me for that gray casket?

Mr. Morgan *(Takes his paper from his pocket)*:
   Now, Misses Tucker, you—

Rosa:
   I mean the one with the golden stars. And the family cars? I figured it would take at least three to hold all of my relatives and closest of friends.

Leroy:
   By God, it aint natcherel, Mamma! It aint natcherel for us to go plannin our own burial.

Rosa:
   I guess it aint—when you don't know it's comin—you might look like you's hurryin it on—*(Silence.)* but when you know, Leroy, I don't see why it haint the natcherelest thing on God's earth to do.

Mr. Morgan:
   The sickest aint always the nearest to the grave, Misses Tucker.

Rosa:
   How much, Mr. Morgan?

Mr. Morgan:
> Well—now—you realize you picked one of the best caskets in the house. That casket by itself at least cost five hundred dollars.

Rosa:
> That's too much!

Mr. Morgan:
> But I'm gonna let you have it at three hundred dollars though.

Rosa:
> And the cars?

Mr. Morgan:
> Each car—let's see—well, it should cost you—say thirty dollars a car—all together ninety dollars.

Rosa:
> That's three hundred and ninety dollars. What's for the chimes on the hearst?

Mr. Morgan:
> Well, now—let me see—the chimes ought to be an additional thirty dollars. But, being it's you, I'll say twenty-five dollars. Now let's see twenty-five dollars for the chimes, plus ninety dollars for the cars, plus three hundred dollars—all total four hundred and fifteen dollars.

Rosa:
> Make it a round four hundred dollars, Mr. Morgan! Oh, my God! Here comes Perry. Now let's all make out like we was just talkin. You all set and keep quiet.

(Perry *enters. He immediately senses something is wrong.* Mr. Morgan *rises.*)

Perry:
> Howdy everybody?!

Mr. Morgan:
>Hydo, Mr. Tucker?

Perry:
>Howdy, Mr. Morgan? *(Looks from Leroy to Rosa.)* What's Mr. Morgan doin out here wid his pad and pencil? *(Leroy turns away.)*

Leroy:
>Mamma wouldn't let me fetch you!

Perry *(Turns to Rosa, who walks away. Turns to Mr. Morgan, who lowers his head.)*:
>Aint somebody's gonna tell me what the buryin man's doin out here on my place? *(Goes to Rosa.)*

Rosa:
>Perry, I sent for him to come here!

Perry:
>Is you shuttin me out on something, Rosa? Why? What you want to see Mr. Morgan about?

Rosa:
>Perry, can't a woman who knows she's gonna die, make the arrangements for her own funeral?

Perry:
>Who's dyin?

Rosa:
>*I'm* dyin! Perry, I'm dyin.

Perry:
>Who said anything about you dyin? *(Turns to Leroy.)* Boy, did you tell your ma—

Leroy:
>Not me, Papa! By God, I never mentioned a word!

Perry *(To Rosa)*:

Who told you such an audacious lie, Rosa? Who in heaven's name—

Rosa:

Taint no lie, Perry, and if anybody told me, it was you! *(Reads his eyes.)* The deep down hurt inside you told me. You told me in everything you did, in everything you said to me—

Perry:

Oh, Good God, have mercy. *(Walks away.)*

Rosa *(Follows him)*:

Don't you know when you hurt deep you can't hide it from me—Perry, this is Rosa! You's been tryin to hold the truth back ever since the doctor told you months ago.

Perry:

Doctors have been wrong before, Rosa, you know that.

Rosa:

This time, the doctors aint wrong! And I know that. You've did your best. You sent me to the hospital and they couldn't do no good! So before I go Perry, I wants to arrange things the way I want them to be...I went down last week and picked out the casket I like. I figured with the family we got, we could get by with the three cars. Other church members, I reckon, will donate their wagons and buggies to accommodate those others who wants to follow me to the buryin ground.

(Leroy takes his handkerchief and weeps quietly.)

Perry:

Rosa, don't bust my heart wide open! Don't you bust my heart, woman!

Rosa:

Leroy, you stop that! Now don't you do that to Perry. *(Goes to Leroy.)* This is the time, boy, to give him your strength, not your weakness.

Leroy:
   Mamma, please—

Rosa:
   Taint no tears, no nothing's gonna change what's gonna happen—so we might as well build ourselves to bear the truth. *(Crosses to* Perry.*)* You come, Perry, sit down over here. *(She leads* Perry *to the step.)*

(Leroy puts an affectionate arm about his father and sits beside him weeping quiety.)

Rosa:
   Now, let's see Mr. Morgan, where was we?

Mr. Morgan:
   We figured the total to be four hundred and fifteen dollars, Misses Tucker.

Rosa:
   We said four hundred dollars even, Mr. Morgan.

Mr. Morgan:
   Yes, that's right, four hundred dollars.

Rosa:
   That's gonna be the cost of my funeral, not a cent over!

Mr. Morgan:
   If you say!

Rosa:
   That's what I say! *(She pulls her apron. For a brief silence she watches* Perry *and* Leroy.*)*

Mr. Morgan:
   No floral pieces?

Rosa:
   Don't worry about the flowers. The Sisters and Brothers of the church will see to that. *(Takes policies from her apron pocket.)* Now, Mr. Morgan, here is all my life insurance paid

up to full. Here's the policy for the Pilgrim's Life, the Metropolitan Life Policy, policy for the Freedom Life—all paid up to full: they should total to two thousand and four hundred dollars.

Mr. Morgan:
Yes, um!

Rosa:
I'm gonna ask you to make a deal with me. If you don't want to do it, you just say so. I don't want no hemmin and hawin about it, if you can't then I'm gonna send for Mr. Kraft at the Sunshine Undertakers—and I'll make the deal with him!

Perry:
No—

Rosa:
My God, Perry don't fight me! *(Above* Perry.*)* Is it a deal, Mr. Morgan?

Mr. Morgan *(Flustered)*:
Well, now—Misses Tucker—I don't—

Rosa *(Sharply)*:
I don't want no hemmin and hawin, Mr. Morgan! Is it a deal or aint it?

Mr. Morgan *(More flustered)*:
Well, I never had no deal like this before. I don't even know if it's legal.

Perry:
It aint legal! It's a sin before God!!! *(Points the way.)* You get off my place, Mr. Morgan! *(He starts for* Mr. Morgan. Rosa *and* Leroy *struggle to stop him.)*

Rosa:
Perry, it aint no sin! . . .

(Stops Mr. Morgan *who has been edging away. She breaks into tears but aborts them.)*

And it's legal all right!

Mr. Morgan:
How do you know, Misses Tucker? How can you tell?

Rosa:
Because it's my life, Mr. Morgan. That's all it's worth. I'm givin it to you in order to save the land!

Mr. Morgan:
Misses Tucker, should a piece of land mean so much to you?

Perry:
Mr. Charlie can have this damn land! I don't want it!

(*A silence. Overcome by tears, he walks abruptly away from* Leroy *who tries to console him, giving the others his back. The others watch his back, seeing him finally gain control.*)

Rosa (*Quietly*):
Is it a deal?

Mr. Morgan (*Finally and quietly*):
It's a deal if that's—what you want.

Rosa:
Very well then. You go down tomorrow and settle the business with the bank and bring the final papers and the remainders of nine hundred dollars to me—(*They hesitate.*) Thank you, Mr. Morgan! You's a good man! (*She shakes his hand and starts for the house. Stops to observe* Perry *and* Leroy.) Leroy, you go home to Sadie and the younguns! Me and Perry wants to be alone . . . for a while.

Mr. Morgan:
I'll drop you off, Mr. Tucker!

Leroy:
Mamma—

(Rosa *moves swiftly and exits into the house.*)

Leroy *(After a moment)*:
>Papa, we shoulda known we could *never* keep her from knowing. *(He slowly moves towards the exit.)* *(Mr. Morgan crosses to Perry.)*

Mr. Morgan:
>You being the man, Mr. Tucker, tell me what to do.

Perry *(Lowers his head)*:
>I wish I knowed . . . *(Looks into the sky.)* I wish I knowed what to tell you . . .

Leroy:
>Coming, Mr. Morgan?

Perry *(More to himself than to Mr. Morgan)*:
>I wish I knowed.

Mr. Morgan:
>Mr. Tucker, God help you. I'll go down to the bank first thing in the morning.

(Mr. Morgan exits. Leroy follows. Perry crosses to sit on the step with his head in his hands. The sun sets more. Soon Rosa enters. She's smoking her pipe. She stands there watching Perry.)

Rosa:
>Perry?

Perry:
>Yes, Rosa?

Rosa:
>You vex with me? *(Perry shakes his head.)* Don't be.

Perry:
>I'm losing you, Rosa . . . What good is the land without you?

Rosa:
>Well, Perry . . . *(Sits next to him.)* for one thing, you won't lose the land to Mr. Charlie! *(Silence.)* I reckon—with all the work we put into this land, we have just about paid for it three or

more times over . . . and to lose it for a little of nothin—you love this land—you love it like some men love a second woman— *(Silence as the two look over the land.)* We've got the grandchildren . . . they ought to have some home place they can return to—there's Carmen and Thomas wantin to come home for a visit . . . and Leroy and his younguns—This land will be a remembrance—We always said every man oughta have a little piece of land to call his own.

Perry:
But, Rosa, to take your life insurance money—

Rosa:
This land is our pride . . . *(Puts her arm around his shoulder.)* Since I was a little girl, each week we paid on them policies. Before I did, my pa did; and since they air called life insurances they ought to go for helpin life! Don't make no sense that all I'm worth should be put into the ground behind me. *(Silence as she studies* Perry.*)*

Perry *(Alarmed)***:**
What's the matter?

Rosa:
Perry, do you believe in the hereafter?

Perry:
I do!

Rosa:
Do you believe that heaven is as light and coolin as a rain shower on a hot summer day?

Perry:
Yes, Rosa, I believe it.

Rosa:
And, do you believe hell is there at the end of eternity in all its bleakness and ugliness for wicked men?

Perry:
What you gittin at, Rosa?

Rosa:
> Oh, Perry, pray for me! I jest can't git it out of my head and heart—Is God any more fairer to us than the white man?

Perry:
> Rosa!

Rosa:
> Perry, I'm falterin.

Perry:
> Now don't talk no more like that!

Rosa:
> Perry, God mustn't be white—God mustn't be white!

Perry:
> God aint got no color at all. God is the spirit of love. Jesus lived and was crucified to teach us to love one another, and he was a white man. *(He holds on to her hands.)*

Rosa:
> Perry, God mustn't be white. *(Holds tightly to Perry. Presently.)* I'm feelin all right now, Perry . . . Look at the sun . . . The day's almost gone . . . Tomorrow, a new day, a new life . . . another beginning . . . *(After a long silence she rises.)* Come on in, and I'll rub your back for you.

Perry:
> I'll come.

Rosa:
> All right. *(Touches him tenderly.)* Don't fret none. I'm all right now.

(She lingers to look off into the sky then exits into the house. The Singer *in silhouette, appears on the horizon.)*

Singer *(As he sings, the light appears in the window.* Perry *slowly rises and exits into the house.)*:
> "Mornin comes afore the noon . . .
> . . . Then evenin comes . . .

And night's too soon . . .
Spring of year is like the morn . . .
. . . And so life goes . . .
When a man is born.

Autumn comes,
And winter chills.
The baby laughs . . .
The young man thrills.
Day starts low;
The noon runs high.
Seasons begin
And seasons die . . ."

(The light in the window goes out. The Singer *continues to sing as he slowly moves across the horizon to completely enshroud the stage.)*

Curtain.

Comments and Questions

1. In a recession or a depression, many people find themselves unable to meet their mortgage payments and unable to hang on to the piece of land that they have struggled for years to maintain. In recent years, the British government has found and paid for housing for people who are unable to continue payments on their mortgages. Would it be better if the government paid the interest payment on the mortgages rather than letting the banks take away the homes of the people? Might this not be a cheaper proposition in the long run? In the United States, there is no such relief for people who are unable to pay their mortgages, and once the bank forecloses, the displaced inhabitants of the house either move in with relatives or join the growing ranks of homeless people. Should the law intervene and stay foreclosure proceedings during a recession or depression? How would this

interfere with the right to contract? Should we protect big businesses or the homeowners? It is readily apparent that those most likely to lose their homes in times of economic strain are those who have the least resources—people like Rosa and Perry. Does Rosa reach the only workable solution to the problem?

2. Rosa sells her life insurance policies in order to pay for her funeral expenses and to ensure that Perry does not lose the house and land after her death. People suffering with AIDS, cancer, and other terminal illnesses are now selling their life insurance policies at a reduced value in order to have money to provide for their medical and living expenses. This practice has been criticized by some as repugnant and socially unacceptable. Why do they feel that way? Is there a concern that if the terminally ill person uses the proceeds from his life insurance policy while he or she is still alive, the state will end up caring for widows, widowers, and orphans who were otherwise already provided for? On the other hand, does not an individual have a right to name any beneficiary he or she chooses? Rosa tells us that the money from the policies "[o]ught to go for helpin life"!

3. Why does Rosa hope that God isn't white? What is significant about the fact that Mr. Charlie is the only white character in the play? Compare and contrast Mr. Charlie with Mr. Morgan.

4. In a subtle way, the play also addresses the medical issue of using aggressive and expensive medical techniques for the terminally ill patient. What is Rosa's attitude toward the doctors who have treated her? It is apparent that the doctors have not told Rosa that she has only a very short time to live. Who should make the decision to inform the patient? The doctor? The relatives? Who appears to have made the decision in this case?

5. What role does religion play in this work? How does Divine law contribute to the theme?